Supply Chain Management

Beiträge zu Beschaffung und Logistik

Series editors
M. Eßig, Neubiberg, Germany
W. Stölzle, St. Gallen, Switzerland

Industrielle Wertschöpfung wird immer komplexer. Der steigende Wettbewerbsdruck zwingt zu differenzierten Angeboten, gleichzeitig nimmt der Kostendruck zu. Unternehmen können diesen gestiegenen Anforderungen nur gerecht werden, wenn sie neben der Optimierung eigener Produktion besonderen Wert auf die Gestaltung effektiver und effizienter Netzwerke legen. Supply Chain Management befasst sich mit unternehmensübergreifenden Wertschöpfungsaktivitäten von der Rohstoffgewinnung bis zur Endkundendistribution. Die Schriftenreihe sieht sich dabei besonders den lange vernachlässigten betriebswirtschaftlichen Teildisziplinen Beschaffung und Logistik verpflichtet, die als Treiber des Supply Chain Management gelten.

Edited by
Prof. Dr. Michael Eßig
Universität der Bundeswehr München
Professur für Materialwirtschaft
und Distribution
Neubiberg, Deutschland

Prof. Dr. Wolfgang Stölzle
Universität St. Gallen
Lehrstuhl für Logistikmanagement
St. Gallen, Schweiz

Weitere Bände in der Reihe http://www.springer.com/series/12359

Irène Kilubi

Strategic Technology Partnering and Supply Chain Risk Management

Five Selected Essays

Springer Gabler

Irène Kilubi
München, Deutschland

Supply Chain Management
ISBN 978-3-658-19917-3 ISBN 978-3-658-19918-0 (eBook)
https://doi.org/10.1007/978-3-658-19918-0

Library of Congress Control Number: 2017955667

Springer Gabler

Printed on acid-free paper

This Springer Gabler imprint is published by Springer Nature
The registered company is Springer Fachmedien Wiesbaden GmbH
The registered company address is: Abraham-Lincoln-Str. 46, 65189 Wiesbaden, Germany

Table of contents

List of abbreviations

ACA	Author Co–citation Analysis
AMR	Advanced Market Research
AL	Alliance
AQ	Acquisition
CA	Consortia
CACM	Communications from Association for Computing Machinery
CIMO	Context–Intervention–Mechanisms–Outcome
CL	Cooperation/Contractual
CLONT	**C**omplementary Capabilities, **L**earning & Exploitation Capabilities **O**rganisational Capabilities, **N**etwork, Alliance, and Partnership Capabilities, **T**echnological, Innovative, and Internal capabilities
CMI	Co-Managed Inventory
CN	Collaboration
CO	Conceptual
CS	Case Study
EE	Evolutionary Economics
ES	Economy/Society
GT	Game Theory
IM	Industry/Market
JIT	Just-in-time
JV	Joint Venture
KBV	Knowledge–based View
LC	Licensing
LR	Literature Review
MDS	Multidimensional Scaling
MIT	Massachusetts Institute of Technology
ML	Multilevel
MR	Merger
MVA	Multivariate Analysis

N/A	Not Applicable
NBF	New Biotechnology Firms
NPD	New Product Development
N/S	Not Specified
NW	Network
OL	Organisational Learning
OM	Operations Management
ON	Organisation
OT	Other Theories
PCA	Principal Component Analysis
RBV	Resourced–based View
R&D	Research and Development
ROT	Real Options Theory
SC	Supply Chain
SCM	Supply Chain Management
SCR	Supply Chain Risk
SCRM	Supply Chain Risk Management
SCT	Social Capital Theory
SLR	Systematic Literature Review
SMEs	Small and medium–sized Enterprise
SNT	Social Network Theory
SSCI	Social Science Citation Index
SPSS	Statistical Package for the Social Sciences
SQ	Survey/Questionnaire
SR	Secondary Database Research
STP	Strategic Technology Partnering/Partnership
TB	Theory Building
TCE	Transaction Cost Economy
TT	Theory Testing
VMI	Vendor Managed Inventory

List of figures

CHAPTER IV
THE STRATEGIES OF SUPPLY CHAIN RISK MANAGEMENT – A SYNTHESIS AND CLASSIFICATION

CHAPTER V
STRATEGIC TECHNOLOGY PARTNERING CAPABILITIES: A SYSTEMATIC REVIEW OF THE EMPIRICAL EVIDENCE OVER TWO DECADES

CHAPTER VI
BRIDGING THE GAP BETWEEN SUPPLY CHAIN RISK MANAGEMENT AND STRATEGIC TECHNOLOGY PARTNERING – INSIGHTS FROM TWO THEORETICAL LENSES

List of tables

CHAPTER III
26 YEARS OF STRATEGIC TECHNOLOGY PARTNERING: INVESTIGATING TRENDS, PATTERNS AND FUTURE PROSPECTS IN RESEARCH THROUGH FREQUENCY ANALYSIS

CHAPTER IV
THE STRATEGIES OF SUPPLY CHAIN RISK MANAGEMENT – A SYNTHESIS AND CLASSIFICATION

CHAPTER V
STRATEGIC TECHNOLOGY PARTNERING CAPABILITIES: A SYSTEMATIC REVIEW OF THE EMPIRICAL EVIDENCE OVER TWO DECADES

CHAPTER VI
BRIDGING THE GAP BETWEEN SUPPLY CHAIN RISK MANAGEMENT AND STRATEGIC TECHNOLOGY PARTNERING – INSIGHTS FROM TWO THEORETICAL LENSES

Chapter I

Summary of the research

1 Introduction

1.1 Motivation and purpose

Modern literature has emphasised the significance of innovation, with "open and closed innovation" (Chesbrough, 2003), and supplier-led innovation (Narasimhan and Narayanan, 2013) being key aspects within supply networks highlighting the need to work in tandem with suppliers. Stakeholders appreciate the need for exploration and exploitation, which helps to perceive how suppliers and supply chain (SC) networks are contributing to commercialisation. Innovation concepts in the operations management (OM) and supply chain management (SCM) context are evolving, drawing on organisational learning theory, knowledge management, network theory, absorptive capacity, social exchange theory, etc. Indeed, considering the prevailing competition, innovation is vital within the OM discipline towards presenting relevant solutions from both perspectives, namely, the theoretical and practical perspective (Narasimhan, 2014). The demands of the market environment and the progression of emerging markets lead to the development of dynamic and complex SC networks (Braunscheidel and Suresh, 2009; Manuj and Mentzer, 2008a; Tummala and Schönherr, 2011; Spekman and Davis, 2004; Zsidisin *et al.*, 2004). Consequently, these effects lead to increased risk exposure; for instance due to short technology and product life cycles, increased demand for just-in-time (JIT) deliveries, reduced inventory buffers and e-business (Brindley, 2004; Fawcett *et al.*, 2011; Giunipero and Eltantawy, 2004; Hallikas *et al.*, 2004; Harland *et al.*, 2003; Narasimhan and Talluri, 2009). Fuelled by several well-documented events, such as natural disasters and events (e.g. Tsunami 2004, Hurricane Katrina 2005, Taiwan earthquakes 1999, 2009,2010), diseases (e.g. foot- and mouth disease in the UK in 2001, the SARS-pandemic 2003/2004, avian influenza 2005, swine influenza 2009) and terrorist attacks (e.g. New York 2001, Madrid 2004, London, 2005, Jakarta 2009), the Iceland volcano eruption in 2010, the nuclear disaster in Fukushima, 2011 and Hurricane Sandy in 2012, interest in supply chain risk (SCR) issues has steadily grown.

The ability to withstand external threats and provide countermeasures to potential risks within SCs occupy primary concern. In spite of the incredible advance in SCRM concepts, parallel progression in theory improvement and endeavours to comprehend the social interactions in SCRM has stayed behind. Although supply chain risk management (SCRM) has become standard in SCM research, the term and concept to establish useful SCRM remains ambiguous and lacks adequate understanding. Apart from that, a generally accepted research or analytical framework is still missing: "The absence of any widely accepted framework for categorizing research in this field reflects the novel and evolving nature of SCRM as well as the SCM field itself" (Zsidisin and Ritchie, 2008, p. 5). Along with increasing SCRs due to environmental and economic changes, answering the question of how to reduce SCRs holds paramount importance (Chen *et al.*, 2013). Collaboration was found to support with environmental uncertainty (e.g. Eden *et al.*, 2008; Vilkamo and Keil, 2003; Dogsen, 1993). Facing fast technological changes and global competition, inter–organisational collaborations have become increasingly important for firms to enhance their competitiveness. Particularly, inter–organisational partnerships are critical for a firm's innovativeness when firms lack sufficient internal research and development (R&D) resources (Un *et al.*, 2010; Smith and Sharif, 2007).

Hence, collaborations in R&D have become a common instrument for securing and leveraging technological competencies (Schulze *et al.*, 2014; Oxley and Sampson, 2004). A major, fundamental factor for wealth creation and superior performance is joint innovation by means of strategic technology partnering (STP) (Bidault and Cummings, 1994; Forrest and Martin, 1992; Kim and Lee, 2003; Lanctot and Swan, 2000; Mukherjee et al, 2013; Sivadas and Dwyer, 2000; Un *et al.*, 2010). Many firms increasingly cooperate in their technological undertakings; they engage in STP for technological, commercial, industrial, or financial reasons. For that reason, STP is deemed imperative for easing the access to strands of technologies that are unknown to a company. Still, there is a paradox: companies frequently fail to reap the anticipated benefits of most of their STPs (Kale and Singh, 2009b). Although the benefits of inter-organisational partnerships have long been recognised, evidence suggests that some organisations are better at creating and capturing value through their strategic partnerships than others (e.g. Heimeriks and Duysters, 2007; Kale *et al.* 2002; Anand and Khanna, 2000). From a resource-based perspective, such performance differentials reflect variance in STP capabilities across organisations. However, in spite of growing interest in this research stream, we lack a systematic theoretical and empirical understanding of those capabilities and their underlying elements (Sarkar *et al.*, 2009).

On this note, Tidd (2014) calls for an enhanced understanding of the inherent mechanism and capabilities that contribute to fruitful interactions and outcomes of collaborative innovation activities. Hence, to encourage companies to secure their SCs, powerful strategies must be settled that fulfil two needs. In the first place, these strategies need to assist firms in minimising costs and enriching customer satisfaction. Second, those strategies need to empower organisations to carry forward their operational activities during and after a severe disruptive incident has happened (Tang, 2006b). Understanding how to respond to and mitigate SCRs comprehensively unveils a supplementary research challenge in SCM (Tang and Musa, 2010). Every organisation follows numerous routine activities, which could relate to how raw materials are processed, or how the executive management reviews the processes are undertaken to account for budgeting or strategy implementation, for example (Grant, 1991).

Considering the significance of both SCRM and STP as competitive features in turbulent and dynamic market conditions, it is to some degree astounding that the link between these two essential research strands has not been sufficiently focused on so far (Bierly *et al.*, 2014). Thus, this research aims at bridging this gap and seeks to combine SCRM and STP. The investigation will be carried out to understand the conditions under which the STP helps reduce and mitigate SCRs. SCRM is about preventing and providing countermeasures to risks and potential disruptions in a supply chain. Hence, SCRM aims at identifying sources and probabilities of risks as well as methods and processes to respond to and mitigate them. STP deals with entering collaborative relationships with other organisations in the area of product design and R&D to achieve higher levels of innovativeness and to maintain the potential to perform in a highly competitive area of high technology. STP, therefore, aims at boosting innovativeness and thus, in turn achieves higher organisational performance. SCRM and STP can be viewed as opposite sides of the same coin, both dealing with an organisation's long-term profitability and viability, but approaching it from opposite angles. In the resource-based view (RBV) of the firm the organisation is viewed as a bundle of valuable resources, encompassing fundamental immaterial assets, which may provide the competitive advantage (e.g. Amit and Schoemaker, 1993). Therefore, the resources of a firm are considered to be a wellspring to the extent they are valuable, rare, distinct, uncommon, and hard to copy or substitute (e.g. Barney, 1991). Likewise, contended that social capital records highly among such immaterial assets and that a distinct incorporation of the role of social capital further fortifies the logical forces of the RBV connected with various issues (Schiele *et al.*, 2015).

Nowadays firms are working increasingly in network environments. By this progress, the network perspective has turned out to be more imperative in SCRM and academic research (Borgatti and Li, 2009; Kim *et al.*, 2011). Therefore, social capital, which analyses the value actors can derive from their network ties, has become increasingly popular in supply chain–related research (Autry and Griffis, 2008; Carter *et al.*, 2007). These issues consist of the comparative benefits of companies as organisational arrangements, the rationale of inter-organisational networks as means to spot business exchanges and the role of social capital as a governance mechanism in such networks (Chisholm and Nielson, 2009). In detail, the present study investigates issues on capabilities aimed at managing the broader SC network and business partnerships. While contemporary and emerging management research acknowledges cooperative partnerships as an enabler for organisational performance, understanding central firm resource configurations has been somehow under-researched. A narrowed emphasis in these research areas lies on solid practices and procedures that empower organisations to excel within interfirm partnerships. Figure I-1 illustrates and explains the outline of the research summary, presented in Chapter I.

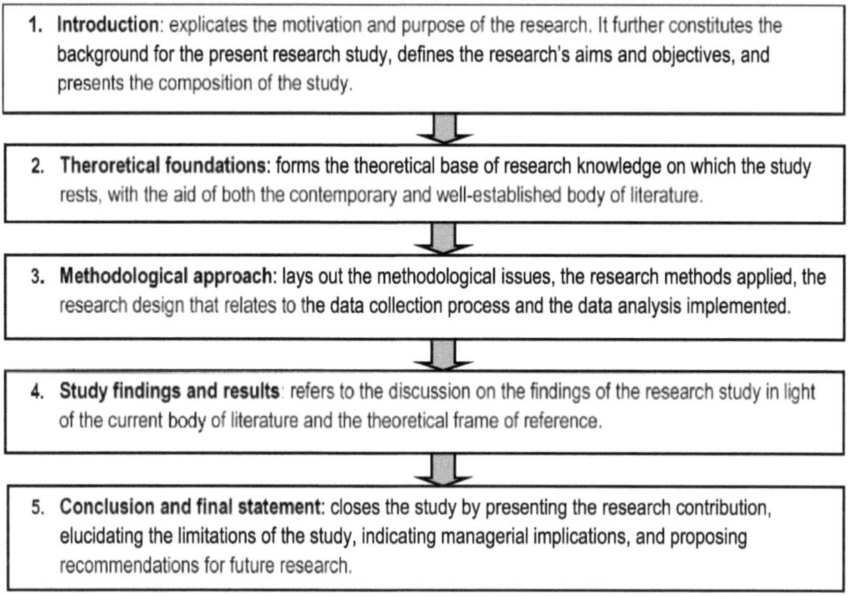

Figure I-1: Outline of the research summary.
Source: Own illustration.

1.2 Thematical boundaries and definitions

The risk of disruptions triggered both from dynamics within SCs and from external environmental action is of vital interest to both practitioners and researchers (Tummala and Schönherr, 2011). There are interruptions of different intensities and types in nearly all SCs (Blackhurst *et al.*, 2005; Greening and Rutherford, 2011). This comprises of interruptions in supply, demand, process, environmental systems, and controls (Christopher and Peck, 2004). Understanding the damaging effects of SCRs on the performance of supply chain networks and the severe consequences associated with these effects can help an organisation design efficient SCRM processes in order to mitigate the detrimental effects caused by these risk sources (Punniyamoorthy *et al.*, 2013). SCRs have been jeopardising the competitiveness and profitability of companies and organisations. As a result, academics and practitioners have become interested in SCRM approaches that support the persistence and efficiency of their SC networks, as well as in practices for evaluating prospective risk sources (Fawcett *et al.*, 2011).The specific network background that we investigate is related to high-tech industries, characterised by the fast technological change that has a remarkable impact on the management of innovation, both within firms and partnerships (Powell, 1998; Hagedoorn *et al.*, 2006). At the node of internal and external technology advancements, one finds STPs where firms internalise capabilities that are at best, to a certain extent, exogenous to them (Hagedoorn and Duysters, 2002). In STPs, firms mainly cooperate closely in the areas of research and new technology development (Hagedoorn, 1993). Therefore, these forms of partnerships have a high influence on the long-term product-market arrangements of the respective firms (Kilubi, 2016; Vilkamo and Keil, 2003). Although STPs were practically unknown before the 1980s, they have turned out a lot more prevailing during the preceding two decades (De Man and Duysters, 2005). Given that R&D alliances may contribute to resource configurations in a different way than other types of alliances do, it is particularly worth examining that form of partnership (Eisenhardt and Schoonhoven, 1996; Schilke and Görzen, 2010) instead of strategic alliances in general. In the following, we are going to define the key terms representing the foundation of the present research study.

1.2.1 Defining Supply Chain Risk Management

The encompassing goal of SCRM is to ensure an efficient and continuous material flow from supplier to end customer (Waters, 2007). SCRM is characterised by a high level of intensity relating to cooperation, partnerships, integrated networks and consciously designed goal setting and planning processes within the SC. Any approach to SCRM should seek to understand, identify, and reduce risks to the SC as a whole through partners' coordination. Despite similar existing definitions of SCRM, an in-depth literature analysis reveals that, at present, there is no commonly and widely accepted definition of what constitutes SCRM. Taking into account the evolution of SCRM definitions, most of the proposals have only been modified slightly, either referring to existing definitions or resulting from theory building processes (Kilubi and Haasis, 2015). A plausible explanation for the deviants arising in the definition process of the elements inherent in SCRM could be that many researchers only use the SCRM definition as a basis for their research, thus, slightly modifying extant definitions without developing a central and consistent definition. Besides, SCRM is a young cross-disciplinary, multi-faceted research field; it should be considered that previous definitions have primarily been developed on a conceptual basis. Therefore, SCRM definitions lack the empirical testing that could impede the creation of an universal definition. Further to this, the conducted research reveals that most researchers rather focus on defining 'supply chain risk' than on proposing a coherent definition of SCRM. Upon reviewing the literature, it becomes apparent that the authors give more consideration to the definition of 'supply chain risk' than to the definition of 'supply chain risk management' (cf. Harland *et al.*, 2003; Sinha *et al.*, 2004; Zsidisin *et al.*, 2004; Zsidisin and Ellram, 2003). A valuable indication of the level of maturity of a discipline is provided by the attitude of researchers concerning the definition of core concepts (Burgess *et al.*, 2009). It suggests that definitional consensus does not exist and that SCRM is still in the evolving stage and has not yet reached maturity. In the context of the present research study, we have embraced the following definition of SCRM:

> *"Supply chain risk management is to [collaborate] with partners in a supply chain apply risk management process tools to deal with risks and uncertainties caused by, or impacting on, logistics related activities or resources." (Norrman and Jansson, 2004, p. 436).*

1.2.2 Defining Strategic Technology Partnering

Farr and Fischer (1992, p. 57) understand cooperation in R&D as "any method by which firms or governments cooperate to make better use of their collective research and development resources to include technical information exchange, harmonising of requirements, codevelopment, interdependent research and development and agreement on standards." Similarly, Ingham and Mothe (1998, p. 250) refer to R&D partnership as "an agreement between independent organisations that combine tangible and/or intangible resources to cooperate in R&D activities". Hagedoorn (2002, p. 478) defines "R&D partnerships as the particular set of different modes of inter–firm collaboration where two or more firms that remain independent economic agents and organisations share some of their R&D activities."According to Vilkamo and Keil (2003, p. 195) "A strategic technology alliance or strategic technology partnering relationship can be understood as "a long–term, continuous and mutually beneficial vertical non–equity relationship where confidential information on future plans and visions are shared proactively to support both companies to focus their resources in the right direction". According to Hagedoorn and Schakenraad (1994, p. 291) "strategic technology partnering is the establishment of cooperative agreements aimed at joint innovative efforts or technology transfer that can have a lasting effect on the product-market positioning of participating companies." All these definitions emphasise the sharing of valuable resources and their combination, at least involving two different parties. In the present study, we are going to use the word strategic technology partnering/partnership (STP) to replace other terms such as alliance, collaboration, or joint venture. Considering the purpose of this study, we define STP as follows:

> *A collaboration between companies that activate and pool their individual tacit and physical assets in the strategic development of technological products to gain mutual benefits and compete in a highly dynamic environment.*

1.2.3 Defining Capabilities

Organisation and management research have emphasised the dynamic capabilities theory (Eisenhardt and Martin, 2000; Teece *et al.*, 1997) as an effective method to profit from inter-organisational partnerships and networks (cf. Kale and Singh, 2007; McGrath and O'Toole, 2013; Mitrega *et al.*, 2012; Möller and Svahn, 2003; Ritter *et al.* 2002; Walter *et al.*, 2006). The firm's capabilities are not solely related to the available resources; they also entail the extent of coordination between the individuals within the organisation and their way of synchronising the accessible resources. The organisational routines within a firm refer to the daily activities that are repeated by the members therein, while capability refers to the summation of multiple routine activities (Nelson and Winter, 1982). Correspondingly, capabilities are complex sets of skills and aggregated knowledge, acquired through organisational processes, that enable companies to leverage their assets (Day, 1994) and refer to "a firm's capacity to deploy resources, usually in combination, using organisational processes to effect a desired end" (Amit and Schoemaker, 1993, p. 35). Eisenhardt and Martin (2000, p. 1107) define 'capabilities' as "the firm's processes that use resources – specifically the processes to integrate, reconfigure, gain and release resources – to match and even create market change". Furthermore, capability is regarded as "the ability to make use of resources to perform some task or activity" (Hafeez *et al.*, 2002, p. 40), for example, Apple's capability to generate radical, breakthrough innovations. These definitions are in line with Wang and Ahmad (2009) who conclude that capabilities are 'first-order', and when companies prove abilities of deploying assets to achieve a wanted target, then those capabilities are likely to result in improved performance. Hence, companies need several skills acquired within and beyond their organisational boundaries to innovate in the light of change and complexity. Along these lines, firm capabilities can be associated with several competitive objectives, such as profitable new market entry, lean and agile SCM, effective new product development (NPD), excellence in manufacturing technology, etc. For the purpose of this research and in accordance with Dosi and Teece (1998, p. 284), we define capabilities as "the reflection of a company's ability to "organize, manage, coordinate, or govern sets of activities".

1.3 Research aims and objectives

The literature on SCRM is highly fragmented, hindering an entire understanding of the current state of research and what to study next (Pfohl *et al.*, 2010). Likewise, discussion on STP capabilities is of broad interest, and the related term can be traced back to different theoretical approaches (Richards and De Carolis, 2003).

Thus, providing a comprehensive overview is challenging. For that reason, we aim to synthesise the existing research findings to provide a clear overview. Despite the increasing attention given to the research area of STP (e.g. Lee *et al.*, 2001; Li *et al.*, 2008; Trott *et al.*, 1995; Mowery *et al.* 1996; Pennings and Harrianto, 1992; Steensma and Corley, 2000), and the recent developments highlighting the interest in and importance of SCRM-related research (cf. Li *et al.*, 2014; Marley *et al.*, 2014; Vilko and Hallikas, 2012; Zhao *et al.*, 2013), the complexity of the intricated issues requires a systematic literature review (SLR), discovering major issues of the extant landscape of empirical, conceptual, as well as theoretical evidence (Kamal and Irani, 2014; Lightfoot *et al.,* 2013; Meier, 2011; Phene and Tallman, 2012) to update and motivate researchers to further investigate this issue. Accordingly, Boote and Bailey (2005) bring forward the argument that in order to promote our shared cognition, scientists must comprehend what has previously been done, the strengths and weaknesses of the existing research, and their underlying meaning. Thus, a thorough literature review is a precondition for doing robust, evident, and valid research.

Cassiman *et al.* (2009, p. 218) correctly pointed out that "as firms increasingly use external relationships to acquire new knowledge, they need to develop the capability for governing these relationships". Hence, the settings above constitute our motivation to analyse current issues and trends in SCRM and STP. There remains noteworthy potential to enrich our knowledge on SCRM and STP since there are many diverse ways of defining concepts. Moreover, the applicability of organisation and management studies in industrial settings is still open to discussion (Daft and Lewin, 1990; Rynes, *et al.* 2001; Tranfield and Starkey, 1998), with a couple of researchers ascribing this issue to deficient communication (e.g. Hambrick, 1994). Some scholars (e.g. van Aken, 2004) attribute the problematic issue to the investigated content being excessively analytical, descriptive and distracted with the hypothetical knowledge to the detriment of enthusiasm for taking care of field problems. It leads to the assumption that typical scientific research in organisation and management has a tendency to concentrate "on analysis and explanation, on problems and their causes" (Denyer *et al.*, 2008, p. 393). Indeed, "it criticises everyday accounts and practices… but does not seek to transform them except in the general sense of demonstrating their incorrectness." (Whitley 1984, pp. 371).

It is required to understand how organisations can achieve as well as maintain their competitive advantage. On the basis of conventional and emerging literature, we suppose that companies engaged in STPs are better able to mitigate and respond to SCRs since uncertainty can be managed through cooperation (Spekman *et al.*, 1998). We focus on creative solutions on how to react to supply chain disturbances which merit more consideration (Bode *et al.*, 2011). In the present study, we argue that both STP and SCRM are critical success factors for company performance and can be seen as massive empowering agents. More precisely, we advocate that the capabilities needed for STP serve as enablers for effective SCRM. On that basis, the study at hand is concerned with the fusion of the two research streams SCRM and STP as an innovative solution to an ever changing world in the industry environment. The economic downturn has triggered a decline in demand, but with the help of supplier networks it has been possible for organisations like Nokia, Ikea and Dell to manage and retain their growth through flexibility. Vertical and horizontal networking are being used by organisations to manage risks, and they pursue knowledge transfer through joint creation of technology and new knowledge (Kogut and Zander, 1996; Powell *et al.*, 1996; Teece, 2000). Thus, the authors devote the following research to the main question: How can the integration of STP and SCRM effectively be used to manage successfully supply chain risks? Stated, the purpose of this analysis is to examine the nexus of linkages between SCRM and STP. Hence, the present study aims at developing a tentative conceptual framework that clusters identified research on conjoint SCRM-STP capabilities that may be, in light of empirical advancement, embraced and further developed into measurement constructs in future research.

With the frame of reference, the spectrum of the scientific concepts and management disciplines to be examined are designed. This design is based on the research questions to be answered and the institutional context of the investigation. Therefore, the objectives of the research study were distilled into five key research questions:

(i) What is the intellectual and conceptual structure of scientific research on SCRM?

(ii) What are the current research paradigms of STP as presented in academic literature?

(iii) What are the strategies for effective supply chain risk management?

(iv) What are the capabilities for effective strategic technology partnering?

(v) What are the major SCRM-STP capabilities that lead to increased performance? And could this help researchers and practitioners to build a more grounded case for implementation?

1.4 Overview of the research study

The present study combines notions from SCM, strategic management, as well as technology and innovation to explore the relationship between SCRM and STP. The study is structured in six chapters (cf. Figure I-2). In the first chapter, the problem statement of the research study is presented. The starting point, in this case, forms the current state of research on SCRM and STP. The overarching objective, the related research questions, as well as the methodological structure of the work, are described. Subsequent to the summary of the research study, Chapter II reviews the role of bibliometric studies and designates the chosen method – that of co-citation. Using a bibliometric study, the most co–cited articles on SCRM are analysed using multivariate statistical techniques, i.e. multidimensional scaling (MDS), cluster analysis, and correspondence factor analysis. Moreover, it entails the presentation and discussion of the findings by describing the intellectual structure of SCRM research discipline attained from the multivariate statistical analysis. In Chapter III, based on the identifications from a frequency analysis, we discuss the classified articles on STP according to theoretical perspectives, methodological approaches, regional focus, the location of study, the level of analysis, types of partnership, and industries considered. Hence, we examine the existing body of knowledge the STP literature that currently exists by tracking current paradigms in STP research and proposing a research agenda. The subsequent Chapter IV deals with the elucidation of SCRM strategies based on the SLR research methodology. Literature is analysed and synthesised, succeeded by the description of the principal findings of the review, resulting in a conceptual classificatory framework for the risk mitigating strategies of SCRM. The study groups and synthesises the various SCRM strategies into proactive and reactive approaches as well as into ante and post disruption state and, additionally, classifies them according to the different supply chain (SC) types, that is to say, efficient SC, risk-hedging SC, responsive SC, and agile SC. Altogether, the findings provide essential practical and theoretical contributions to the strategic responses to adverse incidents. In Chapter V an extensive review, a classification and categorisation of the literature on STP are conducted. It further analyses and synthesises the extant literature and translate the major findings of the present review into a new format. In detail, the review structures extant STP capabilities literature into a proposed classificatory framework referred to as CLONT-framework and highlights its critical importance in strategic management and innovation research from a theoretical, empirical, and practical point of view. Finally, in Chapter VI we use conceptual theory building to create a tentative conceptual framework and to guide future investigation through focused research propositions. Both the resource–based view of the firm and the social capital theory (SCT), serving as a theoretical basis, encourage the dialogue between SCRM and STP and inform the generation of the designed conceptual framework. We examine capabilities that may influence cooperating firms to rely more on STP to deliver countermeasures to potential SCRs.

Figure I-2 illustrates an overview of the core elements that constitute the basis of the present research study. Strategic success potentials such as capabilities are deemed to be essential command variables of strategic management. On the one hand, innovation and technology management lead to opportunities for the sustainable viability of an organisation, on the other hand, they are always associated with risks (Gassmann, 2006). Consequently, a discussion on the concepts and approaches of strategic management, SCRM, as well as on innovation and technology management is required for the consideration of the research questions. An in-depth examination of the overall scope of the relevant concepts and approaches, taking into account its substantive ties, is not possible in the present research study. The conceptual background introduced cannot and does not claim to recreate the full collection of scientific discussions and elucidations in detail and to present a comprehensive depiction of the connections between the research fields so far. The aim of the chapter is rather to prepare the conceptual foundations that are relevant to the subsequent development of a strategic risk management framework for SC networks in a consolidated form. We contribute to the development of the emerging theories of SCRM and STP by integrating notions from the RBV of the firm, the SCT, as well as SCM and strategic management to ease bridging the gap between two principal research disciplines and to highlight the potential value of STP and SCRM to manage risks, disruptions and uncertainties. In the following. we will analyse the theoretical foundations shaping the foundation of the research study that underlines the connection between SCRM and STP.

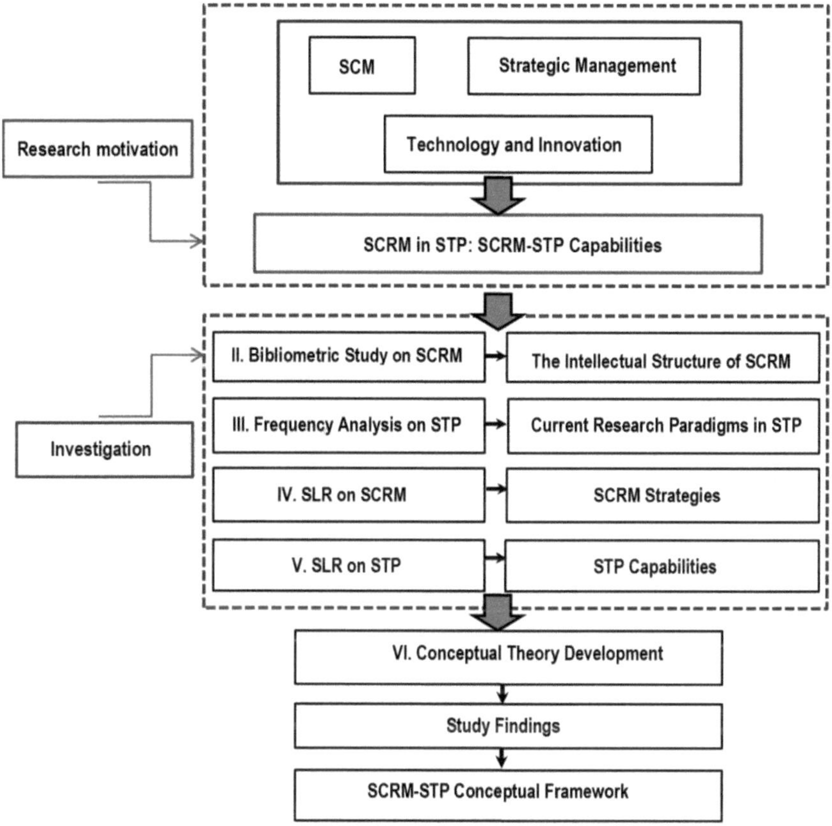

Figure I-2: Overview of the research study.
Source: Own illustration.

2 Theoretical foundations

2.1 Theoretical background of the research

The difficulties and disturbances being part of the SC are managed through the creative ability of an organisation. It must be able to implement long–term solutions to risks and react quickly in the process of solving issues (Mitroff and Alpaslan, 2003) to continue with their value offerings in an efficient manner (Ketchen and Hult, 2007). It is highly risky to carry out technological innovation when there are only a few products that prove to be promising ideas and finally reach the market as services or products for the customers (Hagedoorn and Duysters, 2002). A number of studies claim a positive relationship between external STPs and innovation outcome (Ahuja, 2000; Ahuja and Katila, 2001; Baum *et al.*, 2000), demonstrating that organisations actually make use of external knowledge sources to respond to fast technological changes (Hill and Rothaermel, 2003; Keil *et al.*, 2008). Several researchers have suggested that companies are motivated to enter strategic partnerships: (1) to share and reduce risks (e.g. Chang, 2003; Hagedoorn *et al.*, 2006; Forrest and Martin, 1992; Kotabe and Swan, 1995; Dogsen, 1993); (2) for cost–economizing reasons (e.g. Das *et al.*, 1998;Eisenhardt and Schoonhoven, 1996; Hagedoorn, 2002; Kim and Song, 2007; Lorenzoni and Lipparini, 1999); (3) to boost innovativeness (e.g. Lane and Lubatkin, 1998; Noseleit and de Faria, 2013; Park *et al.*, 2004; Phelps, 2010); and (4) to improve performance (e.g. Fey and Birkinshaw, 2005; Hall and Bagchi–Sen, 2002; Huang and Yu, 2011). In the strategic management literature, STPs are frequently postulated as an important enabler of innovativeness in organisations because STP is strongly interrelated to creating value (Cho and Pucik, 2005), reacting to market uncertainty (Stevens and Dimitriadis, 2004), and overcoming demand fluctuations (Fisher, 1997). Golgeci and Ponomarov (2013) showed that the innovativeness of organisations in rapidly changing business environments is also manifested in the way it handles SCRs. It is vital to reflect not merely the innovativeness role in joint performance but also the increased level of susceptibility towards disruptions and a high degree of adversity (Hult *et al.,* 2004a). Hence, the adverse and disruptive incidents faced by firms can be handled through organisational innovativeness using STP.

In view of unfavourable and uncertain conditions, it becomes essential to understand the capabilities that may enhance the performance of the organisation (Ponomarov and Holcomb, 2009). Any disastrous or disruptive issue subjected to the SC of the organisation can benefit from the building, deployment and leverage of organisational innovativeness (Hearnshaw and Wilson, 2013). For the purpose of the present study, we have decided to use the RBV and the SCT as the two complementary theoretical foundations to perform our research. So far, the RBV has been increasingly used in diverse research disciplines, whereas researchers have only recently begun to adopt the SCT to explain SCM phenomena. Both theories stem from the organisational and management research. One reason for using theories from these adjacent research disciplines is that, in general, organisation and management research is commonly considered as "an applied discipline" (Zald, 1993, p. 514). "The process of systematically applying a theory in diverse settings improves the theory's explanatory power by delineating its boundaries or scope conditions" (Whetten *et al.*, 2009, p. 3). We consider both theories as convenient to explain the mechanisms inherent in both SCRM and STP. In the following, we will elaborate these two underpinning theoretical lenses informing the present study.

2.2 The Resource-based view of the firm in SCRM and STP

Referring to the RBV, it is the rare, valuable and hard to substitute assets that represent the actual competitive advantage (Zhang and Dhaliwal, 2009). When those resources or assets can provide abnormal profits, they are linked to competitive advantage (Wernerfelt, 1984; Peteraf, 1993). The organisation is viewed as a bundle of resources where the related capabilities, competencies, and assets are configured together (Ketchen and Hult, 2007; Vesalainen and Hakala, 2014). Although the RBV entirely focuses on internal resources of an organisation, there are certain researchers that have also emphasised the importance of collaboration with regard to unique resource combinations (Rothaermel and Hess, 2007). They give rise to the question of how an interconnected firm can devote to assets that are not completely possessed or controlled by its interior association. Hence, the classical RBV of a firm has several extensions due to the current dissatisfaction with the purely firm–internal resource perspective (Chisholm and Nielsen, 2009). These theoretical extensions make it possible to view suppliers as a part of firms' valuable resource base (Steinle and Schiele, 2008). Accordingly, the boundaries of firm activities related to the SC and OM have been discussed as part of the resource–based view (e.g. Holcomb and Hitt, 2007). Hence, adopting the RBV perspective, SC linkages that ensure quality materials from suppliers to the organisation or to the customers show valuable resources and provide the organisation with improved operational performance (Rungtusanatham *et al.*, 2003). Both SC linkages and the connection between the SC entities are seen as critical. Similarly, the operational performance impact of the SC interactions can also be clearly understood through the RBV in a pragmatic and conceptual manner (Barratt and Oke, 2007). In this light, R&D co–operation is primarily initiated by firms that are carrying out risky, complex and expensive research projects that are predominantly present in the high–technologies industries (Miotti and Sachwald, 2003).

2.3 The Social Capital Theory in the STP and SCRM context

Gulati and Garguilo (1999) propose that the development of inter-organisational networks (e.g. supply chains) is reliant on endogenous and exogenous variables, as well as on other vital indicators. Moran (2005, p. 1129) advocates that inter-organisational capital "may well prove to be the firm's most enduring source of competitive advantage." The external networks of an organisation, according to the SCT, is a strong contributor towards performance (Leenders and Gabbay, 1999). Similar to differences in STPs, SCs vary with respect to critical competencies such as the learning ability (e.g. McFarland *et al.*, 2008), innovation ability (e.g. Faems *et al.*, 2010), or the ability to respond in a quick and speedy manner to the updated conditions of the market (e.g. Merschmann and Thonemann, 2011).

In this regard, risks and costs can be reduced through the long–term SC effectiveness that has been established through mutually beneficial relationships, shared values, and trust (Vasileiou and Morris, 2006). In other words, social capital in the SC context may be viewed as the information, trust, and norms of mutual benefits inherent within SC structures (Woolcock, 1998). Individuals and organisations within social networks have been the focus of research, and the social capital is used to strengthen supplier relationship (Uzzi, 1996), knowledge transfer promotion (Inkpen and Tsang, 2005), and the regional production networks (Romo and Schwartz, 1995).

Nahapiet and Ghoshal (1998) have developed an approach to cluster attributes of social capital in three distinct categories that has been widely adopted in the fields of operations, SCM and strategic management (e.g. Hagedoorn *et al.*, 2006; and Tsang, 2005; Borgatti and Foster, 2003; Koka and Prescott, 2002; Lawson *et al.*, 2008; Mukherjee *et al.*, 2013; Siu and Bao, 2008). They describe attributes of social capital, clustering them into three categories: a) structural, b) cognitive, and c) relational. The structural element refers to the arrangements of linkages between network members. The cognitive element stands for shared understanding and meaning between the members of the networks; and lastly, the relational element involves partnership, trust, reciprocity, and mutual respect derived from long–term interactions (Yli–Renko, 2001). In the following, we will elaborate each dimension since they form the core of our conceptual framework presented later in Chapter VI.

2.3.1 *Structural dimension of Social Capital*

In total, structural social capital considers the focal points resulting from the arrangement of the system of contacts inside of a given social structure. Partners that upgrade their relations and the communication with different contacts at diverse levels (e.g. technical and managerial) and several functions (e.g. quality, engineering and sales) permit the formation of a social structure that favours both sides of the partnership (Cousins *et al.*, 2006). The structural dimension is a variant of social capital studies in a structuralist and topological manner. At the actor's level, the central position of the actors in the network and the associated benefits constitute the main focus of these studies (e.g., Burt *et al.*, 2000; Powell *et al.*, 1996; Brass and Burkhardt, 1993). Structural capital is often discussed in terms of the wider network of different actors with which a firm holds ties (Autry and Griffis, 2008; Granovetter, 1973). In order to maximise gain, the actor, in this case, is an active agent who exploits his position and is known to be rational (Prusak and Cohen, 2001). The local network topology is the principal function of the actor that provides benefits and ties that are subliminally perceived of as forming leverageable structures (Athanassiou and Nigh, 1999; Markovsky *et al.*, 1993).

2.3.2 Cognitive dimension of Social Capital

The resources that have the ability to provide shared systems of interpretations, representations, and meanings amongst the parties are referred to as the social capital cognitive dimension (Villena *et al.*, 2011). The joint understanding of fundamental assumptions and concepts, as well as shared language, are the basis for cognitive capital (Bolino *et al.*, 2002). Hence, it provides free communication, as well as resource exchange through common interests and objectives (Parra–Requena *et al.*, 2010). Between two actors, there are high levels of cognitive capital according to research while the definition may vary according to the task, network type and outcomes (Lechner *et al.*, 2010).

2.3.3 Relational dimension of Social Capital

Recurrent bonds with familiar companies generate a pattern of interactions in which focal companies can access data about the quality and performance of existing and potential partners (Zaheer *et al.*, 1998; Gulati *et al.*, 2000). SCT, in general, applies to the analysis of inter–organisational relationships as firms endeavour to share data, synchronise their plans and create products conjointly (Galaskiewicz, 2011). In light of the SCT, we conclude that SCRM is – just like STP – an ongoing process that implicates long–term commitment and dedication of all SC members involved (Mahapatra *et al.*, 2010; Giunipero and Eltantawy, 2004; Manuj and Mentzer, 2008b) and requires mutual trust (Bode *et al.*, 2011; Lavastre *et al.*, 2012; Faisal *et al.*, 2006; Tang, 2006a). Mutual interdependence (Adler and Kwon, 2002), actors' similarity (Rivera, 2010) and geographic proximity (Chetty and Michailova, 2011; Felzensztein *et al.*, 2010) are the factors behind the development of relational capital between at least two actors. The social quality of the relationships such as mutual identifications, obligations, relational norms, friendship and trust are part of the relational attributes of the social capital structure (e.g. Cousins *et al.*, 2006; Petersen *et al.*, 2008).

2.4 Merging RBV and SCT

The RBV of the firm and the SCT are the two primary theories being part of many studies (cf. Ahuja, 2000a; Zaheer and Bell, 2005). They have the ability to explain a vast spectrum of concepts becoming visible in research trends and to reduce the gap between research paradigms (Di Guardo and Harrigan, 2012). Hence, the RBV and the SCT are the two complementary theoretical bases used in this study to explore the nexus of SCRM and STP. Within strategic management, the resource–based view is considered most dominant (Barney and Mackey, 2005; Newbert, 2007). The strategic management initiative of RBV revolves around performing better than the competitors and achieving a competitive advantage. Thus, the internal resources such as human, organisational, intangible, technological, physical and financial resources are the competitive benefits of an organisation as part of the classical RBV (Fey and Birkinshaw, 2005; Rothaermel and Hess, 2007). Following Rindova and Fombrun (1999, p. 694), the RBV "attributes advantage in an industry to a firm's control over bundles of unique material, human, organisational and locational resources and skills that enable unique value–creating strategies".

The SCT, on the other hand, is considered as the largest growing area of the organisation network research. This concept has been symbiotically able to return the favour and to increase the interest in social networks (Kim *et al.*, 2011). Social capital describes the benefits that actors may gain from their partnership ties and the network in which they are rooted (Baker, 1990; Burt, 1992; Bourdieu, 1986; Coleman, 1988). We adopt the definition of social capital offered by Nahapiet and

Ghoshal (1998) who regard it as “the sum of the actual and potential resources embedded within, available through, and derived from the network of relationships possessed by an individual or social unit” (p. 243). Relational ties are formed with stakeholders like suppliers, government agencies, unions and competitors as part of the relational resource. The existing variations within the relational resource are considered as a natural outcome of the SC competition (Borgatti and Li, 2009). The proposed extension of the RBV provides a link between the RBV and SCT. We demonstrate the significance of merging the two theories of RBV and SCT while taking into account the inner capabilities of the partners within a network in conjunction with capabilities to exploit the network structure at the same time (Zaheer and Bell, 2005). The theoretical hole between the traditional RBV and SCT is substantial since the RBV centres on the investigation of firms and their internal rent creating assets (member attributes), whereas SCT accentuates the value of external ties (Chisholm and Nielsen, 2009; Lavie, 2006).

3 Methodological approach

3.1 Methodological issues

The ability of SCM to promote knowledge is limited due to our lack of conceptual research; thus, well-implemented conceptual analysis can provide us with the chance to come up and face practical issues rather than staying aloof (Fawcett *et al.*, 2011). Conceptualisation involves abstract thinking and includes the mental representation of an idea. Conceptualisation comes from the Late Latin conceptus and Medieval Latin word *conceptuālis* which means a thought that is only present in the mind and is distinct from the embodiment (American Heritage Dictionary, 2011). Therefore, conceptualisation entails "understanding" or "observing" an abstract aspect in an individual's mind, and conceptual thinking is a process in which a condition or a problem is to be understood abstractly through identification of patterns, relationships, and major fundamental properties (MacInnis, 2011). Empirical and conceptual articles are usually distinguished from each other (Elder and Paul, 2009) in a way that the former includes data. For instance, entirely conceptual articles comprise of 'state-of-the-art' reviews, 'integrative frameworks' and 'theoretical models'. Entirely mathematical works involving in-depth analysis are also considered as theoretical works, bringing about, contrary to verbal statements, mathematical illustrations of the concepts (MacInnis, 2004).

The study at hand relied on conceptual theory building to create a tentative conceptual framework. Initial conceptualisation informed by considering, for instance, real world examples, adjoined with analytical thoughts and related paradoxes (Quinn and Cameron, 1988) along with dialectical antagonisms (Astley and van de Ven, 1983), is labeled as "heterogeneous thought trials" within conceptual theory development in which the sole use of sound logic could suffice if statistical analysis were not available yet (Narasimhan, 2014). We may contend that conceptual articles are, as a wide range of papers seems to be, crucial to the advance of a research discipline. They permit us to move from a smaller scale perspective to a full-scale one; one that focuses on notions that do not currently allow empirical testing and provides better approaches to observing the world (Whetten *et al.*, 2009). In addition to that, one may assume that conceptual articles have the most elevated citation frequencies, proposing they are extensively read and are significant for consecutive empirical research endeavours (MacInnis, 2004). According to Narasimhan (2014, p. 223):

> *"The field of OM can only advance through the generation of "big ideas" leading to home-grown theories. Such ideas can be generated through the use of observational data by synthesizing and integrating past research to provide new conceptualizations of OM issues. It is important to encourage intellectual inquiry unfettered by methodological "musts". A change in mind-set in this regard might expand the reach and resources of OM researchers."*

To begin with, we used bibliometric studies, frequency analysis and the systematic literature review methodology to inform the design of our SCRM-STP conceptual framework.

3.2 Bibliometrics and Co-citation Analysis

One trend is apparent: an increasing number of academic researchers have dedicated their attention to bibliometric studies as an efficient way to evaluate the advance of management disciplines evolving from their juvenile stages. "Scholars devote significant effort to make sense of what has already been done, capture key lessons learned from the past, and identify directions for the future" (Zahra and Sharma, 2004, p. 332). In their review of bibliometric studies in management and organisation from 1993 to 2013, Zupic and Cater (2014) found out that the median year of publication was 2011, i.e., that more than 50 per cent of the articles that employed bibliometric methods were issued within the last three years. While bibliometric is a well-established method used in various scientific fields (Acedo and Cassilas, 2005), management scholars have only recently begun to employ bibliometric and lexicographic techniques increasingly (e.g. Walter and Ribière, 2013; Galvagno, 2011; Backhaus *et al.*, 2010). Bibliometric methods have been applied, for instance, to map the areas of strategic management (e.g. Vogel and Güttel, 2013; Di Stefano *et al.*, 2010; Furrer *et al.*, 2008), organisation (Vogel, 2012; Nosella *et al.*, 2012; Volberda *et al.*, 2011), innovation (e.g. Raasch *et al.*, 2013; Fagerberg *et al.*, 2012; Keupp *et al.*, 2012), entrepreneurship (e.g. Campos *et al.*, 2012; Landström *et al.*, 2012; Kraus, 2011), or operations management (Pilkington and Meredith, 2006).

Although bibliometric studies are widely applied in a diverse range of scientific research – as outlined above – the authors are neither aware of any other bibliometric study in the SCM field except the work of Charvet *et al.*, (2008) nor are they aware of any bibliometric study specifically addressing SCRM.[1] The main purpose of statistical bibliographies is to illuminate the routes and the development trajectory of a discipline, using citation counts and emerging clusters to analyse the various facets of written communications (Eom, 2008). Since the strength of bibliometric studies lies in their unobtrusiveness: they allow for a high level of objectivity (Gmür, 2003) and quantifiability (Durisin *et al.*, 2010) with the means of quantitative analysis (Börner *et al.*, 2003), making declarations about qualitative characteristics (Wallin, 2005). Finally, the outcome is a comprehensive depiction of the subject matter of the research efforts with its conceptual structure as discerned by authors contributing to its intellectual progress (Callon *et al.*, 1993). Therefore, the study relied on *bibliometrics*: "the study of a given field or body of literature using quantitative analysis and statistics to describe patterns of publication" (Vogel, 2012, p. 1019). "The term *bibliometrics* refers to the mathematical and statistical analysis of patterns that appear in the publication and use of documents" (Ramos-Rodriguez and Ruiz-Navarro, 2004, p. 981). The bibliometric technique used herein is that of co–citation analysis which links cited documents (Small, 1973). This method has most commonly been employed to identify core articles in a stream of academic literature (Calero–Medina and van Leeuwen, 2012; Small, 1999; Zitt and Bassecoulard, 1994) and has been fruitfully used by

[1] cf. Zupic and Cater (2014) for a comprehensive overview of bibliometric studies conducted in management and organisation studies, published between 1993 and 2013.

subfields of management and operations science as a tool for enhanced comprehension of the intellectual structure of a given research area (e.g. Carvalho *et al.*, 2013; Leone *et al.*, 2012; Herbst *et al.*, 2011; Martin *et al.*, 2012). Relying on the supposition that the references cited in academic articles are a dependable hint of their relative influence in a given field, co–citation analysis may identify the most influential articles and define the relational associations between them (Teichert, 2010).

3.3 Systematic Literature Review

We conducted a systematic and comprehensive review, consistent with recent suggestions to fortify the methodological rigour of literature reviews in the management and business field (e.g. Briner *et al.*, 2009; Crossan and Aypadin, 2010; Holtbrügge and Dögl, 2012; Macpherson and Jones, 2010). It delivers a general audit trail of procedures, decisions and conclusions made by the reviewers, permitting lucency and the replication of the study (Ordani *et al.*, 2008). Thus, it is a valid technique to generate fresh insights and knowledge by synthesising prevailing academic articles that can be of greater relevance and significance than newer studies (Cooper, 2010). In contrast with the conventional arguably subjective pooling methodologies, a systematic review research method, as adopted in the research study at hand, removes the subjectivity of data collection by using a predefined selection algorithm (Crossan and Aypadin, 2010; Dickersin *et al.*, 1994). This method has been used by several other authors that conducted a SLR in SCM and strategic management as well (e.g. Bakker, 2010; Brandenburg *et al.*, 2014; Felekoglu and Moultrie, 2014; Hassini *et al.*, 2012; Kilubi, 2015). According to Rousseau *et al.* (2008), systematic reviews need to employ critical interpretation with defined criteria aiming to deliver the evidentiary value of previous research. The SLR process was employed for identifying, analysing, synthesising, interpreting and reporting the greatest evidence from the academic literature (Briner *et al.*, 2009; Dickersin *et al.*, 1994; Petticrew, 2001). The scientific rigour in executing each of these steps is of paramount importance for a high-quality review (Starbuck, 2005). Thus, evidence that has been produced from a systematic review using a methodologically rigorous approach has been found to have a strong impact on scientific research and can provide a powerful tool. However, the greatest challenge is to synthesise the review results (Woolf *et al.*, 1990; Denyer *et al.*, 2008). Nonetheless, the SLR methodology offers an evidence-based foundation for literature survey and can thus substantiate a key methodology for investigating secondary data (Briner *et al.*, 2009; Rousseau *et al.*, 2008; Popay *et al.*, 1998).

The strength of these tools to synthesise evidence in existing studies is highlighted by Light and Pillemer (1984) who argue that this method may generate new knowledge and, consequently, must be considered just as valuable as conducting completely new research. We suggest that there are several benefits of the review process as an arrangement of stages, merging narrative synthesis and more conventional methods, where the literature searched for is scant and varied. The iterative research process allowed for a redefinition of review strategy and criteria as well as the use of data extraction templates to examine full papers augmented transparency and consistency during the selection, analysis and synthesis stages. Table I-1 summarises the main differences between systematic literature reviews and conventional reviews.

The systematic literature review method was first introduced in medical sciences and has expanded into the management field since then. Thereby, Petticrew (2001), one of the pioneers, discussed the exploitation of the SLR approach outside of medicine and its applicability to virtually all areas of science. As a result, the SLR approach has finally entered the psychological field and ultimately the management research field (Briner and Denyer, 2012). The new method of the SLR was seen as a contrast and development of the consequently so-called 'traditional narrative reviews' (Tranfield *et al.*, 2003, p. 213). However, SLR has only been used recently and sporadically in the SCRM field (e.g. Gimenez and Tachizawa, 2012; Kamal and Iran, 2014; Pilbeam *et al.*, 2012; Wong *et al.*, 2012).

Systematic literature reviews vs. conventional literature reviews		
Criteria	**Systematic literature reviews**	**Conventional literature reviews**
Defining review questions	Initiate the study with precise questions to be answered or hypothesis to be tested.	At times, also start with accurate questions to be answered, but they usually involve more general discussion of themes with no pre-determined hypothesis.
Searching for relevant studies	Seek to locate all relevant studies to restrict the influence of publication and other biases.	Rarely try to locate all relevant and available literature.
Inclusion and exclusion of studies	Involve in detail the description of what kinds of research studies should be included and which ones excluded to limit bias in selecting.	Typically do not explain the inclusion and exclusion criteria for selecting relevant studies.
Evaluation of study quality	Frequently conduct a quality appraisal for the research methodologies applied to the studies referred to.	Often do not examine differences in research methods or research quality.
Synthesis of study findings	Conclusions are based on the most impeccable studies regarding the methodology employed.	Usually not make a differentiation between methodology impeccable and deficient studies.

Table I-1: Systematic literature reviews vs. conventional literature reviews.
Source: On the basis of the existing literature
(Briner *et al.*, 2009; Denyer *et al.*, 2008; Mulrow, 2001; Popay *et al.*, 1998; Petticrew, 2001; Rousseau *et al.*, 2008).

3.4 Conceptual theory development

Theories derived from qualitative research methodologies could be attributed to conceptual and conjectural processes as a key measure. A close review of real-world scenarios provides the necessary impetus and background for the vast majority of theories drawn up and presented for scrutiny. Thus, Weick (1989) is of the opinion that a sound theory which can justify itself later on – once it is closely evaluated and observed – should include characteristics related to such aspects as (a) the theory should hold true under real world conditions; (b) the supportive arguments should entail a high degree of rationality; and (c) the concepts presented should relate to presumed realities in existence. Theories presented from real world scenarios stand up to scrutiny (Dublin, 1976) since they interrelate the domain of interest in the context of actual scenarios. In Figure I-3, we have depicted how our research fits into the conceptual research process. The nature of reality studied within the present research study is how SCRM and STPs help companies to mitigate and reduce risks in SCs. We identify a research gap that firm innovativeness could be developed, applied, and used to overcome damaging and adverse events that occur in the SC of firms with the means of appropriate capabilities. Therefore, it is important for firms to exhibit innovativeness with the help of STPs in the face of uncertain occurrences in the SCs. Through the abstraction of reality, we model a conceptual framework that depicts the linkage between SCRM and STP to mitigate SCRs and foster innovativeness. The SCT and the RBV, serving as theoretical foundations, encourage the fusion between the two research streams.

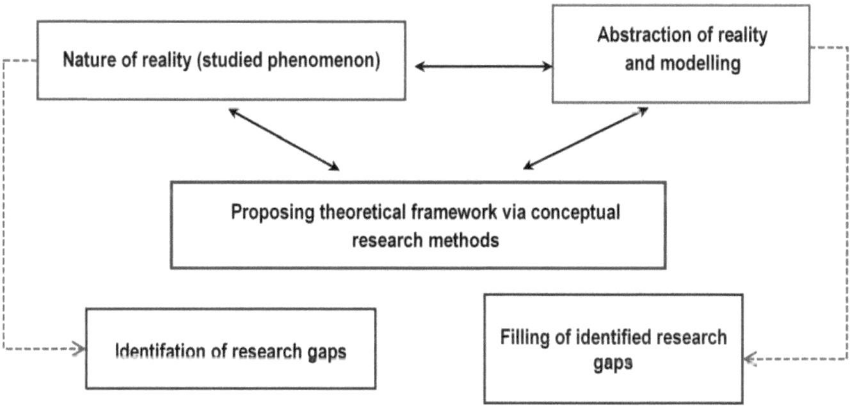

Figure I-3: Elements of the conceptual research process.
Source: Adapted from Narasimhan (2014, p. 218).

SCRM is considered as a significant tool to enhance organisational performance (Ponomarov, 2012). Therefore, SCRM is specifically significant in times when disruptions cannot be predicted beforehand, i.e. precautionary steps cannot be taken (Sheffi and Rice, 2005). Even though the significance of inter-organisational relationships to SC network performance and efficiency has been adequately recognised (Podolny and Page, 1998; Dyer and Nobeoka, 2002; Liker and Choi, 2004), there has been little research performed that has analysed the impact of such a relationship, specifically regarding the social capital that they may involve. However, in the research of some other fields it is suggested that there could be such a linkage (cf. Folke *et al.*, 2002). Further support is provided by anecdotal evidence from the managerial literature. For example, business professionals are encouraged by Mitroff and Alpaslan (2003) to think and perform innovatively so as mitigate the SCRs.

The present study claims that SCRM studies that apply the SCT have been a constrained one because it draws upon only one or two out of three conceptual dimensions presented in Nahapiet and Ghoshal's (1998) inspiring and influential work. Conceptual research is a scientific analysis that depends on an intangible thought process, in contrast to research carried out by empirical means. It is performed to conceptualise, delimit, and solve practical issues (Corley and Gioia, 2011). Therefore, conceptual research is frequently linked with the foremost stage of scientific evaluation, namely identification (bringing forward a new theory). So why should conceptual studies be carried out? As observed in acclaimed journal papers, conceptual articles may have a significant, disparate effect on the discovery of knowledge, and also on the development and involvement of a discipline (Yadav, 2010; MacInnis, 2011). Conceptual studies enable us to view the world and the decision-making process through a new perspective and facilitate to find new ideas for present and emerging activities for resolving real-world issues (Fawcett *et al.*, 2011). After the research prospects have been known, consequent empirical research leads us further towards the discovery of knowledge. Therefore, conceptual research is interlinked with empirical research in which some deficiencies in knowledge could be filled through conceptual research. Yadav (2010) claimed that when a particular key element in the set of inputs is eliminated or considerably changed, there will be an influence on the procedures that foster knowledge – usually in unexpected ways. A research discipline that strives to develop impeccable quality conceptual research might opt for the laborious route to the knowledge identification and its distribution. Empirical studies are not appropriate for some paths to the inquiry; in particular, challenging the shortcomings in knowledge regarding theories we adopt to describe the SCM concept. For instance, if we seek to support real options theory (Bowman and Hurry, 1993) instead of transaction cost economics (TCE) to describe insourcing compared to outsourcing (Williamson, 1991). Rhetorical methods such as analysing the logical consistency of either point of view, assessing the epistemological presumptions which drive each point of view's projections, and assessing the empirical confirmation could lead to the provision of the most appropriate way ahead (Whetten, 1989).

It is observed in evolving research notes that: (1) there is high inconsistency in the empirical attempts to operationalise trust constructs; and (2) that we consequently require new construct development (Seppanen *et al.*, 2007; Jones *et al.,* 2010; Whipple *et al.*, 2013). One of the best ways to deal with emerging problems, for which empirical data is not present because of the emerging nature of our knowledge regarding the phenomena, is conceptual research (Sutton and Staw, 1995). By enabling us to study the rising phenomena, theoretical research help us to: (1) enhance the appropriateness and managerial relevance of our study; and (2) to move further than just presenting the new phenomena to serve an active role in forming the conversation through "sense-giving" – the process of developing the way other scholars and practitioners understand the phenomena under study (Maitlis and Lawrence, 2007). Conceptualisation is a way of bringing about new and maybe even completely different concepts that provide the stimulus for changing a discipline's established models (Kuhn 1996). Likewise, Kilduff (2006) asserted that theoretical papers are useful as they lead to original and significant ideas that could result in the development of additional research queries. Furthermore, using 'methodical conjectures' conceptual research enables academics to study the concepts by applying some thinking tests to discover innovative associations and relationships (Weick, 1989).

One may also discover that it is beneficial to explain the usefulness of our study using conceptual research since it may have a high influence on filling the disparity between theory and practical context (Waller *et al.* 2012). It helps develop the theoretical and expert discussion on new issues that are coming up regarding the relationship between SCRM and STP. This comprises moving further than describing the reasons for the occurrence of the phenomena to formulate reasonable opinions about how we should perceive the phenomena and its interlinking in the future (Weick, 1979). Corley and Gioia's (2011) point out that in studies on management and organisational issues, the hypothetical contributions have not managed to predict effectively (with increased emphasis) the significant conceptual, as well as the practical needs of the society's currently most dominant players that is business and societal enterprises. Organisation studies indulge in taking theories and ideas from other fields, those that are vertical as well as horizontal to it (Whetten et al., 2009). In this case, SCM is not an exemption either, for instance, SC identity salience (Min *et al.*, 2008) and SC capital (Carey *et al.,* 2011). There are some advantages of such borrowing, comprising the improved authenticity of the borrower, better explanation, and enhanced relations between the different disciplines (Morgeson and Hofmann, 1999). All in all, theoretical studies assume a significant role in the current world of knowledge which could motivate the much required empirical assessment.

4 Study findings and results

In the following, we will present the major findings from our research study for each topic separately (Chapter II to Chapter VI). However, in Chapter 5 of the summary of the research we will elaborate the implications and the contributions of our findings on research relating to SCRM and STP in conjunction.

4.1 The intellectual structure of Supply Chain Risk Management

4.1.1 Findings and results from the Cluster Analysis

Following preceding research, we ran a cluster analysis with means of Ward's method (cf. Acedo and Casillas 2005). A hierarchical cluster algorithm was run on the data to generate categories of papers that are closely linked to each other by determining the distance between pairs of articles. The clusters remained stable applying the entire linkage clustering method and three clusters emerged from the resulting dendrogram. The results are visually put into a graph in the dendrogram – which are annexed in Appendix III (of Chapter II) – showing which articles are closest. The cluster analysis generated three groups of articles. To better picture them in a conceptualised and confined region, the groups were overlaid on the MDS graph in Figure 2. The chart demonstrates 1) classifiable clusters that denote primary theoretical research domains; 2) positionings of the groups in relation to one another; and 3) juxtapositions of articles within clusters and across cluster borders. Hence, the papers within a group share mutually related topical research streams. Articles inside a particular group's limits convey a comparative co–reference profile, which implies that those papers address the comparable, broad inquiries – without fundamentally concurring with one another on their findings. Clusters of papers close to the extremes of the chart are, for the most part, interrelated – through co–reference – to fewer neighbours. Similitudes within a cluster depend on the way they are perceived by those authors who referred to the papers conjointly. Put into graphs, the proximity to cluster borders suggests the connection of their intellectual structure to other research domains within the research discipline.

Through co-citation analysis, we examined SCRM by considering different research streams that have emerged from previous research to gauge the state-of-the-art of its discipline and to frame future requirements and research prospects. Four clusters have been identified. Within Cluster One, a large group (Group 1) consists of articles that use simulation and mathematical modelling/programming to explain supply chain risk phenomena and scenarios (n = 9 articles). Their focus lies on supply and demand uncertainty whereby risk management models and optimisation schemes are implemented to illustrate the tradeoff between costs and risks (e.g. Nagurney and Matsypura; 2005; You *et al.*, 2009; Wu and Olsen, 2008). Another group (Group 2) within Cluster One specifically addresses inventory risks arguing that it affects supply efficiency and providing several suggestions on how to avoid the costs of unsold inventory (cf. Agrawal and Seshadri, 2000; Cachon, 2004) (n = 2 articles). The third group (Group 3) in Cluster One consists of conceptual papers and literature reviews (n = 7 articles) that aim at bringing together concepts, models, and frameworks in order to propose risk management and mitigation approaches (e.g. Manuj and Menzer, 2008b; Hallikas *et al.*, 2002; Ritchie and Brindley, 2007a; Trkman and McCormack, 2009). In their longitudinal study of a large retailer based in the UK, Khan *et al.* (2008) suggest a framework for design–led SCRM, thus demonstrating awareness of product design, not just understood as a creative task but rather as a platform to handle risk in SCs. Although the product design stream is relatively young in SCRM and is not commonly related to the SCM field, the article occupies a central positioning in the graph, which means that it is cited evenly by the other articles in its cluster (C1). In summary, for Cluster One (C1) SCRM act as a vehicle to boost the operational performance of supply chain networks. Articles in Cluster Two (C2) deal with various supply and demand risks and propose supply chain and product design methods as means to overcome those risks and manage the complexity related to them (e.g.

Johnson, 2001; Hendricks and Singhal, 2005). Overall, articles in C2 view complex supply chain design and system coordination as a source for risk exposure – but which, effectively managed, can transmute into opportunities for organisations to mitigate risks and disruptions associated with internal and external issues. As a result, a majority of papers in this cluster design methods related to managing disruption risks midst SC entities or co–ordination mechanisms in SC networks (e.g. Hallikas *et al.*, 2002). Finally, Cluster Three (C3) focuses primarily on risk mitigating strategies and encompasses two articles (D1 and D4) – one published in a practitioner–oriented publication outlet (*MIT Sloan Management Review*). A joint feature is an emphasis on identifying and illuminating the variety of risks. Cluster Three shows that effective SCRM is valuable because, in the case of emerging risks, supply chain structures and processes that capture risks and enable to satisfy customer demands are already available.

In sum, the conducted cluster analysis brings forward that the research field is arranged in five different areas of interest: 1) explaining supply chain risk phenomena, concepts, frameworks and insights on SCRM; 2) modelling risks for supply chains; 3) inventory risks affecting supply efficiency; 4) supply chain and product design methods; and 5) supply chain risk mitigating strategies. The identification of factors was reinforced when it was possible to allocate more than two–thirds of the articles into one of the six factors.

4.1.2 Findings and results from the Factor Analysis

The illuminating results of the factor analysis using Ward's method were extracted using Principal Component Analysis (PCA) with the correlation matrix serving as data input (Rowlands, 1999). Additionally, Varimax Rotation, a generally adopted formula, that tries to fit (or loaded) the highest possible amount of papers on the lowest possible amount of factors was run to obtain frugal factors characterised by theoretical importance. The information integrated with correspondence factor analysis were extracted from the correlation matrix. The basic assumption in correspondence factor analysis is that documents that are linked to each other will be cited together again and again in succeeding publications, as opposed to articles which are hardly ever or not at all mentioned together (Teichert, 2010). The correlations among co–citation entries are applied in correspondence factor analysis to decide which papers share universal aspects, with each factor embracing a common facet of the articles that come together (Di Guardo and Harrigan, 2012). Following Eom (2001), an article was included in a factor when its loading (on a –1 to +1 scale) was equal to or above |0.4|. The resulting model of six factors with eigenvalues larger than one was arranged, representing 80.6 per cent of the overall variance. The first three factors account for 65.9 per cent of the variance, explaining most of the variance. "[…] eigenvalues are numerical indicators of the relevance of the factors that suggest the relative importance of these underlying common elements" (Di Guardo and Harrigan, 2012, p. 800).

All 32 articles loaded on at least one factor. Factor One (F1) covers all the articles from Cluster Two (C2) – except that two articles from Cluster One also loaded on it, namely D5 and D21 (Cachon, 2004 and Nagurney and Matsypura, 2005, respectively) – which generated a considerable level of agreement compared with the results of the cluster analysis.

Factor Two (F2) was completely loaded with articles from Cluster One except for one article, namely D1 (Chopra and Sodhi, 2004). The second factor is to a certain degree concerned with the development of SCRM strategy but concentrates on particular aspects, e.g. outsourcing such as article D32 (Lockamy III and McCormack, 2010) or labour turnover, D30 (Jiang, 2009). Factor Three (F3) assembles a few articles from a special issue of the *Journal of Operations Management* on 'Perspectives on risk in supply chains' from 2009, namely D11, D28, and D30 (Braunscheidel and Suresh, 2009; Narasimhan and Talluri, 2009; Jiang *et al.*, 2009). Next, Factor Six (F6) was loaded with two articles from Cluster One, namely D16 and D20 (Cucchiella and Gastaldi, 2006 and Hallikas *et al.*, 2002, respectively), which are located in the middle of the MDS chart – indicating a major interest among scholars from various research streams. Both articles are conceptual or theoretical in nature and provide a framework for the analysis, assessment, and management of risks in SCs designed to mitigate and reduce risks.

From one viewpoint, particular groups and variables seem to indicate that genuine convergence of thought still needs to be established. The groups do not appear to impart an explicit denotation of SCRM, or a reliable perspective on risk management analysis, processes, risk sources, or risk mitigation strategies. From another viewpoint, the different perspectives do not seem to contradict each other or to be incompatible. Results from our statistical analysis demonstrate that the SCRM literature remains disjointed and portrayed by a few assorted, yet vigorous subfields characterised by a few diverse, but robust subfields with a moderate degree of overlaps. That is an encouraging outcome taking into account that multidisciplinary methods for exploring and interpreting a phenomenon deliver a more intensive clarification than uni–path theories. However, unnecessary discontinuity can be a shortcoming because it does not allow for the forthcoming of the research arena to shape as a distinctive discipline.

4.2 Current research paradigms in Strategic Technology Partnering

STPs are prevalent in the today's business world, thus, many professional communities among, scholars, scientists, engineers, and many more have acknowledged the value of inter-organisational networks to strengthen the ability to create innovations in the light of the fast–paced and highly complex market environment (Lee and Cole, 2003; Miles *et al.*, 2005; Wenger, 2000; Chesbrough, 2003). Given the increasing competition, high speed of technological change and discontinuity in most industries, companies enter numerous of strategic partnerships to obtain new resources and access to open new business markets or to reduce risks. Looking into the future, managers are prone to unknown challenges and problems concerning STPs (Kale and Singh, 2009).

More than 70 per cent (41 out of 57) of the reviewed papers were published between 1999 and 2008. The fact that the number of publications started to decrease beginning in 2008 may be because of the global economic crisis that started in 2007. Concerning the regional focus, the evidence is mainly focused on Europe and the USA, with some bias for the period 1999 to 2000 and 2007 to 2008. Industries in the present review focus on high–technology, from which the majority of approximately 40 per cent stem from Electrics and Electronics, Pharmaceutical (e.g. biotechnology), and Manufacturing (e.g. automotive) industries. In those industries creating knowledge is essential to gain competitiveness, where STPs are mainly entered to enhance innovation output marked by a high level of patent use (Schilling and Phelps, 2007; Vonortas, 1997). With regards to the level of analysis applied in the selected papers, one–third of the selected papers used organisational level, followed by industry/market level, and network level as a level of analysis. Nonetheless, most management studies employ a single level of analysis, even though most management issues deal with multi–level phenomena. Even more important, only a couple of academic writers have endeavoured to connect theory or execute research that employs cross–levels of inquiry or investigation. Moreover, the majority of partnership types in the reviewed literature were alliances, collaborations, and cooperation/contractual agreements. Given that R&D alliances are designed to generate new technologies, we expected a larger proportion of joint innovation in R&D alliances than other types of partnerships. This observation is reinforced by a research piloted by Hagedoorn and Duysters (2002) whose analysis demonstrates that the options for a certain type of partnership are influenced by both different environmental circumstances and company–specific settings. They confirm the more companies operate in high–tech sectors, such as ICT, pharmaceuticals, and aerospace, etc., the more they have a disproportionate preference for more flexible organisations like strategic technology alliances. Looking at the theoretical assumptions, we noticed that most articles dealt with the RBV and the KBV and that 54 per cent of the articles have addressed one single theory. The results are not surprising since the resource–based view may be the dominant theoretical standpoint within strategic management (Ketchen and Hult, 2007), and represents a central perspective in the research field of entrepreneurship as well (Alvarez and Busenitz, 2001). However, these two perspectives under consideration have fairly dissimilar concerns regarding the foundations of value creation.

The RBV highlights the internally accrued and combined resources, assets or capabilities (Grant and Baden–Fuller, 2004), and the knowledge–based view conceptualises firms as mechanisms that facilitate knowledge creation, where successful innovations benefit from various knowledge skills (Chesbrough, 2003). Therefore, R&D collaborations provide firms with experience of which they lack, helping them to increase the chance of successfully innovating products (Un and Cuervo–Cazurra, 2004).

Referring to the methodological approaches adopted for researching STP, the trend leans towards the use of secondary databases which has been on the rise from 1992 to 2014; even more sharply from 2005 onwards. We are certain of numerous dynamics that cause the increase in secondary database research: (a) a generally increased awareness of the need for high–quality data, whereas the database is assumed to hold all facts belonging to the domain under study (ACM, 2009) (b) improvements in the costs and quality of data storage/processing; and more importantly, (c) accumulation of high–quality, reliable datasets over the years including simplicity and uniformity of data arrangements (Korth and Silberschatz, 1997). Going into the future, the trend highlights an opportunity for more researchers who cannot afford to collect their own data first–hand to rapidly access simple, easy–to–use interfaces and information with accurate database updates (Korth and Silberschatz, 1997), but also the problem of recycling the same datasets which might lead to snooping. However, given that fact that the majority of journal articles have focused on quantitative studies, we expect a rise in the use of qualitative methods to explore further areas of STP that are alien to the scientific world.

4.3 Supply Chain Risk Management Strategies

SCs are becoming lengthier and more complex as a result of the globalised business environment and vertical integrations. SCRs are interweaved in a way; one mitigation strategy may alleviate other SCRs. For instance, bundling demand reduces anticipated risks, such as inventory and capacity risks. In the present review, eight top SCRM strategies were identified whereof visibility and transparency (n = 26), relationships/partnerships (n = 16), flexibility (n = 15), redundancy (inventory) (n = 13), postponement as well as collaboration (each n = 10), multiple sourcing and flexible contracts (n = 9), and joint planning and coordination (n = 8) were deemed crucial by many researchers. The results are partially in line with extant findings. For instance, this view is supported by the findings of AMR Research's Supply chain risk survey in 2009, which indicates that closer collaboration with supply chain partners and the use of multiple sourcing strategies and redundant suppliers are the most successful methods, frequently adopted to mitigate risks (Tummala and Schoenherr, 2011). Moreover, Kleindorfer and Saad (2005) deemed SCRM strategies such as collaboration, as well as flexibility as crucial for mitigating SCRs. Likewise, Tang (2006b) who mentions slack resources with the means of flexible production processes and product designs, larger inventories, and redundant suppliers that may act as so–called 'shock absorbers'. Next, Lavastre *et al.* (2012) identified multiple sourcing, safety stocks, collaboration, and the sharing of information as one of the most significant ways to deliver countermeasures to risks. Similarly, Wieland (2013) considers multiple sourcing, safety stocks, and flexible transportation as appropriate measures to mitigate SCRs. Finally, according to Sodhi *et al.* (2012), the following general strategies can be adopted for mitigating risks: increasing collaboration with partners including risk sharing, increasing demand, supply and process flexibilities and building buffers, or redundancies across SCs. However, the present investigation exhibits a lack of consistency among different strategies, which may hinder to implement SCRM effectively. Hence, a greater consensus on particular notions and terms concerning SCRM strategies is required.

To categorise and synthesise the SCRM strategies, we are in line with several academics and suggest a grouping that makes a distinction between proactive SCRM approaches for the ex-ante disruptive event and reactive SCRM approaches in the post disruption state for the effectiveness of SCRM and enhanced operational performance (e.g. Kleindorfer and Saad, 2005; Norrman and Jansson, 2004; Thun and Hoenig, 2011; Zsidisin *et al.*, 2000, 2005; Wakolbinger and Cruz, 2011). Moreover, Lee (2002, p. 114) classifies SC strategies as 'efficient', 'risk-hedging', 'responsive', and 'agile' relating them to two SC attributes, namely supply uncertainty and demand uncertainty. For the purpose of the study, we will refer to the attributes as supply-side and demand-side risks. In the following we will use this taxonomy to classify single SCRM strategies and assign them to either the proactive or reactive approach identified in the conventional and emerging academic literature as aforementioned. Since an agile SC regularly undergoes a change in which the customer requests are constantly unsteady, and many suppliers are undependable and restricted, such companies put emphasis on their assets and capacities, quality, delivery reliability, and after-sales service (Braunscheidel and Suresh, 2009; Gligor and Holcomb, 2012; Swafford *et al.*, 2006). Thus, organisations with an agile SC strategy consider both SC attributes (demand-side and supply-side risks) as possessing high levels of risk exposure. According to Lee (2002, p. 114) "agile SCs essentially have strategies in place that combine the strengths of "hedged" and "responsive" supply chains. They are agile because they have the capacity to be responsive to the changing, diverse, and unpredictable demands of customers on the front end while minimising the back-end risks of supply disruptions." An investigation conducted by Wieland and Wallenburg (2012) showed that SCRM using both strategies when appropriate, positively affects organisational performance. On the one hand, their evidence provides insights into the fact that agility, achieved through e.g. flexibility, is essential to cope with customer-related risks. On the other hand, robustness obtained through e.g. redundancy (inventory) is a necessary premise to handle supplier-related risks.

Within the ante disruption state in which the proactive approach is adopted (efficient supply chains and risk-hedging supply chains), we propose appropriate strategies that can help to anticipate and mitigate the impact of SCRs – in this setting, employing proactive procedures is required for managing risks to stabilise SC systems (cf. Figure I-4). Reactive instruments are effect-oriented measurements that strive for mitigating the negative impact of an incident; they do not immediately take action on the risk but aim at capturing the harm instigated by a risk. Accordingly, the reactive SC should be designed in a way that the consequences of an incurred risk are moderated (Tomlin, 2008). Thus, we suggest adequate strategies for effective SCRM in the post disruption state which encompasses the reactive approach (responsive supply chains and agile supply chains) (cf. Figure I-4). In sum, the findings show that visibility and transparency are factors of a central strategy needed in each state of SCRM. Surprisingly, the present study shows that some approaches require nearly the same strategies. However, while some strategies may be more suited for dealing proactively with SCRs, others are more reactive in nature to mitigate SCRs.

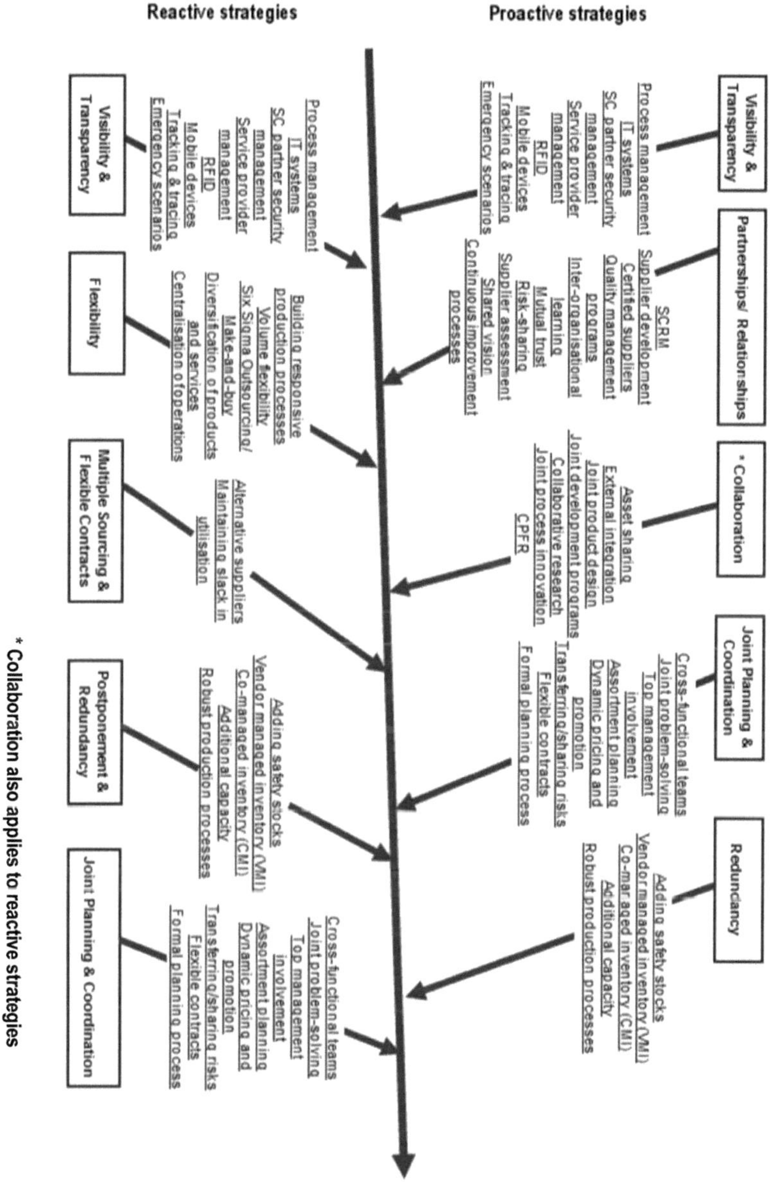

Figure I-4: Supply chain risk management strategies framework.
Source: Adapted from Kilubi and Haasis (2015, p. 44).

4.4 Strategic Technology Partnering Capabilities

As a result, from the selected body of literature (n = 65 articles), our systematic review revealed 38 capabilities across various authors. The largest number of studies deals with technological, innovative, and internal capabilities to ensure STP success. Furthermore, researchers also discuss network, alliance, and partnership capabilities, learning and exploitation, organisational, and complementary as core STP capabilities.

However, we discovered five core STP capabilities that impact performance. In the present review, several capabilities were identified out of which alliance, technological/innovative, complementary, and organisational capabilities were reckoned fundamental by several researchers. This result is partially in line with existent findings. For instance, Wang and Ahmed (2007) drawing on existing empirical findings identified adaptive capability, absorptive capability, and innovative capability as the most frequently declared capabilities in literature. However, the absorptive capability was only mentioned in three of the reviewed articles as an STP capability. A plausible explanation for this might be that the phenomenon of STP capabilities suffers from the deviating wording in literature, thereby restricting the full understanding of STP capabilities. For instance, some authors view capabilities such as alliance capabilities and organisational capabilities as subordinate concepts (or antecedents) of other capabilities such as network and partnership capabilities or internal capabilities. Exemplarily, Lee *et al.* (2001) captured internal capabilities by three variables: technological capabilities, entrepreneurial orientation, and financial resources invested. Moreover, while some of the studies referred to knowledge-based capabilities and others to disseminative capability, endogenous or cognitive capabilities, all have been referring to the same thing. Other examples are interfirm capabilities, integration capabilities, and relational capabilities, all describing elements related to managing a multiple portfolio of networks of partnership. Only a few studies showed clear-cut distinctions among these concepts which were mainly semantics; complementary capabilities, in particular, were clear without ambiguity. Accordingly, we identified a strong need for greater consensus on core capabilities and their related terms that would permit research and, thus, the entire concept of STP to develop and progress more consistently. To further examine the relationship between the capabilities and performance, we applied our unique classificatory framework with the five core STP capabilities to classify and analyse the 65 articles. Thus, we propose a distinctive classificatory framework, referred to as CLONT-framework (***C***omplementary capabilities, ***L***earning & exploitation capabilities, ***O***rganisational capabilities, ***N***etwork, alliance, and partnership capabilities, ***T***echnological, innovative, and internal capabilities), by systematically synthesising the large body of literature.

4.5 Integrating SCRM and STP

In the following we will present the main findings from our conceptual analysis of integrating SCRM and STP through the RBV and SCT. Aspects of SC flexibility have been evaluated by multiple authors (e.g. Vickery *et al.*, 1999; Sánchez and Pérez, 2005; Swafford *et al.*, 2006) who have concluded that a flexible SC model is quickly able to adapt to changing scenarios. Quality and price competitive products are created for the customers, and for this purpose the organisation transacts with suppliers as well as with other partners to attain external resources (Burt, 1992; Pennings *et al.*, 1998; Pennings and Lee, 1999). Swafford *et al.* (2006) propose that SC flexibility impacts organisational capability in multiple ways and is demonstrated by the rate in which organisations respond to sudden changes in the market composition. Following Wheelwright and Clark (1992), new product and process technologies consist of three competitive imperatives for their development; these are speed, quality and efficiency. Likewise, Ketchen and Hult (2007) consider the total value of speed, quality, costs, and flexibility as competitive priorities of best value supply chains. Notwithstanding, the graveness of disturbances may represent a beneficial effect on the activation of an organisation's responsive innovation capabilities since innovative companies are portrayed as ready to react rapidly and adequately (Craighead *et al.*, 2007a). For that reason, firm innovativeness may be constructed, conveyed and utilised against troublesome and adverse happenings occurring in the SC network of the organisation. Thus, firm innovativeness is clearly connected with compelling reaction to exceptional economic changes (Mainela and Puhakka, 2008). This is in line with Feller *et al.* (2013) who concludes that for companies, operating in chaotic and risky business environments, viable competitive advantage derive mainly from their technological capability. Nooraie and Parast (2015), for instance, demonstrate that increased visibility in SCs offers tremendous costs savings when SC disturbances occur. Their results show that high levels of visibility are alluring because it creates efficiency in a SC and reduces both risks and costs. Without visibility of upstream and downstream flows, managers are uncertain about the demand forecasts and order cycle time, etc. To this effect, it can be concluded that risk information sharing, as well as risk sharing mechanisms, contribute to financial efficiency.

Correspondingly, the former is further reinforced by consideration of the duration of the relationship and the extent of the suppliers' trust, while the latter element is reinforced by consideration of correctly perceiving SCRM aspects (Li *et al.*, 2015). Collaboration generates new knowledge through collaborative product design, joint research, or collective process innovation, which enriches the ability of the SC to respond as quickly as possible to environmental changes (Christopher and Holweg, 2012). According to Rajesh *et al.* (2015), the capability of suppliers and their performance are improved, the continuity of supply is ensured and supply–side risks are reduced when the operations of two firms are well–coordinated. In addition to that, when uncertainty is present, communication is enhanced through shared codes based on mutual rules, goals, values, narratives, and common language (Spender, 1989; Inkpen and Tsang, 2005).

Furthermore, a collaborative effort between buyers and their strategic suppliers is maintained through the mutual understanding of development. At this point, the members of the SC share their understandings and explain how improvements may take place and how tasks may be efficiently completed (Handfield and Bechtel, 2002). Companies with better capabilities of securing, embracing, converting and taking advantage of knowledge from external sources may better integrate that gained cognition into new solutions (Kilubi, 2016). Potential advantages of such learning mentioned in the SCM context encompass reciprocal support, risk decline through joint experimentation, exposure to various perceptions and thought-provoking reflections on progress (Bessant *et al.*, 2003). Commitment must also be reinforced by SC members to share valuable information with other SC members as part of visibility (Krause *et al.*, 2007). When a risky situation occurs, trust shows that SC partners allow their fate being taken into the hands of the other party to take action and make appropriate decisions (Inkpen and Tsang, 2005). In this manner, the network actors are willing to share knowledge, and it is trust that plays a crucial role in that process (Powell *et al.*, 1996). The committed exchange partners must provide free information exchange to show their level of trust as the decision makers must not feel that they need to protect themselves from any opportunistic behaviour that may take place by the other party (Blau, 1964; Jarillo, 1988). Consequently, dependence on external knowledge and skills is strongly connected to two elements: the nature of the relationship and the extent of commitment (Siu and Bao, 2008). As a result, trust as a vital constituent of relational capital between network members and a paramount enabler of open information exchange (Gulati and Nickerson, 2008; Ireland and Webb, 2007; Krishnan *et al.*, 2006). We have summarised the main aspects of the conceptual theory building process as an analytical framework, shown in Figure I-5. Using both the RBV and SCT as theoretical foundations of this research study, we have identified conjoint SCRM-STP capabilities for which we have derived six propositions.

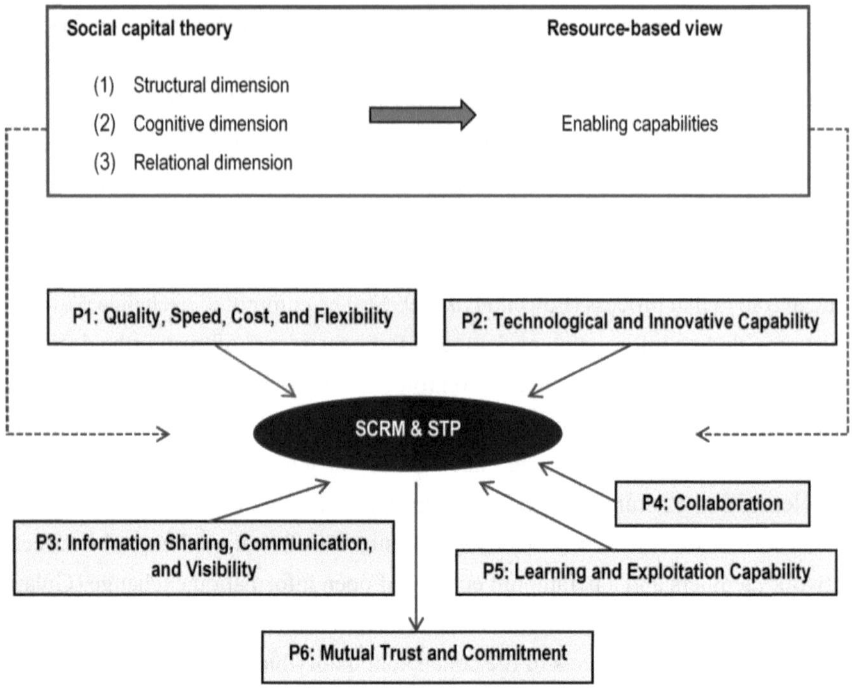

Figure I-5: Analytical framework for the SCRM-STP integration.
Source: Own illustration.

5 Conclusion and final statement

With this investigation, we aimed at answering the following main research question: How can the integration of STP and SCRM effectively be used to manage successfully supply chain risks? To respond to this question, we initially worked out the state of the art SCRM and STP by conducting a bibliometric analysis, frequency analysis, two SLRs, and conceptual theory building. The direct impact of SCRs on performance may be explained by the rising predominance of high complexity and volatility in SCs. SCRM should be deliberately planned and tenaciously kept up to prevent harms for an organisation (Brandman, 2002). The ability to withstand external threats and to mitigate potential disruptions and risks within SCs stand at the forefront. Thus, SCRM carries on to increase in popularity as more scholars and practitioners focus on this significant topic (Sodhi *et al.*, 2012; Thun and Hoenig, 2011; Trkman and McCormack, 2009; Chopra and Sodhi, 2014).

Not surprisingly, our analysis revealed that visibility is required in any settings of useful SCRM. As correctly perceived by Lee *et al.* (2001), open sharing of information provides the cornerstone that holds the SC together. A firm's ability to generate, pool, and make use of information is vital (Trkman and McCormack, 2009). In previous studies, information exchange has already been found to be a critical enabler of SCRM (Kleindorfer and Saad 2005) since it embodies the origin of supply chain collaboration (Bowersox *et al.* 2003) and the counterpart of uncertainty (Chen *et al.*, 2013). To effectively plan for, and answer to, different contingencies SC networks should make every effort to integrate institutional memory into information systems and create collaborative management which both lead to better decisions whether the situation is proactive or reactive (Skipper and Hanna, 2009). Visibility and transparency fortify confidence within the SC and can inhibit overcompensation, pointless interferences, and unproductive decisions after a harmful event has happened (Christopher and Lee, 2004). In addition to that, external collaboration was considered to be of paramount importance when implementing an efficient SCRM system, which highlights the need to work with SC partners to address potential risk exposure instead of trying to tackle the problem in isolation (Skipper and Hanna, 2009). Nevertheless, when demand forecasts are enormously distorted, uncertain or unpredictable, safety stocks can provide a remarkable response to SCRM demands (Lavastre *et al.*, 2012). Profits often emerge when SC partners are open to sharing information and assets to gain mutual benefits; collaboration does also include a reduction in resource sharing, greater response to customer needs, and increased flexibility in adjusting to alterations in the marketplace (Stank *et al.*, 2001). Accordingly, in light of the identified SCRM strategies, we assume that through the smooth exchange of information, firms might achieve better supply chain and financial performance, and in turn achieve higher customer satisfaction.

With the end goal to establish a hypothetical ground for the social interactions of SCRM and STP, we drew from the RBV and SCT and developed a conceptual framework that portrays the social procedures that foster enhanced execution and performance in an managed SC (Min *et al.*, 2008). We considered why a company's organisational performance benefits from a SCRM–STP linkage. This is in line with Feller *et al.* (2013) who employ a mixed–method approach and conclude that for companies operating in chaotic and risky business environments, viable competitive advantage derives largely from their technological capability. With its derivation and development, the complementarity of the SCRM and the STP has been demonstrated. From a social capital perspective, taking a look at SCRM on the one hand, risks and costs can be reduced through the long-term supply chain effectiveness that has been established through mutually beneficial relationships, shared values, and trust. Taking a look at STP on the other hand, quality and innovative products are created for the customers, and for this purpose the respective organisation transacts with suppliers as well as other partners to attain external resources. As a result, the social capital is used to strengthen supplier relationships and to foster knowledge transfer promotion. The suggested framework may well be applied to develop useful SCRM mitigation strategies while engaged in STPs.

Thus, the integration of the two diverse, but yet complementary research streams leads to the achievement of new systems of sustainable competitive advantage that base upon the grounds of the dynamics of the environment.

If the advantages of STPs are so obviously positive, why do not all companies engage in that kind of cooperation? There are various reasons for that; one reason may be the high costs in association with the uncertainty of how the relationship may develop in the course of the business transaction. Another reason results from internal firm–specific factors and the market conditions, in which a company is active (Koza and Lewin, 1998; Park *et al.*, 2002). Through the formation of a STP, a company is prone to opportunistic behaviour by its cooperation partners (Parkhe, 1993). This concern is specially standing out for small and medium–sized enterprise (SMEs) with knowledge–based technologies that possess a low bargaining power compared to large enterprises (Lavie, 2006). To relieve such concerns, trust frequently plays a pivotal role at an early stage alleviating worries of latent opportunistic manners (Adobor, 2005). On the other hand, the relational capital of SMEs, in the form of mutual trust, ought to raise spirits to the formation of STP and lessen worries linked to knowledge outflow and uncertainty (Mukherjee *et al.*, 2013). Investing in new technologies, combined with high volumes, also entails the risk of technologies getting obsolete very soon, which may particularly hinder small firms to enter STPs (Vilkamo und Keil, 2003).

5.1 Practical implications

During the last two decades many disruptive events with detrimental effects, economic or financial crisis, natural disasters or supplier bankruptcies that have caused cumulative risk exposures to organisations have been witnessed. Thus, companies may jeopardise their global competitiveness if they do not learn how to deal with SCRs. The proposed conceptual framework along with its strategies and capabilities can be used to implement managerial procedures to prevent or mitigate SCRs and to identify areas for improvement. Effective SCRM is valuable because, in the case of emerging risks, supply chain structures and processes are already available that capture risks and enable to satisfy customer demands. Resulting from the present findings, we see tremendous potential to improve risk measurement and performance outcomes in diverse settings to provide better guidance to decision-makers. With contemporary globalisation and vertical integration of organisational processes, overseeing risk issues in SCs have turned into a serious issue. It becomes imperative for managers to proactively handle potential SCRs (Rajesh *et al.*, 2015). Organisations can further apply the identified SCRM capabilities in this study to benchmark reactive and proactive SCRM strategies. This guides decision managers towards options as they work out mitigation strategies that are efficient, also less demanding to execute and better brought into line with their organisational capabilities (Talluri *et al.*, 2013). The proposed SCRM strategies framework has amazing potential for indicating strengths and weaknesses to decision-makers. In line with the resource-based approach to strategy analysis (Grant, 1991), firms must first identify their current assets and strong points – what they can accomplish more successfully than their competitors (Pettit *et al.*, 2010). Ultimately, the framework provides managerial assistance for setting priorities to design a strategy for mitigating SCRs. A well-managed firm constantly scans its chaotic and dynamic environment and readjusts its resources quicker than its competitors (Hamel and Valikangas, 2003; Lummus *et al.*, 2006). Consequently, intermittent evaluation of the potential exposure to SCRs is essential. Firms must have a comprehensive plan in place that follow a formal planning process identified by its SC network to ensure relevant planning aspects are incorporated in different functional areas (Schmitt and Singh, 2012). In this context, both Manuj and Mentzer (2008a) and Talluri *et al.* (2013) recommend considering SCRM as an integral element of the organisation's long-term strategic role embedded in managerial decision-making. Top management involvement in proactive planning coupled with mitigation practices will allow the SC network to migrate into recovery modes more smoothly (Guinipero and Eltantawy, 2004; Kleindorfer and Saad, 2005).

STPs cannot be managed sufficiently and efficiently through ad hoc decisions. We agree with Hafeez *et al.* (2002) that capabilities are shaped through integrating and coordinating processes and activities. The findings of this research extend what studies in related research streams have been advocating: in order to leave behind their competitors, companies must cultivate the ability to adjust and share their practices with their partners (Teece *et al.*, 1997; Bruderer and Singh, 1996; Heimeriks *et al.*, 2007). The competitive advantage and performance of an organisation are based on their business networks and relationships (Palmatier, 2008). This is a key asset according to the managerial implications of the present findings. The maximum value of STPs can be extracted through systematic management routines. Organisations engaged in strategic technology partnerships can benefit from the specific management routines that have been stated as part of this research study. Routines outcome from history, experiences, and collective learning within the company.

Toyota's manufacturing capability is such an example where capabilities are deeply embedded in the organisational activities, procedures and operational processes (Hafeez *et al.*, 2002). From a managerial perspective, organisations need to engage in the development and enhancement of their STP portfolio performance for which the present paper analysed the importance of adequate capabilities. Here again, top management team involvement is essential at all levels, they must be committed to the STPs of the organisation at all times, and this commitment must be shown eagerly (Sluyts *et al.*, 2011; Ritala *et al.*, 2009). This activity requires that STP management is regarded as a separate function like finance and marketing (Dyer *et al.*, 2001), where a STP community within the organisation is established that exchanges best practices and provides practical tools in which the organisational knowledge is codified in to make the most of STP relationships. Moreover, firms must set their priorities in which STP capabilities to invest. The STP capabilities inventory provided – as a result of this research study – can help firms to judge the different solutions that may help to increase the efficiency of their STPs (Heimeriks *et al.*, 2009). Hence, it is required that the organisation analyses and implements capabilities, processes and routines that are needed to enhance those business relationships (Mitrega *et al.*, 2012). The previously stated risk mitigation measures can assist companies with a portfolio of selections to complement their specific needs, and we acknowledge that they are effective in responding to and mitigating SCRs. Thus, firms can re-evaluate the impacts of risks of disruptions and invest further in novel solutions to minimise the occurrence of such issues in the future. All in all, the findings of the study at hand may function as a valuable premise for settling on choices as to which variables management should focus on to boost the performance of its organisation (Schilke and Görzen, 2010).

5.2 Limitations and future research

Several theoretical implications may also be extracted as a result of the conducted investigation. On that effect, this research opens the door for further research endeavours since future studies in this field are required to progress our understanding of the SCRM-STP phenomenon. However, this study is accompanied by a few limitations as a result of the research design adopted. First, the academic databases are incessantly being updated with fresh publications as they get published. Thus, the data set collected for this research denotes a 'snapshot' of information in the database during the short period of information accumulation. The sample comprises of articles, based on the postulation that these account to the research fronts of SCRM and STP. Still, further supplementary sources such as books and conference proceedings may also offer insights on risk management in SCs but have not been included in the study (Coombes and Nicholson, 2013). Altered keyword strings when conducting the database searches might have also modified the resulting hits. Nevertheless, it is realistic to expect that the articles studied in the present research are representative of the central research endeavours in the SCRM and STP discipline. Furthermore, future replications may entirely positively influence the recent growth in SCRM and STP works and may even offer an initial appraisal of (fresher) journal publication outlets. The study at hand also gives rise to different associated bibliometric studies. Author co–citation analysis (ACA) (cf. Acedo *et al.*, 2006; Fischbach *et al.*, 2011; Raasch *et al.*, 2013) or co–word analysis (cf. Benavides–Velasco *et al.*, 2011; Leone *et al.*, 2012; Volberda *et al.*, 2010; Wallin, 2012) applied to the literature on SCRM and STP thought could yield supplementary insights. Besides, the propositions and conclusions presented must consider the limitations inherent in the study at hand as well. A profound literature analysis has been submitted as part of this research study as it is a conceptual article; however, some of the details have been entirely based on anecdotal and scant empirical evidence. However, the present research study provides new practical insights into SCRM and STP and advances the current body of literature through the selection, classification and analysis of the SCRM strategies and STP capabilities. Additionally, the executed analysis makes a methodological contribution by combining a bibliometric study by means of multidimensional scaling, cluster analysis and factor analysis with frequency analysis, the systematic literature review methodology, and conceptual theory building to gain valuable insights into SCRM and STP. Table I-2 provides a research agenda for SCRM and STP separately as well as for future studies on SCRM and STP combined.

Further research required	Remarks
Research on Supply Chain Risk Management (SCRM)	
Methodological approach (Case studies)	Conduct qualitative case studies exploring different types of processes related to decision-making and best practices for mitigating SCRs under various levels of uncertainty.
Methodological approach (Quantitative grounded research)	Consider high-quality empirically-based research to quantify the herein reported SCRM strategies (e.g. analytical and network hierarchy process, mathematical or simulation modelling, graph as well as complexity theory).
Methodological approach (Longitudinal studies)	Execute longitudinal studies on SCRM to follow-up, assess, and measure the long-term performance from a regular situation until after a SCR has occurred and develop both qualitative and quantitative constructs.
Research on Strategic Technology Partnering (STP)	
Level of analysis (Multi-level perspective)	We wish future research to emphasise the value of performing multi–level studies that involve the individual or organisation, industry/market, and network level at the same time.

Further research required	Remarks
National and regional effects	We encourage studies conducted based on data sets from multiple regions and countries.
Methodological approach (Mixed method)	Consolidating the strong complementary points of qualitative and quantitative methodologies offers a more comprehensive picture.
Theoretical frame	We suggest exploiting further theories instead of mainly relying on RBV and KBV for strategic technology partnering research.
Industrial settings (Services industry)	More and more firms are entering new markets within the services industry. Hence, researchers may profit from valuable research potential.
Combined research on SCRM and STP	
Methodological approach (Conceptual/theoretical research)	Conceptual articles assume a significant role in the identification stage of improving knowledge.
Methodological approach (Longitudinal studies)	Longitudinal research can offer a valuable contribution to research on the evolution of STP and SCRM capabilities. Given the path– and time–dependent nature of capabilities, it is necessary to investigate the long–term impact of capabilities on performance.
Theoretical frame	Identify and examine a diverse set of capabilities and employ other relevant theories than RBV and SCT (e.g. transaction cost economics, knowledge-based view, etc.) to identify further joint SCRM-STP capabilities.

Table I-2: Research agenda for future studies on SCRM and STP.
Source: Own illustration.

Firstly, we encourage researchers to investigate further the insights of our provided classificatory SCRM framework. Empirical evaluation via large-scale testing of the SCRM strategies presented here on performance is needed to offer validation. In this case, we encourage researchers to conduct high-quality empirically based research to quantify the within reported SCRM strategies, which is of significant interest and calls for much more examination of how to maintain a competitive advantage over time after a SCR has arisen. Finally, further research is necessary to address implementation and measurement issues with the aim to transform this conceptual framework into a fruitful management device. In the past, measuring SCRM itself and measuring its relationship with performance has not received the attention as it deserves. Thus, Hoffmann *et al.* (2013) request for more empirical research in SCRM to explain SC performance with opportunities to operationalise potential into measurable objectives and performance indicators. Researchers have suggested that to assist SC managers in decision-making, empirical research addressing the effectiveness of risk minimising practices is urgently needed (Khan and Burnes, 2007; Li *et al.*, 2015; Tang, 2006b). For that reason, it would likewise be valuable to conduct qualitative studies exploring different types of procedures related to decision-making under various levels of uncertainty (Vilko *et al.*, 2014). Our study might likewise serve as a foundation to start a discourse of how 'risk' is understood within a SCM and a strategic management context. Future research could further investigate shared characteristics and contrasts in the way SCM, operations, logistics, and management articles operationalise SCRs. Such an investigation could unfold essential peculiarities of SCRM that have not yet gained satisfactory research consideration. Besides, such a matter results in value for both new academics of organisation and management studies seeking to deal with the broad range of the research area and to recognised scientists whose dedicated research undertakings have made it challenging to keep well–informed of developments in other subfields. Maybe in the event that we take more into consideration the underlying elements of SCRM within this structure, how they are correlated, and what they represent, SCRM conferences and publishers will reach the fame and status that is compulsory to create an academic discipline to take seriously.

We also recommend exploring best practices for mitigating SCRs; thus, we strongly advocate researchers to develop both qualitative and quantitative constructs to identify, assess and evaluate SCRM and its effect on performance, which can give potentially new data in order to create fundamental knowledge and gain new valuable insights. Several researchers have suggested requirements for improved SCRM, empirically grounded research (Jüttner *et al.*, 2003), analytical and network hierarchy process respectively (Vanany *et al.*, 2009), quantitative techniques such as mathematical or simulation modelling (Rao and Goldsby, 2009), graph as well as complexity theory (Colicchia and Strozzi, 2012), and general development of well-grounded models by considering other interdisciplinary research approaches (Ghadge *et al.*, 2012). Nevertheless, no matter which research method is chosen, an integrated approach to SCRM requires the incorporation of risk matters from industrial practice (Tang and Musa, 2011). With more qualitative and quantitative research, it is possible to validate the framework presented in this research study and to generate a set of generalisations based on variables like organisational and industry characteristics (Brannen, 2005). For that reason, we suggest exploiting mixed method research designs, for instance, case studies and surveys/questionnaires conjointly to make evidence of theoretical concepts. Accordingly, a couple of researchers call on the implementation of mixed method research designs to adequately address SC phenomena (Craighead *et al.*, 2007b; Golicic and Davis, 2012; Mangan *et al.*, 2004; Seuring, 2011). Moreover, we advocate conducting longitudinal studies on SCRM to follow-up, assess and measure the long-term performance from a regular situation until after a SCR has occurred. According to Barr (2004) major contributions from strategic management research have been made from qualitative research, despite quantitative methods being more frequently adopted. However, management and organisation studies rely on a variety of research methods that proves beneficial to advancing our knowledge and promoting research progress in this field (Molin–Azorin, 2010). We are certain of that empirical methods to advance STP understanding, in particular mixed–method approaches in combination with case study research for further exploration of unknown phenomena within the STP field will provide valuable theoretical as well as substantial managerial implications.

Hence, case study methodologies and conceptual studies show promising ways for further exploration of issues regarding new phenomena (Wassmer, 2010). Conceptualisation is quite significant for the progress of academic disciplines, whether it is solely present in conceptual papers or papers involving a mix of theoretical and empirical approaches (Yadav, 2010). Besides, our field appears to be moving towards the direction of giving more significance to empirical rather than conceptual aspect (e.g. Webster 2005; Stewart and Zinkhan, 2006). It is important that academic conferences and specialised meetings that solely address theory development and analysis in various considerable areas are established as everlasting elements of nationwide conferences. As presented earlier on, there exists a significant role of conceptual articles in the identification and validation stage of improving knowledge (MacInnis, 2011).

We further wish to emphasise the value of performing multi–level studies that involve the individual or industry/market, organisation and network level perspective (cf. Powell, 1996; Hagedoorn, 2006; Rothaermel, 2007). Researchers usually execute studies at a single level of analysis (for instance, the individual, the team, or the organisation), in spite of the fact that they regularly turn to the following lower level for explanatory mechanisms. Management scientists have a long history of perceiving that organisational phenomena unfold within complex structures, hitherto our scientific world commonly disregards the multi–level dynamics of these social organisms (Kozlowski and Klein, 2000). We have learned that simultaneous and explicit reflection of multi–levels of analysis, and 'dialogue' between research on different levels, can enhance our understandings of inherently cross-level (inter)– and intra–organisational phenomena (Capaldo, 2007). Hence, for management to keep propelling as a research discipline in which academics strive for to clarifying the behaviours of individuals, teams, and organisations, we need to magnify our theories and empirical studies to incorporate multilevel effects. We propose that powerful comprehension of social and organisational dynamics requires regard to higher and lower levels of investigation simultaneously (Hackman, 2003). The use of the micro or a macro perspective only produces fragmented comprehension at either level. New bits of knowledge may be obtained by imaginative studies that transfer microlevel theories to spectacles typically inspected the macro level; moreover, using macrolevel theories to microlevel events might produce novel insights (Hitt *et al.*, 2007). Numerous international management scientists bring up that collaborations between participants of distinctive countries are getting progressively predominant in the modern commercial environment (cf. Spicer and Bailey, 2007). Thus, Cadogan (2010) encourages studies conducted based on data sets from multiple regions and countries, respectively. Consequently, future studies may consider integrating territorial effects in its examinations to analyse whether territorial effects explicate a larger part of the deviation in foreign affiliate' performance than donation effects (Makino *et al.*, 2004). Studies from a national perspective recognise essential contrasts between distinctive social behaviour in their attitudes to reaching ethical decisions (Ralston *et al.*, 1997; Robertson and Crittenden, 2003; Vitell *et al.*, 1993). In addition to that, we suggest exploiting further theories instead of mainly relying on RBV and KBV for STP research. For instance, the SCT suggests that a firm's external networks represent a significant contributor to its organisational performance (Leenders and Gabbay, 1999), which could be further explored in the context of both SCRM and STP. Lastly, we advise researchers to pay more attention to the services industry since it is still underrepresented in management studies. More and more firms are entering new markets within the services industry characterised by low barriers to entry along with high margins (PwC, 2014). Hence, researchers may miss out valuable research potential.

Directions for future research must also be included with regards to the SCRM-STP integration. At first, future research must take into account the question of how an organisation's innovative capability can be used to reduce the disruptions in the SC. The SCT gives an awareness that the benefits and cooperation among firms could be attributed to a great extent by the grant of network resources and their positions within the networks (e.g. cliques, centrality) (Chang, 2003), while the RBV provides the firm with essential capabilities to exploit their valuable resources in an efficient manner (Kale and Singh, 2007; Ettlie and Pavlou, 2006; Santangelo, 2000). In terms of the SCT, all three underlying dimensions and their ability to affect the performance outcomes have been included for improved understanding of how those mechanism work. On the one hand, from the perspective of the suppliers, the social capital must be analysed in a much more thorough manner (Schiele *et al.*, 2015). On the other hand, the contingency factors that affect relationship performance and social capital like environmental uncertainty may be analysed through future research to gain additional insights (Carey *et al.*, 2011).

All through our discourse, it has become apparent that social capital is a multi–level occurrence (Adler and Kwon, 2002; Oh *et al.*, 2006). It would accordingly be advantageous to examine more in–depth how relationships within individual boundary spanners in a SC network form relationships at the firm–level. The proposed conceptual framework is the first concept to connect SCRM and STP to one research stream. The complementarity of the two research streams directs towards a new strategic approach, which should be validated and empirically tested in a large–scale quantitative study. Contrasted with the transaction cost economics perspective that predominates in the SC literature, the social capital perspective provides an open door for the extended comprehension of the complexities of SC connections (Krause *et al.*, 2007). The subject matter to focus on is the process through which the capabilities can be created as well as sustained (Zollo *et al.*, 2002). A longitudinal comparative case analysis is needed for a thorough understanding of the mentioned processes. Longitudinal research can potentially offer a valuable contribution to research on the evolution of STP and SCRM capabilities since capability development (such as by investing in R&D) does not necessarily produce immediate performance effects (McGrath and O'Toole, 2013). Given the path– and time–dependent nature of capabilities, it is necessary to investigate the impact of capabilities on long–term performance, which could be measured by the organisation's key (both financial and market) performance indicators in comparison to its main competitors or the industry average over a period of five to ten years (Duysters *et al.*, 2012). Moreover, complex challenges ask for exceptional approaches that can be accomplished by strategic thinking and activities in the context of SCRM and STP (Johnson *et al.*, 2013). Building on existing organisational theory, namely on social capital and the resource–based view, we allied the two concepts and applied them to SCRM within STP relationships. We are confident of that by drawing together the RBV and SCT we gain a fuller and richer explanation of organisational–level effects within strategic networks in SCs. In the end, this investigation has released a novel line of inquiry into this essential zone of SCM and strategic management research.

Next, future research could identify and examine other capabilities as the ones explicated in this study and could employ other relevant theories (e.g. transaction cost economics, knowledge-based view, etc.) to identify further joint STP-SCM practices and their corresponding capabilities (Li *et al.*, 2015). As a result, the research study at hand makes vital contributions to the theoretical understanding of the SCRM-STP relationship and proposes insights on practical applications that may lead to improved business profitability. All in all, SCRM and STP are still blossoming fields of research marked by diverse viewpoints. At the end, we hope that the integration of SCRM and STP has a significant potential to advance theory and practice in managing SCRs and, therefore, constitutes an innovative and novel concept in times of an uncertain business environment.

Chapter II

Investigating current paradigms in supply chain risk management – a bibliometric study

Abstract

This paper aims at analysing the intellectual structure and research fronts of supply chain risk management (SCRM), in order to identify the knowledge groups in the research area to date, as well as to reveal any relationships between these subfields and the central, influential trends. By means of a bibliometric study, the 32 most co-cited articles on SCRM published in 16 top business-related academic journals are analysed using multivariate statistical techniques, i.e. multidimensional scaling (MDS), cluster analysis, and correspondence factor analysis. The results demonstrate a clearly identifiable structure as a result of the performed co-citation analysis. The conducted cluster and factor analysis bring forward that the research field is arranged in five different areas of interest: 1) explaining supply chain risk phenomena, concepts, frameworks and insights into SCRM; 2) modelling risks for supply chains; 3) inventory risks affecting supply efficiency; 4) supply chain and product design methods; and 5) supply chain risk mitigating strategies. Overall, the intellectual structure of SCRM is first examined through a bibliometric approach using quantitative techniques – for improved understanding of its origins and to identify the state of the science – as well as to offer suggestions for future studies that could cover current gaps.

1 Introduction

Supply chain risks (SCRs) appear to be a major problem as unsettled economic environments. High volatility in supply and demand, coupled with rapid technological changes, and unforeseeable disturbances, are common issues these days (e.g. Barry, 2004; Christopher and Holweg 2011; Tang and Tomlin, 2008; Waters, 2007). Judging by the increased number of articles published in scientific journals and germane trade periodicals, supply chain risk management (SCRM) is an area of growing importance (Chopra and Sodhi, 2004; Trkman and McCormack, 2009; Wieland and Wallenburg, 2013). The globalisation of markets, increased outsourcing and offshoring, reliance on external sources of know–how and new solutions, coupled with the emergence of information and communication technologies required to coordinate extended supply chain networks, are just a few reasons why this topic is relevant today (Lockamy III and McCormack, 2010; Narasimhan and Talluri, 2009; Pujawan and Geraldin, 2009; Ritchie and Brindley, 2007a, b). SCRM can be seen as a strategic activity undertaken by companies as SCRs can directly affect, business, financial, and operational performance of organisations (Narasimhan and Talluri, 2009). These trends have expressed themselves through an increase of best cost country sourcing and collaboration with global SC partners (e.g. Lee, 2002; Martha and Subbakrishna, 2002; Norrman and Jansson, 2004). In an industrial environment mired in considerable uncertainty and complexity, firms are obliged to manage their supply chain (SC) in an efficient manner to advance reactivity and flexibility (Christopher and Lee, 2004; Manuj and Mentzer, 2008a,b; Peck, 2005; Wagner and Bode, 2008). As a consequence, risks, disruptions, disturbances, and uncertainties are evidence that the field of SCRM is ever broadening, and the theories, concepts, processes, and practices must develop with it (Cavinato, 2004; Neiger *et al.* 2009; Tang and Musa, 2010; Thun and Hoenig, 2011; Zhao *et al.*, 2013). Although the significance of SCRM research is not in question, diverse viewpoints concerning its intellectual contributions to the numerous research areas it relies on do exist (Pfohl *et al.*, 2010). We aim to contribute to the SCRM literature by examining the intellectual structure of SCRM for improved understanding of its origins and its state of the science.

We use a well–established quantitative method to postulate the intellectual structure of SCRM (i.e. the shared theories, methodologies, findings/results, and implications). Therefore, the study relies on *bibliometrics*: "the study of a given field or body of literature using quantitative analysis and statistics to describe patterns of publication" (Vogel, 2012, p. 1019). "The term *bibliometrics* refers to the mathematical and statistical analysis of patterns that appear in the publication and use of documents" (Ramos–Rodriguez and Ruiz–Navarro, 2004, p. 981). This study does not focus on a particular definition of SCRM as the focal point of the paper. Rather, we refer to the term 'supply chain risk management' and its use in the scientific literature. While the definitions of SCRM differ, understanding the scope of its use and the inherent structure of related models is worthwhile. The present paper examines SCRM by considering different research streams that have emerged from previous research to gauge the state–of–the–art of its discipline and to frame future requirements and research prospects.

Therefore, the main objectives are to: (1) outline the intellectual and conceptual structure of scientific research on SCRM as embodied in the scientific literature and analyse the intellectual structure of this research domain to date (i.e shared or complementary methodological approaches, findings/results, etc.); (2) define research streams that form both the intellectual structure and knowledge groups in the field as well as to reveal any relationships between these subfields; and, (3) chart and illustrate the intellectual arrangement in a bi–dimensional sphere in order to evaluate the clusters to support future academic research endeavours.

The paper at hand is composed of four core sections. The first provides a background for the present research, reviewing the role of bibliometric studies and designating the chosen bibliometric method – that of co–citation – reported herein. The second one contains an outline of the method adopted, specifically, the co–citation technique. Section three entails the presentation and discussion of the findings and results obtained from the multivariate analysis (MVA). And, finally, section four provides a summary and the conclusions arising from this study, indicates existing limitations, and offers suggestions for future research.

2 Methodological background of the research

2.1 Bibliometrics

One trend is apparent: an increasing number of academic researchers have dedicated their attention to bibliometric studies as an efficient way to evaluate the advance of management disciplines evolving from their juvenile stages. "Scholars devote significant effort to make sense of what has already been done, capture key lessons learned from the past, and identify directions for the future" (Zahra and Sharma, 2004, p. 332). In their review of bibliometric studies in management and organisation from 1993 to 2013, Zupic and Cater (2014) found out that the median year of publication was 2011, i.e., that more than 50 percent of the articles that employed bibliometric methods were issued within the last three years. While bibliometric is a well-established method used in various scientific fields (Acedo and Cassilas, 2005), management scholars have only recently begun to increasingly use bibliometric and lexicographic techniques (e.g. Backhaus *et al.*, 2010; Galvagno, 2011; Walter and Ribière, 2013). Bibliometric methods have been applied, for instance, to plot the areas of strategic management (e.g. Di Stefano *et al.*, 2010; Furrer *et al.*, 2008; Vogel and Güttel, 2013), organisation (e.g. Nosella *et al.*, 2012; Vogel, 2012; Volberda *et al.*, 2011), innovation (e.g. Fagerberg *et al.*, 2012; Keupp *et al.*, 2012; Raasch *et al.*, 2013), entrepreneurship (e.g. Campos *et al.*, 2011; Kraus, 2011; Landström *et al.*, 2012), and operations management (Pilkinton and Meredith, 2006). Although bibliometric studies are widely applied in a diverse range of scientific research – as outlined above – the authors are neither aware of any other bibliometric study in the SCM field except the work of Charvet *et al.*, (2008) nor are they aware of any bibliometric study specifically addressing SCRM.[2]

---

[2] cf. Zupic and Cater (2014) for a comprehensive overview of bibliometric studies conducted in management and organization studies, published between 1993 and 2013.

The main purpose of statistical bibliographies is to illuminate the routes and development trajectory of a research discipline by clustering and analysing the various facets of written communications (Eom, 2008). Since the strength of bibliometric studies lies in their unobtrusiveness, they allow for a high level of objectivity (Gmür, 2003) and quantifiability (Durisin *et al.*, 2010) with the means of quantitative analysis (Börner *et al.*, 2003), making declarations about qualitative characteristics (Wallin, 2005). Finally, the outcome is a comprehensive depiction of the main issues of the research efforts with its conceptual structure as discerned by authors contributing to its intellectual progress (Callon *et al.,* 1983).

2.2 Co–citation Analysis

Co–citation analysis which links cited documents (Small, 1973), is the method most commonly applied for identifying core articles in a stream of academic literature (Calero–Medina and van Leeuwen, 2012; Small, 1999; Zitt and Bassecoulard, 1994) and has been fruitfully used by subfields of management and operations science as a tool for enhanced comprehension of the intellectual structure of a given research area (e.g. Carvalho *et al.*, 2013; Leone *et al.*, 2012; Herbst *et al.*, 2011; Martin *et al.*, 2012).

Relying on the supposition that the references cited in academic articles are a dependable hint of their relative influence in a given field, co–citation analysis can identify the most influential articles and define the relational associations between them (Teichert, 2010). A co–citation analysis is not more indicative of whether or not an article is critical of academic literature compared to citation counts. However, a major postulation of co–citation analysis is that the more frequently two articles are jointly cited, the more likely that they embody a complementary or similar intellectual stream (Verbeek *et al.*, 2002). Co–citation analysis supposes that: (1) citation infers use; (2) citation and frequent use are grounded on the level of impact and merit; (3) co–citation echoes content similarity, and that (4) each citation is equally relevant (Pierce, 1990). Co–citation analysis is therefore viewed as a possibility for identifying high–density areas in a network of citations by clustering highly co–cited articles that are reasonably homogenous, setting up the intellectual foundation of a research domain (Jarneving, 2005; Franklin and Johnston, 1988; Vogel, 2012). On this note, a graphical chart of which available publications are likely to be conjointly cited helps to ascertain various research disciplines – represented by clusters of academic work (Ponzi, 2002). The many–sidedness of the method, its validity for exploring the intellectual structure of an academic discipline and its acceptance by diverse researchers makes it suitable for the present study.

3 Research methodology and data collection

The general process for co–citation analysis adopted in this research follows a six–step approach (cf. Figure II-1): (1) selection of the database that contains bibliometric data and the journals to be included in the analysis, (2) identification of the most relevant work within the area of study by using articles as unit of analysis, (3) compilation of raw co–citation matrix to calculate similarity between pairs of referencing articles, using co–citation counts, (4) multivariate statistical analysis of the co–citation matrix using multidimensional scaling (MDS), cluster analysis, and factor analysis, (5) output preparation by using visualisations, and (6) use of the resulting visualisation for discussion and evaluation (Boyack and Klavans, 2010; Chabowski *et al.*, 2013; Zupic and Cater, 2014). Once the results are at hand, the analysed articles are allocated to the different paradigms identified.

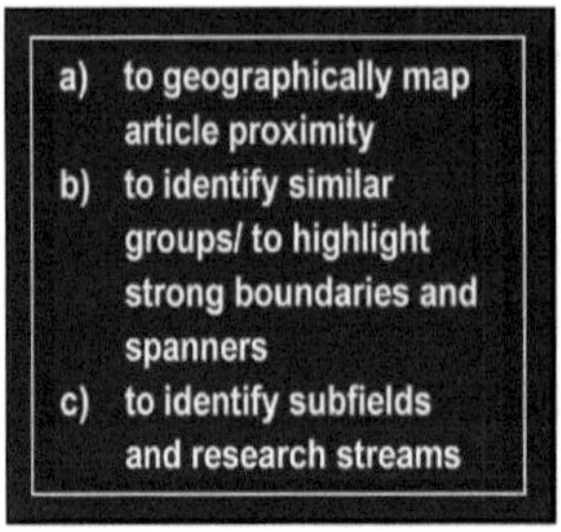

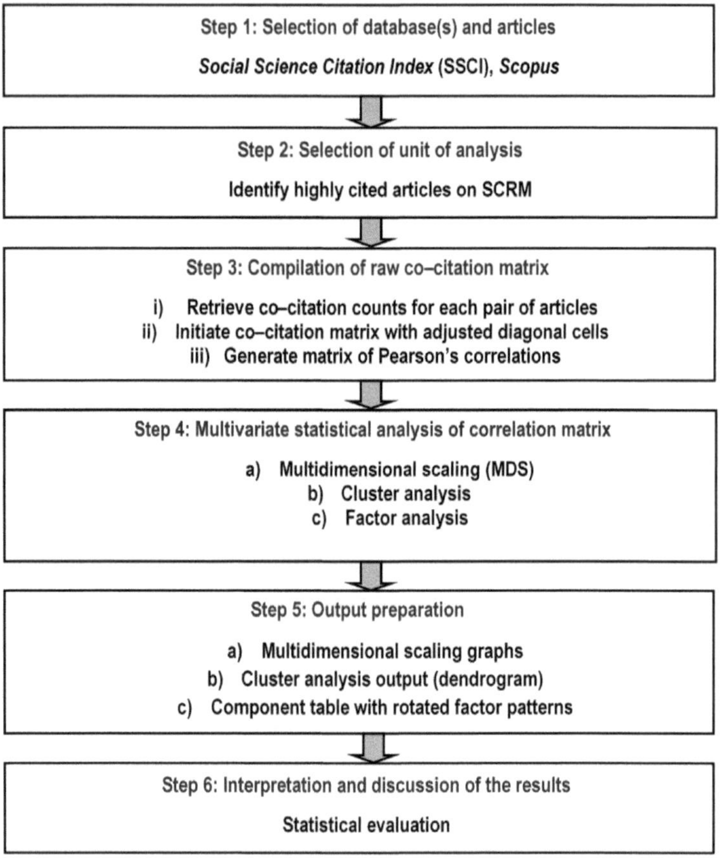

Figure II-1: Co–citation analysis process.
Source: According to Boyack and Klavans (2010), Chabowski *et al.* (2013), Zupic and Cater (2014).

3.1 Database selection

The *Social Science Citation Index* (SSCI) is by far the most common source of bibliometric information, and it is likely to be the most frequently used source for reference retrieval (Zupic and Cater, 2014) which covers index information and citation lists (Pilkington and Meredith, 1999). Since the database, SSCI of *Thomson Reuters* has become available for the large–scale analysis of citation structures, co–citation analysis has emerged as a school of research for the empirical investigation of the underlying structures and progression in scientific communities and areas (Gmür, 2003). Following Nerur *et al.* (2008), Di Guardo and Harrigan (2012), and Chabowski *et al.* (2013), the SSCI was applied to identify papers for inclusion. However, the scope of journals encompassed by the SSCI is restricted, even though most of the quality journals are incorporated. It takes a while for fresher journals to become integrated into the SSCI. Thus, it does not cover data from recently launched publications. Although the SSCI enables an easy retrieval of co–citation frequencies, a lot of journal publications in the operations and logistics area are not covered by the database.[3] Thus, the data provided by SSCI was used for the present study if available, but as the SSCI does not encompass all issues of the included journals, the missing information had to be acquired and provided through other sources. An alternative source is the *Scopus* database – the second most frequently used database right after the SSCI – that we used to complement the citation results yielded by SSCI (cf. Gerdsi *et al.*, 2013; Hamish and Wald, 2012; Walter and Ribière, 2013).

3.2 Journal article selection

As a general rule, scholars choose terminologies being representative of the body of knowledge to be investigated. The authors proceeded as follows; firstly, keywords were defined as search criteria in the SSCI and *Scopus* databases. Some of the keywords were selected from the current academic literature; others resulted

[3] Two representative examples of missing journals in SSCI: International Journal of Operations and Production Management (IJOPM) and International Journal of Physical Distribution and Logistics Management (IJPDLM).

from a brainstorming session with university professors and post–doctoral researchers including the validation and quality assessment of keywords to enhance the accuracy and focus of the co–citation analysis. The initial search criteria were specified to encompass all academic (peer–reviewed) articles enclosing the keyword strings *supply chain risk management* in any of the *Title (TI), Abstract (AB)* or *Author–Supplied Keywords (KW)* fields with no time restriction. While the implementation of an increasing number of keywords may slightly enhance the sample, it may also reinforce the tendency to add irregularities regarding non–relevant journal articles. Thus, this initial search turns out to be increasingly challenging from a practical point of view (Charvet *et al.*, 2008). Being interested in outlining the fundamentals of the multidisciplinary field of SCRM, we selected articles published in academic journals in the areas of management, business, operations, logistics, and economics. Secondly, as the focus bases upon peer–reviewed articles, all editor notes, conference and working papers, books, and dissertations, etc. were excluded from the analysis (cf. Chabowski *et al.*, 2013).

Highly cited articles represent fundamental themes, concepts, research streams, and methods in science (Verbeek *et al.*, 2002). To further restrict the composition of primary articles, one of the most frequently adopted approaches is to either pick out the most highly-cited documents on the basis of a pre–determined maximum, to choose papers that include a minimum per centage or a minimum number of co–citations amongst all leading articles, or to apply a mixture of both (e.g. Martin *et al.*, 2012; Shafique, 2013). We have learned that high citation rates correlate with peer judgments about scientific merit and excellence and the significance of contributions (Wallin, 2005). However, there are no quantitative measures or tools that can be applied to determine the appropriate number of papers straightforward. Altogether, a preliminary set of 5358 articles was obtained (SSCI 2710 hits, *Scopus* 2548 hits) which was reduced to the most frequently cited ones. Firstly, following Acedo and Casilla (2005), articles with a minimum citation frequency of 15 were involved in the analysis of the present study to smoothen the running of the later execution of the factor analysis and to strengthen the likelihood of its achievement (Pilkinton and Liston–Heyes, 1999). Secondly, articles were manually filtered to establish whether read abstracts met the criteria for inclusion. Next, all those articles that clearly referred to thoughts associated with SCRM in the title or abstract were extracted (as of January 2015). Finally, the selection process resulted in a total of 75 articles from 2000 to 2011 and is biased for elder articles since newer articles need time to obtain a fair amount of citation rates.

3.3 Selection of unit of analysis

Each research that studies co–citations must start with a set of documents or authors being involved in the creation of the foundation of the concept or discipline under investigation (Canon *et al.*, 1995) and use this as a basis to further create the co–citation matrix for subsequent analysis. Influence can be gauged by adopting different units of analysis such as a document, which can be a book or paper (e.g. Cacique, 2013; Pilkington and Meredith, 2009; Ramos–Rodriguez and Ruiz–Navarro, 2004; Vogel and Güttel, 2013), an author (e.g. Nerur *et al.*, 2008; Landström *et al.*, 2012; Raasch *et al.*, 2013), or a journal (Podsakoff *et al.*, 2005; Vogel, 2012; Wallin, 2012). According to the suggestions of White and Griffith (1981), it was determined to apply articles in lieu of authors since the former permit for a more accurate ascertainment of the research fronts in this area. Hence, the bibliometric technique employed in the present study is the co–citation analysis using documents in which the unit of analysis is the referenced journal article and the kind of relations investigated are the co–cited articles. Note that, taking authors as a unit of analysis could entail the risk of receiving non–homogeneous results, since authors can write on diverse themes associated with the same subject matter (Durisin *et al.*, 2010). More precisely, for the present research which is targeted at a definite research field, it is favourable to perform the investigation in terms of papers, so that the results are protected against biases due to the possible circumstance that the same author may have written on various research streams (Acedo *et al.*, 2006).

3.4 Compiling of co–citation matrix

Following the approach afore–mentioned, the frequencies of co–citations were gained for each pair of papers. Co–citation analysis is based on grouping together documents that are frequently cited in pairs and represent counts of the frequency with which two existing documents are mentioned together in a new paper (Bayer *et al.* 1990). A co–citation is existent in case two authors or references show up in the same reference list (see Figure II-2). It can be understood as the quota for relatedness of the subject matter of two co–cited authors or texts which enable us to say something about the manner of interaction between one and another author (Gmür, 2003).

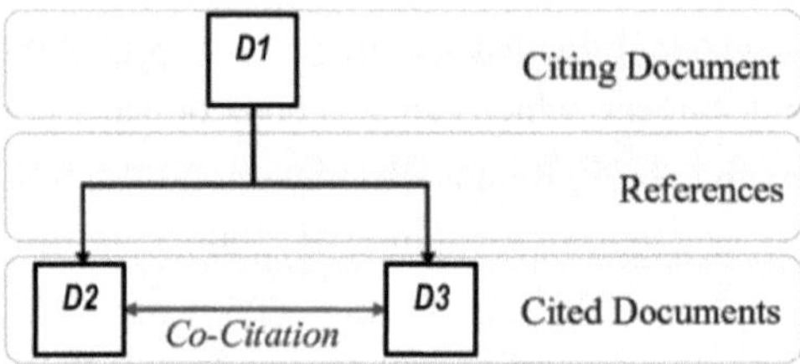

Figure II-2: Example of a co–citation.
Source: Adapted from Vogel (2012, p. 1021).

In this study, we conduct a typical co-citation analysis as proposed, for instance, by Landström *et al.* (2012), Shafique (2013) and Vogel (2012). Hence, a co–citation between two articles (for instance, *D2* and *D3*) takes place when a reference *D2* that is cited in article *D1* also cites article *D3* (cf. Figure II-2), that is, the rate of co–citations between *D2* and *D3* and represents the frequency of citations of *D2* that correlate with cited references of *D3* (Eom, 2008). Co–citation analysis is predicated on the basis of the distribution rates gained from counting the citations, by creating all the pairs possible from the 75 most frequently cited articles and totaling all the papers that reference both articles. For a full list of the most frequently co-cited articles used for the present analysis please refer to the Appendix I. Therefore, by the co-citations, the assembled data describe the number of times at which two papers are cited jointly. These counts are then composed of a 75 ×

75 square, symmetrical matrix in which the core diagonal row stays indeterminate with the value zero since no article can be cited by itself (Di Guardo and Harrigan, 2012). Contrariwise, a zero cell outside of the diagonal row indicates that one of the articles was not jointly cited with the other one (Rowlands, 1999). The applied co-citation matrix is represented in the Appendix II.

3.5 Conversion of raw co–citation matrix

In co–citation analysis, the co–cited article counts are the prime input data (see Table II-1) in which the co–citation count configuration creates a raw co–citation frequency matrix (Eom, 2008). Hence, co–citations were set out for each of the 75 articles. More than half of the articles had a small co–citation rate due to the fact that they were either unlikely to have had a meaningful impact on the development of the research domain or were too recently published to have had time to influence the extant academic literature (Pilkinton and Liston–Heyes, 1999). Consequently, the size of the sample was reduced from 75 to 32 items by excluding papers with more than two–third of zeros in the row of the matrix, resulting in a final 32 x 32 raw co–citation matrix.

	D1	D2	D3	D4	D5	D6
D1	**0**	5	4	6	1	8
D2	5	**0**	4	11	0	5
D3	4	4	**0**	5	1	2
D4	6	11	5	**0**	2	9
D5	1	0	1	2	**0**	1
D6	8	5	2	9	1	**0**

Table II-1: The applied raw co–citation matrix (extract).
Source: Own illustration.

Noteworthy is the fact that 59 per cent of the most co–cited journal papers were published in the International Journal of Production Economics (n = 7), Journal of Operations Management (n = 4), Production and Operations Management, International Journal of Physical Distribution & Logistics Management, Management

Science, and Supply Chain Management: An International Journal (each n = 2). Two articles are published in a practitioner–oriented journal (California Management Review and MIT Sloan Management Review); the remainder are all available from publications with a more prominent scientific tendency (cf. Table II-2).

Journal publication	Number of articles	Percentage
Production and Operations Management (POM)	2	6.3 %
International Journal of Production Economics (IJPE)	7	21.9 %
International Journal of Physical Distribution & Logistics Management (IJPDLM)	2	6.3 %
Management Science (MS)	2	6.3 %
Journal of Operations Management (JOM)	4	12.5 %
Supply Chain Management: An International Journal (SCMIJ)	2	6.3 %

Table II-2: Publishing journals of the most co–cited articles.
Source: Own illustration.

There are two main options to process the core diagonals when computing correlation coefficients. The first one implicates taking the sum of the three highest scores and dividing them by two; that provides a general sign of the relative meaning of a particular work within the research discipline (White and Griffith, 1981). The other way is to use the criterion of deleting the two pairs and merely to consider them as missing values (McCain, 1990). For the purpose of the present research, after having experimented with both approaches, the latter option was chosen because no substantial dissimilarities had been observed in the resultant patterns (cf. Ramos–Rodriguez and Ruiz–Navarro, 2004). For the subsequent analysis, the *r–Pearson* correlation matrix was estimated for the standardisation of data and to minimise potential scale effects in addition to the count of zero cells in the matrix (Moya *et al.*, 1998; Rowlands 1999). Bibliometric methods produce a co–occurrence frequency matrix that is then converted to a correlation matrix with a Pearson correlation coefficient usually being used as the measure of similarity.

Since correlation coefficients epitomise a measure of similarity (not dissimilarity) between two papers, the following rule of thumb applies: the greater the positive correlation, the closer the proximity and the closer the two papers are located in the chart (Leydesdorff and Vaughan, 2006; White and McCain, 1998). Table II-3 shows the most cited articles included in the co-citation analysis ordered by citation rates.*[4]

Code	Author	Year	Citation counts
D1	Tang	2006a	312
D2	Kleindorfer and Saad	2005	267
D3	Tomlin	2006	237
D4	Chopra and Sodhi	2004	221
D5	Cachon	2004	175
D6	Hendricks and Singhal	2005	164
D7	Hallikas *et al.*	2004	130
D8	Faisal *et al.*	2006	111
D9	Agrawal and Seshadri	2000	90
D10	Wu and Olson	2008	82
D11	Braunscheidel and Suresh	2009	78
D12	Manuj and Mentzer	2008a	78
D13	Johnson	2001	76
D14	Manuj and Mentzer	2008b	67
D15	Tang and Tomlin	2008	67
D16	Cucchiella and Gastaldi	2006	57
D17	Ritchie and Brindley	2007a	53
D18	You *et al.*	2009	50
D19	Finch	2004	49
D20	Hallikas *et al.*	2002	43
D21	Nagurney and Matsypura	2005	43
D22	Rao and Goldsby	2009	42
D23	Sodhi	2005	42
D24	Sinha *et al.*	2004	41

[4] At this point it should be noted that we have conducted a co-citation analysis and not a citation analysis, i.e. we were concerned with the frequencies of those articles that have been most cited with other articles conjointly.

Code	Author	Year	Citation counts
D25	Trkman and McCormack	2009	41
D26	Bogataj and Bogataj	2007	38
D27	Neiger *et al.*	2009	35
D28	Narasimhan and Talluri	2009	34
D29	Thun and Hoenig	2011	32
D30	Jiang *et al.*	2009	31
D31	Khan *et al.*	2008	24
D32	Lockamy III and McCormack	2010	23

Table II-3: Set of the 32 most co–cited articles listed by the number of citations.
Source: Own illustration.

3.6 Multivariate statistical analysis

Following Acedo and Casillas (2005), Charvet *et al.* (2008), and Di Guardo and Harrigan (2012), three distinctive multivariate statistical methods were used by means of the *Statistical Package for the Social Sciences* (SPSS) to gather useful data from the correlation matrix: Firstly, metric MDS was applied to investigate the probability of the model's instability and to reduce data for simplicity (cf. Chabowski *et al.*, 2013). Additionally, non–metric MDS was used to create a map in order to detect any sort of interrelation amongst the single studies by ascertaining the elements that best describe the similarities and dissimilarities between individual variables (Wilkinson, 2002). Next, cluster analysis was run to group similar articles, thus attaining a series of noteworthy groups of articles. Cluster analysis involves a technique that generates groupings from data that are initially unclassified (Jarneving, 2005). Finally, factor analysis was conducted to connect individual articles with a specified element as well as to derive subfields from the co–citation matrix and to identify which studies frame each factor and their level of contribution or loading as an estimate of the relative dominance that each study has within a paradigm (Nerur *et al.*, 2008). Moreover, we were able to analyse the way they are interrelated, how significant their connexions are, and how far away from or close to the centre of their group factor they are located (Nosella *et al.*, 2012). Even though the application of all these methods together might seem to be superfluous, each one of them allows us to define some supplementary traits of the link between the studies. Moreover, it allows for screening the reliability of the results acquired (Acedo and Casillas, 2005). After applying all these methods, we can determine the relational characteristics of the intellectual structure of research on SCRM.

4 Results and discussion of the multivariate analysis

4.1 Discussion of the results: Multi–dimensional scaling and cluster analysis

4.1.1 Putting into graphs the selected articles

SPSS's PROXSCAL procedure was used to execute metric multidimensional scaling on the co–citation matrix. According to conventional practice in bibliometric analysis regarding the importance of network modelling, we used a stress rate of 0.10 or lower as a guiding value for an appropriate model fit (Ramos–Rodriguez and Ruiz–Navarro, 2004). The stress index is a measure that symbolises the discrepancy between the plotted distances as opposed to the original closeness matrix; thus, a lower stress index directs to a more appropriate fit (Charvet *et al.*, 2007). Next, to choose the correct dimension, Kruskal's stress I index was plotted for different dimensionalities. In MDS, a trade–off exists selecting the numbers of dimensions: while more dimensions enhance the goodness–of–fit, two or three dimensions enable a simplified visual depiction of the results. Although the stress value shows a significantly higher effect for the three–dimensional answer (S = 0.704), the model of fit is more satisfactory with two dimensions (S = 0.663) with a higher congruence coefficient. Both The Dispersion Accounted For (D.A.F. = 0.559) and the Shephard Plot suggest realistic fit (cf. Lattin *et al.*, 2003). Additionally, the explained variance (RSQ = 0.80) shows this representation to be a good approximation of the reality (cf. Chabowski *et al.*, 2013). After comparing the two– and three–dimensional solution, we decided to forward the two–dimensional chart since the three–dimensional one did not deliver any additional insight. In Figure II-3, the MDS chart is plotted for the 32 key papers by using the information collected from the generation of a correlation matrix. To facilitate the subsequent analysis, the outcomes of the multidimensional scaling can be transferred to a diagramme in a two–dimensional space. Articles located in the middle of the diagramme signify those papers that can be associated with diverse schools of thought with mixed co–citation patterns. Next, a hierarchical cluster algorithm was run on the data to generate categories of papers that are closely linked to each other by determining the distance between pairs of articles.

As a result, the cluster analysis produced three groups of articles. To better picture them in a conceptualised and confined region, the groups were overlaid on the MDS graph, shown in Figure II-2. The chart demonstrates: 1) classifiable clusters that denote primary theoretical research domains; 2) positionings of the groups in relation to one another; and 3) juxtapositions of articles within clusters and across cluster boundaries. Hence, the papers within a group share mutually related topical research streams. Articles inside a particular group's limit convey a comparative co–reference profile which implies that those papers address comparable, broad inquiries – without fundamentally concurring with one another on their findings. Clusters of papers close to the extremes of the chart are, for the most part, interrelated through co–reference to fewer neighbours. Similitudes within a cluster depend on the way they are perceived by those authors who referred to the papers conjointly. The centrality of a group – how nearly it is located on the axes starting point – advocates that the cluster's papers are viewed to be of concern to many neighbouring clusters. In the case of Cluster One (C1), groups straddling around the centre of the MDS graph are highly dense, mirroring scientists' solid inclinations to refer to these papers conjointly. However, it does not happen to papers within the clusters C2 and C3 where articles are scattered over multi–dimensional space proposing that these clusters cover academic influences from less related research domains. The articles in Cluster C1 focus on diverse aspects of SCRM using different kinds of research methods – in particular, we can find here most of the conceptual papers and literature reviews aiming at bringing together several research perspectives. Papers with that kind of central positioning have a higher probability of being cited by the adjacent two groups (C2 and C3). On the one hand, areas that overlap – as in the case of Cluster One (C1) and Cluster Two (C2) – indicate a significant connection between the clusters' research streams. On the other hand, clusters with minor or no overlap with other clusters – as in the case of Cluster One (C1) and Cluster Three (C3) – indicate strands that have less in common. We can only identify two articles within Cluster C3 – one provides a literature review on simulations and mathematical modelling in SCRM, namely article D1 (Tang, 2006a), and the other one is a practical paper that suggests SCRM practices for effective SCRM, namely article D4 (Chopra and Sodhi, 2004). The articles grouped into the three clusters are listed in Table II-4. The explanations and interpretations referring to each cluster are elucidated in the following.

Cluster One (C1)	Cluster Two (C2)	Cluster Three (C3)
D5: Cachon (2004)	**D2:** Kleindorfer and Saad (2005)	**D1:** Tang (2006a)
D8: Faisal *et al.* (2006a)	**D3:** Tomlin (2006)	**D4:** Chopra and Sodhi (2004)
D9: Agrawal and Seshadri (2000)	**D6:** Hendricks and Singhal (2005)	
D10: Wu and Olson (2008)	**D7:** Hallikas *et al.* (2004)	
D11: Braunscheidel and Suresh (2009)	**D13:** Johnson (2001)	
D12: Manuj and Mentzer (2008a)	**D19:** Finch (2004)	
D14: Manuj and Mentzer (2008b)	**D24:** Sinha *et al.* (2004)	
D15: Tang and Tomlin (2008)		
D16: Cucchiella and Gastaldi (2006)		
D17: Ritchie and Brindley (2007a)		
D18: You *et al.* (2009)		
D20: Hallikas *et al.* (2002)		
D21: Nagurney and Matsypura (2005)		
D22: Rao and Goldsby (2009)		
D23: Sodhi (2005)		
D25: Trkman and McCormack (2009)		

Cluster One (C1)	Cluster Two (C2)	Cluster Three (C3)
D26: Bogataj and Bogataj (2007)		
D27: Neiger *et al.* (2009)		
D28: Narasimhan and Talluri (2009)		
D29: Thun and Hoenig (2011)		
D30: Jiang *et al.* (2009)		
D31: Khan *et al.* (2008)		
D32: Lockamy III and McCormack (2010)		

Table II-4: Categories of articles generated through both MDS and cluster analysis.
Source: Own illustration.

4.1.2 Identifying relevant clusters

Following preceding research, we ran a hierarchical cluster analysis with means of Ward's method (cf. Acedo and Casillas 2005). The clusters remained stable when applying the entire linkage clustering method. As a result, three clusters emerged from the resulting dendrogram and are shown on the MDS in Figure II-3. The results are visualised in a graph in the dendrogram – which are annexed in Appendix III – illustrating which articles are the closest ones. A dendrogram is a graphical representation of the merger or division of elements of a hierarchical cluster analysis in the form of a tree structure with the dimensions elements and distance index. The dendrogram illustrates the path of hierarchical cluster analysis by graphically identifying at what stage which clusters have been united or divided (Duran and Odell, 2013).

Cluster One (C1)

Cluster One (C1) comprises the newest articles within the highly cited article set with about 61 per cent published from 2006 onwards and represents the largest group (n = 23 articles) within the article set. Articles within Cluster One are positioned in the centre of the MDS graph featuring a high level of density where dominant issue dealt with pertains to adopting SCRM to reduce firm's exposure to uncertainties and increase operational performance. Surprisingly, we found that Cluster One could be divided into four thematic groups. One large group (Group 1) uses simulation and mathematical modelling/programming to explain supply chain risk phenomena and scenarios (n = 8 articles). Their focus lies on supply and demand uncertainty whereby risk management models and optimisation schemes are implemented to illustrate the tradeoff between costs and risks (e.g. Nagurney and Matsypura; 2005; Wu and Olson, 2008; You *et al.*, 2009). For instance, Sodhi (2005) suggests two risk measures, referred to as "demand–at–risk" (DaR) and "inventory–at–risk" (IaR) and two linear programming models to handle demand uncertainty. Tang and Tomlin (2008) have examined the benefits of different flexibility strategies in the SCRM context. They showed that through mitigation of supply, process, and demand risks, most of the benefits are achieved at low levels of flexibility. Neiger *et al.* (2009) elucidate a unique methodology for detecting process–oriented SCRs. Another group (Group 2) within Cluster One specifically addresses inventory risks, arguing that it affects supply efficiency and provides several suggestions on how to avoid the cost of unsold inventory (cf. Cachon, 2004; Agrawal and Seshadri, 2000) (n = 2 articles). In addition to that, the correlation matrix discloses that the two articles D5 and D9 exhibit a greater degree of shared citations compared to the other articles within this group.

The third group (Group 3) in Cluster One consists of conceptual papers and literature reviews (n = 7 articles) that aim at bringing together concepts, models, and frameworks in order to propose risk management and mitigation approaches (e.g. Hallikas *et al.*, 2002; Manuj and Menzer, 2008b; Ritchie and Brindley, 2007a; Trkman and McCormack, 2009). In their qualitative study referring to a manufacturing SC context, Manuj and Mentzer (2008a), for instance, provide discernments into the practicability of six SCRM strategies with regards to environmental settings and the importance of moderators. These papers consolidate the work in an emerging strand of SCM. Both the empirical and theoretical work in the SCM field and other related fields foster a better understanding of risk management in SC networks. "It is recognized in the literature that risk can be studied as a 'mathematical construct' (Cachon, 2004; Tomlin, 2006), 'conceptual construct' (Svensson, 2004; Zsidisin and Smith, 2005) or a combination of the two approaches (Wu and Knott, 2006)." (Narasimhan and Talluri, 2009, p. 115).

The last group within Cluster One (Group 4) deals with external risks that affect SCs using miscellaneous research methodologies and is marked by high heterogeneity in how SCRs are handled (n = 6 articles). Braunscheidel and Suresh (2009) conclude that SC agility enables companies to respond successfully to unexpected changes in the business market. Moreover, they state that it acts as a risk mitigation strategy for handling disruptions in a SC (Chopra and Sodhi, 2004; Christopher and Towill, 2001; Kleindorfer and Saad, 2005). Faisal *et al.* (2006) present an approach that acts as a countermeasure to risks in SC by recognising the dynamics among different enablers. Using interpretive structural modelling, they propose a hierarchy–based model including reciprocal relationships among various enablers for risk mitigation. The study by Jiang *et al.* (2009) investigates the problem of labor turnover as a source of SC disruption risk in the context of outsourcing. Next, Lockamy III and McCormack (2010), who apply the mixed method research, provide an approach to analysing risks in networks of supply to simplify decisions concerning outsourcing. In their longitudinal study of a large retailer based in the UK, Khan *et al.* (2008) suggest a framework for design–led SCRM. Thus, they demonstrate the importance of product design, not only understood as a creative task but rather as a platform to handle SCRs. Although the product design stream is relatively young in SCRM and is not commonly related to the SCM field, the article occupies a central positioning in the MDS graph, i.e., that it is cited evenly by the other articles in its cluster (C1). Lastly, Thun and Hoenig (2011) use survey questionnaires to validate SCRM practices empirically. Specifically, groups are generated representing two different ways to handle supply chain risks, namely, responsive and proactive SCRM. In summary, with respect to the articles in Cluster One (C1), SCRM acts as a vehicle to boost the operational performance of supply chain networks and leans towards SCRM practices and managerial decision–making.

Cluster Two (C2)

A second cluster (C2) with seven articles was identified – three out of which adopting the case study methodology. Four out of seven papers were published in the *Production and Operations Management* journal – applying the rarely used event study methodology – and in *Supply Chain Management: An International Journal* (each n=2). One article (D13) in this cluster was published in a practitioner journal, namely *California Management Review* (Johnson, 2001). The papers in Cluster Two (C2) were published between 2001 and 2005. Articles in C2 deal with various supply and demand risks and propose SC and product design methods as means to overcome those risks and manage the complexity related to them (e.g. Hendricks and Singhal, 2005; Tomlin 2008). Two general categories of risk affecting SC design become obvious: (1) risks arising from complications of both planning and coordinating supply and demand, and (2) risks arising from disruptions to ordinary actions (Hallikas *et al.*, 2002).

Kleindorfer and Saad (2005), for example, offer a conceptual framework that mirrors the shared activities of assessing and mitigating the risks that are fundamental to disruption risk management in SCs. Based on the results, they discuss the implications for the design of management procedures envisioned to deal with SC disruption risks. Another commonality of the papers within this cluster is the fact that most look at one particular industry; e.g., toys (Johnson, 2001), aerospace (Sinha *et al.* 2004), manufacturing (Hallikas *et al.,* 2004), or chemicals (Kleindorfer and Saad, 2005).

The approaches adopted to manage disruption risks should 'match' with characteristics and requirements of the elementary background of decision; and different SC contexts will require different process methods of assessing and mitigating risks (Sinha *et al.*, 2004). Given that, a SC member may have requests laid down by another SC partner that opposes that of another partner. To respond to this issue, Finch *et al.* (2004) present a generic prescriptive methodological procedure for risk mitigation that shall provide a mechanism to lessen conflicting objectives. Hallikas *et al.* (2004) aimed at discovering a) what kind of risks arises from network collaboration and b) how SCRM processes do function in collaborations surrounded by networks. According to them, the ideal strategy is to strive for shared and balanced rewards of risks between firms. Besides, companies should also minimise their dependency on a single organisation or network entity. Overall, articles in Cluster Two (C2) view a complex supply chain design and the required system coordination as a source for risk exposure, but which, effectively managed, can transform into opportunities for organisations to mitigate risks and disruptions associated with internal and external issues. As a result, a majority of papers in this cluster designs methods relating to managing disruption risks midst SC entities or co–ordination mechanisms in SC networks (e.g. Hallikas *et al.*, 2002).

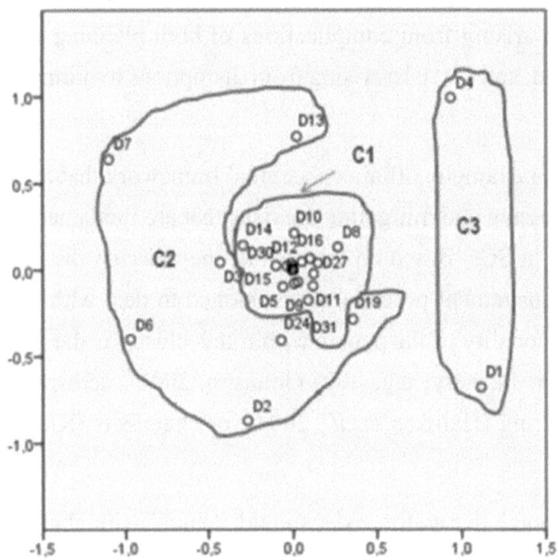

Figure II-3: Chart generated through both MDS and cluster analysis.
Source: Own Illustration.

Cluster Three (C3)

Cluster Three (C3) primarily focuses on risk mitigating strategies and encompasses two articles (D1 and D4) – one published in a practitioner–oriented publication outlet (*MIT Sloan Management Review*). A joint feature is an emphasis on identifying and illuminating the variety of risks. The two articles in this cluster deal with different categories of risk sources and risk drivers with the aim of identifying appropriate risk reduction and risk mitigating strategies. Tang's (2006a) review paper on SCRM has a dominant position and is, overall, the most frequently cited journal article at the same time. Tang (2006a) reviews previous literature with regard to a number of quantitative models that deal with SCRs and relates various SCRM strategies identified in the academic landscape to real practices. He classifies SCR into disruption and operational risks. He further claims that SCRs result from unreliable economic changes, natural catastrophes, and consumer demands. The related mitigation approaches are then grouped into demand management, supply management, information management, and product management. For each mitigation plan, Tang (2006a) defines both tactical and strategic plans to mitigate risks affecting SCs.

Chopra and Sodhi (2004) distinguish between supplier–related, customer–related, and internal risks that may have a different impact on different categories of risk source, such as disruption risks, procurement risk, or information processing risks. Similar to Tang (2006a), they propose adequate mitigation approaches linked to tailored strategies, for each class of risk source. In sum, articles in Cluster Three (C3) confirm that well-managed SCRM is effective because when risks occur, SC plans are accessible to mitigate those risks.

4.2 Discussion of the results: Factor analysis

The illuminating results of the factor analysis using Ward's method were extracted by means of Principal Component Analysis (PCA) with the aid of the correlation matrix (Rowlands, 1999). Additionally, Varimax Rotation, a generally adopted formula that tries to fit (or loaded) the highest possible amount of papers on the lowest possible amount of factors, was run to obtain frugal factors characterised by their theoretical importance which are displayed in Table II-5.

LOADINGS OF FACTORS (WITH A MINIMUM OF 0.4 TAGGED)
Rotated Component Matrix

Articles	Principal Component						
	Journal	F1	F2	F3	F4	F5	F6
D2: Kleindorfer and Saad (2005)	*POM*	.789				.407	
D5: Cachon (2004)	*MS*	.784			.444		
D24: Sinha *et al.* (2004)	*SCMIJ*	.767		.413			
D6: Hendricks and Singhal (2005)	*POM*	.725	.426				
D21: Nagurney and Matsypura (2005)	*TRP E*	.639	.308				
D19: Finch (2004)	*SCMIJ*	.605	.418	.477			
D7: Hallikas *et al.* (2004)	*IJPE*	.591	.371	.382		.345	
D3: Tomlin (2006)	*MS*	.567	.478			.441	
D13: Johnson (2001)	*CMR*	.536	.438	.358		.313	
D8: Faisal *et al.* (2006a)	*BPMJ*		.780	.475			
D23: Sodhi (2005)	*POM*	.398	.767		.331		
D4: Chopra and Sodhi (2004)	*MIT*		.757	.305			
D32: Lockamy III and McCormack (2010)	*IJPR*	.576	.687				
D12: Manuj and Mentzer (2008a)	*IJPDLM*	.491	.599			.352	
D30: Jiang *et al.* (2009)	*JOM*		.576			.520	.328
D28: Narasimhan and Talluri (2009)	*JOM*			.920			
D11: Braunscheidel and Suresh (2009)	*JOM*			.872			
D25: Trkman and McCormack (2009)	*IJPE*			.859			.329
D15: Tang and Tomlin (2008)	*IJPE*			.772		.409	
D27: Neiger *et al.* (2009)	*JOM*	.423	.505	.580			

Articles	Principal Component						
	Journal	F1	F2	F3	F4	F5	F6
D10: Wu and Olson (2008)	*IJPE*	.393	.317	.578			
D9: Agrawal and Seshadri (2000)	*IIE Trans*				.913		
D31: Khan *et al.* (2008)	*IJPDLM*	.348	.449		.637		
D26: Bogataj and Bogataj (2007)	*IJPE*	.310	.463		.622		
D1: Tang (2006a)	*IJPE*	.367	.422	.312	.433		
D14: Manuj and Mentzer (2008b)	*JBL*					.889	
D16: Cucchiella and Gastaldi (2006)	*JMTM*						.905
D20: Hallikas *et al.* (2002)	*IJPE*	.523					.713

Table II-5: Results of the factor analysis applying Varimax Rotation.
Source: Own illustration.

The basic assumption in correspondence factor analysis is that documents that are linked to each other will be cited together again and again in succeeding publications, as opposed to articles which are hardly ever or not at all mentioned together (Teichert, 2010). The correlations among co–citation entries is applied in correspondence factor analysis to decide which papers share universal aspects, with each factor embracing a common facet of the articles that come together (Di Guardo and Harrigan, 2012). Following Eom (2001), an article was included in a factor when its loading (on a –1 to +1 scale) was equal to or above |0.4|. The resulting model of six factors with eigenvalues larger than one was arranged, representing 80.6 per cent of the overall variance, depicted in Table II-6. The first three factors account for 65.9 per cent of the variance, explaining most of the variance. "[…] eigenvalues are numerical indicators of the relevance of the factors that suggest the relative importance of these underlying common elements" (Di Guardo and Harrigan, 2012, p. 800). All 32 articles were loaded on at least one factor. Factor One (F1) covers all the articles from Cluster Two (C2) – except that two articles from Cluster One were also loaded on it, namely D5 and D21 (Cachon, 2004 and Nagurney and Matsypura, 2005, respectively) – which generated a considerable level of agreement compared to the results of the cluster analysis. Both articles are simulation–based and focus on facilitating decision–making when faced with supply and demand uncertainty. The analysis highlights that within the other papers included in Factor One there are two distinctive approaches to the study of SCRM strategy. The first is concerned with the wider question of the role of risk management in SCM in general, while the second group debates the necessity of SCRM to be an integral part of organisation's strategic decision–making (e.g. Hallikas, 2004; Sinha *et al.*, 2004).

Factor Two (F2) was completely loaded with articles from Cluster One except for one article, namely D1 (Chopra and Sodhi, 2004). The second factor is, to a certain degree, concerned with the development of SCRM strategy, but focuses on particular aspects, e.g. outsourcing parameters such as article D32 (Lockamy III and McCormack, 2010) or labor turnover, D30 (Jiang, 2009). Factor Three (F3) assembles a few articles from a special issue of the *Journal of Operations Management* on 'Perspectives on risk in supply chains' from 2009, namely, D11, D28, and D30 (Braunscheidel and Suresh, 2009; Narasimhan and Talluri, 2009; Jiang *et al.*, 2009). Note that three articles from the *International Journal of Physical Distribution and Logistics Management,* D15, D25, D10 (Wu and Olson, 2008; Tang and Tomlin, 2008; Trkman and McCormack, 2009) join the cluster of *Journal of Operations Management* articles. All three papers focus on the linkage between SCM and traditional risk management and hence prove that the third cluster is not simply an artifact of the special issue. Factor Three (n = 6 articles) was completely loaded with articles from Cluster One, namely D10, D11, D15, D25, D27, and D28 (Wu and Olson, 2008; Braunscheidel and Suresh, 2009; Tang and Tomlin, 2008, Trkman and McCormack, 2009, Neiger *et al.*, 2009; Narasimhan and Talluri, 2009, respectively). The advancement of SCRM strategy influences the articles within this group. However, these articles do not question the necessity of a SCRM strategy; they rather deal with what shapes or involves an 'optimal' strategy and propose several mechanisms that may foster superior value and support risk mitigation, such as flexibility (e.g. Tang and Tomlin, 2008) or agility (e.g. Braunscheidel and Suresh, 2009).

	Factor One (F1)	Factor Two (F2)	Factor Three (F3)	Factor Four (F4)	Factor Five (F5)	Factor Six (F6)
Cluster One (C1)	2	5	6	3	1	2
Cluster Two (C2)	7	0	0	0	0	0
Cluster Three (C3)	0	1	0	1	0	0

Table II-6: Sum of journal articles from MDS clusters being loaded on each factor.
Source: Own illustration.

5 Conclusion and implications

Several conclusions and implications may be extracted as a result of the conducted analysis. Moreover, this research opens the door for further research endeavors. Accordingly, the subsequent conclusions and implications respond to the research objectives mentioned at the beginning of this paper. The main objectives were to: (1) outline the intellectual and conceptual structure of scientific research on SCRM as embodied in the scientific literature analysing the intellectual structure of this discipline to date (i.e shared or complementary methodological approaches, findings/results, etc.); (2) define research streams that form both the intellectual structure and knowledge groups in the field as well as to reveal any relationships between these subfields; and (3) to chart and illustrate the intellectual arrangement in a bi–dimensional sphere in order to evaluate identified clusters to support future academic research endeavors. In the following, we will present the conclusions that address these research objectives.

(1) Firstly, we can observe an accentuation on modelling and theoretical papers showing a bias in favour of conceptualising and depicting supply chain risk phenomena. Apparently, there are manifold broad research streams that individually differ from each other. One area has strong ties to the operations field and consists mainly of modelling and simulation articles – the focus lies on what risks are in the supply chain context of organisations and how risks related to networking can be analysed. A second cluster views supply chain design and network coordination as a source of risk exposure and proposes different methods and mechanisms to deal with complexity. A third cluster is concerned with the variety of risk sources and ways how to mitigate them. As a result, each group considers different aspects, processes and stages of SCRM (for instance risk identification or risk assessment). The presence of several of relatively individual approaches to SCRM is not per se a negative manifestation. However, scholars must carefully recognise the leading advances in the streams that correspond to their particular selected research

area. While not comprehensive, the key works identified in the present bibliometric analysis may be a helpful starting point or a reference framework. Although the statistical analysis revealed three distinct clusters, we could reveal three sub-clusters within the large group of Cluster One (C1), resulting in five groups of clusters. Hence, we have identified a high level of correspondence between the cluster analysis and the factor analysis in which Factor One (F1) covered all the articles from Cluster Two (C2) – except that two articles from Cluster One were also loaded on it. Likewise, Factor Two (F2) was completely loaded with articles from Cluster One except for one article. Next, Factor Four (F4) was loaded with three articles from Cluster One (C1). Finally, Factor Six (F6) was loaded with two articles from Cluster One. In this context, the identification of factors was reinforced when it became possible to allocate more than two-thirds of the articles into one of the identified clusters. In sum, the conducted cluster and factor analysis bring forward that the research field of SCRM is arranged in five different areas of interest: 1) explaining supply chain risk phenomena, concepts, frameworks and insights of SCRM; 2) modelling risks for supply chains; 3) inventory risks affecting supply efficiency; 4) supply chain and product design methods; and 5) supply chain risk mitigating strategies.

(2) From one viewpoint, particular groups and variables seem to indicate that genuine convergence of thought still needs to be established. The groups do not appear to impart a predictable denotation of SCRM, or a reliable perspective on risk management analysis, processes, risk sources, or risk mitigation strategies. From another viewpoint, the different perspectives do not seem to contradict each other or to be incompatible. In the event that this is purely an artifact of the advancement of SCRM academic writings within explicit, entrenched disciplines, we should be convinced that awesome potential is to be found in improved reconciliation between the distinctive research streams. Despite what might be expected, if apparently incompatible perspectives on principal issues yield rival paradigms for SCRM, it is significant to spot them

at an early stage. Furthermore, the lack of substantial bridging articles suggests that researchers still have to reinforce their efforts to unite the diverse existing viewpoints and to build a few connections between them. Results from our statistical analysis demonstrate that the SCRM literature remains disjointed, being portrayed by a few assorted, yet vigorous subfields characterised by a few diverse, but robust subfields with a moderate degree of overlaps. This is an encouraging outcome taking into account that multidisciplinary methods for exploring and interpreting a phenomenon deliver a more intensive clarification than uni–path theories. Overall, unnecessary discontinuity can be a shortcoming because it shapes the forthcoming of the research arena as a distinctive discipline. The results mirror the extensive multiplicity of research approaches and themes that constitute the investigation on SCRM.

(3) In fact, conducting parallel cluster and factor analysis may seem dispensable; but each method provides particular parameter value that offers supplementary information concerning relations among papers (Biehl *et al.*, 2006; Teichert, 2010). However, researchers recommend that a combination of different methods is especially promising "because it can triangulate the findings and allow scholars to strengthen the methodological rigor and thus the theoretical validity of their reviews" (Keupp *et al.*, 2012, p. 383). The strong point of factor analysis rests on the ability to discover shared, underlying dimensions of which elements might be positioned while the power of cluster analysis method rests on the ability to point to group affiliation. With respect to the present study, cluster analysis was applied to detect the various research streams within the SCRM literature out of which three have been identified while factor analysis suggests the intellectual connections between the selected articles. The SCRM arena is still comparatively new, and the analysis has demonstrated that it possesses an emerging structure. Maybe if we take more into consideration the underlying elements within this structure, how they are correlated, and what they represent, SCRM conferences and

publishers will gain the fame and status that is compulsory to create an academic discipline which will be taken seriously. In the following, we will use these shortcomings to present a couple of suggestions for future research.

6 Limitations and future research

With this paper, the latent structure fundamental to the SCRM literature was explored. The assumptions for the current investigation are that: (1) research on SCRM is a foundation for the understanding of risks inherent network environments, and (2) bibliometric methods provide an appropriate device for analysing the intellectual structure of a given literature. Co–citation analysis is especially enlightening in diagramming out the intellectual structure and research streams of connected colleges (i.e. the existence of an invisible school of thought) in the SCRM research. Findings in the study at hand can support the community of SCRM scholars to identify the core literature that may function as chief wellsprings of motivation for defining new research inquiries and developing new viewpoints. A shortcoming in co–citation study is that authors here and there refer to each other not so much because they have used each other's work for their research, but for some very different reasons. However, a recent research shows the growing significance of citations because references to citation counts may be an integral part of competitive contests among researchers (Aksnes and Rip, 2009). Different diverse intentions may induce citations (Gundolf and Filser, 2013), and, possibly, some will undermine the assumption that co–referencing is an appropriate measure of the resemblance and scholarly connection between articles (Hoffman and Holbrook, 1993).

Still, the major value of using a bibliometric methodology is its quantitative and objective nature. As mentioned previously in this article, a bibliometric research is virtuously one of the devices offered to scholars who are interested in the progress of SCRM. Since the study reported herein was limited to academic work, future research could likewise supplement and contrast the findings to the practitioner's view of SCRM. Besides conventional surveys, Delphi studies may prove predominantly useful here. Making use of qualitative methods to investigate the state–of–the–art and current developments in the intellectual structure of SCRM school of thought permits the approval of the recognised structures or disclosure of different patterns. The keyword 'supply chain risk management' was chosen as an exclusive keyword to stay as impartial as possible. Yet it is essential to highlight again that the definite goal is not to establish a list of 'top' SCRM papers. However, the ultimate aim was to leverage co–citation profiles to investigate the intellectual structure of SCRM. In this respect, the bibliometric analysis at hand was able to extricate a couple of clusters and articulate some of their principle attributes. A co–citation analysis entails the identification of the arrangement of core documents. Irrespective of the approach or decision tenets that are applied, a certain level of subjectivity cannot fully be excluded at this stage (McCain, 1990). Considering the multi–disciplinary nature of SCRM, the analysis was not restricted to a couple of publications or the inclusion of expert views. Both methods could lead to a possible predisposition due to journals' or researchers' contextual background. Thus, databases were used from the whole accumulation of academic and scientific publications covered by SSCI online database supplemented by the *Scopus* database. Minimum citation and co–citation share boundary values were defined as to encompass a vast set of papers while ensuring sufficient co–citation counts. Minor increases or decreases of these boundary share values do not fundamentally influence core groupings. Keeping in mind the end goal to increase full esteem through this bibliometric analysis, intermittent replication of the approach to disclosing the changing intellectual structure or convergence of fundamental ideas may be desirable. Such longitudinal study may make use of the present research as a benchmark. Furthermore, future replications may entirely positively influence the recent growth of SCRM works and may even offer an initial appraisal of (fresher) journal publication outlets with a distinct focus on SCRM. Finally, the study at hand also gives rise to different associated bibliometric studies. Author co–citation analysis (ACA) (cf. Acedo *et al.*, 2006; Fischbach *et al.*, 2011; Raasch *et al.*, 2013) or co–word analysis (cf. Benavides–Velasco *et al.*, 2011; Leone *et al.*, 2012; Volberda *et al.*, 2010; Wallin, 2012) applied to the literature of SCRM school of thought could yield supplementary insights. A methodical analysis of the cognitive structure of plan setting research by examining fundamental papers and their intellectual relationships have allowed for improved assessment of the

SCRM's contextual profiles and also of its future prospects. Particularly on the account of the development and the increasing number of research conducted on the highly significant topic of SCRM, characterised by an absence of adequate systematisation.

We consolidated distinctive quantitative techniques – multidimensional scaling, cluster analysis and factor analysis – to triangulate the findings and, therefore, validate our assertions. Improved triangulation ought to enhance the capacity of academics to make inferences from their studies. The application of multiple research methods to a subject may bring about more robust and generalisable results (Scandura and Williams, 2000). The outcomes of the examination have indicated various inconsistencies and possible knowledge gaps that still obstruct a full understanding of SCRM. Based on the results, we projected out promising avenues for further research which can contribute noticeably to the advancement of the research discipline. These explanations may facilitate research endeavours that have the potential to offer tremendous contributions that help SCRM move forward as a research field more consistently. The present analysis additionally makes a methodological contribution by combining multidimensional scaling, cluster analysis and factor analysis to gain valuable insights into SCRM. The methodology adopted affirms and prolongs former articulations about the value of bibliometric and lexicographic procedures (e.g. Furrer *et al.* 2008; Nag *et al.* 2007; Nerur *et al.* 2008). The opportunities for future research that we have discussed may additionally stimulate the development of valuable insights that may notify managers about organisational options. Our study might likewise serve as a foundation to start a discourse of how the term risk is understood within a SCM background. Future research could further investigate shared characteristics and contrasts in the way SCM, operations, logistics, and management articles define and operationalise supply chain risks. Such an investigation could unfold essential peculiarities of SCRM that have not yet gained satisfactory research consideration.

This greater consistency, thus, would encourage the improvement of the understanding of how distinctive sub–forms of supply chain risks ought to be directed advantageously, and it would likewise allow scholars to create more decisive guidance for managers.

Chapter III

26 years of strategic technology partnering: Investigating trends, patterns and future prospects in research through frequency analysis

Abstract

Many firms are increasingly cooperating in their technological undertakings. They engage in strategic technology partnering (STP) for technological, commercial, industrial and financial reasons. STP is deemed to be imperative for easing access to strands of technologies that are unknown to a company. This frequency analysis of STP is based on a systematic literature review (SLR) approach and provides a thorough review of 57 articles published in highly ranked peer-reviewed journals spanning a 26-year period from 1988 to the beginning of 2014. Research on STP is somewhat fragmented, which renders some of the research studies irreconcilable and impedes a greater understanding and consistency of the discipline. There is still a growing body of literature on the subject matter from various disciplinary perspectives which adopt various theoretical and methodological lenses at diverse levels of analysis. In the current paper, we analyse among other things the various methodological, research and theoretical issues underpinning STP and propose a research agenda. Hence, we contribute to the existing body of knowledge on STP literature by offering a state- of-the-art overview of current research and elaborating on promising areas for further investigation.

1 Introduction

Collaborating is deemed of paramount importance to deal with environmental uncertainty (Dogsen, 1993; Eden *et al.*, 2008; Vilkamo and Keil, 2003). Facing fast technological changes and global competition, inter–organisational collaborations have become increasingly important for firms to enhance their competitiveness. Particularly, inter–organisational partnerships are critical for a firm's innovativeness when firms lack sufficient internal research and development (R&D) resources (Smith and Sharif, 2007; Un *et al.*, 2010). Hence, R&D partnerships have become a standard mechanism for safeguarding and exploiting technological proficiencies (Oxley and Sampson, 2004; Schulze *et al.*, 2014).

Farr and Fischer (1992, p. 57) understand cooperation in R&D as "any method by which firms or governments cooperate to make better use of their collective research and development resources to include technical information exchange, harmonising of requirements, codevelopment, interdependent research and development, and agreement on standards." Similarly, Ingham and Mothe (1998, p. 250) refer to R&D partnership as "an agreement between independent organisations that combine tangible and/or intangible resources to cooperate in R&D activities". Hagedoorn (2002, p. 478) defines "R&D partnerships as the particular set of different modes of inter–firm collaboration where two or more firms that remain independent economic agents and organizations share some of their R&D activities." According to Vilkamo and Keil (2003, p. 195) "a strategic technology alli ance or strategic technology partnering relationship can be understood as" a long–term, continuous, and mutually beneficial vertical non–equity relationship where confidential information on future plans and visions is shared openly and proactively in order to help both companies to focus their resources to the right direction". All these definitions emphasise the sharing of valuable resources and their combination, at least involving two different parties. For the purpose of this paper we define STP as follows:

> *A strategic technology partnership is a collaboration between companies that activate and pool their individual tacit and physical assets in the strategic development of technological products to gain mutual benefits and compete in a highly dynamic environment.*

There are various ways through which international technology co-operation and transfer are taking place today. The terms, such as strategic partnership, strategic alliance collaboration, joint R&D, consortia, cooperation, can be explored throughout the academic literature (e.g. Ingham and Mothe, 1998; Mukherjee *et al.*, 2013) and have often been considered as synonyms and used interchangeably (Forrest and Martin, 1992; Kale *et al.*, 2002). Nevertheless, for the purpose of the study at hand we will use the word strategic technology partnering/partnership (STP) to replace other terms such as alliance, collaboration or joint venture. Starting from the 1980s, the formation of strategic technology partnerships, alliances, and joint ventures between firms has significantly increased in a great number of industries at a major rate over the last three decades (Dyer *et al.* 2004; Hagedoorn *et al.*, 2006; Li *et al.*, 2008; Noseleit and de Faria, 2013). One of the most widely cited motives for strategic partnerships is the acquisition and sharing of new technical skills, technological or organisational capabilities from partner firms (Bidault and Cummings, 1994; Bstieler and Hemmert, 2008; Mowery *et al.*, 1996; Kim and Song, 2007; Un *et al.*, 2010). In fact, this sharing of knowledge has even been identified to be the dominant objective for companies to form partnerships (e.g. Caloghirou *et al.*, 2004; Cassiman *et al.*, 2009; Duysters *et al.*, 1999; Huang *et al.*, 2011; Meier, 2011; Zhang and Baden–Fuller, 2010), especially in high technology markets (Ettlie and Pavlou, 2006; Kalaignanam *et al.*, 2007).

The recent devotion given to strategic technological partnering in a variety of commercial and management contexts has developed quicker than our thorough understanding of how such arrangements work. Cassiman *et al.* (2009, p. 218) correctly pointed out that "as firms increasingly use external relationships to acquire new knowledge, they need to develop the capability for governing these relationships". Hence, the settings above constitute our motivation to analyse current issues and trends in SCRM and STP. In spite of the substantial number of research studies that have been conducted in this particular area since the 1980s, little effort has been undertaken to convert those findings systematically into an inclusive literature review. There remains noteworthy potential to enrich our knowledge on SCRM and STP since there are many diverse ways of definitions and concepts in the literature. Consequently, this field of research lacks paradigmatic consensus. Therefore, we conduct a systematic and transparent review, consistent with recent suggestions to fortify the methodological rigor of literature reviews in the management and business field (e.g. Briner *et al.*, 2009; Mulrow, 2001; Rousseau *et al.*, 2008).

The present paper is organised as follows: the proceeding section deals with the elucidation of the rigorous SLR method and explicates the fundamental criteria used to select and evaluate scientific databases, as well as academic journals and articles. Next, based on these identifications, we discuss the classified articles according to theoretical perspectives, methodological approaches, regional focus, the location of study, the level of analysis, type of partnership, and industries considered. The paper closes by providing the underlying theoretical implications and indicating possible directions for future research.

2 Methodology and analysis of the reviewed literature

A comprehensive review on STP was conducted incorporating papers published over a 26–year period in multiple management disciplines. The analysis is inspired by the general methodology of systematic reviews (cf. Denyer and Neely 2004; Kilubi, 2015; Meier, 2011; Mulrow *et al.* 2001; Walker, 2010). In contrast to the conventional literature reviews, a systematic review research method, as adopted in the present paper, removes the subjectivity of collecting data by employing a predefined selection algorithm (Crossan and Aypadin, 2010). From a methodological perspective, a literature review is a systematic, replicable, and explicit procedure for the identification, evaluation, and interpretation of the existing landscape of a research study (Fink, 2005). It provides a necessary audit trail of decisions, procedures and conclusions of the reviewers, allowing for transparency and research replication (Ordanini *et al.*, 2008). Although this research methodology is accompanied by many challenges – such as challenges of data synthesis from numerous disciplines or large amounts of documents to review (Pittaway *et al.*, 2004) – we considered it necessary to apply a methodology that is capable of coping with the vast scope of the strategic technology partnering field. Following Tranfield *et al.* (2003), we conducted a three–phase procedure: planning, execution, and reporting. The review process being part of the execution process comprises three main parts, namely, data collection, data analysis, and data synthesis. The scientific rigour in executing each of these steps is of paramount importance for a high–quality review (Rousseau *et al.*, 2008; Starbuck, 2005). In the course of the planning stage, we decided to confine our data source to top–ranked peer–reviewed journal articles since these can be regarded as confirmed knowledge and are expected to have the highest influence in the field (Podsakoff *et al.*, 2005). Denyer and Tranfield (2009, p. 682) used the acronym 'CIMO' (Context–Intervention–Mechanisms–Outcome) to specify the four distinctive dimensions to be scrutinised in order to accomplish the subsequent phases of a well–designed systematic literature review. Table III-1 presents the CIMO–logic adopted to inform the present study.

Element	Rationale(s)
Context (C)	The increase of interfirm cooperation can be credited to the shifting business and technology market environment. Indeed, a chaotic and turbulent environment obliges to increase the motivation to innovate in cooperation with external partners (Zhang and Baden-Fuller, 2010; Kotabe and Swan, 1995). As a result, firms actively search for knowledge externally to jointly develop their innovations with other institutions (Noseleit and Faria, 2013; Phelps, 2010) because individual firms in isolation cannot control the growing complexity and the fast technological changes of these days (Phene and Tallman, 2010; Chang, 2003; Forrest and Martin, 1992; Dogsen, 1993).
Interventions (I)	The triggering forces for entering cooperations are: (1) mounting R&D costs, (2) ever-shortening technology life cycles, (3) accelerating complexity of technological solutions (e.g. Belderbos *et al.* 2006; Huang and Yu, 2011), (4) ever-expanding globalisation of industrial markets (e.g. Rothaermel and Hess, 2007; Sampson, 2007), (5) increasing customer demands (e.g. Duysters *et al.*, 1999; Lambe and Spekman, 1997), and intense global competition (e.g. Lanctot and Swan, 2000; Smith and Sharif, 2007).
Mechanism (M)	In strategic technology partnerships companies predominantly cooperate tightly in the area of R&D in technology. The central argument is that no company will have an all-embracing competence in every field of technology (Kale and Singh, 2007; Hagedoorn, 1993). The primary motivation to enter an inter-organisational cooperation of any kind is that firms together can achieve benefits they would not gain unaccompanied (Chen *et al.*, 2011; Spekman *et al.*, 1998).
Outcomes (O)	Within the STP domain of inquiry, academics have often considered strategic alliances as sources of novel capabilities and innovativeness (Kim and Song, 2007; Zollo *et al.*, 2002). An Ernst & Young (2009) study affirms the increased value of alliances, with a larger part of executives hoping to commit more corporate consideration and organisational assets to future strategic partnerships.

Table III-1: CIMO–logic applied to the present SLR.
Source: Own illustration.

2.1 Data collection

Firstly, we looked up 15 papers as suggested by researchers within the field to frame the study of our field. In line with Grégoire *et al.* (2011) and Patton (1990), we applied criterion sampling and defined inclusion and exclusion criteria for the articles to be incorporated in the SLR. The date of publication was unrestricted (as of March 2014). Following suggestions, we limited our references to academic peer–reviewed journals that are written in English (Kilubi, 2015; Podsakoff *et al.*, 2005). Finally, in accordance with Nag *et al.* (2007), we excluded *Harvard Business Review* because it predominantly addresses the managerial audience. Since the same rule also applies to *California Business Review* we omitted it as well.

Inclusion criteria	Rationale for inclusion or exclusion
All countries and regions	Consider all countries and regions to achieve a comprehensive overview.
All types of strategic partnerships	Include collaborations (CN), alliances (AL), cooperations/contractual agreements (CL), acquisitions (AQ), mergers (MR), joint ventures (JV), consortia (CA), and licensing (LC).
Commercial partnering (B2B)	Exclude articles on alliances of governmental and public sector organisations, or the participation of universities. Following recommendations, it is determined that the SLR should concentrate on business–to–business partnerships.
High–technology industry	Companies in the high-technology industries are best for studies on STPs because existence and return on investment are critically dependent upon an organisation's capability to generate and commercialise innovations rapidly and proficiently. Consequently, firms in these industries proactively form partnerships in pursuit of their future innovation activities (Schilling and Phelps, 2007).
Journal ranking	Include articles with a ranking of 4 or 3 as defined by the ABS (*Association of Business Schools)* are included in the review.
Level of analysis	We are only concerned with the macro and micro level, i.e. economy/society, industry/market, network, organisation, thus we exclude the individual level, e.g. groups, teams, and single persons.
Organisational form	Exclude papers that compare different organisational forms with each other as well as work by researchers solely interested in STP evolution.

Inclusion criteria	Rationale for inclusion or exclusion
Partnering life cycle	Exclude articles on the choice between alternative organisational forms and on partnership termination.
Publication of full–length journal article	Following Grégoire *et al.* (2011) and Müller–Seitz (2012), we exclude book reviews, short research summaries (less than five pages), editorial pieces, monographs, as well as replies to previously published articles.
Publication in peer–reviewed academic journals	Include peer–reviewed academic journals that publish high–quality research.
Either qualitative or quantitative paper (empirical studies or theoretical studies)	Focus on capturing all evidence, both empirical and theoretical, since different approaches have contributed to the research area of strategic technology partnering.
Time horizon	Include all evidence from 1988 to the beginning of 2014 (as of March 2014). The year 1988 is chosen as the starting point for collecting the relevant data because the very first relevant article on STP was identified in this year, referring to the inclusion and exclusion criteria of the present study (cf. Nueno and Oosterveld, 1988).

Table III-2: Inclusion and exclusion criteria for the present SLR (in alphabetical order).
Source: Own illustration.

For the review at hand, only a selection of top–tier peer–reviewed journal publications with an *ABS* (*associationofbusinessschools.org)* ranking of *4* or *3* were included in the present SLR.*[5] We focused our attention on several electronic reference databases, such as Web of Science, Business Source Complete, and ScienceDirect (cf. Figure III-1).The defined unit of analysis is the strategic technology partnership. We performed keyword searches using the term *strategic partner* OR *R&D partner* AND *technology* given the multitude of meanings ingrained in the term 'strategic technology partnership' and contemplating that

[5] ABS, the *Association of Business Schools* is the representative body for leading economic faculties (business schools) from universities, independent business schools, and higher education institutions in the UK. The ABS is the publisher of the ABS Academic Journal Quality Guide which ranks academic journals. The journals are ranked from 1 till 4; the number 4 signifying the best category and 1 the worst one.

scholars may have utilised this term in a multifaceted way. Thus, articles were not discarded by incorporating the keyword "alliance" or "collaboration", for instance. Besides, the following categories have been chosen, document type "article" and 'review' (but not "book review"); language "English"; subject area "business", "management", and "economics". The articles were selected according to the pre–determined exclusion and inclusion criteria (see Table III-2). The search strings developed were utilised as selection criteria to search for the title, abstract and author–provided keywords. To ensure an unbiased view and to support the reliability and validity of the review, three researchers (the two authors and one research assistant) formed part of the article selection and data extraction process. According to Nag et al. (2007), the articles were selected by rating each article's abstracts and conclusions on a four–point anchored scale. The average Cohen's kappas of 0.81 and 0.87, respectively, indicated a highly significant inter–rater agreement (Conger, 1980; Landis and Koch, 1977). We considered an article as relevant if the average score across all coders was at least 3.0 on both scales (cf. Keupp et al., 2012).

One major limitation of executing a literature search using keywords is that relevant studies that have not incorporated the selected keywords but investigated a similar topic might be overlooked or missed out. Therefore, a few manual inclusions were discussed and added to the SLR by the consensual agreement of the two authors and the research assistant (cf. Felekoglu and Moultrie, 2014; Thorpe *et al.,* 2005). As a result, a total list of 57 peer–reviewed articles in 22 key journal publications, spanning from the beginning of 1988 to the beginning of 2014 (listed in the Appendix by journal, author, and year, etc.), met the selection criteria and were included in the review process. The year 1988 was chosen as the starting point for collecting information because it was the year in which the very first relevant article on STP was identified referring to the inclusion and exclusion criteria of the present study (cf. Nueno and Oosterveld, 1988). The first quarter of the year 2014 is determined as the end time to take account of the latest publications. Figure III-1 outlines our rigorous journal article selection process.

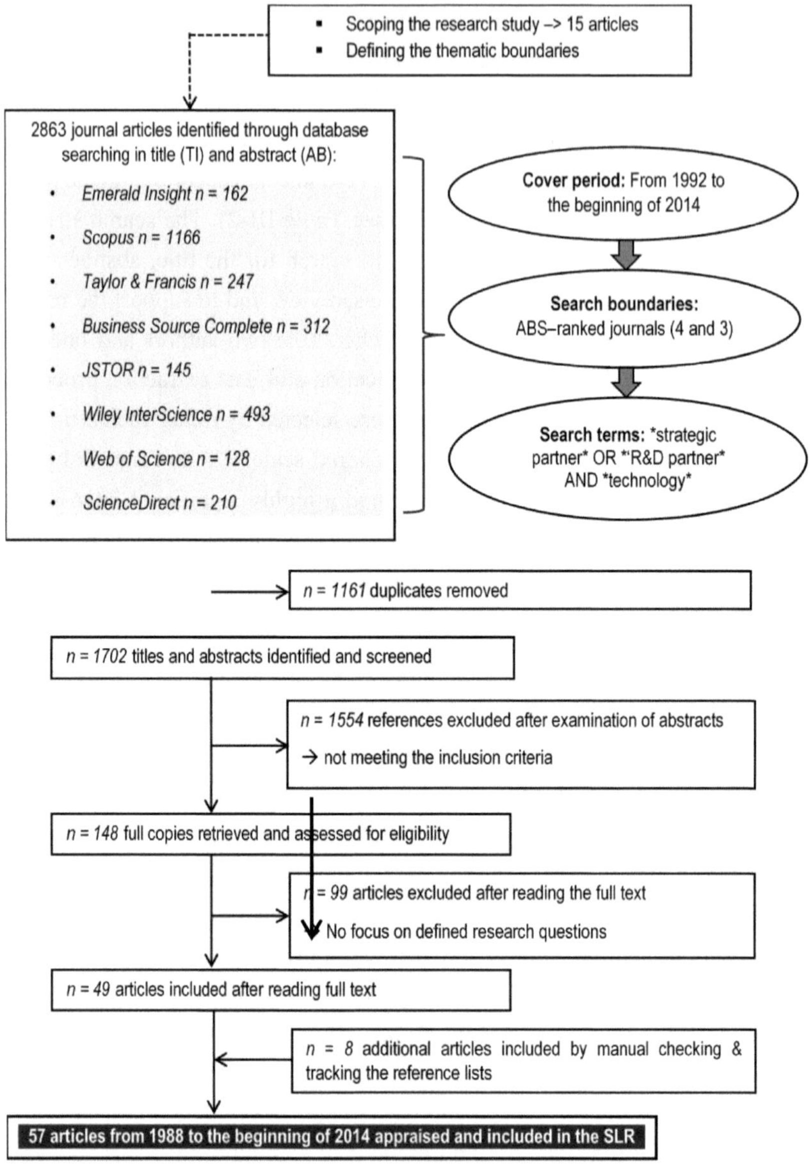

Figure III-1: Summary of the SLR journal article selection process.
Source: Own illustration.

2.2 Data analysis

First, we devised a two–tier review scheme for systematic evaluation, to reduce subjective bias and enhance validity (Keupp *et al.*, 2012). While some authors evidently favour meta–analyses due to the stronger capability to validate findings in opposition to literature reviews (e.g. Stanley *et al.*, 2008), others caution against inaccurate conclusions derived from meta–analyses when they are designed without the required discretion (Durlak and Lipsey, 1991; Rozas and Klein, 2010) and underline their restricted field of application being unable to handle non–randomised studies or qualitative research (Petticrew, 2001; Seuring and Gold, 2012). Apart from that, due to the heterogeneous and highly dispersed nature of the existing literature, a meta–analysis was not possible. Nevertheless, the focus was not on the quantitative data analysis of articles, but rather on gaining conceptual and methodological clarity, and on identifying research gaps (Rashman *et al.*, 2009). Consequently, a narrative synthesis of the reviewed articles was performed. In a narrative synthesis, the interactions between studies with different theories, foci, and methodologies are thematically explored whereby primarily relying on the use of words and text to collect and explain the findings of the synthesis (Mays *et al.*, 2005). This SLR intends to present a comprehensive outline, along with a conceptual instead of an empirical consolidation. Therefore, we are methodologically restricted to descriptive methods, instead of considering statistical techniques in evaluating the findings of our study.

Among existing qualitative analysis techniques, pattern–matching and explanation building (Yin, 1994) were chosen for this review. It is the principal value–added product of a systematic review as it creates new knowledge based on methodical data collection and vigilant analysis. According to the suggestions of Popay *et al.* (2006), we analysed each study with regard to the year of publication, author's country, regional focus, industry, level of analysis, theoretical perspective, explanatory mechanism, types of outcomes, and methodology. In the following, we will evaluate and synthesise the findings from our frequency analysis.

3 Study findings

The sample of 57 selected journals in this SLR was published in 22 interdisciplinary academic journals. In detail, 15 of the selected journals are included in the top 50 of most cited technology innovation management journals as ascertained by Linton and Thongpapanl (2004). Moreover, eight of the journals are among the 45 used by the Financial Times for ranking global business schools (FT.com, 2010). Table III-3 provides a summary of the number of published articles linking the number of papers issued per journal and per year (only journals appearing at least twice have been displayed). Top five journal publications being relevant to our studies were identified (see Figure III-3), along with further journals containing less than three publications. Considering the *Social Sciences Citation Index* (SSCI) and evaluating aspects relating to the prominence, the reputation, and the quality of the content in the respective journals, the publication sources of the selected articles indicate the high degree of scientific relevance (Gundolf and Filser, 2013).

Academic Journal	1988-1992	1993-1994	1995-1996	1997-1998	1999-2000	2001-2002	2003-2004
Academy of Management Journal	0	0	0	1	1	0	0
Administrative Science Quarterly	0	0	1	0	1	0	0
Journal of Business Research	0	0	0	0	0	0	0
Journal of International Business Studies	0	0	0	0	0	0	0
Journal of Product Innovation Management	0	1	0	0	0	0	0
Long Range Planning	1	0	0	0	0	0	0
Management Science	0	0	0	0	0	0	0
Organization Science	1	0	0	0	0	1	0
R&D Management	2	1	0	1	2	0	3
Research Policy	0	1	0	0	1	1	1
Strategic Management Journal	0	1	1	0	1	2	0
Technovation	0	0	1	0	0	0	2

Table III-3: Number of articles per year published by academic journal (extract).
Source: Own illustration.

2005-2006	2007-2008	2009-2010	2011-2012	2013-2014	No. of articles	Percentage
0	2	1	0	0	**5**	9.62 %
0	0	0	0	0	**2**	3.85 %
0	0	0	0	2	**2**	3.85 %
0	1	0	1	0	**2**	3.85 %
0	1	1	1	1	**5**	9.62 %
0	0	1	0	0	**2**	3.85 %
0	2	0	0	0	**2**	3.85 %
0	1	0	0	0	**3**	5.77 %
0	0	0	0	0	**9**	17.31 %
0	0	0	0	0	**4**	7.69 %
0	1	0	0	0	**6**	11.54 %
0	1	0	1	0	**5**	9.62 %

Larger numbers of publications were obviously released in certain years which could be due to the fact that certain academic journals had released call for papers on the topic of STP or strategic alliances, etc. Figure III-2 shows the development of literature over time with the years 2007 to 2008 (19 per cent, n = 11) marking the peak in number of articles published, followed by 1999 to 2000 (12 per cent, n = 7), 2003 to 2004 (10.5 per cent, n = 6), and finally the years 1993 to 1994 (9 per cent, n = 5). More than 75 per cent of all selected articles were published from 1999 to 2000. The small number of papers for the period 1988 to 1998 could result from the meagre coverage in the academic databases.

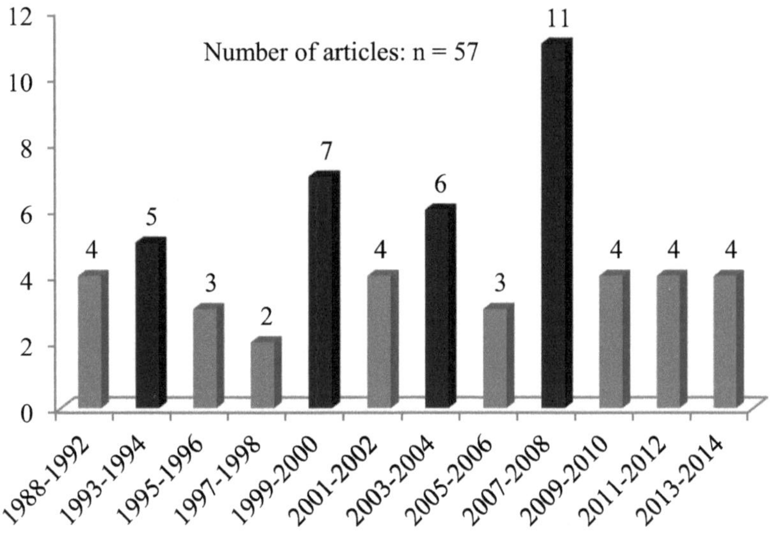

Figure III-2: Distribution of STP publications.
Source: Own illustration.

The key journals contributing to the present SLR elucidate the fields of research that explain the concepts related to STP (Figure III-3). More precisely, the five key academic journals concerning their coverage of this subject were *R&D Management* (15.79 per cent, n = 9), *Strategic Management Journal* (10.53 per cent, n = 6), *Academy of Management Journal, Journal of Product Innovation Management,* and *Technovation* (each 8.77 per cent, n = 5).

Figure III-3: Summary of journals contributing to the review (appearing at least twice).
Source: Own illustration.

We make a distinction between cross–cultural studies according to the following two categories: 1) whether the study is conducted by authors from a single region or different regions and nations, respectively; 2) whether the data is collected worldwide or limited to a particular geographic area. Thus, we focus on a) location of study and b) regional focus of study in the following. We referred to the location of study as 'international' when at least two authors of an article came from different regions, i.e., for example, one author comes from the USA and one from Europe. Note that, for the papers classified as, e.g. 'Europe' or 'Asia', it implies that all the authors reside within the same region. Figure III-4 shows that the majority of authors who contribute to the selected journal articles come from Europe with 44 per cent of the total sample (n = 25), followed by North America with 33 per cent (n = 19). However, only 7 per cent of the articles were written by authors with an 'international' background (n = 12), and finally only 11 per cent (n = 6) of the reviewed articles have been contributed by authors from the Asian area.

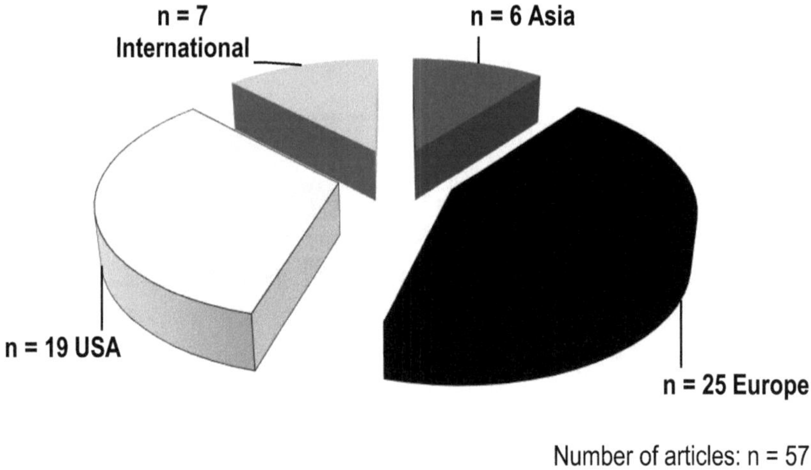

Figure III-4: Number of articles classified by the location of each study.
Source: Own illustration.

Next, we analysed the regional focus of the study for each journal article included in the present review (see Figure III-5). We referred to the regional focus as 'international' when the data obtained came at least from two different regions, i.e., for example, data was collected from the USA and Europe. Note that, for the papers classified as e.g. 'Europe' or 'Asia', it implies that data came from the same region. Moreover, we referred to the regional focus of a study as either 'Not specified (N/S)' 16 per cent (n = 9) in case no conclusions could be drawn from that information or as 'Not applicable (N/A)' 4 per cent (n = 2) in case the study was conceptual or a literature review. The analysis shows that 33 per cent (n = 19) of the papers include data based internationally, 16 per cent (n = 9) based in the USA, whereas 16 per cent (n = 9) of the journal articles did not specify the regional focus of their study. Europe is quite highly represented with 23 per cent (n = 13), illustrating that European scholars have made an elevated contribution to the topic. It must be remarked, however, that articles concentrating on Asia only represent 9 per cent (n = 5).

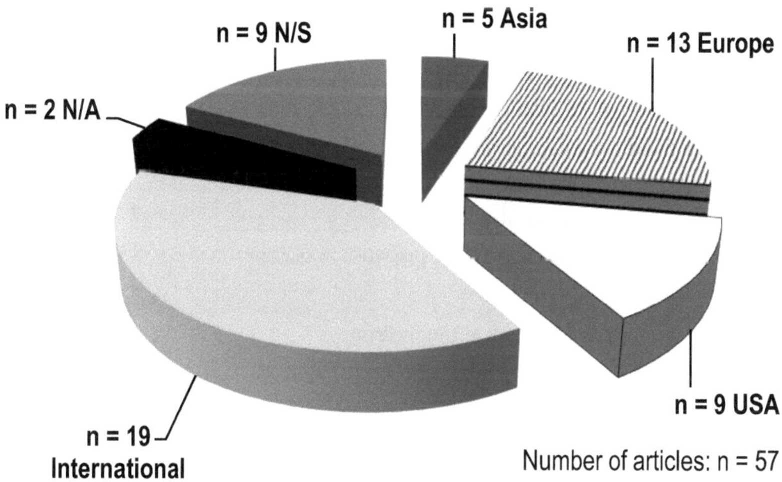

Figure III-5: Number of articles classified by the regional focus of each study.
Source: Own illustration.

Table III-4 highlights the industries under investigation and the frequency of articles relating to each industry. The total sample of articles in the review is obviously biased towards electrics and electronics (18.31 per cent, n = 26) and pharmaceutical industries (11.27 per cent, n = 16), followed by manufacturing companies (9.86 per cent, n = 14) and the chemicals industry with 6.34 per cent (n = 9). However, the services industry only represents 2.8 per cent (n = 4) of the overall sample.

Industry		In no. of articles mentioned	Percentage
Chemicals & Chemical Products		**9**	6.34 %
Electrics & Electronics		**26**	18.3 %
	Computers & Software	4	2.82 %
	General	5	3.52 %
	Information & Communications Technology	2	1.41 %
	Information Technology	3	2.11 %
	Semiconductor	4	2.82 %
	Telecommunications	8	5.63 %
Manufacturing Industries		**14**	9.86 %
	General	2	1.41 %
	Aerospace Equipment	1	0.70 %
	Automotive	4	2.82 %
	Mechanical Engineering Medical & Healthcare Equipment Petroleum Refinement & Production	4 2 1	2.82 % 1.41 % 0.70 %
Pharmaceutical Industries		**16**	11.27 %
	General	8	5.63 %
	Biotechnology	8	5.63 %

Industry		In no. of articles mentioned	Percentage
Services Industries		**4**	2.82 %
	Communication Services	1	0.70 %
	Financial Services	1	0.70 %
	Software- & Computer-related Services	2	1.41 %
Not applicable (N/A)		2	1.41 %
Not specified		9	6.34 %
Other(s)		2	1.41 %

Table III-4: Sectoral analysis of journal articles reviewed.
Source: Own illustration.

Most of the partnership types were alliances, corresponding to 39 per cent (n = 28) of the total sample, followed by collaborations with 26 per cent (n = 19), and co-operation's/contractual agreements with 19 per cent (n = 14). Next, acquisitions and joint ventures each made up 6 per cent (n = 4) of the total number of papers reviewed. Note, however, consortia, licencing agreements, and mergers only corresponded to each 1 per cent (n = 1) of the total article set (cf. Figure III-6).

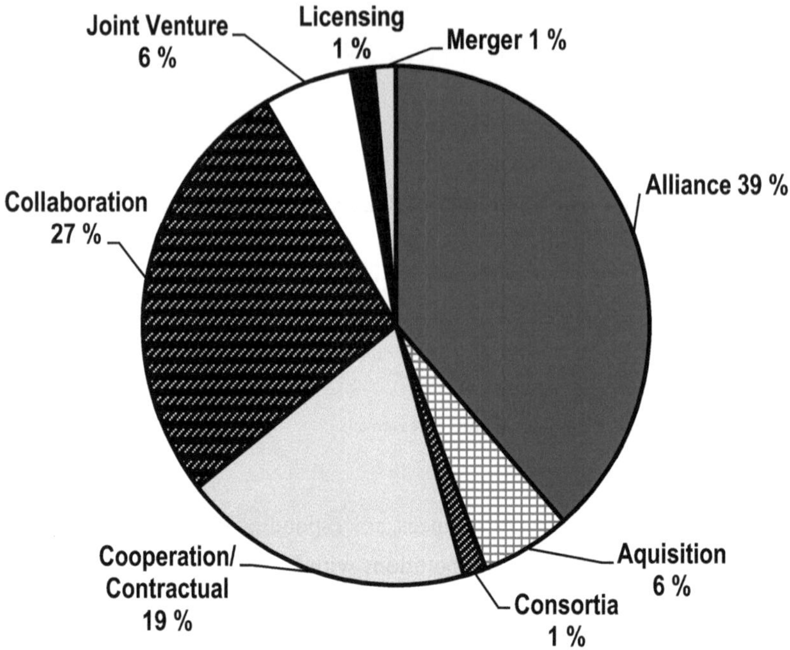

Figure III-6: Variety of partnership types used in the included studies for review.
Source: Own illustration.

From 1988 to 1996 most of the theories focused on the resourced–based view (RBV) (37 per cent, n = 19) and knowledge–based view (KBV) (25 per cent, n = 13), followed by the social network theory (SNT) (17 per cent, n = 9), and organisational learning (OL) (13 per cent, n = 7). From 1997 to 2005 the focus on KBV and RBV further increased, whereas the one on SNT reached its highest point at the commencement of the new millennium but started to decrease from then on. Noteworthy, from 2001 onwards – with a progressive growth – transaction cost economy (TCE) began to play a role in STP research. Still, TCE did not appear that often, with only in 8 per cent (n = 4) of all articles mentioned, but evolutionary economics (EE) and the real options theory (ROT) appeared even less frequently, with each 4 per cent representation (n = 2). However, the focus on OL remained stable during that period. From 2006 onwards all theories were used more often –

which can be seen in Figure III-7 showing an upward trend of the frequency of all theories applied – except for SNT as previously mentioned. Surprisingly, evolutionary economics, social capital theory, and the real options theory were each only used twice in the selected articles. Moreover, in five papers other theories were applied of which three were accompanied by at least one of the theories mentioned above.

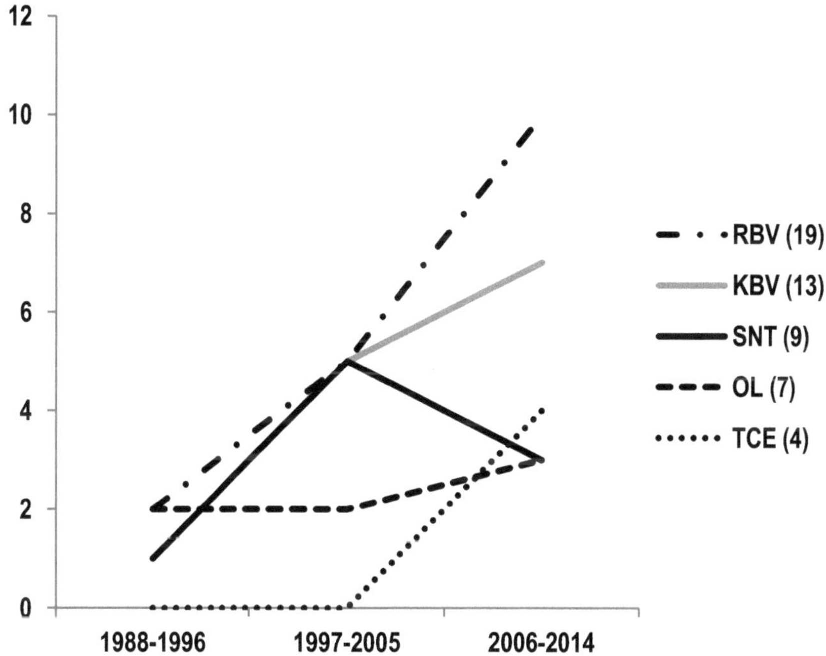

Figure III-7: Most frequently used theories related to years of publication.
Source: Own illustration.

Our analysis revealed that 54 per cent (n = 31) of the articles reviewed have addressed one single theory, whereas 26 per cent (n = 15) have focused on at least two theories at the same time. However, a significant proportion of 19 per cent (n = 11) did not specify the theory applied to their research (see Figure III-8).

Although several authors adopted a few theories, the lack of an explicit and coherent theoretical foundation becomes apparent.

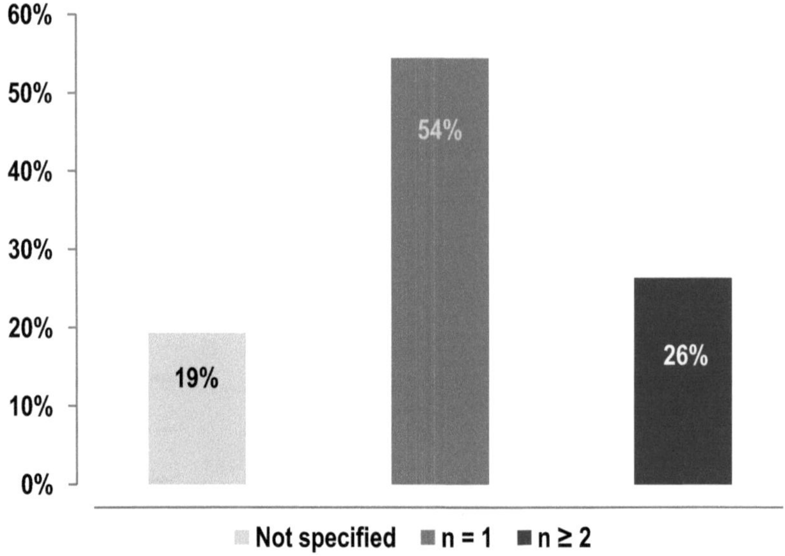

Figure III-8: Percentage of theories used in each article classified into three groups.
Source: Own illustration.

We also analysed the level of analysis applied in each selected journal article, which is shown in Figure III-9. Our analysis revealed that the articles mainly focused on the organisational level with 33 per cent (n = 19), the industry/market level with 26 per cent (n = 15) and the multilevel of analysis with 21 per cent (n = 12). Next, attention was focused on the network level of analysis with 14 per cent (n = 8). Surprisingly, only 5 per cent (n = 3) of the reviewed articles focused on economy and society respectively.

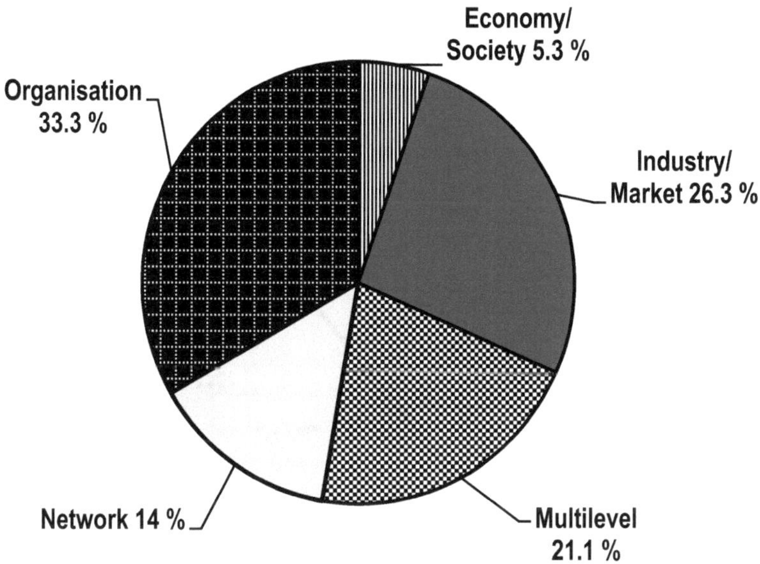

Figure III-9: Breakdown of articles by level of analysis.
Source: Own illustration.

Concerning the research methodologies applied to the surveyed papers, we classified the approaches to investigate STP literature into five categories. Consistent with Seuring (2004) and Keupp *et al.* (2012), five research methodologies were classified. The five classifications included: (1) theoretical/conceptual papers; (2) case studies; (3) surveys; (4) literature reviews; but instead of modelling papers – which is not common in STP research – our fifth category was secondary database research. The highest proportion was captured by empirical articles, with a certain focal point on testing theory with 55 per cent, including both secondary database research with 42 per cent (n = 24) and surveys/questionnaires with 32 per cent (n =18). However, theory building (case studies) was considered less with 23 per cent (n = 13) representation. Literature reviews and conceptual papers made up the smallest share (2 per cent, n = 1 for each methodology). Thus, our results found that empirical research, more precisely theory testing with the means of secondary database research and surveys/questionnaires, has been the preferred methodology to explore the topic of STP within the last 26 years (42 out of 57). Figure III-10 displays the methodologies used in the selected papers.

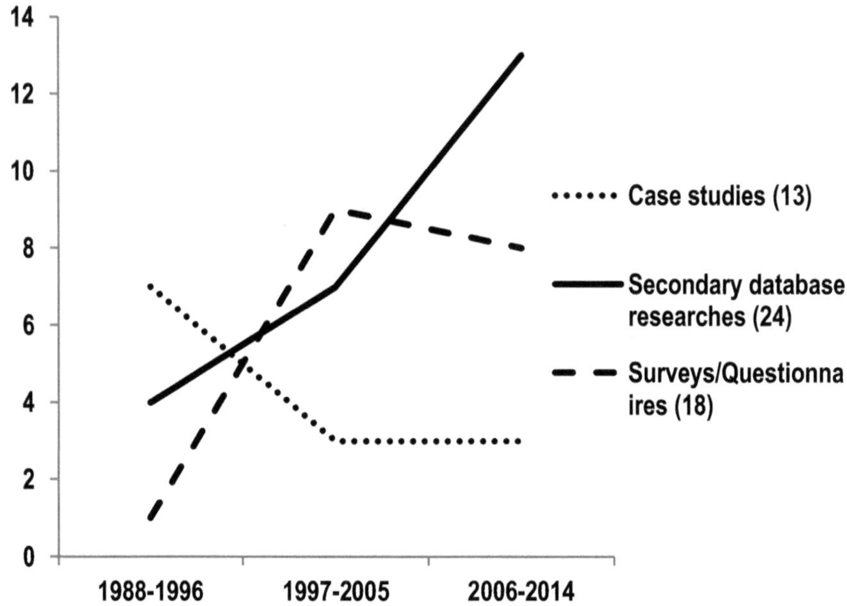

Figure III-10: Breakdown of articles by most frequently applied methodological approaches. Source: Own illustration.

All in all theory testing has been consistently used as a primary method in previous studies. Moreover, it can be seen that a growing number of researchers conducted either secondary database research or surveys/questionnaires. Secondary database research had a sharp increase since 1992 and has been growing exponentially, whereas surveys/questionnaires showed a steady increase from 1992 until 2003. From 2003 on, the latter started to show a downward trend. In contrast, case study research in STP literature had its peak between 1988 and 1994 and gradually decreased until 2003 reaching a point where the number remained stable until today.

Interestingly, literature reviews and conceptual papers have infrequently been used over time. The distribution of theories by the level of analysis may be of interest, too (cf. Table III-5). However, the SLR at hand did not disclose a particular theory for STP that may function at multiple levels. For instance, both RBV and KBV, are used at the industry/market level and the organisational level. However, those papers not specifying or not using a theoretical base adopted either the multilevel or the organisational level approach. Nonetheless, more theoretical development should be conducted to integrate the macro levels.

Theories	Multilevel (ML)	Economy/ Society (ES)	Industry/ Market (IM)	Network (NW)	Organisation (ON)
Economics and Evolution (EE)			Kim and Song (2007); Zollo *et al.* (2002)		
Social Network Theory (SNT)	Ahuja (2000a)	Ciu *et al.* (2002)	Ketchen *et al.* (2007)	Schilling and Phelps (2007)	Ahuja (2000b)
Resource-based View (RBV)	Rothaermel and Hess (2007); Santangelo (1999)	Miotti and Sachwald (2003)	Chang (2003); Ketchen *et al.* (2007); Kim and Song (2007); Mowery *et al.* (1996); Noseleit and Faria (2013); Phene and Tallman (2012)	Chen *et al.* (2011); Ettlie and Pavlou (2006); Huang and Yu (2011); Lee *et al.* (2001)	Ahuja (2000b); Caloghirou *et al.* (2004); Dogsen (1993); Kale and Singh (2007); Tidd (2014); Trott *et al.* (1995); Vilkamo and Keil (2003)
Knowledge-based View (KBV)	Ingham and Mothe (1998)		Bayona (2001); Ketchen *et al.* (2007); Li *et al.* (2008); Mowery *et al.* (1996); Phene and Tallman (2012); Un *et al.* (2010); van de Vrande *et al.* (2011);	Kim and Lee (2003); Phelps (2010)	Dogsen (1993); Fey and Birkinshaw (2005); Kale and Singh (2007); Sampson (2007); Saxton (1997); Schulze *et al.* (2007); Sividas and Dwyer (2000);

Theories	Multilevel (ML)	Economy/ Society (ES)	Industry/ Market (IM)	Network (NW)	Organisation (ON)
			Zhang and Baden-Fuller (2010)		Steensma and Corley (2000)
Transaction Cost Economy (TCE)			Li *et al.* (2008); Mukherjee *et al.* (2013); Phene and Tallman (2012)		Sampson (2007)
Social/Relational Capital Theory (SCT)	Hagedoorn *et al.* (2006)		Mukherjee *et al.* (2013); Siu and Bao (2008)	Lee *et al.* (2001)	
Real Options Theory (ROT)			Ketchen *et al.* (2007); van de Vrande *et al.* (2011)		
Game Theory (GT)	Häussler *et al.* (1994)			Kim and Lee (2003)	Cassiman (2009)
Other Theories (OT)	Zhou and Li (2008); Zollo *et al.* (2008)				Dogsen (1993)
N/S and N/A	Bstieler and Hemmert (2008); Kalaignanam *et al.* (2007); Rothaermel (2001)	Nueno and Oosterveld (1988)	Forrest and Martin (1992)	Carr (1999)	Bidault and Cummings (1994); Bonaccorsi and Lipparani (1994); Farr and Fischer (1992); Hagedoorn and Schakenraad (1994); Duysters *et al.* (1999)

Table III-5: Level of analysis used by theory.
Source: Own illustration.

4 Discussion

More than 70 per cent (41 out of 57) of the reviewed papers were published between 1999 and 2008. The fact that the number of publications started to decrease at the beginning of 2008 may have resulted from the global economic crisis that had started in 2007. Our analysis revealed that more than 50 per cent of the articles in our SLR were contributed by leading academic journals, namely *R&D Management, Strategic Management Journal, Journal of Product Innovation Management, Academy of Management Journal*, and *Technovation.* In order to further highlight the vital importance and interdisciplinary role of the STP phenomenon, we found a wide range of journals from various disciplines that have published relevant studies. Over the last decades, the formation of technology partnerships has grown remarkably (e.g. Anand and Khanna, 2000; Dyer *et al.* 2004; Hagedoorn, 2002; Grant and Baden–Fuller, 2004). In the same way, the quantity of associated studies in the management and innovation literature has grown at an unprecedented rate. STPs have turned into an important research subject incorporating a wide range of theoretical frameworks and viewpoints (Saxton, 1997; Un *et al.*, 2010).

Hence, scholars and practitioners have started to devote to understanding reasons that explain why companies enter STPs and how some of them outperform others. Various arguments for companies entering STPs have been elaborated such as to gain moderate and share costs and risks, and to access external knowledge (Grant and Baden–Fuller, 2004; Meier, 2011). As stated by Link and Siegel (2007), inter-organisational partnerships in the profit–making business areas have been expanding increasingly over the last two decades which can be attributed to economic changes such as (1) investments in public–private partnerships including start–ups, innovation parks, and small and family–owned business programs; (2) recreation of antitrust enforcement to foster collaborative research; (3) enactment of legislation designed to endorse prompted technological transmission from institutions of higher education and public laboratories to companies (Ketchen *et al.*,

2007); and (4) accelerating movements in globalisation and information technology (Friedmann, 2005). In addition to that, the growth of inter-organisational partnerships is fueled by the shifting commercial and technological environment where the driving forces for STPs are: (1) rising R&D expenditure, (2) ever–shortening product life cycles, (3) rising complexity of technological solutions, and (4) the progressing globalisation of business markets and product offerings (Chang, 2003). An Ernst & Young (2009) study confirmed the continuously growing value of STPs, with a majority of executives planning to dedicate corporate devotion to future collaborations. Many professional communities among scholars, scientists, engineers, and many more have acknowledged the value of inter-organisational networks to strengthen the ability to create innovations in the light of the fast–paced and highly complex market environments (Chesbrough, 2003; Miles *et al.*, 2005; Lee and Cole, 2003; Wenger, 2000).

If the advantages of STPs are so obviously positive, why do not all companies engage in that kind of cooperation? There are various reasons for that; one reason may be the high costs in association with the uncertainty of how the relationship may develop in the course of the business transaction. Another reason results from internal firm–specific factors and the market conditions under which a company actively operates (Koza and Lewin, 1998; Park *et al.*, 2004). Through the formation of a STP, a company is prone to opportunistic behaviour of its cooperation partners (Parkhe, 1993). This concern is a principal feature of small and middle–sized enterprises (SMEs) with knowledge–based technologies that possess a low bargaining power compared to large enterprises (Lavie, 2007). To relieve such concerns, trust frequently plays a pivotal role at an early stage by alleviating worries of latent opportunistic manners (Adobor, 2005). On the other hand, the relational capital of SMEs, in the form of mutual trust, ought to inspire the formation of STP and lessen worries linked to knowledge outflow and uncertainty (Mukherjee *et al.*, 2013). Investing in new technologies combined with high volumes also entails the risk of technologies getting obsolete very soon which may particularly hinder small firms to enter STPs (Vilkamo und Keil, 2003).

4.1 Geographical issues

Concerning the regional focus, the evidence is mainly focused on Europe and the USA, with some bias for the period 1999 to 2000 and 2007 to 2008. Regrettably, 16 per cent (n = 9) did not specify the regional focus of their study. We can only assume that those articles either based their study globally or focused on the location of the study. Referring to the location of study involved in our selected body of literature, the paper at hand identified that primary authors from Europe and USA (two–third) conducted research on STP. Consequently, the results show that only a few journal articles were published by authors from Asia and other regions. Since emerging economies such as Asia and Latin America will experience remarkable growth in the global economy within the next years, researchers may be missing out on high potential. With the growth of emerging–market companies and global competition (Cuypers and Martin, 2010), STPs both local and global are critical to business success (Ketchen *et al.*, 2007).

The KPMG's Global Manufacturing Outlook 2012 reveals that as the costs of manufacturing technology continue to decrease, the barriers to entry are getting lower for smaller players. Another key finding of the KPMG study is that strategic technology partnering has been becoming more important to international producers in case innovation is imperative. Hence, manufacturers in emerging economies like those in India have to make substantial efforts to maintain cost–effective as more and more multinationals from developed markets have been on the verge of conquering their markets (KPMG, 2012). Moreover, cross–national academics exploit information from diverse societal settings in an attempt to find underlying generalisations. Their core belief is that cross–national comparisons are conceivable and that there are similar patterns of explanations and principles across the wide diversity of cultures (Spicer and Bailey, 1997). The careful selection of countries for sampling is also an issue to make sure that the complete ranges of the country–level variables of interest are encompassed. It is possible that in this context, aspects of country–level variables may be recognised as potential explanations why the identified variances emerged which, furthermore, may direct to future research necessities that require more in–depth investigation (Cadogan,

2010). Makino *et al.* (2004) demonstrate that nation effects are as significant as industry effects and that both nation and industry effects are even more prominent in emerging nations. National economists, though contend that territorial contrasts may be more notable within than between nations (e.g., Krugman, 1991; Markusen, 1995). Likewise, a study conducted by Lenartowicz and Roth (2001) shows that organisational performance differs considerably across cultures within a nation.

4.2 Industries considered

STPs have been fast growing since the early 1980s in particular in high–tech industries (Hagedoorn *et al.*, 2006; Kim and Song, 2007). Cross–industry cooperations and collaborations occur in a wide range of industries and merge very diverse technologies (Bidault and Cummings, 1994). The concentration of collaborative arrangements in knowledge-intensive sectors points to technology occupying a major function in STP formation (Dickson and Weaver, 1997; Doz, 1988). Industries in the present review focus on high–technology, from which the majority of approximately 40 per cent stem from electrics and electronics, pharmaceutical (e.g. biotechnology), and manufacturing (e.g. automotive) industries. In these industries which are mainly penetrated by STPs to enhance innovation output being marked by a high level of patent use, the creation of knowledge is essential to gaining competitiveness (Schilling and Phelps, 2007; Vonortas, 1997). Furthermore, high–technology industries are constantly under pressure due to short product–life–cycle and reduced time–to–market to quickly anticipate shifting customer requirements and to embrace novel technological innovations (Duysters *et al.*, 1999). In the emerging digital and electronics areas where fast new product introduction and creative product solutions represent fundamental innovative, strong points, companies proactively join networks of complementary resources (Miotti and Sachwald, 2003). Particularly, we can experience a rise of technology–based strategic partnering in knowledge–based scientific fields such as ICT (Duysters and Vanhaverbeke, 1996; Hagedoorn und Schakenraad, 1994; Santangelo, 2000). Firstly, considering the dynamic and multi–faceted nature of companies rooted in the technology–intensive industry such as electronics, manufacturing, and chemicals, organisations count on other organisations that can provide the lacking expertise that is necessary to achieve global competitiveness. Likewise, the electrics and electronics, as well as the automotive industry, are characterised by intricate new product launches. "Second, there is a trend toward changing the locus of innovation in the sector of the economy, moving upstream in the supply chain from assembly (buyer) firms like General Motors Corporation and Toyota to first–tier suppliers like Delphi and Visteon" (Ettlie and Pavlou, 2006, pp. 126–127). In the biotechnology industry, for instance, high level of costs incur for R&D and are fuelled by a complex and a tedious process of product authorisation as well as a high rate of product failure, thus many organisations thrive for collaboration in order to overcome those challenges (Phene and Tallman, 2012; Rothaermel, 2001). Besides, the biotechnology industry is one of the industries with large amounts of technological breakthroughs and is characterised by high research concentration (Katila und Ahuja, 2002). This industry lies at the interface of many diverse technological disciplines and domains, such as immunology, bioinformatics, molecular biology, genetics, chemical, agriculture, food, etc. (Phene *et al.*, 2006), making STP a necessary prerequisite for inter-organisational collaborations (Higgins und Rodriguez, 2006). Thirdly, as new technological knowledge in the biotechnology sector is dispersed among incumbent companies, new biotechnology firms (NBFs), and universities/research institutes, therefore, the industry is characterised by very high levels of alliances (Zhang and Baden–Fuller, 2010). However, we also noticed that the services industry is underrepresented in STP research. During the last two decades, service industries have been a sector of importance and growth in an increasingly competitive environment. For instance, today the service industry represents one of the major drivers for growth in the economy and accounts for 70 per cent of the gross domestic product in the USA (Ellram *et al.,* 2007). Due to the fact that more and more firms are entering new markets within the services industry characterised by low entry barriers with high margins (PwC, 2014), researchers will have to pay more attention to the development of STPs in the services industry in the near future.

4.3 Levels of analysis

Generally speaking, the level of analysis is a matter of organisation of scientists because they regularly pick between contending levels of analysis (Rousseau, 1985). One–third of the selected papers used organisational level, followed by industry/market level, and network level as a level of analysis. Although most management issues deal with multi–level phenomena, nonetheless, most management studies employ a single level of analysis. Even more important, only a couple of academic writers have endeavoured to connect theory or execute research that employs cross–levels of inquiry or investigation. Multi–level datasets and methods emphasise contentions regarding nations, different country groupings, and so on (Hitt *et al.*, 2007). Progress in multi–level analysis permit improved accuracy in the quantitative global business research and open up new methodological and reasonable potential outcomes (Peterson *et al.*, 2012). As the management literature matures, yet, scientists gain a more intricate understanding of phenomena by using multi–level lenses Luckily, more advanced techniques for investigating multilevel information have been created, for example, inside and between investigation (cf. Dansereau and Yammarino, 2000), and cross–level operator techniques (James and Williams, 2000). Firms have been challenged more and more by augmented bureaucratisation and fast technological change. The open doors for new multilevel studies are numerous, and they emerge from methodological and theoretical contemplations. For instance, there are opportunities to examine whether particular phenomena show up at different levels of examination (cf. Schneider *et al.*, 2003). Therefore, several researchers suggest that research may become conceivably profitable by examining the role of inter-organisational partnerships within networks or between STP associates in the development and design of new technologies and products, etc. (Almeida and Phene, 2004; Yamin and Otto, 2004); this distinction raises the necessity for research that incorporates cross–level analysis. Theoretically and empirically linking a phenomenon that fundamentally includes cross–levels of analysis, is an issue that has attracted growing consideration in the organisational science literature (cf. for instance, Earley and Brittain (1993), Klein and Kozlowski (2000), the special issue of the *Academy of*

Management Review (1999, Vol. 24 No. 2), and the statement of direction for *The Journal of Organizational Behaviour* (Rousseau and Fried, 2001)).

4.4 Partnership types

The majority of partnership types in the reviewed literature were alliances, collaborations, and cooperation/contractual agreements. Given that R&D alliances are designed to generate new technologies, we expected a larger proportion of joint innovation in R&D alliances than other types of partnerships. This observation is reinforced by a research piloted by Hagedoorn and Duysters (2002) whose analysis demonstrates that the options for a certain type of partnership are influenced by both different environmental circumstances and company–specific settings. They confirm the more companies operate in high–tech sectors, such as ICT, pharmaceuticals, and aerospace, etc., the more they have a disproportionate preference for more flexible organisations such as strategic technology alliances. In summary, concerning the overall sample of evidence in the paper at hand numerous significant conclusions can be drawn. Starting from the early 1980s, organisations gradually have become mindful of the focal points of collaborating with capable partners (Duysters *et al.*, 1999). Regarding the industries analysed in the selected journal articles, the evidence base is somewhat dominated by a focus on electrical/electronics, pharmaceutical, and manufacturing industries. In the past, firms mainly relied on mergers and acquisitions to avail themselves of their particular core competency areas, whereas strategic partnerships were mainly used to reinforce or contract out non–core competence areas (Hagedoorn and Duysters, 2002).

These days, a growing exploitation of STP (contractual agreements, strategic alliances, joint ventures) can be observed to generate vitally radical innovations or to enter emerging business markets (Duysters and Vanhaverbeke, 1996). Alliance–based and collaboration–based relationships dominate the network in the STP literature. Joint efforts in cutting-edge commercial enterprises commonly reflect more than merely a formal contractual trade (Powell *et al.*, 1996). Collaboration frequently comprises incalculable results and depends highly on trust and a joint vow to adhere to ethics of trustworthiness and even–handed management (Von Krogh, 1998). Collaboration may be heading for any commonly craved goal: detecting and then tackling an issue, solving a problem, designing a new invention, and much more. Within a shared network system, ideas are open–source prospects, where each entity may use the thoughts to formulate promising projects within its partnership network (Lee and Cole, 2003). The connection between the partnering companies is tighter because they commonly profit from the effective advancement of technologies (Schönmakers and Duysters, 2006). Ohmae (1989) was one of the first researchers to promote international strategic alliances as a compelling reaction to globalisation while underlining the significance of mutual trust and engagement. In today's fast–moving, knowledge–intensive sphere, research and development alliances have turned into a mainstream vehicle for leveraging technological capabilities. Furthermore, business people perceive that intensive interaction with STP associates open doors for profit-yielding business development. Along these lines, the shaping of an incredible network of alliances turns into a foundation of their corporate strategy, in which they implement a network–sustaining strategy to enrich exchanges and increment common reliance (Siu and Bao, 2008). Joint development agreements regularly involve more elevated amounts of organisational relationship and happen when two or more organisations liaise with each other to generate new products by merging their reciprocal abilities (Robertson and Gatignon, 1998). Then again, such cooperations lead to sensitive difficulties linked to the safeguard of technological expertise, since effective accomplishment of STP goals regularly demands of a company to put valuable skills and know–how at risk of being captured by innovation partners. Hence, companies must choose the right balance between upholding open knowledge exchange to advance the technological development objectives of the STP, and controlling information streams to elude unintended release of profitable innovations (Oxley and Sampson, 2004).

4.5 Theoretical lenses

Looking at the theoretical assumptions, we noticed that most articles dealt with the RBV and the KBV and that 54 per cent of the articles have addressed one single theory. The resulting conclusions correspond with the expectations considering the dominance of the resource-based view from a theoretical standpoint within strategic management theories (Ketchen *et al.*, 2007). Correspondingly, this is also a major consideration in entrepreneurship (Alvarez and Busenitz, 2001). However, these two perspectives under consideration have fairly dissimilar concerns regarding the foundations of value creation. The RBV highlights the internally accrued and combined resources, assets or capabilities (Grant and Baden–Fuller, 2004) and the knowledge–based view conceptualises firms as mechanisms that facilitate knowledge creation, where successful innovations benefit from various knowledge skills (Chesbrough, 2003). Therefore, R&D collaborations provide firms with experience of which they lack, helping them to increase the chance of successfully innovating products (Un and Cuervo–Cazurra, 2004). In RBV, technological capabilities constitute the welfare of a company's viable competitive advantage, since these capabilities can comprise protected patents, technological know–how, and trade secrets, etc., that are valuable and hard to imitate by competitors (Fey and Birkinshaw, 2005; Rothaermel and Hess, 2007). Such capabilities are certainly even more critical in high–technology companies (Un *et al.*, 2010). In the context of the emerging knowledge–based international economy, both supply and demand for new technology have been growing at the global level (Miotti and Sachwald, 2002). Otherwise, the social network research captures a relational viewpoint (Dyer and Singh, 1998) and provides insights that the success and performance of a STP may be mostly influenced by the configuration of network resources and their positioning within the networks (e.g., centrality, cliques) (Chang, 2003).

Organisational learning (OL), on the one hand, has assumed a dominant role within the organisational theory (Argyris and Schön, 1978). Previous research has put emphasis on the critical success factor for learning in developing new products (e.g. Aggeri and Segrestin, 2007; Eisenhardt and Martin, 2000; Elmquist and Le

Masson, 2009; Lynn *et al.*, 2000). In essence, OL is an ongoing development through which companies create new knowledge (Li *et al.*, 2008; Tippins and Sodhi, 2003). The transaction–cost–based STP literature, on the other hand, has tended to concentrate on appropriation concerns (Gulati and Singh, 1998; Hennart, 1988) as drivers of governance. Indeed, White and Lui (2005) suggest that studies investigating STP arrangements should explicitly include the cost of cooperation besides typical appropriation concerns. Anticipated coordination cost in STPs is the outcome of the level of interdependency needed for STP partners to fulfil certain tasks (Phene and Tallman, 2012). The transaction cost economics (TCE) perspective analyses the conditions under which cooperative arrangements bring about the most effective system of an organisation (Hennart, 1988, 1991; Stuckey, 1983). TCE has long been the central theory for examining transaction risks and the related contractual answers (Leiblein, 2003). Previous studies in TCE advocate that the choice of a suitable governance structure that companies apply is one mechanism to promote knowledge exchange in STPs (Oxley and Sampson, 2004). Several essential contributions can be credited to TCE, among others: (1) it has attracted attention to the multiplicity of contracts in high–level performance economies; and (2) it has provided an efficiency–based argument for this multiplicity (Raynaud *et al.*, 2009; Wever *et al.*, 2012). However, several researchers argue that the limited focus of TCE on reducing costs ignores the tactic and organisational learning factors of inter-organisational cooperation (Eisenhardt and Schoonhoven, 1996; Powell *et al.*, 1996). Most often, the elementary motives of creating a STP are more intricate than pure cost contemplations. Intentions such as know-how and skill transfer between STP entities that enhance the organisations' abilities using cooperative learning can be a vital aspect (Ozman, 2009).

4.6 Methodological approaches

In recent years, the number of scholars, academics, and scientists employing large volumes of data has increased significantly (CACM, 2009). Referring to the methodological approaches adopted for researching STP, it can be observed that the trend leans towards the use of secondary databases which has been rising from

1992 to 2014; even more sharply from 2005 onwards. We are certain of numerous dynamics that cause the increase in secondary database research: (a) a generally increased awareness of the need for high–quality data, whereas the database is assumed to hold all facts belonging to the domain under study (CACM, 2009) (b) improvements in the cost and quality of data storage/processing; and more importantly, (c) accumulation of high–quality, reliable datasets over the years including simplicity and uniformity of data arrangements (Korth and Silberschatz, 1997). Going into the future, the trend highlights an opportunity for more researchers who cannot afford to collect their own data first–hand to rapidly access simple, easy–to–use interfaces and information with accurate database updates (Korth and Silberschatz, 1997), but also the problem of recycling the same datasets which might lead to snooping. However, given that the majority of journal articles have focused on quantitative studies, we expect a rise in the use of qualitative methods to further explore areas of STP that are alien to the scientific world. In order to conduct exploratory research with the purpose of developing knowledge that is highly related to practice and the real world, the case study technique is, in particular, applicable and appropriate (Wassmer, 2010). In any case, we can observe a diminishing pattern in the adoption of longitudinal research methods. This decay has happened despite various calls for more longitudinal studies; that even although researchers postulate that the larger the amount of sources of confirmation supporting hypothesis is, the more significant the deductions are that can be made (Scandura and Williams, 2000). Above and beyond, our findings advocate that research in the management field needs to adopt more triangulation on research methodologies. Thus, it may be valuable for scholars to step outside the prevailing approaches of their basic scientific zones and to attempt using methods employed in other disciplines. In strategic management, the use of both qualitative and quantitative research methods can be observed. However, the application of large–scale operationalised research design prevails (Molina–Azurin, 2010). Nevertheless, to become attractive to a scientific audience, research in management and organisation should be 'counterintuitive' to challenge conventional theory (Bartunik *et al.*, 2006). Clearly, there is a substantial opportunity for wider implementation of mixed method research designs within organisation and management studies (Bazeley, 2008; Östlund *et al.*, 2011). Recapitulatory, the overall aim and core proposition of mixed methods research is that the conjoint adoption of qualitative and quantitative research designs may render an improved understanding of research issues and multifaceted phenomena than either research design alone offers (Bryman, 2007; Creswell *et al.*, 2007; Johnson and Onwuegbuzie, 2004), uniting the strengths of both approaches and lessening some of the complications relating to singular approaches (Johnson *et al.*, 2007; Molina–Azurin, 2010).

5 Conclusion

We conducted frequency analysis based on a systematic literature review on STP following the suggestions of Denyer and Tranfield (2009), as well as Macpherson and Jones (2010) that methodological rigor of literature reviews should be strengthened. SLRs have advantages over ad-hoc, traditional literature reviews as they augment: (1) the validity of a literature review by offering guiding rules that enable to reproduce the study (Denyer and Neely, 2004; Thorpe *et al.,* 2006); (2) the rigor of a review by featuring systematically produced evidence supporting the arguments (Pittaway *et al.* 2004); and (3) the generalisability of the results by permitting the accrued knowledge in the discipline to be systematically synthesised and analysed (Wang and Chugh, 2014). STPs are prevalent in the today's business world. Given the increasing competition, the high speed of technological change and discontinuity in most industries, companies enter numerous strategic partnerships to obtain new resources, and to gain access to new business markets, or to reduce risks. Looking into the future, managers are prone to unknown challenges and problems concerning STPs (Kale and Singh, 2009).

Due to the economic changes and the ways how firms compete in such an environment, firms have been increasingly put under pressure to align their resources and, thus, often seek valuable input from external sources. Thus, for firms entering into STPs may contribute to ensuring that companies are successful over the long run. We suggest that there are several benefits of the review process as an arrangement of phases merging narrative synthesis and more conventional methods, where the literature searched for is scant and varied. The iterative research process allowed for a redefinition of the review strategy and the used criteria. Moreover, the use of data extraction templates to examine full papers augmented transparency and consistency during the selection, analysis and synthesis stages. As a result, our first contribution is the execution of a transparent literature review technique. A systematic and replicable approach was undertaken to explore a large and fragmented body of literature crossing multiple fields. Moreover, we highlight the research gaps in the extant literature that arrange for meaningful opportunities for further investigation that are presented in the following.

6 Theoretical implications and future research

Even though predicated on a literature review, the analysis should suggest some implications for further investigation. Future studies in this field will be necessary to progress our in-depth knowledge of the STP phenomenon. To begin with, we wish to emphasise the value of performing multi–level studies that involve the individual or organisation, industry/market, and network level at the same time. We would have wanted to highlight papers that present this perspective, but there were only three studies that applied such an approach (cf. Hagedoorn, 2006; Powell, 1996; Rothaermel, 2007). Researchers usually execute studies at a single level of analysis, here, they regularly turn to the following lower levels of explanatory mechanisms (for instance, the individual, the team, or the organisation). Management scientists have a long history of perceiving organisational phenomena unfolding within complex structures, hitherto our scientific world commonly disregards the multi–level dynamics of these social organisms (Kozlowski and Klein, 2000).

We have learned that a simultaneous and explicit reflection of multi–levels of analysis, and a sustained 'dialogue' among research being based on different analysis levels may enhance our understanding of inherently cross level (inter)– and intra–organisational phenomena (Capaldo, 2007). Hence, for management to keep propelling as a research discipline in which academics strive for clarifying the behaviours of individuals, teams, and organisations, we need to magnify our theories and empirical studies to incorporate multilevel effects. Researchers propose that powerful comprehension of social and organisational dynamics requires simultaneous consideration of higher and lower levels of investigation (e.g. Hackman, 2003). The use of the micro or a macro perspective only produces fragmented comprehension at either level. Hitt *et al.* (2007) recommend the following: (1) employing multi–level approaches to current models, taking into account bottom–up effects, (2) teaming up crosswise on multidisciplinary topics, and (3) considering significant real–world phenomena through multi–level methods. New bits of knowledge may be obtained by imaginative studies that transfer microlevel theories to spectacles that inspect the macro level; moreover, applying macrolevel theories to microlevel events might produce novel insights (Peterson *et al.*, 2012). Numerous international management scientists bring up that collaborations between participants of distinctive countries have been getting progressively predominant in the modern commercial environment (cf. Spicer and Bailey, 2007). Thus, Cadogan (2010) encourages studies to employ data sets from multiple regions and countries, respectively. Future studies may consider integrating territorial effects in its examinations to analyse whether territorial effects explicate a larger part of the deviation in foreign affiliates' performance than domestic effects (Makino *et al.*, 2004). Studies from a national perspective recognise essential contrasts between distinctive social behaviours in the ways to reaching ethical decisions (Ralston *et al.*, 1997; Robertson and Crittenden, 2003; Vitell *et al.*, 1993).

Next, according to Barr (2004) major contributions from strategic management research have been made from qualitative research, despite quantitative methods have been more frequently adopted. However, management and organisation studies rely on a variety of research methods that proves beneficial to advancing our knowledge and promoting research progress in this field (Molina–Azorin, 2010). Regarding both the qualitative and quantitative evaluations offers a more perspicacious and comprehensive picture (Arora and Stoner, 2009) and may also support to highpoint the consistencies and disparities between specific factors of a phenomenon (Bernardi *et al.*, 2007). "Because management research asks a large variety of questions, draws on numerous theoretical paradigms from a range of disciplines, and is characterised by investigations involving multiple levels of analysis, there is a benefit in combining the complementary strengths of quantitative and qualitative approaches" (Bazeley, 2008, p. 134). Moreover, guidelines for managers could be prepared with better precision and assurance (Scandura and Williams, 2000). We are certain that empirical methods will advance STP understanding, in particular mixed–method approaches in combination with case study research for further exploration of unknown phenomena within the STP field, and will provide valuable theoretical as well as substantial managerial implications.

Hence, case studies or survey methodologies show promising ways for further exploration of issues regarding new phenomena (Wassmer, 2010). In addition to that, we suggest exploiting further theories instead of mainly relying on RBV and KBV for STP research. For instance, SCT that advocates that a company's external networks represent a significant contributor to its organisational performance (Leenders and Gabbay, 1999), could be further explored in the context of STP. Lastly, we advise researchers to pay more attention to the services industry since it is still underrepresented in STP studies. More and more firms have been entering new markets within the services industry characterised by low barriers to entry along with high margins (PwC, 2014). Hence, researchers may miss out valuable research potential. Finally, in Table III-6 we provide a short research agenda summarising major points that should be addressed in future research.

Major research points	Remarks
Level of analysis (Multi-level perspective)	We wish future research to emphasise the value of performing multi–level studies that involve the individual or industry/market, organisation, and network level at the same time.
National and regional effects	We encourage studies conducted based on data sets from multiple regions and countries.
Methodological approach (Mixed method research)	Consolidating the strong complementary points of qualitative and quantitative methodologies offers a more comprehensive picture.
Theoretical frame	We suggest exploiting further theories instead of mainly relying on RBV and KBV for strategic technology partnering research.
Industrial settings (Services industry)	More and more firms are entering new markets within the services industry. Hence, researchers may profit from valuable research potential.

Table III-6: Research agenda for future research on strategic technology partnering.
Source: Own illustration.

The present literature study has the potential to contribute significantly to the current literature both in appraising the current state of strategic technology partnering and in providing a platform for future developments in the research field. Such a matter will result in value for both new and established academics of strategic management seeking to deal with the broad range of the research area and to recognised scientists whose devoted research endeavours are a challenge to stay well–informed of developments in other subfields. We hope that the current research will in turn contribute to further studies investigating the interrelationships of the various factors concerning STP, providing valuable contributions.

Chapter IV

The strategies of supply chain risk management – a synthesis and classification

Abstract

This paper conducts an in-depth systematic literature review (SLR) of 86 peer-reviewed academic journal articles on supply chain risk management (SCRM) strategies from 2000 to mid 2015. The findings reveal that there is a variety of fragmented supply chain risk (SCR) mitigation strategies and that there is a need for an explicit terminology. Moreover, the analysis also indicates a lack of empirical evidence regarding the relationship between SCRM strategies and performance, since most studies have been simulation-based or qualitative in nature. The current study groups and synthesises the various SCRM strategies into proactive and reactive approaches for the ante and the post disruption state and classifies them according to the different supply chain (SC) types; namely, efficient SC, risk-hedging SC, responsive SC, and agile SC. Altogether the findings provide essential practical and theoretical contributions to strategic responses to adverse incidents by creating a unique conceptual framework of SCRM strategies and providing direction towards promising areas of research.

1 Introduction

Supply chain risk management (SCRM) is a young emerging area of research within the supply chain management (SCM) context (Nooraie and Parast, 2015). SCRM deals with risk as a situation and entails exposure to two fundamental elements: an incident and the uncertainty regarding the conceivable implication (Bandaly *et al.*, 2014; Vilko *et al.*, 2014). Nowadays, in the chaotic and highly dynamic market environment, every organisation in the supply chain (SC) is susceptible to disruptive events (Knemeyer *et al.*, 2009). This turbulence creates a situation in which SCRM becomes paramount for organisational survival and wealth (Wildgoose *et al.*, 2012). However, taking into account diverse confirmations collected by other academics and practitioners, many executives feel it is hard to legitimise some pricey strategies for protecting against supply chain risks (SCR) that eventually do not come about (Ambulkar *et al.*, 2015). Hence, to encourage companies to secure their SCs, powerful strategies must be settled that fulfil two needs. In the first place, these strategies need to assist firms in minimising costs and enriching customer satisfaction. Secondly, these strategies need to empower organisations to carry forward their operational activities during and after a severe disruptive incident has happened (Tang, 2006b). The understanding of how to mitigate and respond to SCRs comprehensively unveils a supplementary research challenge in SCM (Tang and Musa, 2010). For the purpose of the present literature study we embrace the following definition of SCRM:

> *"Supply chain risk management is to [collaborate] with partners in a supply chain apply risk management process tools to deal with risks and uncertainties caused by, or impacting on, logistics related activities or resources" (Norrman and Jansson, 2004, p. 436).*

Since misleading evaluations and poor judgments may prompt unforeseen developments – which may have critical outcomes when identified at short notice –

uncertainties and potential disruptions should be continuously observed and overseen (Heckmann *et al.*, 2014). The intricacy of the contemporary SCs and the amplified dependence on the competitive benefit of the SC as a whole leads to an augmented exposedness to risks (Hoffmann *et al.*, 2013; Manuj *et al.*, 2014). These developments highlight the interest in and importance of SCRM-related research (cf. Li *et al.*, 2014; Marley *et al.*, 2014; Vilko and Hallikas, 2012; Zhao *et al.*, 2013). Academics have done research to provide knowledge about SCRs sources (e.g. Christopher and Peck, 2004; Harland *et al.*, 2003; Manuj and Mentzer, 2008a, b; Yu *et al.*, 2009), perceptions and perspectives on SCRs (e.g. Jüttner, 2005; Lavastre *et al.*, 2012; Lockamy III, 2010; Sodhi *et al.*, 2012), performance implications of SCRs (e.g. Hendricks and Singhal 2005; Ritchie and Brindley 2007a,b; Thun and Hoenig, 2011; Zhao *et al.*, 2013), and risk mitigation strategies (e.g. Hallikas *et al.*, 2002; Kleindorfer and Saad, 2005; Spekman and Davis, 2004; Wieland and Wallenburg, 2012).

Effective SCRM strives for monitoring and overseeing unpredicted disruptions by deliberately adopting appropriate measures in order to mitigate and manage SCRs (Jüttner *et al.,* 2003; Jüttner, 2005; Norrman and Jansson, 2004). The impact of SCRs on organisational performance can be attributed to the rising prevalence of high complexity and instability in global SCs. The ability to withstand external threats and potential countermeasures and risks within SCs are of primary concern. We aim to analyse and synthesise the research findings to arrange for a clear-cut overview. By addressing these essential knowledge gaps, the present study delivers a systematic literature review (SLR) on SCRM strategies by adopting a robust research methodology such as proposed by Rousseau *et al.* (2008) and Denyer and Tranfield (2009). For the similar purpose, the systematic review approach has been applied in other SCM literature reviews lately (e.g. Delbufalo, 2012; Gligor and Holcomb, 2012; Gosling and Naim, 2009). With the present research we aim at answering the following main question: What are the strategies for effective supply chain risk management?

Hence, the study has two objectives to accomplish:

a) To develop a framework to classify SCRM literature, focusing on risk-reducing and risk mitigating strategies,

b) To study future trends to provide insights for academics to set up new research areas, and for practitioners to explore related benefits to arrange for a business case regarding SCRM implementation.

The present paper is organised as follows: Section 2 describes the methodology used for analysing the academic literature. Section 3 discusses the study findings including the descriptive analysis of the reviewed papers and presents the conceptual framework that was developed for classifying SCRM strategies into a new format. Section 4 discusses the study findings in light of previous research and the contribution to theory and practice. In section 5 the managerial implications of the study are outlined. Finally, recommendations for future research are given in Section 6.

2 Review methodology and data collection

In the present paper, a SLR of SCRM is arranged that ensures document reliability and quality, adopting a visible and scientifically replicable approach, which is in line with calls for greater methodological rigor in management literature reviews (e.g. Briner *et al.*, 2009; Rousseau *et al.*, 2008). We adopt an explicit SLR process suggested by Tranfield (2003) and Denyer and Tranfield *et al.* (2009) since that approach is systematic, replicable, transparent, and, thus, favourable for evidence-informed knowledge investigation. This method has been used by several other authors that conducted a SLR in SCM and strategic management as well (e.g. Bakker, 2010; Brandenburg *et al.*, 2014; Hassini *et al.*, 2012; Kilubi, 2015). We employ the SLR process for identifying, analysing, synthesising, interpreting and reporting the greatest evidence from the academic literature (Briner *et al.*, 2009; Dickersin *et al.*, 1994; Petticrew, 2001) on SCRM strategies which is addressed in five distinctive phases as shown in Figure IV-1: (a) formulating the research question, locating studies, (b) selecting and evaluating relevant studies, (c) analysing and synthesising findings and (d) reporting and making use of results.

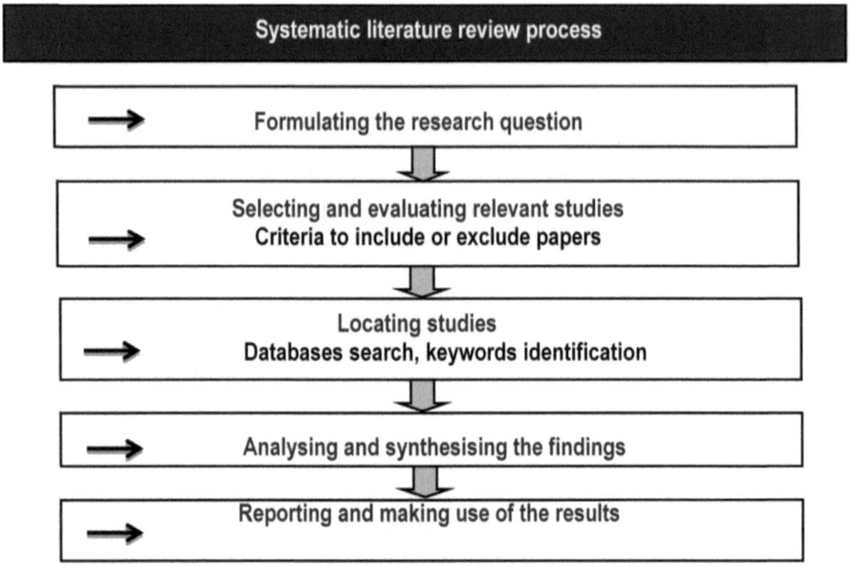

Figure IV-1: Research methodology for the present systematic literature review.
Source: Adapted from Denyer and Tranfield (2009).

2.1 Formulating the research question

The present review precisely addresses research questions that have been specified with an explicit and reliable focus (Light and Pillemer, 1984). In the first phase, the scope of the research in adherence to the objectives and the underlying study questions are defined.

As previously mentioned, the overall aim of the present paper is to review systematically the development of the extant literature based on focused research questions in order to identify what issues have been addressed and where the potential for future studies can be located. In line with Rousseau *et al.* (2008), the questions underlying the review have been precisely formulated to avoid any ambiguity. Therefore, the objectives of the study were distilled into one key research question: What are the strategies for effective supply chain risk management? The substance of the papers was further evaluated through descriptive analysis: (1) How has the distribution of the articles been over time? (2) In which journals have the papers been published? (3) What research methodologies have been adopted?

2.2 Locating studies

A major challenge was to capture and include the most relevant extant research in this review. More specifically, we needed to identify relevant articles that are in alignment with the research questions. We searched *Science Direct (Elsevier), Scopus*, *Taylor & Francis Group*, *Business Source Complete (EBSCO Host),* and *ABI/Inform Global (ProQuest)* for articles published before July 2015 without any other limitations concerning the publication date. Following Seuring and Müller (2008), the search was limited to articles in English, i.e. articles available in other tongues were not taken into account. Given that the context of the study is the supply chain, these were identified as the databases with the best coverage of this research field and have been utilised in similar studies (cf. Burgess *et al.*, 2006; Natarajarathinam *et al.*, 2009; Nordin and Agndal, 2008).

Although many types of publications exist, we chose to focus our literature review on articles published in academic journals, because these can be considered as "certified knowledge" (Denyer and Tranfield, 2009, p. 684) and are the most capable of gauging knowledge in a field (Ordanini *et al.,* 2008; Podsakoff *et al.*, 2005; Ramos-Rodriguez and Ruíz-Navarro, 2004). Furthermore, "Established influential journals [...] tend to shape the theoretical and empirical work in a field by setting new horizons for inquiry within their frame of reference" (Furrer *et al.*, 2008, p. 2). Therefore, in the next step, we took into account quality and citation rankings of peer-reviewed SCM and logistics journals provided by Charvet *et al.* (2008), Giunipero *et al.* (2008), and Chapman and Ellinger (2009) in order to validate the journal selection.

The ranking applied was the current version of the *VHB Jourqual Ranking 3* which is also widely recognised (Schrader and Henning-Thurau, 2009). For the present research only the inclusion of peer-reviewed journals with a *VHB* ranking (vhb.online.org/startseite)[6] of A +, A, B or C were defined as one of the criteria. After the initial reduction of the four lists, the shortlist was again discussed with experts and the most relevant journals about the present subject were selected. To further direct the study, four distinct disciplines for analysis were identified; Logistics/SCM, Operations/Production Management, Operations Research, and Management Science.

2.3 Selecting and evaluating relevant studies

To ensure an unbiased view and strengthen the review, three researchers formed part of the article selection and data extraction process. First of all, we scanned the selected electronic databases under the terms of the defined keywords, with no time limit. In line with previous similar systematic literature reviews (cf. Colicchia and Strozzi, 2012; David and Han, 2004; Rashman *et al.*, 2009), this paper defined keywords as search criteria. Our unit of analysis was "supply chain risk management". In pseudo code, we used the search phrases "supply chain risk(s)" OR "supply chain risk management" in the article title (TI) solely, as well as together with the keyword "performance" in the abstract (AB), keywords (KW) and title (TI) search. Next, we redefined our search process; the necessary criterion was that a paper had to cover the phrase "supply chain" with at least one of the keywords "risk(s)" OR "risk management"; for example, "supply chain' AND 'risk(s)' OR 'risk management'. Then, every article in each of the previously 27 selected journals (from 2000 to mid 2015) was initially considered. The search resulted in 1833 articles at first; however, these numbers should not be seen as mutually exclusive as several studies were incorporated into more than one database. Subsequently,

[6] VHB, the *Association of University Professors for Business Research*, represents the umbrella organisation of university professors in german-speaking countries in the field of Business Administration. The VHB ranking is based on an assessment of economically relevant journals by the members of the VHB (Adler and Harzing, 2009). The journals are ranked from A till E; the letter A signifying the best category and E the worst one.

we omitted duplications of articles to avoid integrating an article twice in our analysis (cf. Nijmeijer *et al.*, 2012). In this case, 1472 duplicates were removed, and 261 articles remained.

We read the abstracts and conclusions to determine scholars' relevance to SCRM; thus, after the examination we excluded 208 references that did not seem relevant to the formulated research questions. For instance, by applying the criteria mentioned above, SCRM articles that did not focus on SCR reduction and mitigation strategies were discarded. According to Nag *et al.* (2007), the articles were selected by rating each article's abstract on a four–point anchored scale, where the average Cohen's kappas of 0.82 and 0.86, respectively indicated a highly significant inter–rater agreement. We considered an article as relevant if the average score across all coders was at least 3.0 on both scales (cf. Keupp *et al.*, 2012). For a SLR, it is particularly important to define clear borders to confine the study. In this connection, five important in- and exclusion criteria are determined as presented in Table IV-1.

Inclusion criteria	Rationale for inclusion or exclusion
Either qualitative or quantitative paper (e.g. empirical studies, theoretical studies	We focused on capturing all evidence, both empirical and theoretical since different approaches have contributed to the research area.
Journal ranking	For the present research, only the inclusion of peer–reviewed journals with a *VHB* ranking (vhb.online.org/startseite)[1] of A +, A, B or C were defined as one of the criteria with no time restriction.
Publication of full-length journal article	Following Grégoire *et al.* (2011) and Müller-Seitz (2012), we excluded book reviews, short research summaries (less than five pages), editorial pieces, monographs, as well as replies to previously published articles.
Publication in peer-reviewed academic journals	We only included peer-reviewed that publish high-quality scientific studies in English with a focus on management (Seuring and Müller, 2008). In this regard, we excluded books, book chapters, conference proceedings, dissertations, editorials, research notes (with less than five pages in length), and working papers.
Time horizon	Include all relevant evidence from before July 2015.

Table IV-1: Inclusion and exclusion criteria for the present SLR (in alphabetical order).
Source: Adapted from Kilubi and Haasis (2016).

The abstracts with likely relevance were individually assessed by each reviewer and hesitations on the subject of in- or exclusion were talked over until a consensus was found. Several articles (n = 208) were excluded because they perceptibly did not meet the pre-determined inclusion criteria. Given that, journal articles had to show a clear focus on SCRM strategies and the purpose of the study at hand. In order to warrant the rigor of this SLR, every article was autonomously read by each member of the review panel to minimise potential bias and add to validity. The resulting 153 studies were reviewed in full-text and summarised by applying a semi-structured data mining template. Finally, all journal articles were read completely again by each member of the review panel independently. Articles that seemed non-relevant to the essential criteria of the review were removed to ensure a reliable focus. Here again, 84 articles were excluded, whereas 79 articles were identified after reading the full text. By performing snowball sampling of the included papers, we found seven supplementary relevant studies. At the end of the day, 86 articles were included in the analysis (cf. Figure IV-2). The final result is a total database of 86 peer-reviewed academic articles listed in the systematic review over a period of 15 years from 2000 to mid 2015. These articles were then analysed in-depth and synthesised in order to address the underlying research questions of the present systematic literature review.

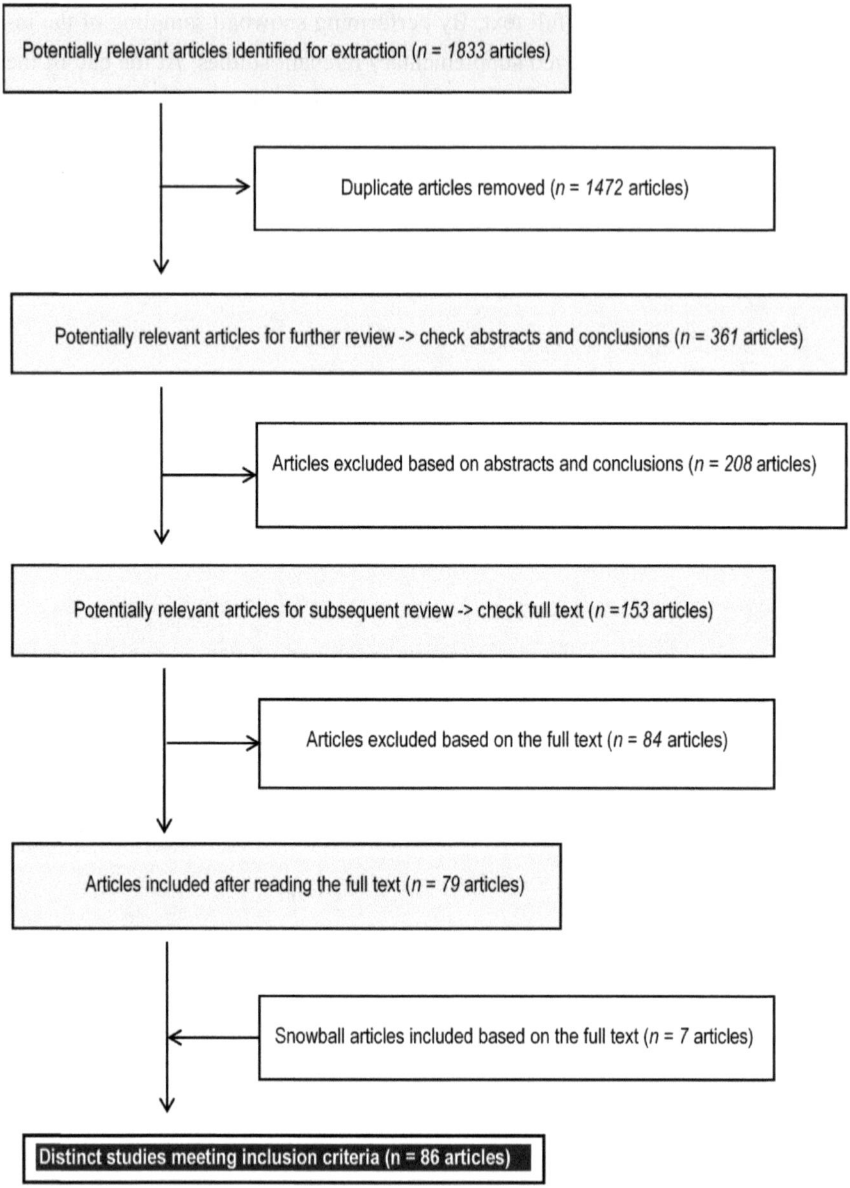

Figure IV-2: Flow diagram of article selection process.
Source: Own illustration.

3 Study findings

On the one hand, the aim of the investigation was to evaluate single studies and explore how they relate to each other. On the other hand, synthesis aims to align the findings derived regarding a particular topic from multiple sources. Hence, it can allow for a higher degree of comprehension and reliability to the conclusions derived, which in turn can provide a greater input of conceptual or theoretical progress in comparison to that obtained from a single empirical study (Campbell *et al.*, 2003). Accordingly, synthesis is the core element of a systematic review–a process that accumulates the findings from the series of assimilated research to arrive at conclusions predicated on the body of evidence (Popay *et al.*, 2006). The intention in this SLR is a comprehensive outline and a conceptual, rather than an empirical, consolidation. Therefore, we are methodologically restricted to descriptive rather than statistical methods in the description of the findings. According to Gammelgaard and Flint (2012), qualitative research methods should be used when questions about a phenomenon presuppose them. However, the goal was to analyse and evaluate the vast body of literature while synthesising it "into a new or different arrangement and developing knowledge that is not apparent from reading the individual studies in isolation" (Denyer and Tranfield, 2009, p. 685). Hence, below we break down our findings by answering our research questions, followed by a critical discussion.

3.1 Descriptive features of the reviewed SCRM literature

In the first stride of the examination, descriptive features were considered to classify the articles. The substance of the papers was further evaluated through descriptive analysis. For these classifications, each paper was assigned to exactly one category, where the deliberate procedure and systematic method made sure the objectivity of the study (Seuring and Müller, 2008). As aforementioned, reliability was taken notice of by involving four researchers in all iterations of the formal investigation. The 86 journal articles determined through the SLR are evaluated in this section in regard to the year of publication, the journal publication, and the methodology adopted towards perceiving the literature regarding SCRM and related strategies. We can discern that more focus has been accorded to SCRM processes, especially triggered after disasters like the USA terrorist attacks in 2001 (Barry, 2004). As a result, a rising number of papers focused on SCRM from 2001 onwards. An analysis of the years in which the 86 selected articles were published manifests that the first articles appeared in 2000. In fact, nearly 90 per cent of the surveyed journal articles (77 out of 86) were published from 2004 onwards. The years 2004 (12 per cent, n = 10), followed by 2015 (10 per cent, n = 9), 2011, 2013, 2014, and 2012 (each 8 per cent, n = 7), 2006, 2008, and 2009 (each 7 per cent, n = 6) marked the peaks, providing evidence for the fact that research interest in SCRM is still further growing (see Figure IV-3). Special issues can explain some peaks on SCRM-related topics.

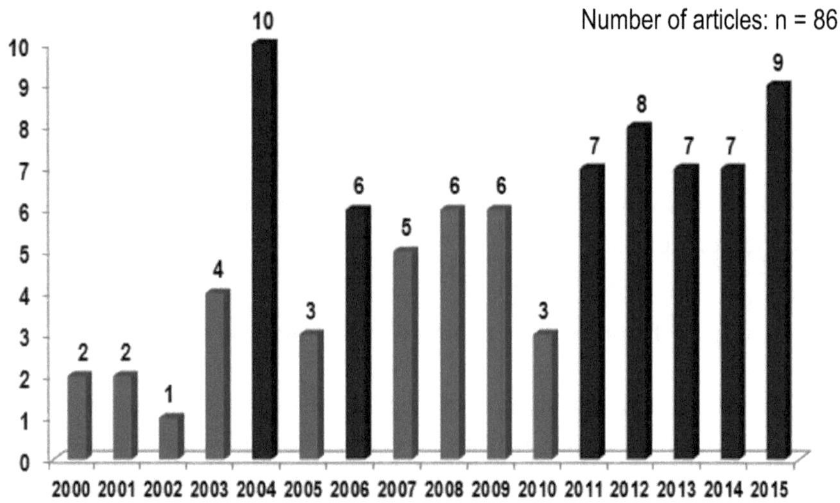

Figure IV-3: Distribution of the articles included in the SLR.
Source: Own illustration.

The sample of 86 scientific papers in this SLR were published in 27 business-related academic journals; 20 of them were among the journals returning the most SCM hits as identified by Charvet *et al.* (2008) in their bibliometric study of the intellectual structure of SCM. In detail, the largest proportion of journal articles (43 per cent) originated from the *International Journal of Physical Distribution & Logistics Management* and the *International Journal of Production Economics* (each n = 13), followed by *Supply Chain Management: An International Journal* (n = 12) and the *International Journal of Production Research* (n = 7). That indicates high interest among peer-reviewed academic journals in this highly relevant research domain. Note, however, that three articles originated from practitioner-oriented journals, *MIT Sloan Management Review* (cf. Chopra and Sodhi, 2004 and Sheffi and Rice, 2005, respectively) and *California Management Review* (cf. Johnson, 2001). Thus, we identified the top 4 journals in which the selected articles were published (cf. Table IV-2). Besides that top four ranking, any other journal shows less than five article publications. Note, however, the quality, the eminence, and standing of the journal publications in which the analysed articles were issued demonstrate the high level of scientific relevance and significance.

Academic Journal	No. of articles	Percentage
European Journal of Operational Research	**3**	3.49 %
International Journal of Logistics Research and Applications	**2**	2.33 %
International Journal of Physical Distribution and Logistics Management	**13**	15.12 %
International Journal of Production Economics	**13**	15.12 %
International Journal of Production Research	**7**	8.24 %
Journal of Business Logistics	**4**	4.65 %
Journal of Enterprise Information Management	**2**	2.33 %
Journal of Operations Management	**4**	4.71 %
Journal of Purchasing & Supply Management	**2**	2.33 %
Journal of Supply Chain Management	**2**	2.33 %
Management Science	**2**	2.33 %
Omega	**3**	3.49 %
Production and Operations Management	**3**	3.49 %
Supply Chain Management: An International Journal	**12**	13.95 %

Table IV-2: Number of articles in alphabetical order (appearing at least twice).
Source: Own illustration.

Next, we performed a citation analysis by using citation counts extracted via Google Scholar and Web of Science to find out which articles have been most cited by researchers in the SCRM field focusing on risk mitigation strategies. Then again, articles showing up in Web of Science have been contended to be specific with an observed bias towards American journals (Brown, 2011; Johnstone, 2007), and some suggest that the free citation service offered by Google Scholar arranges for the breakdown of a more extensive scope of publications (Franceschet, 2010). The simple conjecture fundamental to citation analysis is that citations act as a proxy for the comparative influence within a research area (Backhaus *et al.*, 2011; Coombes and Nicholson, 2013). In this manner, built on a representative sample, the aggregated references to individual articles, authors, or journals surrenders a satisfactory representation of the articles', authors', or journals' influence on a relating research field (Culnan, 1986). Besides, citations are taken as a measure of merit and impact. If a paper is intensely referred to, it is viewed as important. This suggestion builds on the presumption that authors cite articles which they contemplate vital for their work (Zupic and Cater, 2014). Some preliminary assumptions may be drawn from the citation frequencies between 2000 and the beginning of 2015 (cf. Table IV-3). However, cautiousness is needed on the interpretation of the effects. Moreover, the citation frequencies are in fact biased towards elder articles since newly published articles have not had the opportunity yet to establish themselves. For the purpose of simplicity, we have only displayed those articles with a minimum citation count of 100 (a complete list is available from the authors upon request).

We identified three top cited papers; these papers have in common that they attempt to answer and address a number of SCRM issues in a single article and to capture the whole SC mitigation process. Among others, this may be the reason that those papers have been commonly cited by other researchers because such papers form a good starting point for strategically based and business-oriented discussions on SCRM. The most frequently cited paper is the well-established one of Chopra and Sodhi (2004), which has been published in a practitioner journal, but has gained remarkable prominence in the academic world as well (citation counts n = 1095). This article presents a wide-ranging application framework for dealing successfully with SC disruptions. The framework encompasses the complete SCRM process from SCR analysis to the selection of the appropriate SCR mitigation strategy. Next, we have the study of Kleindorfer and Saad (2005) who aimed to achieve three goals within their research (citation counts n = 978). Firstly, to design a conceptual framework for analysing, assessing and mitigating SCRs. Secondly, to examine accident history of the U.S. Chemical Industry from 1995 to 2000 using secondary database. Thirdly, to convey implications for the establishment of management systems to handle SC disruptions. The third highly cited paper is the one of Jüttner *et al.* (2003) which is a literature review (citation counts n = 727); they were the pioneers in providing a comprehensive definition of SCRM that has also been mostly referred to. In defining SCRM, Jüttner *et al.* (2003) adopt four theoretical constructs: a) sources of risk, which result in b) detrimental consequences of risk, originated from c) drivers of risk and probably counterbalanced by c) risk mitigation strategies. These constructs form the basis of their proposed research agenda and has opened new directions for further studies on SCRM.

Author	Year	Journal	Title	Citation Counts
Chopra and Sodhi	2004	*MIT Sloan Management Review*	"Managing risk to avoid supply chain breakdown"	1095
Kleindorfer and Saad	2005	*Production and Operations Management*	"Managing disruption risks in supply chains"	978
Jüttner *et al.*	2003	*International Journal of Logistics Research and Applications*	"Supply chain risk management: Outlining an agenda for future research"	727
Harland *et al.*	2003	*Journal of Purchasing & Supply Management*	"Risk in supply networks"	653
Christopher and Lee	2004	*International Journal of Physical Distribution & Logistics Management*	"Mitigating supply chain risk through improved confidence"	622
Hendricks and Singhal	2005	*Production and Operations Management*	"An empirical analysis of the effect of supply chain disruptions on long-run stock price performance and equity risk of the firm"	609
Tang	2006a	*International Journal of Production Economics*	"Perspectives in supply chain risk management"	578
Norrman and Jansson	2004	*International Journal of Physical Distribution & Logistics Management*	"Ericsson's proactive supply chain risk management approach after a serious sub-supplier accident"	565
Sheffi and Rice	2005	*MIT Sloan Management Review*	"A supply chain view of the resilient enterprise"	523

Author	Year	Journal	Title	Citation Counts
Hallikas *et al.*	2004	*International Journal of Production Economics*	"Risk management process in supplier networks"	511
Tang	2006b	*International Journal of Logistics Research and Applications*	"Robust strategies for mitigating supply chain disruptions"	455
Manuj and Mentzer	2008b	*International Journal of Physical Distribution & Logistics Management*	"Global supply chain risk management strategies"	427
Choi and Krause	2006	*Journal of Operations Management*	"The supply base and its complexity: Implications for transaction costs, risks, responsiveness, and innovation"	419
Zsidisin *et al.*	2004	*International Journal of Physical Distribution & Logistics Management*	"An analysis of supply risk assessment techniques"	354
Braunscheidel and Suresh	2009	*Journal of Operations Management*	"The organizational antecedents of a firm's supply chain agility for risk mitigation and response"	353
Manuj and Mentzer	2008a	*Journal of Business Logistics*	"Global supply chain risk management"	348
Tang and Tomlin	2008	*International Journal of Production Economics*	"The power of flexibility for mitigating supply chain risks"	336
Tomlin	2006	*Management Science*	"On the value of mitigation and contingency strategies for managing supply chain disruption risks"	336
Spekman and Davis	2004	*International Journal of Physical Distribution & Logistics Management*	"Risky business: Expanding the discussion on risk and the extended enterprise"	319

Author	Year	Journal	Title	Citation Counts
Giunipero and Eltantawy	2004	*International Journal of Physical Distribution & Logistics Management*	"Securing the upstream supply chain: A risk management approach"	305
Faisal *et al.*	2006	*Business Process Management Journal*	"Supply chain risk mitigation: Modeling the enablers"	297
Zsidisin and Ellram	2003	*Journal of Supply Chain Management*	"An agency theory investigation of supply risk management"	282
Wagner and Bode	2008	*Journal of Business Logistics*	"An empirical investigation of supply chain performance along several dimensions of risk"	281
Johnson	2001	*California Management Review*	"Learning from toys: Lessons in managing supply chain risk from the toy industry"	273
Trkman and McCormack	2009	*International Journal of Production Economics*	"Supply chain risk in turbulent environments – A conceptual model for managing supply chain network risk"	236
Agrawal and Sheshadri	2000	*IIE Transactions*	"Risk intermediation in supply chains"	232
Wilson	2007	*Transportation Research Part E: Logistics and Transportation Review*	"The impact of transportation disruptions on supply chain performance"	227
Ritchie and Brindley	2007a	*International Journal of Operations & Production Management*	"Supply chain risk management and performance: A guiding framework for future development"	222
Tang and Musa	2010	*International Journal of Production Economics*	"Identifying risk issues and research advancements in supply chain risk management"	221

Author	Year	Journal	Title	Citation Counts
Cavinato	2004	*International Journal of Physical Distribution & Logistics Management*	"Supply chain logistics risks: From the back room to the board room"	217
Goh *et al.*	2007	*European Journal of Operational Research*	"A stochastic model for risk management in global supply chain networks"	212
Finch	2004	*Supply Chain Management: An International Journal*	"Supply chain risk management"	209
Knemeyer *et al.*	2009	*Journal of Operations Management*	"Proactive planning for catastrophic events in supply chains"	204
Thun and Hoenig	2011	*International Journal of Production Economics*	"An empirical analysis of supply chain risk management in the German automotive industry"	199
Yu *et al.*	2009	*Omega*	"Single or dual sourcing: Decision–making in the presence of supply chain disruption risks"	197
Sinha *et al.*	2004	*Supply Chain Management: An International Journal*	"Methodology to mitigate supplier risk in an aerospace supply chain"	170
Neiger *et al.*	2009	*Journal of Operations Management*	"Supply chain risk identification with value–focused process engineering"	165
Christopher and Holweg	2011	*International Journal of Physical Distribution & Logistics Management*	"Supply Chain 2.0": Managing supply chains in the era of turbulence"	154
Agrell	2004	*International Journal of Production Economics*	"Risk, information and incentives in telecom supply chains"	132
Sodhi and Tang	2007	*Production and Operations Management*	"Researchers' perspectives on supply chain risk management"	129

Author	Year	Journal	Title	Citation Counts
Schoenherr *et al.*	2008	*Journal of Purchasing & Supply Management*	"Assessing supply chain risks with the analytic hierarchy process: Providing decision support for the offshoring decision by a US manufacturing company"	128
Tummala and Schoenherr	2011	*Supply Chain Management: An International Journal*	"Assessing and managing risks using the Supply Chain Risk Management Process (SCRMP)"	128
Ellis *et al.*	2010	*Journal of Operations Management*	"Buyer perceptions of supply disruption risk: A behavioral view and empirical assessment"	124
Barry	2004	*International Journal of Physical Distribution & Logistics Management*	"Supply chain risk in an uncertain global supply chain environment"	113
Bogataj	2009	*International Journal of Production Economics*	"Measuring the supply chain risk and vulnerability in frequency space"	107
Lai *et al.*	2009	*Omega*	"Sharing inventory risk in supply chain: The implication of financial constraint"	103

Table IV-3: Most cited journal articles ordered by frequency (only citations with a frequency of at least 50 are displayed).
Source: Own illustration.

In order to analyse the research methodologies of the reviewed journal articles, we distinguished seven methodologies. Similar to Seuring and Müller (2008), this study analyses the following research methodologies applied to the articles discussed: 1) surveys/questionnaires, 2) case studies 3) secondary databases, 4) simulations/modeling, 5) conceptual/theoretical papers, and 6) mixed methods. Other than Seuring and Müller (2008), we decided to exclude literature reviews and add two further research methodologies instead, namely the secondary database and mixed method research. Figure IV-4 displays the allocations of the articles to the respective research methodologies.

The analysis revealed that simulation/modeling was the primary methodology adopted to study SCRM issues over the last decade (23 out of 86 articles). Moreover, researchers have frequently applied the case study research approach (17 out of 86 articles) and the survey/questionnaire design (20 out of 85 articles), followed by conceptual/theoretical research design (15 out of 86 articles). We consider the former finding as the necessity of theory development in SCRM, bearing in mind that it is a relatively underexplored research domain. The fact that case study is the second most used research methodology shows the relatively fresh research discipline of SCRM in which researchers first need to comprehend the phenomena in full (da Mota Pedrosa *et al.,* 2012; Hassini *et al.*, 2012). However, the mixed method research design was only conducted in 7 out of 85 articles (case studies supplemented by surveys/questionnaires, in particular), or secondary database research in only 4 out of 85 articles. When reviewing the literature on SCRM, two major research streams become apparent. One contains exploratory studies (that includes case studies, conceptual papers, and literature reviews), and the other one is mathematical modelling. In the first stream, researchers attempt to explore and arrange managerial issues connected with SCRs, whereas the second stream is concerned with modelling and simulation to devise decision options for well-defined risk-mitigating techniques. All in all, early research in SCRM has primarily been case-based, theoretical, or survey-based in nature. In the latest years, the emphasis has more switched over to simulation models (Talluri *et al.*, 2013). In light of this view, the significance of the SCRM topic and the need for further expanding research in this field – especially using combined qualitative and quantitative research to create new evidentiary knowledge – is manifested.

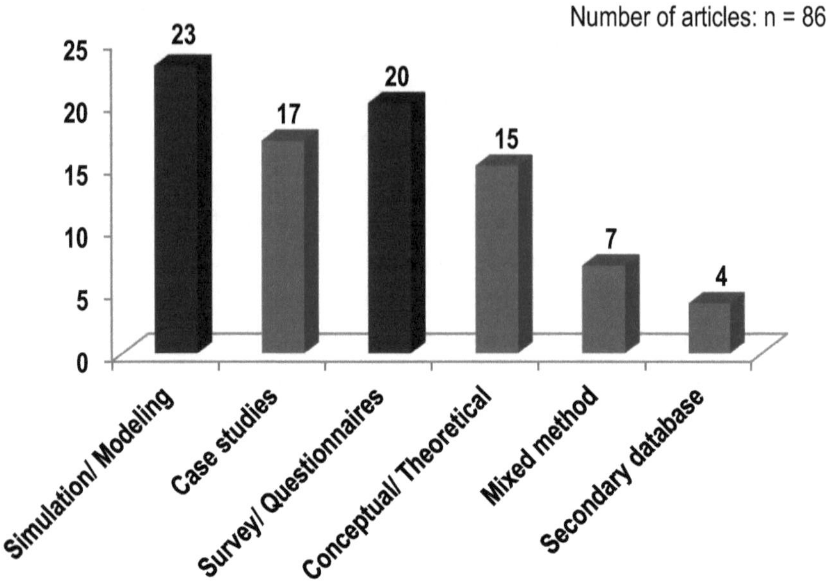

Figure IV-4: Research methodologies applied to the SCRM articles included for review.
Source: Own illustration.

3.2 Strategies for an effective Supply Chain Risk Management

SCs have become lengthier and more complex as a result of the globalised business environment and vertical integrations. SCRs are interweaved in a way; one mitigation strategy may alleviate other SCRs. For instance, bundling demand reduces anticipated risks, such as inventory and capacity risks. In the present review, eight top SCRM strategies were identified whereof visibility and transparency (n = 26), relationships/partnerships (n = 16), flexibility (n = 15), redundancy (inventory) (n = 13), postponement as well as collaboration (each n = 10), multiple sourcing and flexible contracts (n = 9), and joint planning and coordination (n = 8) were deemed crucial by many researchers. Table IV-4 illustrates the top eight strategies that represent a total share of approximately 65 per cent of the selected papers. The results are partially in line with extant findings. For instance, the findings of AMR's (Advanced Market Research) supply chain risk survey in 2009 indicate that closer collaboration with supply chain partners and the use of multiple sourcing strategies and redundant suppliers are the most successful methods that have been frequently adopted to mitigate risks (Tummala and Schoenherr, 2011). Moreover, Kleindorfer and Saad (2005) deemed SCRM strategies such as collaboration as well as flexibility as crucial for mitigating SCRs. Likewise Tang (2006b), who mentions slack resources with the means of flexible production processes and product designs, larger inventories, and redundant suppliers that may act as so-called 'shock absorbers'and are considered the most effective ways to deliver countermeasure to SCRs. Next, Lavastre *et al.* (2012) identified multiple sourcing, safety stocks, collaboration, and information sharing as the most important ways to control risk exposure

Strategies	Frequency	Author(s)
Visibility and-Transparency (e.g. Information Sharing, Communication)	**26**	Johnson (2001); Bode *et al.* (2011); Spekman and Davis (2004); Finch (2004); Kleindorfer and Saad (2005); Faisal *et al.* (2006); Sinha *et al.* (2004); Ritchie and Brindley (2007a b); Lavastre *et al.* (2012); Li *et al.* (2015); Christopher and Lee (2004); Yang and Yang (2010); Jüttner *et al.* (2003); Manuj and Mentzer (2008a, b); Bandaly *et al.* (2014); Tang (2006b); Tang and Tomlin (2008); Rajesh *et al.* (2015); Wagner and Bode (2008); Tang (2006b); Speier *et al.* (2011); Zsidisin *et al.* (2004); Khan *et al.* (2008); Norrman and Jansson (2004)
Flexibility	**15**	Talluri *et al.* (2013); Knemeyer *et al.* (2009); Braunscheidel and Suresh (2009); Jüttner *et al.* (2003); Kleindorfer and Saad (2005); Sinha *et al.* (2004); Christopher and Holweg (2011); Skipper and Hanna (2009); Johnson (2001); Khan *et al.* (2008); Tang (2006b); Knemeyer *et al.* (2009); Tang and Tomlin (2008); Thun and Hoenig (2011); Wieland (2013)
Relationships/ Partnerships	**16**	Giunipero and Eltantawy (2004); Faisal *et al.* (2006); Ritchie and Brindley (2007a, b); Lavastre et al (2012); Tang (2006b); Speier *et al.* (2011); Grötsch *et al.* (2013); Li *et al.* (2015); Kleindorfer and Saad (2005); Hallikas *et al.* (2002); Lavastre et al (2012); Jüttner *et al.* (2003); Khan *et al.* (2008); Spekman and Davis (2004); Vilko and Hallikas (2012)

Strategies	Frequency	Author(s)
Postponement	**10**	Kleindorfer and Saad (2005); Yang and Yang (2010); Jüttner *et al.* (2003); Manuj and Mentzer (2008a, b); Bandaly *et al.* (2014); Manuj *et al.* (2014); Tang (2006b); Tang and Tomlin (2008); Wagner and Bode (2008)
Multiple Sourcing and Flexible Contracts	**9**	Sinha *et al.* (2004); Jüttner *et al.* (2003); Knemeyer *et al.* (2009); Norrman and Jansson (2004); Tang (2006b); Zsidisin and Ellram (2003); Kleindorfer and Saad (2005); Ritchie and Brindley (2007a, b)
Redundancy (Inventory)	**13**	Marley *et al.* (2014); Bode *et al.* (2011); Talluri *et al.* (2013); Zsidisin *et al.* (2000); Lavastre et al (2012); Zsidisin and Ellram (2003); Tang (2006b); Kleindorfer and Saad (2005); Tomlin (2006); Sheffi and Rice (2005); Knemeyer *et al.* (2009); Schmitt and Singh (2012); Zsidisin and Wagner (2010)
Collaboration	**10**	Jüttner *et al.* (2003); Spekman and Davis (2004); Khan *et al.* (2008); Kleindorfer and Saad (2005); Christopher and Holweg (2011); Lavastre *et al.* (2012); Vilko and Hallikas (2012); Rajesh *et al.* (2015); Rajesh and Ravi (2015); Chen *et al.* (2013)
Joint Planning and Coordination	**8**	Braunscheidel and Suresh (2009); Ritchie and Brindley (2007a, b); Knemeyer *et al.* (2009); Hallikas *et al.* (2004); Speier *et al.* (2011); Lavastre *et al.* (2012); Sinha *et al.* (2004); Jüttner *et al.* (2003)

Table IV-4: Overview of most frequently mentioned SCRM strategies from 2000 to mid 2015. Source: Own illustration.

Similarly, Wieland (2013) considers multiple sourcing, safety stocks, and flexible transportation as appropriate measures to reduce SCRs. Finally, Sodhi *et al.* (2012) advocate that for preventing risks, the following general strategies can be adopted: increasing collaboration with partners including risk sharing, increasing demand, supply and process flexibilities and building buffers or redundancies across SCs. However, the examination of the systematic review demonstrates a lack of consistency regarding SCRM strategies, which may hinder the ability to implement SCRM effectively. One good example of the discrepancies in wording is the fact that some authors talk about awareness of risks while others mention 'common understanding of risks'. Another example is that some of the studies reviewed referred to redundancy, while others referred to holding inventory, stockpiling, safety stock, strategic stock, extra inventory, backup, overcapacity, or capacity, although all researchers might have meant the same. Also, some strategies mentioned are pretty vague, without deeper specifying the domain such as mobility, speculation, imitation, formal procedures, risk acceptance, and training. Only a few had clear-cut distinctions among these concepts which were mainly semantics. Hence, the results indicate that a greater consensus on particular notions and terms concerning core SCRM strategies is required which would allow the academic literature and, therefore, the entire concept of SCRM to progress more consistently.

3.3 Grouping and synthesis of SCRM Strategies

To categorise and synthesise the SCRM strategies, we are in line with several academics and suggest a grouping that makes a distinction between proactive SCRM approaches for the ante disruptive event and reactive SCRM approaches in the post disruption state for the effectiveness of SCRM and enhanced operational performance (e.g. Kleindorfer and Saad, 2005; Norrman and Jansson, 2004; Thun and Hoenig, 2011; Wakolbinger and Cruz, 2011; Zsidisin *et al.*, 2000, 2005). Reactive SCRM implies taking actions after an incident has occurred. Nevertheless, arrangements that are taken ahead of time, for example, plans of action enable a less demanding and speedier reaction to the emergency (Knemeyer *et al.,* 2009). Consequently, reactive SCRM is labelled by measures that are somewhat effect-related as opposed to cause-related. Reactiveness includes a portion of the preparatory components of proactiveness, yet it does not achieve its maximum capacity on the grounds that it concentrates on minimising the consequence of a risk instead of the likelihood of its event (Thun and Hoenig, 2011). Therefore, proactiveness in SCRM can be communicated through two elements: actions set in motion ex-ante with a specific target to moderate the likelihood that SCRs occur as well as actions induced ex-ante meant for lessening the impact of SCRs as they emerge (Wakolbinger and Cruz, 2011; Zsidisin *et al.* 2005). Then again, proactive SCRM means arranging ahead to alleviate hazards before they arise (Mitroff and

Alpaslan, 2003). Several scholars have continually proposed managing SCRM proactively to avoid their potential occurrence (e.g. Trkman and McCormack, 2009). Along these lines, proactive SCRM focuses not only on identifying potential misfortunes relating to certain SCRs and defining their probability but also on planning and activating appropriate counteractions before an adverse event occurs (Craighead *et al.*, 2007a; Li and Barnes, 2008). In this context, Lee (2002, p. 114) classifies SC strategies as 'efficient', 'risk-hedging', 'responsive', and 'agile' relating them to two SC attributes, namely supply uncertainty and demand uncertainty.

He further makes a distinction between low and high parameter value pertaining to the uncertainty attributes. For the purpose of the study, we will refer to the attributes as supply-side and demand-side risks. Table IV-5 provides a compilation of supply-side and demand-side risk sources that have been identified in the reviewed articles.

Supply chain risk sources	Description	Examples	Author(s)
Supply-side risks	Supply-side risks are grounded on instabilities of flow on behalf of suppliers and refer to substantial or inacceptable letdowns with incoming goods and services.	Disruption of schedules, supply, inventory, and technology access, quality problems, capacity constraints, high capacity utilisation, inflexibility of the supply source, currency fluctuations, technological uncertainty, product complexity, etc.	Zsidisin *et al.* (2000); Johnson (2001), Goh *et al.* (2007); Manuj and Mentzer (2008a, b); Tang and Tomlin (2008); Wagner and Bode (2008); Lockamy III and McCormack (2010); Tummala and Schoenherr (2011); Zsidisin and Wagner (2010); Wever *et al.* (2012); Zsidisin and Smith (2005); Punniyamoorthy *et al.* (2013); Schoenherr *et al.* (2008); Vilko and Hallikas (2012)
Demand-side risks	Demand-side risks involve disturbances on behalf of the consumers. Those risks are interrelated to losses caused e.g. by processing errors, technical failures, and quality problems.	New product introductions, variations in demand, reputation risks, receivables risks, product shortages, product recalls, industry or market risks (e.g. volatility of customer demand).	Johnson (2001); Goh *et al.* (2007); Manuj and Mentzer (2008a, b); Wagner and Bode (2008); Tang and Tomlin, (2008); Wever *et al.* (2012); Tummala and Schoenherr (2011); Zsidisin and Smith (2005); Punniyamoorthy *et al.* (2013); Schoenherr *et al.* (2008)

Table IV-5: Supply-side and demand-side risk sources.
Source: Own illustration.

In the following, we will extend the taxonomy of Lee (2002) making a distinction between the ante disruption and the post disruption state and between the proactive and reactive strategy approach to classifying single SCRM strategies identified in the conventional and emerging academic literature as aforementioned and assign them to the respective type of supply chain (see Figure IV-5).

Figure IV-5: SCRM strategies framework.
Source: Own illustration.

An efficient SC is, therefore, low on demand-side risks and supply-side risks. Efficient SCs are typically characterised by constant and foreseeable demand, lengthy product life cycles and lesser net revenues. In this manner, organisations with efficient supply chains necessitate a lower degree of responsiveness to prompt design feature changes and demand fluctuations (Fisher, 1997). Since those products return lesser margins, such SCs should set higher priorities on cost efficiency. However, due to efficient procurement processes, the supply base is well-settled (Wu *et al.*, 2014). A company that goes for the risk-hedging SC is highly exposed to supply-side risks, but little to demand-side risks. Thus, companies that apply a risk-hedging SC strategy approach usually hedge themselves against supplier uncertainty (Lai *et al.*, 2009). These organisations encounter obstacles concerning, for instance, the delivery reliability and lengthy cycle time from supply to production (Lee, 2002).

Organisations that set up a responsive SC strategy follow the goal of reacting flexibly to demand fluctuations, mirroring an adequate level of price and service awareness (Mason-Jones *et al.*, 2000). Along these lines, responsive SCRM is regularly connected with redundancies and security stock so as to minimise harm (Sheffi and Rice, 2005). Therefore, a responsive SC consequently beholds the demand-side attribute as possessing high levels of risk exposure during low levels of risk exposure for the supply-side attribute. There are likewise situations in which elevated amounts of flexibility and responsiveness to the commercial area are required (Choi and Krause, 2006). Since an agile SC regularly undergoes a change in which the customer requests are constantly unsteady, and many suppliers are undependable and restricted, such companies put emphasis on their assets and capacities, quality, delivery reliability, and after-sales service (Braunscheidel and Suresh, 2009; Gligor and Holcomb, 2012; Swafford *et al.*, 2006). Consequently, organisations with an agile SC strategy consider both SC attributes (demand-side and supply-side risks) as possessing high levels of risk exposure. According to Lee (2002, p. 114) "agile SCs essentially have strategies in place that combine the strengths of "hedged" and "responsive" supply chains. They are agile because they have the capacity to be responsive to the changing, diverse, and unpredictable demands of customers on the front end while minimising the back-end risks of supply disruptions." An investigation conducted by Wieland and Wallenburg (2012) showed that SCRM using both strategies when appropriate, positively affects organisational performance. On the one hand, their evidence provides insights into the fact that agility, achieved through e.g. flexibility, is essential to cope with customer-related risks. On the other hand, robustness obtained through e.g. redundancy (inventory) is a necessary premise to handle supplier-related risks.

Within the ante disruption state in which the proactive approach is adopted (efficient supply chains and risk-hedging supply chains), we propose four strategies that can help anticipate and mitigate the impact of SCRs. In this setting, employing proactive procedures is required for managing risks to stabilise SC systems–which are presented in the following:

(1) ***Visibility and Transparency*** through information sharing may take place through process management, IT systems, and service provider management, for instance (Speier *et al.*, 2011; Thun and Hoenig, 2011). For the adequate assessment and response to disruptive events, a high level of transparency is necessary (Hendricks and Singhal, 2012). Further devices of information transmission and connectivity through the supply chain for greater transparency and visibility are RFID or mobile devices for minimising the probability of SCRs occurrence (Byrne, 2005; Sheffi and Rice, 2005).

(2) ***Partnerships/Relationships*** in terms of supplier relationship management (SRM) can help reduce supply-side uncertainties and may guarantee high quality and a high on-time delivery ratio (Ellis *et al.*, 2010; Giunipero and Eltantawy, 2004; Khan *et al.*, 2008; Vilko and Hallikas, 2012). Swink and Zsidisin (2006), as well as Cheng and Kam (2008), suggest that strong ties to key suppliers enable proactive SCRM because relational governance fosters close information exchange and shapes trust.

(3) ***Redundancy*** (inventory) through adding external safety stocks is an excellent alternative to increased storage costs, risk of obsolescence, capital waste caused by internal surplus stock, and protecting from unforeseen disruptions and demand variance (Rajesh *et al.*, 2015; Rajesh and Ravi, 2015; Schmitt and Sing, 2012; Kleindorfer and Saad, 2005). One solution is vendor managed inventory (VMI) or co-managed inventory (CMI) (Lavastre *et al.*, 2012).

(4) ***Joint Planning and Coordination*** with a motivated cross-functional team which possesses a broad spectrum of functional expertise is beneficial because risks are usually spread across the SC and necessitate joint problem-solving (Hallikas *et al.*, 2004; Speier *et al.*, 2011). In addition, the team may need to look outside experts, for instance, by sharing or transferring risks which can happen through outsourcing and closing flexible contracts (Manuj and Mentzer, 2008b; Sinha *et al.*, 2004).

Reactive instruments are effect-oriented measurements that strive for mitigating the negative impact of an incident; they do not immediately take action on the risk but aim at capturing the harm instigated by a risk. Accordingly, the respective SC should be designed in a way that the consequences of an incurred risk are moderated (Tomlin, 2008). Thus, we propose the following six strategies for effective SCRM in the post disruption state which encompasses the reactive approach (responsive supply chains and agile supply chains):

(1) ***Visibility and Transparency*** through information sharing may take place through process management, IT systems, and service provider management, for instance (Speier *et al.*, 2011; Thun and Hoenig, 2011). For the adequate assessment and response to disruptive events, a high level of transparency is necessary (Hendricks and Singhal, 2012). Further devices of information transmission and connectivity through the supply chain for greater transparency and visibility are RFID or mobile devices for minimising the probability of SCRs occurrence (Byrne, 2005; Sheffi and Rice, 2005).

(2) ***Collaboration*** generates new knowledge through joint product design, collaborative research, or collective process innovation which enhances the ability of the SC to respond promptly to environmental changes (Chen *et al.*, 2013; Christopher and Holweg, 2011; Christopher and Peck, 2004). According to Rajesh *et al.* (2015), the capability of suppliers and their performance are improved, the continuity of supply is ensured and supply-side risks are reduced when the operations of two firms are well-coordinated.

(3) ***Redundancy*** (inventory) through adding external safety stocks is an excellent alternative to increased storage costs, risk of obsolescence, capital waste caused by internal surplus stock, and protecting from unforeseen disruptions and demand variance (Rajesh *et al.*, 2015; Rajesh and Ravi, 2015; Schmitt and Sing, 2012; Kleindorfer and Saad, 2005). One solution is vendor managed inventory (VMI) or co-managed inventory (CMI) (Lavastre *et al.*, 2012).

(4) ***Flexibility*** in building responsive production processes to respond to any external changes has become immanent (Braunscheidel and Suresh, 2009; Datta, 2007; Lavastre *et al.*, 2012). Another way to increase flexibility is outsourcing to external providers to gain extra capacity when needed and transform fixed cost into variable costs (Choi and Krause, 2006). For instance, *DHL* is working with several vehicle producers to establish joint aftermarket logistics structures (Christopher and Holweg, 2011).

(5) ***Multiple sourcing and flexible contracts*** can be another way to reduce risks by using alternative suppliers. If one vendor drops out because of quality or other delivery problems, at least, one other supplier is still available ensuring the delivery of parts while maintaining slack in utilisation (Knemeyer at al., 2009; Ritchie and Brindley, 2007a, b; Thun and Hoenig, 2011).

(6) ***Postponement*** by holding the base materials, subassemblies, and modules as strategic backup inventory and configuring or assembling the product late against actual orders leads to reduced inventory costs and lower logistics costs (Bandaly *et al.*, 2014; Christopher and Holweg, 2011; Manuj and Mentzer, 2008b; Yang and Yang, 2010).

The findings direct that *visibility and transparency* is a central strategy needed in each state of SCRM. Surprisingly, the present study shows that some approaches require nearly the same strategies. However, while some strategies may be more suited for dealing proactively with supply chain risks, others are more reactive in nature to mitigate SCRs. Table IV-6 shows the assignment of the strategies to each type of supply chain.

Type of Supply Chain	Supply chain risk management strategies
Efficient Supply Chains	Visibility and Transparency, Partnerships/Relationships
Risk-hedging Supply Chains	Joint planning and Coordination, Redundancy (Inventory), Visibility and Transparency
Responsive Supply Chains	Postponement, Visibility and Transparency, Redundancy (Inventory), Multiple Sourcing and Flexible Contracts, Collaboration, Flexibility
Agile Supply Chains	Flexibility, Postponement, Visibility and Transparency, Multiple Sourcing and Flexible Contracts, Redundancy (Inventory), Collaboration

Table IV-6: Most frequently mentioned SCRM strategies from 2000 to mid 2015 assigned to each type of supply chain.
Source: Own illustration.

4 Discussion

With this investigation, we aimed to answer the following primary research question: What are the strategies for effective supply chain risk management? To respond to this question, we worked out the state of the art in risk management concerning SCM by conducting a systematic literature review. SCRM should be deliberately planned and tenaciously kept up to prevent harms for an organisation (Brandman, 2002). The present research is guided by a SLR approach proposed by (among others) Briner *et al.* (2009), Dickersin *et al.* (1994), and Rousseau *et al.* (2008) to ensure substantial evidentiary value. A comprehensive review of extant literature is a useful tool for providing a comprehensive overview by further structuring, refining, and synthesising the extant knowledge on a particular research subject (Carter and Ellram, 2003). Our conclusions resulting from the systematic literature review of 86 peer-reviewed journal articles from 2000 to mid 2015 illustrate the importance of adopting a broader scope of and view on SCRM strategies.

The direct impact of SCRs on performance may be explained by the rising predominance of high complexity and volatility in supply chains. The ability to withstand external threats and to deliver countermeasure to potential disruptions and risks within supply chains stands at the forefront. Thus, SCRM continues to increase in popularity as more researchers and practitioners focus on this important topic (e.g. Chopra and Sodhi, 2014; Sodhi *et al.*, 2012; Thun and Hoenig, 2011; Trkman and McCormack, 2009). An examination of the literature discloses that the greater part of the research in SCRM is rather qualitative in nature. Quantifying the strategies for SCRM mitigation to find the causal linkages between them is not considered in the literature. Furthermore, the analysis of the 86 journal articles demonstrates a lack of consistency among different strategies, which may hinder the ability to implement SCRM effectively. Hence, a greater consensus on particular notions and terms concerning SCRM strategies is required. Consequently, we grouped and synthesised the different terms into reactive and proactive SCRM methods and assigned them to different supply chain types as proposed by Lee (2002). The reactive strategy is appropriate for dealing with supply-side risks and internal risks whereas the proactive should be applied for demand-side and external risks. For the ante disruption state, the proactive approach (efficient and risk-hedging SC) constitutes of strategies of visibility and transparency, partnerships/relationships, collaboration, multiple sourcing and flexible contracts, and redundancy (inventory). In contrast, for the post disruption state, the reactive approach (responsive and agile SC) includes strategies of visibility and transparency, flexibility, multiple sourcing and flexible contracts, redundancy (inventory), and joint planning and coordination, collaboration, and postponement.

However, within both approaches (reactive and proactive) the strategies comprise several elements. Not surprisingly, our analysis revealed that visibility and transparency is required in any settings of useful SCRM. As correctly perceived by Lee *et al.* (2001), open sharing of information provides the cornerstone that holds the SC together. A firm's ability to generate, pool, and make use of information is vital (Trkman and McCormack, 2009). Already in previous studies information exchange was found to be a critical enabler of SCRM (Kleindorfer and Saad, 2005) since it represents the starting point of SC collaboration (Bowersox *et al.,* 2003) and the counterpart of uncertainty (Chen *et al.*, 2013). To effectively plan for, and answer to, different contingencies SC networks should make every effort to create institutional memory into information systems and collaborative management which leads to better decisions about whether the situation is proactive or reactive (Skipper and Hanna, 2009). Visibility and transparency fortify confidence within the SC and can inhibit overcompensation, pointless interferences and unproductive decisions after a harmful event has happened (Christopher and Lee, 2004). External collaboration was also judged to be of paramount importance when implementing an efficient SCRM system, which highlights the need to work with SC partners to address potential risk exposure instead of trying to tackle the problem in isolation (Skipper and Hanna, 2009). Nonetheless, when forecasts are enormously uncertain, unpredictable or distorted by external happenings, safety stocks can provide a remarkable response to SCRM demands (Lavastre *et al.*, 2012).

Profits often emerge when SC partners are open to sharing information and assets to gain mutual benefits. Collaboration also includes greater response to customer needs and increased flexibility in adjusting to alterations in the marketplace (Stank *et al.*, 2001). Accordingly, in light of the identified SCRM strategies, we assume that through the smooth exchange of information, firms might achieve improved SC and financial performance, and achieve higher customer satisfaction. Thus, empirical research investigating the relationship between SCRM and performance is certainly on the agenda.

5 Managerial implications

The findings of the SLR also have rich implications for executives and managers. During the last two decades many disruptive events with detrimental effects, economic or financial crisis, natural disasters or supplier bankruptcies which have caused cumulative risk exposures to organisations have been witnessed. Thus, companies may jeopardise their global competitiveness if they do not learn how to deal effectively with SCRs. The proposed conceptual framework along with its strategies can be used to implement managerial procedures to prevent or mitigate SCRs and to identify areas for improvement. Effective SCRM is valuable because when risks occur, supply chain structures and processes are already available that capture risks and enable to satisfy customer demands. Resulting from the present findings, we see tremendous potential to improve risk measurement and performance outcomes in diverse settings, thus providing better guidance to decision-makers. Without visibility of upstream and downstream flows, managers are uncertain about the demand forecasts and order cycle time, etc.

According to Bowersox *et al.* (2003) and Chen *et al.* (2013), information sharing is the starting point of supply chain collaboration. The importance of top management support for this process is an advice to managers to better respond to risks by developing and implementing an effective SC contingency planning process with appropriate mitigation measures within their organisations (Tomlin, 2006; Wever *et al.*, 2012; Wong, 2011). Organisations can further apply the identified SCRM strategies in this study to benchmark reactive and proactive SCRM strategies. With contemporary globalisation and vertical integration of organisational processes, overseeing risk issues in SCs have turned into an serious issue. It becomes imperative for managers to proactively handle potential SCRs (Rajesh *et al.*, 2015). The proposed SCRM strategies framework has incredible potential for indicating decision-makers their strengths and weaknesses. In line with the resource-based approach to strategy analysis (Grant, 1991), firms must first identify their current assets and strong points – what they can accomplish more successfully than their competitors (Pettit *et al.*, 2010).

At last, the framework offers managerial assistance for setting priorities to design a strategy for mitigating SCRs. This guides decision managers towards options as they work out mitigation strategies that are efficient and also less demanding to execute and better brought into line with their organisational capabilities (Talluri *et al.*, 2013). Thus, a well-managed firm constantly scans its chaotic and dynamic environment and readjusts its resources quicker than its competitors (Hamel and Valikangas, 2003; Lummus *et al.*, 2006). Consequently, intermittent evaluation of the potential exposure to SCRs is essential. Firms must have a comprehensive plan in place that follow a formal planning process identified by the SC network to ensure that relevant planning aspects are incorporated in different functional areas (Schmitt and Singh, 2012).

In this context, both Manuj and Mentzer (2008a) and Talluri *et al.* (2013) recommend considering SCRM as an integral element of the organisation's long-term strategic role embedded in managerial decision-making. Top management involvement in proactive planning coupled with mitigation practices will allow the SC network to migrate into recovery modes after disruptions more smoothly (Guinipero and Eltantawy, 2004; Kleindorfer and Saad, 2005).

6 Avenues for future research

Apart from describing existing contributions, the present systematic literature review provides new practical insights into SCRM and advances the current body of literature through the selection, classification and analysis of SCRM strategies. Hence, the present paper offers insights into the development of research disciplines and indicates at which points further research is required on the highly relevant topic of SCRM (Pfohl *et al.*, 2010). Firstly, with means of a detailed SLR we have identified eight unique categories of SCRM strategies that may add to the enhanced effectiveness of SCRM. Therefore, the second contribution of this research was to interpret and transfer single SCRM approaches into the SCRM strategies framework (cf. Figure IV-5) to create a useful management device for improving performance. The third contribution was to extend Lee's proposed framework by including the element of categorising SCRM strategies into proactive and reactive strategies, as well as into ante disruption and post disruption state to classify the findings. The previously stated risk mitigation measures can assist companies with a portfolio of selections to complement their specific needs, and we acknowledge that they are effective in responding to and mitigating SCRs.

However, this study has a few limitations resulting from the research design. First, the academic databases have been continuously updated with new publications as they get published. Thus, the data set collected for this research denotes a 'snapshot' of information in the database during the short period of information accumulation. The sample comprises articles, based on the postulation that these account to the research fronts of SCRM. Still, further supplementary sources such as books and conference proceedings may also offer insights into risk management in SCs but have not been included in the present study (Coombes and Nicholson, 2013). Altered keyword strings when conducting the database searches might have also modified the resulting hits. Nevertheless, it is realistic to expect that the articles included in the present research are representative of the central research endeavours in the SCRM discipline. Firstly, we encourage researchers to further investigate the insights of our provided classificatory SCRM framework. In the past, measuring SCRM itself and measuring its relationship with performance has not received the attention it deserves. Thus, Hoffmann *et al.* (2013) request more empirical research in SCRM to explain SC performance. Researchers have suggested that, to support and facilitate supply chain managers in decision-making, empirical research focusing on the effectiveness of risk reduction strategies and practices is eagerly needed (Khan and Burnes, 2007; Li *et al.*, 2015; Tang (2006b). For that reason, it would likewise be valuable to conduct qualitative studies exploring different types of procedures relating to decision-making under various levels of uncertainty (Vilko *et al.*, 2014). Empirical evaluation through large-scale testing of the SCRM strategies presented herein on performance is needed to offer validation. Finally, further research is necessary to address implementation and measurement issues with the aim to transform this conceptual framework into a profit-yielding management device. SCRM is an obligatory assignment of each SC to remain viable and enables to assimilate to change and prosper in the long run (Pettit *et al.*, 2010).

We also recommend exploring best practices for mitigating risks; thus, we strongly advocate researchers to develop both qualitative and quantitative constructs to identify, assess and evaluate SCRM and its effect on performance which can generate potentially new data in order to create fundamental knowledge and gain new valuable insights. Several researchers have suggested requirements for improved SCRM, empirically grounded research (Jüttner *et al.*, 2003), analytical and network hierarchy process respectively (Vanany *et al.*, 2009), quantitative techniques such as mathematical or simulation modelling (Rao and Goldsby, 2009), graph as well as complexity theory (Colicchia and Strozzi, 2012), and general development of well-grounded models by considering other interdisciplinary research approaches (Ghadge *et al.*, 2012). Nevertheless, no matter which research method is chosen, an integrated approach to SCRM requires the incorporation of risk issues from industry practice (Tang and Musa, 2011).

With more qualitative and quantitative research, it will become possible to validate the framework presented in this paper and to generate a set of generalisations based on variables such as organisational and industry characteristics (Brannen, 2005). For that reason, we also propose to exploit methodologically mixed method research designs such as case studies in combination with surveys/questionnaires to validate and evidence theoretical concepts. Accordingly, a couple of researchers call on the implementation of mixed method research designs to adequately address SC phenomena (Craighead *et al.*, 2007b; Golicic and Davis, 2012; Mangan *et al.*, 2004; Seuring, 2011). Moreover, we recommend to conduct longitudinal studies on SCRM to follow-up, assess and measure the long-term performance of a conventional situation until after a SCR has occurred. Since an in-depth analysis of the presented citations' counts was outside our scope, it would be interesting to analyse the intellectual structure, the research fronts and research paradigms of SCRM over time.

The SLR at hand makes vital contributions to the theoretical understanding of SCRM strategies and proposes insights for practical applications that may lead to improved business profitability. In this light, we encourage researchers to conduct high-quality empirically based research to quantify the within reported SCRM strategies which is of significant interest and calls for much more examination of how to maintain a competitive advantage over time after a SCR has arisen. In this context, Ishfaq (2012) contended that supply chain resilience could be accomplished without restrictively excessive operational expenses. While SCRM principally manages risk mitigation, some researchers have discussed supply chain resilience and its significance in SCRM research (Zsidisin and Wagner, 2010; Blackhurst *et al.*, 2011; Tukamuhabwa *et al.,* 2015; Wieland, 2013). Grötsch *et al.* (2013, p. 2846) stated that SCRM's "particular objective is to build and maintain resilient supply chains." Thus, a few studies state that supply chain resilience may result in lasting competitive advantage by persistently adjusting and creating capabilities to make a SC more resilient (Ponomarov and Holcomb, 2009; Pettit *et al.*, 2010).

The present paper contributes a rigorous and systematic review on the highly significant topic of SCRM strategies. Besides the methodological contribution, we provide evidentiary value and knowledge as a fundamental basis to further explore this highly relevant subject. All in all, SCRM is still a blossoming field of research characterise by diverse viewpoints. In this respect, the imperatives for future research on SCRM strategies and their effect on performance are established.

Chapter V

Strategic technology partnering capabilities: a systematic review of the empirical evidence over two decades

Abstract

Strategic technology partnering (STP) is considered to be significant for the access to novel technologies that are unknown to organisations. However, the performance heterogeneities within organisations can be explained by STP capabilities. Hence, the aim of this paper is threefold: a) to provide a classificatory framework by categorising the various STP capabilities b) to draw conclusions from the analysis of the empirical findings and c) to guide further publications and identify future research needs. The present paper adopts a systematic literature review (SLR) methodology. In this research, the extant empirical research on STP capabilities will first be classified and integrated within a classificatory framework. Lastly, the review insights will provide methodological suggestions along with theoretical themes for future research that have not yet been explored. The study findings show that there is a strong need for a clear and unified terminology for the distinctive capabilities of STP and research has mainly highlighted certain common capabilities while other essential ones lack analysis. The SLR further reveals that most research has been quantitative in nature relying on secondary database research. This systematic literature review provides a thorough overview of prior research on STP capabilities investigating 65 articles published in highly ranked peer-reviewed journals, spanning a 22-year period from 1992 to 2014. In sum, this review structures extant STP capabilities literature into a proposed classificatory framework referred to as CLONT-framework and highlights its critical importance in strategic management and innovation research from a theoretical, empirical and practical point of view.

1 Introduction

Why are some organisations more successful with their strategic technology partnerships than others? Although the benefits of interfirm partnerships have long been recognised, evidence suggests that some organisations are better at creating and capturing value through their strategic partnerships (Anand and Khanna, 2000; Heimeriks and Duysters, 2007; Kale *et al.,* 2002). From a resource-based perspective, such performance differentials reflect variance in STP capabilities across organisations. However, in spite of growing interest in this research stream, we lack a systematic empirical and theoretical understanding of those capabilities and their underlying elements (Sarkar *et al.*, 2009). An essential factor to create wealth and superior performance is joint innovation by means of STP (Bidault and Cummings, 1994; Forrest and Martin, 1992; Kim and Lee, 2003; Lanctot and Swan, 2000; Mukherjee et al, 2013; Sivadas and Dwyer, 2000; Un *et al.*, 2010).

Hence, in recent years, researchers have paid a lot of attention to studying capabilities of strategic technology partnerships (STP) and understanding how firms benefit from it (e.g. Huang and Yu, 2011; Phelps, 2010; Schreiner *et al.*, 2009; Vesalainen and Hakala, 2014). The underlying theoretical claims are that firms with greater innovation achievements are presumed to have superior capabilities (e.g. Kim and Song, 2007; Lee *et al.*, 2001; Mowery *et al.*, 1996) and that STP capabilities are vital antecedents of overall business performance (e.g. Fey and Birkinshaw, 2005; Kale and Singh, 2007; Rothaermel and Hess, 2007). The specific network background that we investigate is to be found in the high-tech industries – characterised by fast technological change – that has a significant influence on the management of innovation (Hagedoorn *et al.*, 2006; Powell, 1998). At the node of internal and external technology advancements, STP can be found where firms internalise capabilities that are at best, to a certain extent, exogenous to them (Hagedoorn and Duysters, 2002). Therefore, the capability to create and coordinate partnerships and to find new partners is important in many industries but especially in so-called high-tech industries (Hagedoorn, 1993). In STPs firms mainly cooperate closely in the areas of R&D. Therefore, these kinds of partnerships have a high influence on the long-term product-market arrangements of the respective firms (Hagedoorn and Duysters, 2002). Alliances were virtually unknown before the 1980s and have become much more prevalent during the past two decades (De Man and Duysters, 2005). Given that R&D alliances may contribute to resource configurations in a different way than other types of alliances do, it is particularly worth examining that kind of partnership (Eisenhardt and Schoonhoven, 1996; Schilke and Görzen, 2010) and not strategic alliances in general.

STP capabilities have been found, for instance, to foster superior innovation performance (Häussler and Higgins, 2014; Huang and Yu, 2011), as well as to enhance both R&D and new product development (NPD) process effectiveness and efficiency (Noseleit and de Faria, 2013; Schulze *et al.*, 2014). In that context, external resources for innovative know-how help complement capabilities and allow firms to handle sophisticated technologies through combined resources with the aim to rise innovative performance (Duysters *et al.*, 1999; Fey and Birkinshaw, 2005; Ketchen *et al.,* 2007; Un *et al.*, 2010). Thus, companies need several skills from within and outside their organisational boundaries to innovate in the light of change and complexity. Accordingly, we posit that companies need specific capabilities within STP that enable them to govern successfully their interorganisational relationships.

Capabilities are complex sets of skills and aggregated knowledge, educated through organisational processes, that enable companies to leverage their assets (Day, 1994) and refer to "a firm's capacity to deploy resources, usually in combination, using organisational processes to effect a desired end" (Amit and Schoemaker, 1993, p. 35). Eisenhardt and Martin (2000, p. 1107) define 'capabilities' as "the firm's processes that use resources – specifically the processes to integrate, reconfigure, gain and release resources – to match and even create market change." Furthermore, capability is regarded as "the ability to make use of resources to perform some task or activity" (Hafeez *et al.*, 2002, p. 40); for example, Apple's capability to generate radical, breakthrough innovations. These definitions are in line with Wang and Ahmad (2009) who conclude that capabilities are 'first-order', and when companies prove the abilities of deploying assets to achieve a wanted target, then those capabilities are likely to result in improved performance. Yet there exist a paradox: companies frequently fail to reap the anticipated benefits of most of their STPs (Kale and Singh, 2007). However, despite the increasing attention being given to this research area (e.g. Lee *et al.*, 2001; Li *et al.*, 2008; Pennings and Harrianto, 1996; Steensma and Corley, 2000), the complexity of the issues requires a systematic literature review (SLR) discovering major issues of the extant landscape of empirical as well as conceptual and theoretical evidence (Ettlie and Pavlou, 2006; Meier, 2011; Phene and Tallman, 2012) to update and motivate researchers in the field for further investigation. According to Hagedoorn and Schakenraad (1994, p. 291) "strategic technology partnering is the establishment of cooperative agreements aimed at joint innovative efforts or technology transfer that can have a lasting effect on the product-market positioning of participating companies." Similarly, Hagedoorn (2002, p. 478) defines "R&D partnerships as the specific set of different modes of inter-firm collaboration where two or more firms that remain independent economic agents and organisations, share some of their R&D activities". On this note, Tidd (2014) calls for an enhanced understanding of the inherent mechanisms and capabilities that contribute to fruitful interactions and outcomes of collaborative innovation activities.

Discussion on STP capabilities is of broad interest, and the related term can be traced back to different theoretical approaches (Richards and De Carolis, 2003). Literature is thus fragmented, and providing a comprehensive overview is challenging. The present paper supports a better understanding of STP capabilities by offering – to the best of our knowledge – the first review of the literature investigating STP capabilities and their effect on performance. Thus, this state-of-the-art systematic literature review (SLR) forms an accessible pool of knowledge that is of high relevance for future research on STP (Kilubi, 2015). Accordingly, the systematic review approach has been recently applied in other business- and management-related literature reviews (cf. Bakker, 2010; Felekoglu and Moultrie, 2014;

Keupp *et al.*, 2012). Therefore, the primary purpose of the present paper is to deliver a systematic review, by identifying, reviewing, and organising key conceptual and empirical research on STP capabilities and providing in-depth analysis concerning the noteworthy topic, whereby the research effort in this article primarily focuses on papers published in major scholarly peer-reviewed journals.

Hence, the present study has three objectives to accomplish: (a) to develop a classificatory and an integrated framework that clusters existing capabilities of STP and that may be, in light of empirical advancement, embrace and further develop into measurement constructs in future research, (b) to draw conclusions from the analysis of the empirical findings, and (c) to establish a research agenda by exploring main research issues in areas where further research is required. The overall core question determines the present SLR: Why do some organisations have greater, overall STP success than other organisations? The organisation of the paper at hand is structured as follows: In the succeeding section, we describe our rigorous, SLR methodology, the method that was used to conduct the extensive review, classification and categorisation of the literature. In the third section, we analyse and synthesise the literature and present the major findings of the present review, including the STP capabilities framework development. Further, we discuss the classified articles according to theoretical perspectives and methodological approaches applied. Finally, the paper summarises the underlying implications of the investigation for managerial practice and discusses promising theoretical themes for future research in the fourth section.

2 Review methodology and data collection

2.1 Research approach

We conduct a systematic and comprehensive review, consistent with recent suggestions, to fortify the methodological rigor of literature reviews in the management and business field (e.g. Crossan and Aypadin, 2010; Holtbrügge and Dögl, 2012; Macpherson and Jones, 2010). From a methodological perspective, a systematic literature review is a) a replicable and an explicit procedure for the identification, evaluation, and interpretation of the existing landscape of a research study (Fink, 2005). Furthermore, a systematic review is b) a well-thought-out process to examine the background of a specific literature that aims at circumventing possible biases occurring from virtuously narrative analysis and applies an unambiguous algorithm, contrarily to a heuristic, to conduct an examination of the literature (Petticrew, 2001; Thorpe *et al.*, 2005). A SLR delivers a general audit trail of procedures, decisions and conclusions made by the reviewers, permitting lucency and the replication of the study (Ordani *et al.*, 2008). Thus, it is a valid technique to generate fresh insights and knowledge by synthesising prevailing academic articles that can be of greater relevance and significance than newer studies (Cooper, 2010). The methodology applied in the present study follows the works of Bakker (2010), Felekoglu and Moultrie (2014), and Keupp *et al.* (2012). The execution phase in the present study review process encompasses six process steps and discusses issues of time horizon, database selection, journal selection, article selection, article categorisation, and article analysis, as shown in Figure V-1. The scientific rigor in performing each of these steps is of paramount importance for a high-quality review (Rousseau *et al.*, 2008; Starbuck, 2005).

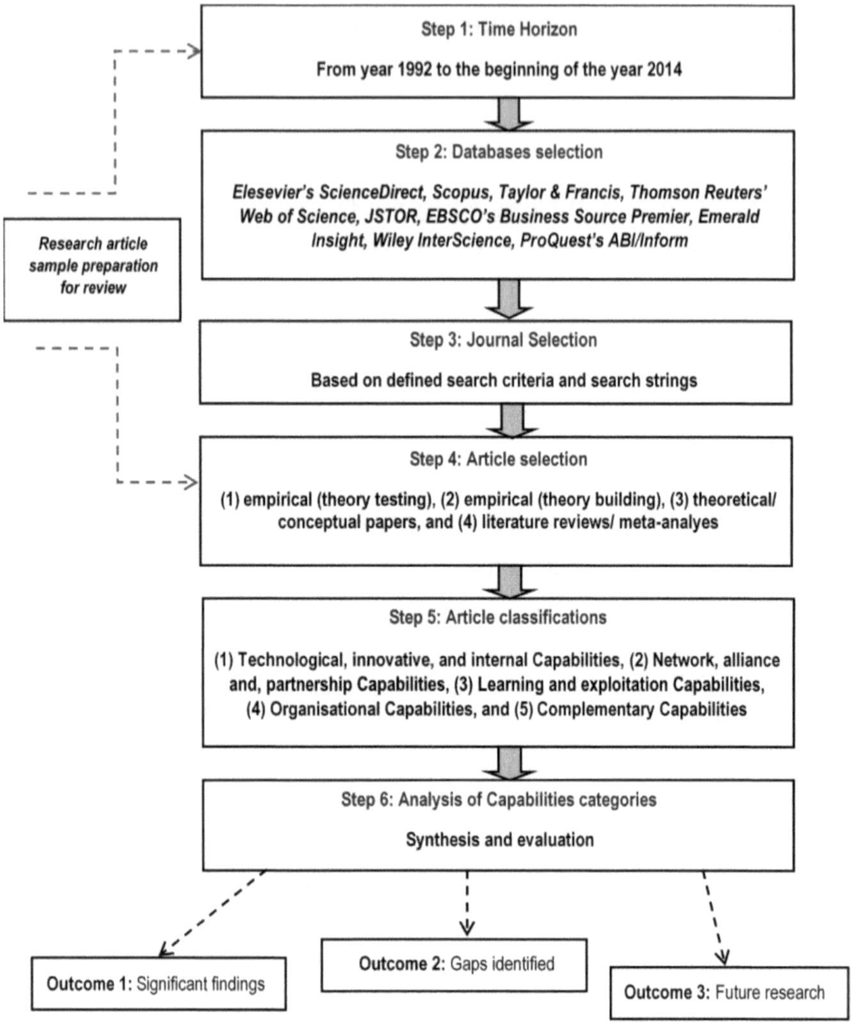

Figure V-1: Research methodology for the present systematic literature review.
Source: Adapted from Bakker (2010), Felekoglu and Moultrie (2014), and Keupp *et al.* (2012).

2.2 Time horizon of articles publication

Articles published over the 22-year period from 1992 to mid 2014 by journals recorded in the subject categories of nine databases encompassing business, economics, and management studies were examined (as of July 2014). The year 1992 is determined as the starting year for collecting the relevant data because from that year onwards the topic of STP has started to attract the attention of several key authors (e.g. Bidault and Cummings, 1994; Bonaccorsi and Lipparini, 1994; Forrest and Martin, 1992; Pennings and Harianto, 1992). Since the aim was to capture all relevant articles, as well as the most recent academic journal publications addressing this highly significant topic, June 2014 was chosen as the end point.

2.3 Identification and selection of relevant databases

Given the interdisciplinary subject of the review (i.e. strategic technology partnerships), we focused our attention on six electronic reference databases, namely, (1) *EBSCO's Business Source Complete,* (2) *Elsevier's ScienceDirect,* (3) *Scopus,* (4) *Thomson Reuters' Web of Science,* (5) *Wiley InterScience, and* (6) *ProQuest's ABI/Inform* in order to detect pertinent articles across a designated range of journals. Those selected electronic databases are widely provided by academic institutions (Felekoglu and Moultrie, 2014). Additional potential articles were identified by searching Google Scholar. To test the validity of *Google Scholar*, a search was conducted in both *Google Scholar* and *EBSCO's Business Source Complete*. *Google Scholar* included all, and more, of the papers listed on *EBSCO's Business Source Complete*. This is consistent with studies that note that *Google Scholar* is more comprehensive than other databases; however, it still suffers from limitations such as incomplete references and, therefore, it was decided not to rely solely on it for the article search (e.g. Kousha and Thelwall, 2007; Walters, 2007).

2.4 Selection of relevant journals

To begin with the systematic review, we looked up 12 initial papers as recommended by experts in the field to scope the research. We used criterion sampling as suggested by Grégoire *et al.* (2011) and Patton (1990) to identify a valid sample of STP articles, whereas the tool in the article search process was the databases search. The search covered peer-reviewed academic articles written in English. We decided to limit the references to peer-reviewed journals because those are perceived as confirmed knowledge and are supposed to have the utmost influence on the research field (Podsakoff *et al.*, 2005; Ramos-Rodriguez and Ruíz-Navarro, 2004), neglecting books, conference proceedings, working papers, and other grey literature (Ordanini *et al.,* 2008). For the present research, only the inclusion of top-tier peer-reviewed journals with an *ABS* (*associationofbusinessschools.org)* ranking of *4* or *3* were defined as one of the criteria, since higher-prestige journals publish more high-value articles and very prestigious academic journals publish quite a few low-value journal articles (McKinnon, 2013; Starbuck, 2005).

At the end, 26 business- and management-related academic journals were identified to search for in the relevant databases: *Academy of Management Journal, British Journal of Management, Decision Sciences, Economic Management Review, Industrial Marketing Management, International Journal of Innovation Management, Journal of Business Research, Journal of Business Venturing, Journal of Economics & Management Strategy, Journal of International Business Studies, Journal of International Management, Journal of Management, Journal of Management Studies, Journal of Marketing, Journal of Product Innovation Management, Journal of Technology Transfer, Long Range Planning, Management Science, Organisation Science, Organisation Studies, R&D Management, Research Policy, Strategic Entrepreneurship Journal, Strategic Management Journal, and Technovation.*

2.5 Identification of relevant articles

Our unit of analysis is the strategic technology partnerships. To ensure an unbiased view and to strengthen the process of the review, we set up a review panel, consisting of a university professor, two research assistants, and a Ph.D. student. Firstly, we defined keywords as search criteria in academic databases. Some of the keywords were selected from the present academic literature, while others resulted from a brainstorming session with the review panel including the validation and quality assessment of keywords to enhance the accuracy and the focus of the present SLR. Next, we performed keyword searches using the term *strategic partner* OR *'R&D partner* AND *technology* OR *innovation* OR *product development* AND *capabilities* given the multiplicity of meanings rooted in the term 'strategic technology partnering' and taking into account that academics might have applied the term in many different ways. Therefore, papers were, for example, not excluded from having the keyword "alliance" or "collaboration" – indeed, a sizeable proportion of the papers in the review did have alliances or collaborations as their primary focus as a type of partnership. The afore-mentioned search strings were used as a selection criterion for the topic to be searched in the title, abstract and author-provided keywords. The database search yielded an initial sample 907 hits/papers, of which 784 duplicates were removed. The remaining 123 titles were identified, screened and analysed in compliance with the exclusion and inclusion criteria as presented in Table V-1.

Inclusion criteria	Rationale for inclusion or exclusion
All countries	Consider all countries and regions to achieve a comprehensive overview.
All types of strategic partnerships	Include collaborations (CN), alliances (AL), cooperations/contractual agreements (CL), acquisitions (AQ), mergers (MR), joint ventures (JV), consortia (CA), and licensing (LC).
Commercial partnering (B2B)	Exclude papers on strategic partnerships of governmental and public sector organisations, or the participation of universities. Following recommendations, it was agreed that the review should concentrate on business-to-business partnerships.
High-technology industry	Firms in those businesses are ideal for investigation on STPs because continuity and effectiveness are crucial regarding a firm's capability to generate and commercialise innovations rapidly and proficiently. Consequently, firms in these industries proactively form partnerships in pursuit of their future innovation activities (Schilling and Phelps, 2007).
Journal ranking	Include articles with a ranking of 4 or 3 as defined by the *ABS* (*Association of Business Schools*).[7]
Level of analysis	We are only concerned with the macro and micro level, i.e. economy/society, industry/market, network, organisation, thus we exclude the individual level, e.g. groups, teams, and single persons.
Organisational form	Exclude papers that compare different organisational forms with each other as well as work by researchers solely interested in STP evolution.
Partnering life cycle	Exclude articles on the choice between alternative organisational forms and on partnership termination.
Publication in peer-reviewed academic journals	We include peer-reviewed journals that publish high-quality academic research.
Publication of full-length journal article	Following Grégoire *et al.* (2011) and Müller-Seitz (2012), we exclude books, book chapters, conference proceedings, dissertations, editorials, research notes (with less than five pages in length), and working papers.

[7] ABS, the *Association of Business Schools* is the representative body for leading economic faculties (business schools) from universities, independent business schools, and higher education institutions in the UK. The ABS is the publisher of the ABS Academic Journal Quality Guide which ranks academic journals. The journals are ranked from 1 till 4; the number 4 signifying the best category and 1 the worst one.

Inclusion criteria	Rationale for inclusion or exclusion
Either qualitative or quantitative paper (e.g. empirical studies, theoretical studies)	We focus on capturing all evidence, both empirical and theoretical since different approaches have contributed to the research area.
STP capabilities	Examine the capabilities that ensure the success of STPs.
STP outcomes	Examine how STP capabilities influence performance.
Time horizon	Include all evidence from 1992 to mid 2014 (as of July 2014). The year 1992 is selected as the starting point for gathering the relevant data because from that year on the topic of STP began to attract the attention of several key authors (e.g. Bidault and Cummings, 1994; Bonaccorsi and Lipparini, 1994; Forrest and Martin, 1992; Pennings and Harianto, 1992).

Table V-1: Inclusion and exclusion criteria for included papers in the systematic review (in alphabetical order).
Source: Adapted from Kilubi and Haasis (2016).

For instance, by applying the criteria mentioned above, articles focusing on smaller units of analysis, as well as articles treating STP as being formed by individuals or by actors other than firms, such as universities, were discarded. Articles (n = 39) that did not comply with the inclusion criteria were excluded after examination of the abstracts and the conclusions. At this point, 84 papers were brought forward to the next stage; the full copies were extracted and evaluated for appropriateness by reading the text entirely. Articles had to show a clear connection between STP capabilities and performance. We looked in detail at the aim of the study, the research methodology, definitions of key terms, etc. Consequently, 25 articles were removed because they did not focus on the research questions. However, 59 articles were included in our SLR after having read the full text and having been found to meet elementary criteria of relevance and value. One limitation to article search by defined keywords is the fact that relevant studies that have not incorporated the selected keywords but investigated a similar topic might be overlooked or missed out. Hence, as some relevant references can be unexploited owing to the rigid process of the keywords search (Leseure *et al.* 2004; Thorpe *et al.*,

2005), a few manual inclusions were evaluated and included in the SLR after a fundamental consensus of all members of the review panel. Through manual checking and citation tracking, six additional articles were included in our literature review, resulting in a total list of 65 peer-reviewed articles in 24 academic publications, covering the period from 1992 to the beginning of 2014. These articles were included in the present SLR to ensure high quality and comprehensiveness. Figure V-2 outlines the applied detailed journal article selection process.

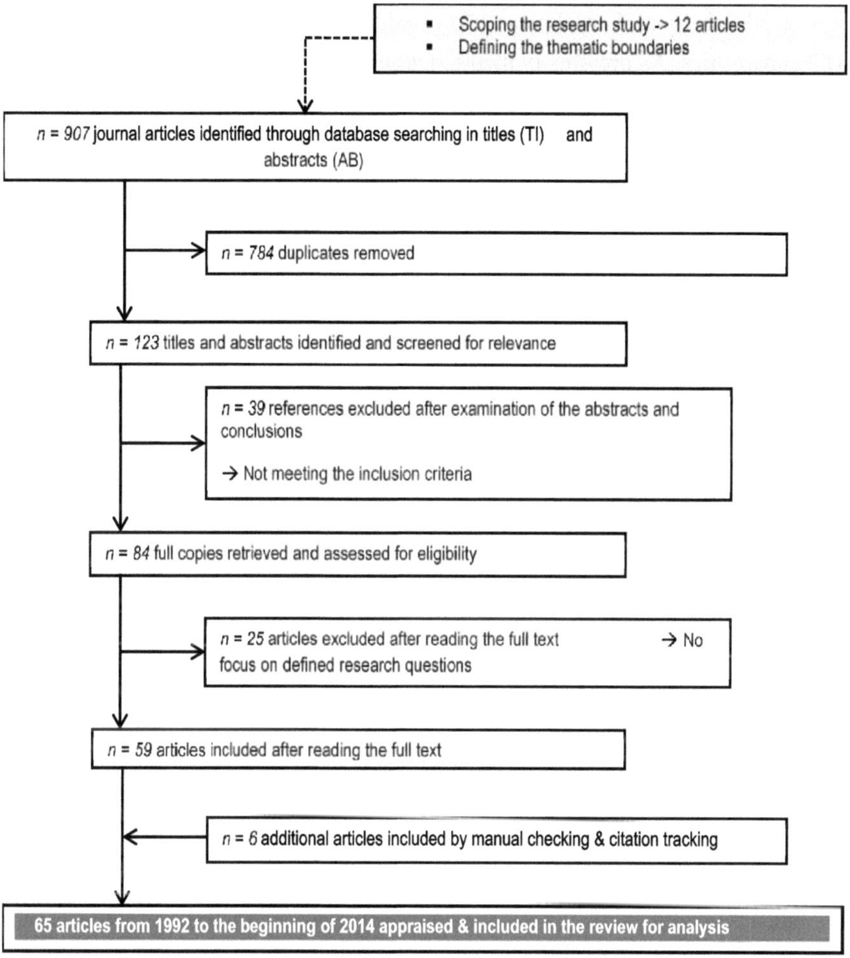

Figure V-2: Summary of the SLR journal article selection process.
Source: Own illustration.

2.6 Article classifications

In the following, the final sample of 65 business and economics journal articles were analysed in depth and logically structured according to the different capability features delineated in the subsequent section. To organise the selected database of 65 academic journal articles, we identified, analysed and aggregated the various STP capabilities. As previously mentioned, the studies of several researchers that have hitherto investigated STP capabilities issues were reviewed. In the present literature review, 38 STP capabilities were identified which were then grouped into five distinct core capabilities. In particular, the arrangement was guided by the works of Ingham and Mothe (1998), Deeds *et al.* (1999); Ettlie and Pavlou (2006), Häussler and Higgins (2014), Huang and Yu (2011), Kale and Singh (2007), Lee *et al.* (2001), and Sampson (2007) in order to identify critical STP capabilities that positively influence performance.

The most frequently mentioned capabilities in the extant literature explaining the STP phenomenon are 1. *technological, innovative, and internal capabilities* (e.g. Feller *et al.*, 2013; Huang and Yu, 2011; Ritala *et al.*, 2009; Zhang and Baden-Fuller, 2010; Häussler *et al.*, 2012), 2. *network, alliance, and partnership capabilities* (e.g. Duysters, 2012; Häussler and Higgins, 2014; Faems, 2010; Mitrega *et al.*, 2012; Schilke and Görzen, 2010; Sluyts *et al.*, 2011), 3. *learning and exploitation capabilities* (e.g. Fey and Birkinshaw, 2005; Hagedoorn *et al.*, 2006; Lorenzoni and Lipparini, 1999; Schulze *et al.*, 2014), 4. *complementary capabilities* (e.g. Noseleit and de Faria, 2013; Un *et al.*, 2010; Tidd, 2014), and 5. *organisational capabilities* (e.g. Cassiman *et al.*, 2009; Ketchen *et al.*, 2007; Kim and Song, 2007; Phene and Tallman, 2012). All these authors identify several STP capabilities such as organisational, network, coordination, relational, internal, knowledge, managerial, and technological capabilities. Thus, we screened for the various core capabilities mentioned by the authors and synthesised them into five core capabilities dominating the present academic literature. In the Appendix, we have attached all capabilities as originally mentioned in the 65 selected articles, prior to synthesising them. These core capabilities enable scholars to better understand the differences between the different forms of STP capabilities and will allow future studies to be more explicit regarding the particular STP core capability that is being studied and how each particular capability affects performance. As a result, we propose a distinctive classificatory framework, referred to as CLONT-framework (***C***omplementary capabilities, ***L***earning & exploitation capabilities, ***O***rganisational capabilities, ***N***etwork, alliance, and partnership capabilities, ***T***echnological, innovative, and internal capabilities), synthesising the large body of literature into five core STP capabilities as displayed in Table V-2. It provides a description of each STP core capability, as well as the frequency in which it occurs and the corresponding author(s).

STP Core Capabilities	Frequency	Description	Author(s)
(1) Complementary capabilities	**12**	Complementary capabilities imply the pooling of distinct skills and know-how, or technological diversity between partners which inspire creativity and novel approaches to prevalent challenges. Thus, they constitute the extent to which companies get along and appreciate anticipated synergies that are critical to an operation's success.	Deeds *et al.* (1999); Kale and Singh (2007); Malik (2002); Noseleit and de Faria (2013); Phelps (2010); Sampson (2007); Santangelo (2000); Saxton (1997); Tidd (2014); Un *et al.* (2010); Vilkamo and Keil (2003); Zollo *et al.* (2000)
(2) Learning and exploitation capabilities	**13**	Firms with superior capabilities of obtaining, integrating, converting, and leveraging knowledge from external sources are better in transforming the assimilated knowledge into superior innovations. Thus, learning and exploitation capabilities are seen as endogenous capabilities. The central point is that over time organisations build up a body of knowledge and skills through experience and learning-by-doing.	Fey and Birkinshaw (2005); Hagedoorn *et al.* (2006); Huang and Yu (2011); Ingham and Mothe (1998); Ketchen *et al.* (2007); Lorenzoni and Lipparini (1999); Miotti and Sachwald (2003); Mowery *et al.* (1996); Phene and Tallman (2012); Powell *et al.* (1999); Sampson (2007); Schulze *et al.* (2014); Trott *et al.* (1995)

STP Core Capabilities	Frequency	Description	Author(s)
(3) Organisational capabilities	**12**	The organisational capabilities base upon practiced routines and represent a set of functional capabilities, coordinated through business processes and activities. As a result, the necessary organisational capabilities for the generation and application of new technology typically become embodied in a set of experienced processes, structures, and formalised procedures within a firm.	Cassiman *et al.* (2009); Deeds *et al.* (1999); Ettlie and Pavlou (2006); Forrest and Martin (1992); Ketchen *et al.* (2007); Kim and Song (2007); Malik (2002); Pennings and Harianto (1992); Sivadas and Dwyer (2000); Trott *et al.* (1995); Phene and Tallman (2012); Zollo *et al.* (2002)
(4) Network, alliance, and partnership capabilities	**23**	Are defined as the abilities of a company to effectively manage a multitude of interfirm partnerships. They can be understood as company-specific capabilities that enable an organisation to position itself in a broad portfolio and network of partnerships with various firms and the capacity to handle, build, and manage relationships. Hence, network and partnership capabilities are predominantly related to the particular brainpower of firms concerning their network arrangements and the selection of the right external partners.	Capaldo (2007); De Man and Duysters (2005); Duysters *et al.* (1999); Duysters (2012); Ettlie and Pavlou (2006); Faems (2010); Feller *et al.* (2013); Hagedoorn *et al.* (2006); Häussler and Higgins (2014); Heimeriks and Duysters (2007); Kalaignanam *et al.* (2007); Kale *et al.* (2002); Kale and Singh (2007); Lorenzoni and Lipparini (1999); Mitrega *et al.* (2012); Rothaermel and Deeds (2006); Sarkar (2009); Schilke and Görzen (2010); Schreiner *et al.* (2009); Sivadas and Dwyer (2000); Siu

STP Core Capabilities	Frequency	Description	Author(s)
			and Bao (2008); Sluyts *et al.* (2011); Heimeriks *et al.* (2009)
(5) Technological, Innovative, and internal capabilities	**31**	Refer to the level of expertise within a technological territory that encompass the different scientific techniques available to the organisation; i.e. the ability to continually create new products, technologies, and processes depends on a company's technological and scientific capabilities. Furthermore, they point to skills for the successful transformation of inputs into outputs.	Ahuja (2000a); Bayona *et al.* (2001); Caloghirou *et al.* (2004); Cassiman *et al.* (2009); Carr (1999); Ciu *et al.* (2002); Deeds *et al.* (1999); Duysters *et al.* (2012); Faems *et al.* (2010); Feller *et al.* (2013); Fey and Birkinshaw (2005); Häussler *et al.* (2012); Häussler and Higgins (2014); Hagedoorn and Duysters (2002); Hagedoorn and Schakenraad (1994); Huang and Yu (2011); Ketchen *et al.* (2007); Malik (2002); Lanctot and Swan (2000); Lee *et al.* (2001); Li *et al.* (2008); Miotti and Sachwald (2003); Mowery *et al.* (1996); Powell *et al.* (1996); Rothaermel (2001); Ritala *et al.* (2009); Rothaermel and Hess (2007); Steensma and Corley (2000); Zhang and Baden-Fuller (2010); Zhou and Li (2008); Capaldo (2007)

Table V-2: Description of the five identified core STP capabilities.
Source: Own illustration.

2.7 Analysis of categories

In the final step, the classified journal articles were compared and critically evaluated. In order to organise and synthesise valuable insights from the extant academic literature, we concerned ourselves with building distinctive STP core capabilities to create a comprehensive classificatory framework. Next, a critical analysis and discussion of the various contributions relating to capabilities in STP based on the research methodology, theories adopted, and their main findings were conducted. Given that the paper is descriptive by nature and the purpose is to analyse and categorise existing literature on STP capabilities and to identify areas for future research, we did not use statistical methods to cluster the selected journal articles. In the final step of our analysis, we explicitly targeted our efforts on analysing the classified articles to conceptualise the STP capabilities landscape and to further shape the framework. The review panel analysed each of the papers with respect to its thematic and descriptive content. Prior to that, the panel members who all reviewed a sizeable sample of the papers, discussed their findings, before splitting the papers between them. The emerging capabilities of STP were identified and synthesised through thematic analysis (Rousseau *et al.*, 2008). More precisely, a descriptive deductive analysis was conducted in which the papers were categorised on a per year basis, on the theoretical base, and the methodological approach. Five major STP capabilities have been identified through the SLR which are elaborated in the following section (cf. Figure V-3). Before analysing the existing research in each of these five core STP capabilities, we briefly outline the theoretical and methodological lenses that have been used to study STP capabilities.

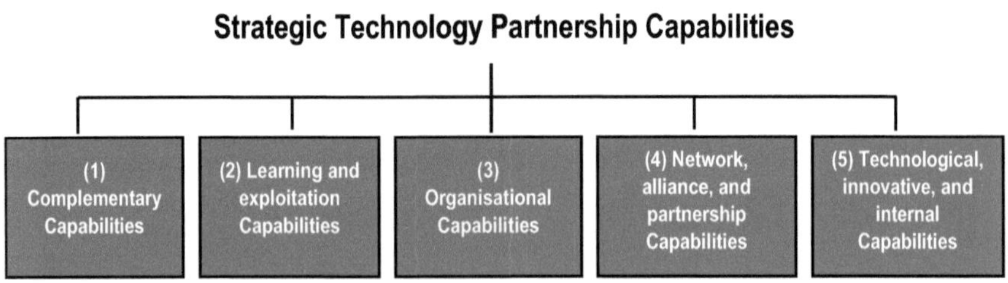

Figure V-3: Classificatory framework (CLONT-framework).
Source: Own illustration.

3 Study findings

3.1 Background of papers

In order to further highlight the vital importance and interdisciplinary role of the STP capabilities phenomenon, we found a broad range of journals from various disciplines that have published relevant studies. The sample of 65 selected journal articles in this SLR was issued in 26 leading academic journals. In detail, the largest number of articles appeared in *Strategic Management Journal* (n = 10), *Technovation* and *Academy of Management Journal* (each n = 6). Next, *R&D Management* (n = 5), followed by both *Journal of Product Innovation Management* and *Organisation Science* (each n = 4). Then succeeded by *Journal of Business Venturing, International Journal of Innovation Management,* and *Research Policy* (each n = 3). Lastly, *Journal of Business Research, Journal of Management Studies, and Industrial Marketing Management* (each n = 2).

3.1.1 Years of publication

More than 57 per cent (37 out of 65 articles) of the reviewed papers were published between 1999 and 2008, with 2007 marking the peak of 12 per cent (8 out of 65 articles). We started the literature review in the year 1992, approximately around the time when STP began attracting more and more researchers (e.g. Bidault and Cummings, 1994; Bonaccorsi and Lipparini, 1994; Forrest and Martin, 1992; Pennings and Harrianto, 1992). The fact that the number of publications started to decrease from 2008 onwards may be caused by the global economic and financial crisis that began in 2007; companies were reluctant to enter any forms of partnerships and were more concerned with the viability of their active business. But since 2011, we have observed an upward trend, with already three articles published in the first quarter of 2014 (Häussler and Higgins, 2014; Schulze *et al.*, 2014; Tidd, 2014).

3.1.2 Methodological approaches

Concerning the research methodologies applied to the surveyed papers, we classified the approaches used similar to Crossan and Apaydin (2010) into four categories: (1) empirical (theory testing), (2) empirical (theory building), (3) theoretical/conceptual papers, and (4) literature reviews/meta-analyses. Empirical papers that test theory include surveys/questionnaires and secondary database research (Keupp *et al.*, 2012). Empirical papers that build theory rely on the case study methodology (Seuring and Müller, 2012). Contrariwise, theoretical papers contain conceptual, modelling or simulation methods (Pilbeam *et al.*, 2012). We consider this as an indication for the necessity of theory development in STP to further advance the discipline and to explore unknown phenomena. The highest proportion was captured by empirical articles, with a particular emphasis on theory testing with 72 per cent. Next, the focus was on both secondary database research (38 per cent, n = 22) and surveys/questionnaires (34 per cent, n = 22), but less on theory building (case studies) with 25 per cent (n = 16) representation. Theoretical and conceptual papers showed the smallest share (3 per cent, n = 2). Surprisingly, the mixed-method approach has been used only once recently (cf. Feller *et al.*, 2013). The breakdown of articles by theories is depicted in Figure V-4.

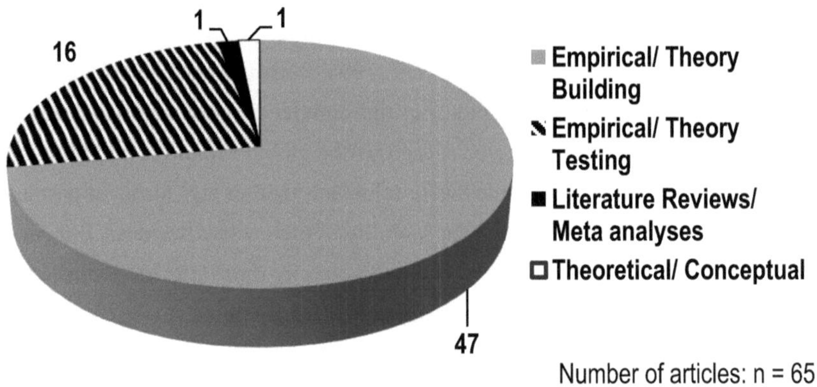

Figure V-4: Methodological approaches applied to the journal articles included for review. Source: Own illustration.

The quantitative studies were apparent during the entirely defined period. More precisely, in the years 1994, 1997, 2000-2001, 2004-2005, 2008, as well as in the years between 2011 and 2014, among the selected papers only quantitative articles were issued, whereas qualitative research studies were more published between 1992 and 2000 and between 2009 and 2010. The reason for that may be that when the topic is in its infant stage the phenomenon needs to be explored and theories should to be developed. Thus, when STP reached a more mature level at the beginning of the 21st century, the findings and emerged theories from the former decade needed to be tested and validated using quantitative approaches. Given the fact that the majority of journal articles have focused on quantitative studies, we may expect a rise in the use of qualitative methods to explore further areas of STP that are alien to the scientific world.

3.1.3 Theory of papers

Due to the multidisciplinarity of STP research, the prevalence of management-related theories is noteworthy (see Figure V-5). Overall, the resource-based view (RBV) was represented in 49 per cent (n = 32) of all journal articles on study, whereas the knowledge-based view (KBV) was represented in 23 per cent (n = 15), followed by social network theory (SNT) and TCE with each 8 per cent (n = 5) representation. Next in the ranking was organisational learning (OL) with 5 per cent (n = 3). However, the evolutionary economics (EE) and the social capital theory (SCT) did not often appear, each only twice (3 per cent). Moreover, in one study the theoretical base was not specified (N/S).

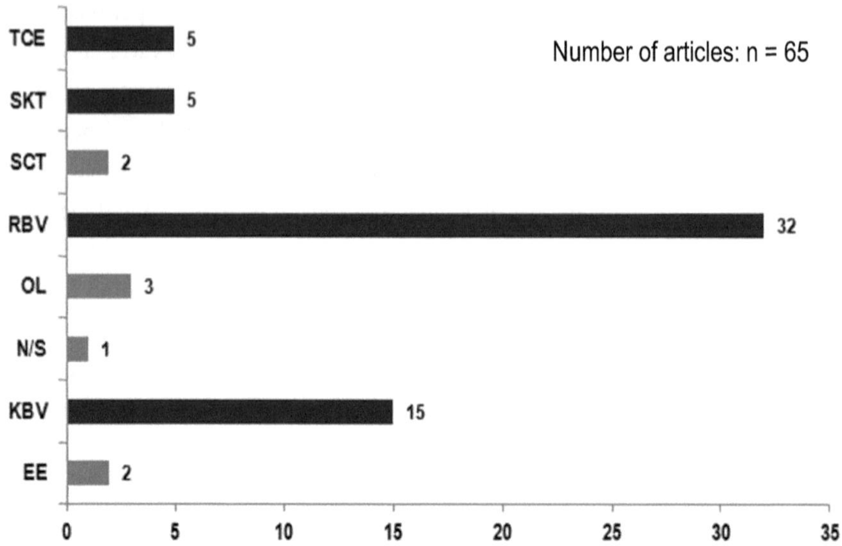

Figure V-5: Theories applied to the journal articles included for review.
Source: Own illustration.

It is not surprising that most papers dealt with the RBV and KBV since both theories stem from the organisational theory. Furthermore, the resource-based view is possibly the governing theoretical viewpoint within strategic management (Ketchen *et al.*, 2007), and also represents a fundamental perspective in the entrepreneurship field (Alvarez and Busenitz, 2001). However, these two perspectives have deviating concerns with the origins of value creation, with RBV highlighting the unique internally accumulated and combined resources, assets or capabilities that foster sustained performance distinctions with other firms (Eisenhardt and Schoonhoven, 1996; Grant and Baden-Fuller, 2004; Park and Song, 2004), and the KBV conceptualising firms as mechanisms that facilitate knowledge creation with the means of exploiting internal and/or external sources (Birkinshaw, 2005; Contractor and Ra, 2002; Un and Cuervo-Cazurra, 2004). As a result, most of the papers that adopt the RBV empirically analyse the relationship between STP capabilities, in particular, technological capabilities, and innovativeness by using data gathered from secondary databases (e.g. Ettlie and Pavlou, 2006; Fey and Birkinshaw, 2005; Häussler *et al.*, 2012). Papers using the KBV as a theoretical framework, on the other hand, mainly investigate how firms can effectively absorb and disseminate knowledge gained from external sources focusing on learning and exploitation capabilities that foster effective NPD (e.g. Kale and Singh, 2007; Phelps, 2010; Schulze *et al.*, 2014). The analysis reveals that 59 per cent (n = 33) of the articles reviewed have addressed one single theory (e.g. Cassiman *et al.*, 2009; Feller *et al.*, 2013; Zhang and Baden-Fuller, 2010), whereas 27 per cent (n = 15) have focused on at least two theories at the same time (e.g. Kale *et al.*, 2002; Lorenzoni and Lipparini, 1999; Phene and Tallman, 2012). Although research on STP has grown over the last two decades and quite a few theories were adopted by several authors, the lack of an explicit, coherent and common theoretical foundation outweighs (Reus and Rottig, 2009).

Several researchers advocate that the strategic importance of STP capabilities rests upon their evident role in sustainable business and higher profitability (e.g. Mukherjee *et al.*, 2013; Phelps, 2010; Phene and Tallman, 2012; Rothaermel and Hess, 2007; Un *et al.*, 2010). This is in line with our findings that indicate the increasing significance of STP capabilities in adapting to fast technological change in industrial markets to remain globally competitive (e.g. Huang and Yu, 2014; Kim and Song, 2007; Mowery *et al.*, 1996; Noseleit and de Faria; 2013). Having developed the classificatory framework, we now carry on aggregating and analysing conceptual and empirical findings which are pertinent to the topic. Our examination focuses on studies investigating factors relating to STP performance. The intention was to analyse and evaluate the vast body of academic literature while synthesising it "into a new or different arrangement and developing knowledge that is not apparent from reading the individual studies in isolation" (Denyer and Tranfield, 2009, p. 685). The consequential synthesis is a knowledgeable elucidation of what the scientific evidence reveals concerning the defined research questions and related issues that emerged during the review process (Rousseau *et al.*, 2008). Thus, given below we break down our findings by describing the five STP core capabilities while examining their linkage to performance in order classify and analyse the 65 selected journal articles.

3.2 Synthesis and categorisation of STP Capabilities

As a result, in the selected body of literature, our systematic review revealed 38 capabilities across various authors. The largest number of studies deals with technological, innovative, and internal capabilities to ensure STP success. Furthermore, researchers also discuss network, alliance, and partnership capabilities, learning and exploitation, organisational, and complementary as core STP capabilities being displayed in Figure V-6.

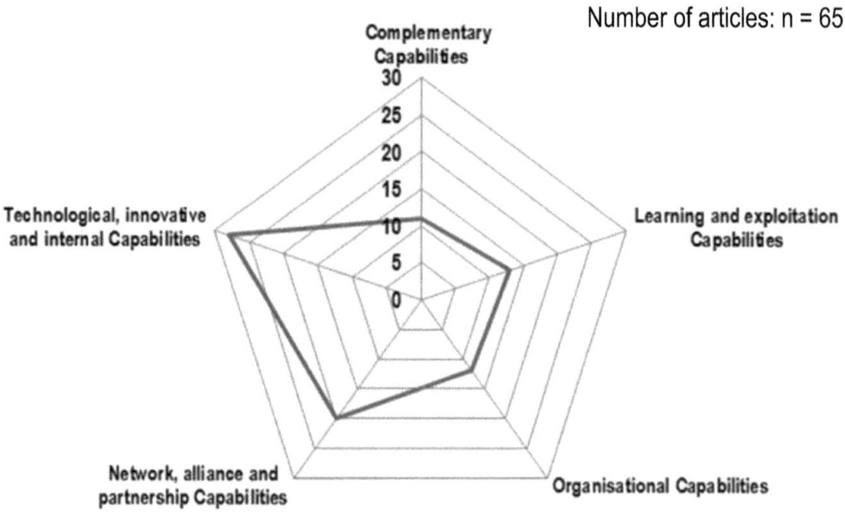

Figure V-6: Top STP capabilities by frequency.
Source: Own illustration.

Thus, we discovered five core STP capabilities that affect performance. In the present review, several capabilities were identified out of which alliance, technological/innovative, complementary, and organisational capabilities were reckoned fundamental by several researchers. This result is partially in line with existent findings. For instance, Wang and Ahmed (2007), drawing on existing empirical findings, identified adaptive capability, absorptive capability, and innovative capability as the most frequently declared capabilities in the literature. However, the absorptive capability was only mentioned in three of the reviewed articles as an STP capability. A plausible explanation for this might be that the phenomenon of STP capabilities suffers from deviating wording in literature, thereby restricting the full understanding of STP capabilities. For instance, some authors view capabilities, such as alliance capabilities and organisational capabilities as subordinate concepts (or antecedents) of other capabilities, such as network and partnership capabilities or internal capabilities. Exemplarily, Lee *et al.* (2001) captured internal capabilities by three variables: technological capabilities, entrepreneurial orientation, and financial resources invested. Moreover, while some of the studies talked about knowledge-based capabilities and others about disseminative capability, endogenous or cognitive capabilities, all have been relating to the same thing. Other examples refer to interfirm capabilities, integration capabilities, and relational capabilities, all describing elements being involved in the management of a diverse set of networks or partnership portfolios. Only a few studies showed clear-cut distinctions between these concepts which were mainly semantics; complementary capabilities, in particular, were clear without ambiguity. Accordingly, we identified a strong need for greater consensus on core capabilities and their related terms that would permit research and, thus, the entire concept of STP to develop and progress more consistently. To further examine the relationship between the capabilities and performance, we applied our unique classificatory framework with the five core STP capabilities (see Appendix V for the descriptions) to classify and analyse the 65 articles. We will present the findings in the following.

3.2.1 Complementary Capabilities

Technology usually necessitates the simultaneous use of different sets of soft skills and knowledge bases in the innovation process. Accordingly, in a longitudinal study of 98 alliance partnerships Saxton (1997) considers partner reputation, the level of conjoint decision-making, trust and commitment, as well as strategic similarities between partners to have a significantly positive effect on profits from STP participation. According to Santangelo (2000), companies are keen on entering STPs to obtain partner's capabilities associated with their areas of competencies; therefore, companies with coinciding sets of technological expertise are more expected to form a partnership. Based on secondary data from a longitudinal study of the ICT (information and communication technology) industry, different prerequisites that help foster successful partnership formation are discussed and point to partner's similarity, mutual interaction, technological diversification on partners' technological convergence, and companies sharing technological commonalities. Others have conducted longitudinal studies using a secondary database and found a conceptually similar result that technological similarity between strategic technology partners increases firm patenting (e.g. Kim and Song, 2007). In addition to that resource sharing, combining knowledge, skills, and physical assets, as well as complementarity and collaborative linkages positively, affect network effectiveness and innovation output (e.g. Ahuja, 2000b). This is in line with similar investigations that reveal that STPs engender long-term relationships with suppliers, customers and support respective firms with complementary resources and capabilities to complement their internal capabilities (Rothaermel, 2001; Zollo *et al.*, 2002).

Nevertheless, if firms aim at reducing risks and costs, they will aggregate similar assets; if companies aim instead at managing technological conjunction, they will pool complementary assets (Miotti and Sachwald, 2003). Enablers towards higher flexibility and greater efficiency through complementary capabilities mentioned by Vilkamo and Keil (2003) comprise risk sharing, common objectives of partners, and explicit contributions from partners. Likewise, Sampson (2007) found out that partners with varied capabilities can learn more from one another than associates with quite comparable capabilities, inspiring novel ideas and creativity. By means of a sample of 463 R&D alliances in the telecommunications equipment industry, their findings show that companies profit most from STP when the capabilities of partners are moderately dissimilaras to enable efficient absorption. Accordingly, recent studies provide increasing evidence that firms that combine internal and external activities outdo those companies only active in a single activity (Cassiman *et al.*, 2009; Un *et al.*, 2010). In his longitudinal investigation of 77 telecommunications apparatus producers, Phelps (2010) points out that diversity and dissimilar knowledge increase the potential for highly novel and exploratory innovation. Similarly, Phene and Tallman (2012) ponder experience in related technology to enrich firm ability to integrate external technology with organisation processes. Noseleit and de Faria (2013) highlight that partnership with parties from the same and related industries increase internal R&D efficiency, with related industry partnerships being most beneficial, leading to a positive impact on innovation performance. Their findings base on a longitudinal study of 781 R&D collaborations.

3.2.2 Learning and exploitation Capabilities

The point is that over long periods of time, organisations develop a range of knowledge and expertise through learning by doing and gaining experience (Trott *et al.*, 1995). Ingham and Mothe (1998) have conducted three case studies demonstrating that among other things learning by doing, trust between partners, member's involvement, and motivation are necessary prerequisites to foster a culture of learning. The findings of Fey and Birkinshaw (2005) suggest that openness to new ideas emerge as the single most significant predictor of R&D performance, with a direct influence on performance and also with a positive moderating effect on the linkage between partnering and performance. Hagedoorn *et al.* (2006) point out that if a firm is effective in establishing endogenous capabilities, it may steadily develop and enhance its capabilities even more to execute its commercial tasks efficiently and outperform its competitors. Kale and Singh (2007) use survey data from a large sample of US-based enterprises to test their theoretical arguments, that is, the STP learning process acts as one of the primary mechanism through which the STP management function leads to significant STP success. Next,

Huang and Yu's (2011) findings allude that learning in R&D partnerships can profoundly contribute to innovativeness. Companies with better capabilities of acquiring, assimilating, transforming and exploiting knowledge from external sources may better incorporate that attained cognition into novel ideas and solutions. Moreover, Schulze *et al.* (2014) have empirically tested the significance and impact of knowledge transfer to R&D alliances and indicate that disseminative capability leads to enhanced NPD process effectiveness and efficiency. A company can go a step further and codify its accumulated STP management know-how in the form of usable memorised knowledge objects, such as management manuals, guidelines, and checklists that integrate best practices to manage the different phases and decisions in the STP life cycle (Sluyts *et al.,* 2011). Several learning mechanisms can be installed by organisations in which the STP learning mechanisms may include STP training, evaluation tools, or manuals (Draulans *et al.*, 2003; Heimeriks *et al.*, 2009; Heimeriks and Duysters, 2007). Within organisations, it is essential to formalise and transfer the lessons learned and best practices within the organisation. Partnership success rates can be increased through STP evaluations, STP training, and STP specialists hiring and that, especially, when learning by doing has reached its maximum (Draulans *et al.*, 2003). Indeed, a STP department within the organisation may prove to be a repository for the STP best practices learning and stimulation which in return increases the success of alliances (Kale *et al.*, 2002).

3.2.3 Organisational Capabilities

Organisations may accumulate an extensive range of competencies over time which induce the competitive edge, and, as such, recognising and quantifying organisational capabilities have turned into a fundamental part of several research endeavours (cf. Vilkamo and Keil, 2003). Following Pennings and Harrianto (1992) organisations are repositories of routines. In their case study of a chemical company, Trott *et al.* (1995) argue that mechanisms, such as an 'open' and informal style of management, creation of enthusiasm, sense of excitement, 'spirit' within the business, good working relationships, fostering mutual respect and credibility, the provision of extensive library facilities, and favourable operating environment lead to greater competitiveness. Their conclusions hint at the importance of non-formalised "activities and effective communications between credible boundary-spanning individuals for the assimilation of new knowledge" (p. 38). In their empirical research Deeds *et al.* (1999) show that those organisational capabilities that constitute the competitive edge are not 'simple' resources, but collected resource arrangements which shape in the long run and are characterised by path dependency. Accordingly, Sivadas and Dwyer (2000) using survey questionnaires have studied semiconductor and healthcare alliances and propose that organisational routines and procedures, such as clarity of agreement or clear-cut agreements, engaging in mutually dependent partnerships, fostering clan and formalised relationships, cooperative competency, institutional support, standardisation of processes, and the use of formalised control may all lead to higher innovation success. Kim and Song (2007) emphasise that the organisational capabilities required for the design and generation of new technology typically becomes embodied in a range of company routines which then form and frame further decision-making regarding technology development. As a result, organisational capabilities have been considered as a set of valuable assets and competencies (Wang and Ahmed, 2007). For STP organisational capabilities to work out, the involvement of the top management team is extremely crucial. They have the ability to provide extensive support to the system, and may eventually enhance the STP performance of the organisation at large (Sluyts *et al.*, 2011). With close top management commitment, innovative culture, and openness, it is possible to motivate individuals to share their experiences and thoughts. The STP performance of the organisation can also be enhanced by investing in deliberate organisational tools for developing the required STP capabilities (McGrath and O'Toole, 2013).

3.2.4 Network, alliance, and partnership Capabilities

Closer collaboration, more effective and efficient partnerships as pioneered by Toyota and Japanese firms, in general, tend to pay off considerably. Following

Ingham and Mothe (1998), companies that build capabilities to manage their external STP are perceived to outperform their competitors when it comes to lowering transaction costs, improving the flexibility of their collaborative relationships, and reducing their dependence on the market environment. Duysters *et al.* (1999) outline that the required alliance capabilities should be tailored to the particular overall strategy of a company. As a result, they have designed a framework that puts emphasis on the need for a balanced alliance portfolio management, building business communities with partners, establishing adequate collaboration capabilities, improved partner selection, sharing of risks, setting clear goals for the alliance, and policies designed by the board. Moreover, the results of Kale *et al.* (2002) suggest that firms that invest in an alliance management function to oversee and coordinate a firm's overall STP activity can enhance the probability of success. For example, *BMW* has appointed a department "Strategic Cooperation Partnerships" with its staff and resources. Ultimately, having such a function can improve firms' alliance abilities in terms of identifying appropriate alliance partners, screening alliance partners more efficiently, and attracting alliance partners that are more robust and compatible (Kale and Singh, 2007). In their longitudinal study employing secondary database research, Hagedoorn *et al.* (2006) found statistical evidence for the role of various networking capabilities in the biotechnology industry. Next, Ettlie and Pavlou (2006) showed that interfirm partnership capabilities, such as intensive interactions are significantly related to critical NPD success outcomes. Rothaermel and Deeds (2006) have empirically investigated the relationship between alliance-specific and firm-level factors on a high-technology partnership alliance management capability within a longitudinal study on a sample of 325 global biotechnology firms. Indeed, the results demonstrate that those firms with greater STP experience achieve higher levels of NPD. Similarly, Kalaignanam *et al.* (2007) in their longitudinal research on larger and smaller firms involved in new technology alliances – adopting the event study methodology on data encompassing 167 asymmetric alliances in the ICT industry – figured out that the greater the STP experience the greater the rentability of the organisations. Equally, Heimeriks and Duysters (2007) surveyed 2600 alliances and found supporting evidence for their hypothesis, stating that a company's alliance capability is positively related to its alliance performance, in particular regarding sales figures. Moreover, using data from longitudinal case studies of three companies in the packaging machine industry, Lorenzoni and Lipparini (1999) studied the beneficial ability to coordinate competencies and pool knowledge across companies. Schreiner *et al.* (2009) investigated the influence of alliance management capability on relevant alliance outcomes and advise that companies achieve greater joint action and fulfilment of key strategic goals within a partnership. Besides, Cassiman *et al.* (2009), after having conducted a case study of a microelectronics company, confirm that alliance capability is hard to imitate, nourishing competitive advantage in innovativeness over time. Counting on data from 105 R&D partnership engagements in the global telecommunication industries, Feller *et al.* (2013) assume that the development of alliance capabilities requires joint learning and the continuous developing of routines and mechanisms to accrue, store, assimilate and disseminate relevant knowledge. Häussler and Higgins (2014) conducted a survey of biotechnology firms and found that superior alliance performance emanates from STP capabilities. As a result, they contend that the ability to interrelate with other firms exhibits relevant positive effects on firm growth and innovativeness. Not surprisingly, since alliance experience constitutes an important antecedent for building and developing network and collaborative know-how (Anand and Khanna, 2000; Heimeriks and Duysters, 2007; Hoang and Rothaermel, 2005; Kale *et al.*, 2002).

3.2.5 Technological, innovative, and internal Capabilities

The received acumen on inter-firm capabilities subliminally supposes that the acquisition of technology-based capabilities is a necessary and desired outcome of cross-company collaboration. Hagedoorn and Schakenraad (1994) results indicate that firms attracting technology through their alliances and businesses focusing on R&D cooperation have noteworthy higher rates of revenue. Two years later, Powell *et al.* (1996) tested hypotheses on a sample of purposive biotechnology companies and claimed that multifunctional teams, formal repositories, powerful task forces, informal seminars, and exercising of routines led to novel innovations and the generation of products, and thus in turn to higher sales. Next, using secondary database research from partners in bilateral STPs, Mowery *et al.* (1996) propose among other things that developing and maintaining active environmental scanning, the possession of relevant technical skills that facilitate inward technology transfer, and overlapping technological capabilities are the foundations for successful innovation. Similarly, Deeds *et al.* (1999) who analysed the relationship between companies' product development capabilities and firm performance concluded that both research capabilities and the capabilities of the R&D team are of paramount importance for the organisation's ability to absorb, disseminate, and exploit research being executed externally. Accordingly, Lanctot and Swan (2000) stated in their study that the degree of appropriability, the dominance of the product design, as well as the complementary of assets directly impact business performance in a positive manner. Likewise, Lee *et al.* (2001), who examined the influence of internal capabilities in combination with external networks on firm performance by surveying 137 Korean technological start-up companies, revealed that several interaction terms between internal capabilities and external partnership connections had a statistically significant effect on performance leading to firm growths and high returns. Bayona (2001) on the other hand, affirmed that firms with individual internal capacities in R&D have a higher probability of realising cooperative R&D. Hence, maintaining technological capability has a major importance for global competitiveness since those capabilities deal with the specific competence and skills concerning the development and introduction of novel products and services (Hagedoorn and Duysters, 2002). Caloghirou *et al.*'s (2004) results from their evaluations express a solid positive linkage between the R&D intensity and innovation output. Furthermore, their results indicate that internal capabilities, as well as openness towards new ways of thinking and knowledge sharing, are essential for enhancing innovative performance. Ways of improving internal capabilities include, for instance, training and development of human skills, and efforts for establishing interaction mechanisms. Using an unusually comprehensive panel database of pharmaceutical companies over a 22-year period

(1980–2001), Rothaermel and Hess (2007) posit that a proliferation in the degree of intellectual human capital results in a commensurate increase in R&D capability. According to Häussler *et al.* (2012), those capabilities are knowledge-based and lie upon companies' prior experiences and learning processes, whereby in high technology industries this capacity is typically manifested in a company's scientific skills, know-how, and competencies. Hence, they hypothesise that the impact of STP on product development is determined by the degree of specialisation and on the organisation's technological capabilities. Häussler *et al.* (2012) are in line with Feller *et al.* (2013), who employ a mixed-method approach and conclude that, for companies operating in chaotic business environments, viable competitive advantage largely derive from their technological capability. Table V-3 evaluates each of the 65 selected journal articles from 1992 to mid 2014, as well as the frequency of each of the STP categories.

Author(s)	Year	Journal (abbreviation)	STP Capability categories				
			(1)	(2)	(3)	(4)	(5)
Overall results	**65**		**12**	**13**	**12**	**23**	**31**
Ahuja	2000	SMJ					x
Bayona *et al.*	2011	RP					x
Caloghirou *et al.*	2004	TNV					x
Cassiman *et al.*	2009	LRP			x		x
Carr	1999	RDM					x
Capaldo	2005	SMJ				x	x
Cui *et al.*	2002	RDM					x
Deeds *et al.*	1999	JBV	x		x		x
De Man and Duysters	2005	TNV				x	
Duysters *et al.*	1999	RDM				x	x
Duysters *et al.*	2012	EMIR				x	x
Ettlie and Pavlo	2006	DS			x	x	
Faems *et al.*	2010	JIM				x	x
Feller *et al.*	2013	OS				x	x

Author(s)	Year	Journal (abbreviation)	STP Capability categories				
			(1)	(2)	(3)	(4)	(5)
Fey and Birkinshaw	2005	JOM		x			x
Forrest and Martin	1992	RDM			x		
Hagedoorn and Duysters	2002	JMS					x
Hagedoorn and Schakenraad	1994	SMJ					x
Hagedoorn *et al.*	2006	BJM		x		x	
Häusler & Higgins	2012	JEMS					x
Häussler *et al.*	2014	JBV				x	x
Heimeriks & Duysters	2007	JOM				x	
Heimeriks *et al.*	2009	LRP				x	
Huang and Yu	2011	JTT		x			x
Ingham and Mothe	2002	RDM		x			
Kalaignanam *et al.*	2007	MS				x	
Kale and Singh	2007	SMJ	x			x	
Kale *et al.*	2002	SMJ				x	
Ketchen *et al.*	2007	SEJ		x	x		x
Kim and Song	2007	TNV			x		
Lanctot and Swan	2000	JIM					x
Lee *et al.*	2001	SMJ					x
Li *et al.*	2008	AMJ					x
Lorenzoni and Lipparini	1999	SMJ		x		x	
Malik	2002	TNV	x		x		x
Miotti and Sachwald	2003	RP		x			x
Mitrega *et al.*	2012	IMM					
Mowery *et al.*	1996	SMJ		x		x	
Noseleit and de Faria	2013	JBR	x				
Pennings and Harianto	1992	OS			x		
Phelps	2010	AMJ	x				
Phene and Tallman	2010	AMJ		x	x		
Powell *et al.*	1996	ASQ		x			x

Author(s)	Year	Journal (abbreviation)	STP Capability categories (1)	(2)	(3)	(4)	(5)
Ritala *et al.*	2009	IJIM					x
Rothaermel	2001	SMJ					x
Rothaermel and Deeds	2006	JBV				x	
Rothaermel and Hess	2007	OS					x
Sampson	2007	AMJ	x	x			
Santangelo	2000	RP	x				
Sarkar *et al.*	2009	OS				x	
Saxton	1997	AMJ	x				
Schilke & Görzen	2010	JOM				x	
Schreiner *et al.*	2009	SMJ				x	
Schulze *et al.*	2014	JPIM		x			
Siu and Bao	2008	JPIM				x	
Sivadas and Dwyer	2000	JM			x	x	
Sluyts *et al.*	2011	IMM				x	
Steensma and Corley	2000	AMJ					x
Tidd	2014	IJIM	x				
Trott *et al.*	1995	TNV		x	x		
Un *et al.*	2010	JPIM	x				
Vilkamo and Keil	2003	TNV	x				
Zhang and Baden-Fuller	2010	JMS					x
Zhou and Li	2008	JIBS					x
Zollo *et al.*	2002	OS	x		x		

Table V-3: Evaluation of the 65 selected journal articles from 1992 to mid 2014.
Source: Own illustration.

4 Discussion

The SLR at hand puts forward that concepts of STP capabilities have not been clearly defined yet. The same observation was already made more than one decade ago by Hafeez *et al.* (2002). But what happens if an organisation does not possess distinctive capabilities? Briefly speaking, it is no more able to differentiate itself positively along any magnitude that is vital to its customers than the average of its competitors. If an industry is at a deadlock and none of its opponents has a significant focal point, then the benefits of the business will settle at the level of industry average standard (Porter, 1998). In the more probable occasion that diverse contenders have realised distinctive capabilities and can offer better quality, more reliable service, or more sophisticated products, then an organisation has no plan of action, however, to bring down its costs to balance the absence of advantages (Day, 1994). Thus, we may assume an existing direct relationship between the mastery of capabilities and superior market performance.

The results of the SLR at hand show that publications on STP capabilities have gradually increased over the last two decades and reached a peak in 2007. Since 2013, we can observe an upward trend with already three articles published in the first quarter of 2014. The articles reviewed examine a broad variety of issues and employ various research methodologies. Concerning the latter, the methodological approach is shifting away from case studies to the application of large-scale, multiple-industry dataset proofs. In particular, the majority of papers focuses on theory testing and is based on secondary databases and surveys/questionnaires. Considering the fact that between 2011 and 2014 only quantitative papers were published, the topic may need more qualitative research to explore new insights. However, we observe a lack of multiple methods – only one of the selected articles focused on the propandagised mixed-method theory (cf. Feller *et al.*, 2013). Another interesting aspect relates to the reflection that present empirical studies on STP frequently study capabilities at a static point in time. Therefore, longitudinal studies can significantly contribute to the evolution of STP capabilities since capability development (such as by investing in R&D) does not necessarily produce immediate performance effects (McGrath and O'Toole, 2013). Additionally, longitudinal studies may highlight how organisations implement STP structures, improve information tools and processes, share knowledge among organisations, focus on collaborated goals, and stimulate common understanding over time (Niesten and Jolink, 2014). Given the path- and time-dependent nature of capabilities and the fact that they evolve over time, it is meaningful to examine the impact of capabilities on long-term performance. This can be measured by the organisation's key (both financial and market) performance indicators in comparison to its main competitors or the industry average over a period of five to ten years (Duysters *et al.*, 2012; Wang and Ahmed, 2007). Likewise, previous works by Powell *et al.* (1996) and Teece *et al.* (1997) illustrate the complexity of capability development which does not happen automatically and takes time to build. This will facilitate cross-comparison of research findings and thus enhance the 'collective power' of research outcomes.

The examination of the 65 journal articles revealed 38 different STP capabilities and points to a lack of consistency that might hinder the understanding of the necessary capabilities to form successful STPs. In response, we grouped and synthesised the different unique capabilities into five STP core capabilities. Most of the journal articles focus on three STP capabilities, namely (1) technological, innovative, and internal capabilities (31 out of 65 articles), (2) network, alliance, and partnership capabilities (23 out of 65 articles), (3) learning and exploitation capabilities (13 out of 65 articles). Many of the articles in the first group investigate the 'technological, innovative, and internal capabilities' in combination with 'complementary capabilities' or 'network, alliance, and partnership capabilities' and how it impacts STP success, in particular regarding the level of innovativeness. Surprisingly, complementary capabilities and organisational capabilities (each 12 out of 65 articles) received the lowest frequency rate among the reviewed journal articles. Although several researchers emphasise the importance of organisational capabilities and consider it as an accumulation of assets and competencies over time being a major predictor of competitiveness, we notice that this capability area was given less attention than the other two ones. The rising interest in these topics underlines the strategic importance of fostering the required capabilities to manage successfully technology partnership and in turn boost performance. Furthermore, it provides evidence for the significance of the topic and its related issues and proposes a direction towards more publications in the identified STP capabilities categories.

5 Conclusion

The objectives of this article were to review the existing research on STP capabilities, to organise major findings and to develop a research agenda by identifying existing gaps in the current understanding and highlighting future research opportunities. Over the last two decades, research on STP and its related issues have received increased devotion in a broad range of prominent business- and management-related academic journals. In this paper, we analysed STP capability issues over the last two decades. The topic's significance is due to various industrial trends at this time: globalisation of markets and business activities, fast technological changes, increased time-to-market, and increased customer expectations, just to name a few (e.g. Eden et al., 2008; Park et al., 2004; van de Vrande et al., 2011). Furthermore, the number of international STPs has increased during the last two decades because they have become a major opportunity for acquiring and developing technological assets (Li et al., 2008; Narula and Duysters, 2004). Extant research has suggested that firms are motivated to enter STP, for instance, to accrue and gain market power (e.g. Grant and Baden-Fuller, 2004), to share and reduce risks (e.g. Hagedoorn et al., 2006), for cost-economising reasons (Kim and Song, 2007), to establish new skills and competencies (Meier, 2011), to access new technologies (Huang and Yu, 2011), to boost innovativeness (Phelps, 2010) and to foster NPD (e.g. Noseleit and de Faria, 2013). The growing devotion given to STP capabilities, in various economic and management contexts, has developed more rapidly than the general exhaustive understanding of how such settings function. Our research was driven by the overall main question: Why do some organisations have greater, overall STP success than other organisations? In response, we conducted an SLR to contribute towards a better understanding of the key factors of STP capabilities issues in existing academic studies. In our classificatory framework, we identify five core capabilities that helped us organise and structure the literature landscape on STP capabilities.

5.1 Managerial implications

Organisations require tangible and intangible resources to manage competition in the markets, and through strategic networks it is possible to attain them. Thus, entrepreneurs and practising managers must recognise their importance. In the contemporary world today, STPs are a part of the daily business activities and not an unusual event that can be overlooked (Bamford and Ernst, 2002). STPs cannot be managed sufficiently and efficiently through ad hoc decisions. We agree with Hafeez *et al.* (2002) that capabilities are formed through the assimilation and steerage of procedures and activities. The findings of this SLR extend what studies in related research streams have been advocating: in order to leave behind their competitors, companies must cultivate the ability to adjust and share their practices with their partners (Bruderer and Singh, 1996; Heimeriks *et al.*, 2007; Teece *et al.*, 1997). The competitive advantage and performance of an organisation are based on the business networks and relationships of the organisation. This is a key asset according to the managerial implications of the present findings (Palmatier *et al.*, 2008). The maximum value of STPs can be extracted through systematic management routines. Organisations engaged in strategic technology partnerships can benefit from the specific management routines resulting from history, experiences, and collective learning within the company. Toyota's manufacturing capability is such an example that shows that capabilities are deeply embedded in the organisational activities, procedures and operational processes (Hafeez *et al.*, 2002).

From a managerial perspective, organisations need to engage in the development and enhancement of their STP portfolio performance for which the present paper has highlighted the importance of STP capabilities. It may also be beneficial for organisations to establish alignments with those partners who are already STP capable. Hence, the identified STP core capabilities may also be applied to assess the criteria in choosing the potential strategic technology partners (Schilke and Görzen, 2010). The STP management process should be managed efficiently, and a strong focus should be devoted to the management to improve the STP performance throughout the lifecycle of the STP. The STP manager plays a vital role in updating and implementing relevant and appropriate mechanisms. Knowledge sharing initiatives must be encouraged by those managers as they may act as the central knowledge stock. The top management team involvement is essential at all levels; they must be committed to the STPs of the organisation at all times, and this commitment must be shown eagerly (Ritala *et al.*, 2009). This activity requires that STP management is regarded as a separate function such as finance and marketing (Dyer *et al.*, 2001). Establishing an STP community within the organisation that exchanges best practices and provides practical tools in which the organisational knowledge is codified in is of paramount importance to make the most of previous STP relationships. The existing knowledge can be dispersed using codification tools like guidelines, databases, checklists and manuals which help replicate the best practices within the organisation. Moreover, through sharing mechanisms, such as workshops, seminars, task forces, job rotation or, employees are motivated to exchange best-practices, STP-related data and information, and know-how to their colleagues (Heimeriks *et al.*, 2009). Assembling best-practices in manuals, offering a few principles on the most proficient method to handle certain STP procedures or enabling job-rotations turn out to be more effective than attempting to get individuals to lucid their insight through authority briefings or reports (Sluyts *et al.*, 2011).

Evaluations must be carried out by organisations to realise if they use their STP experience to expand and leverage knowledge across the organisation. Furthermore, firms must set their priorities in which STP capabilities are to be invested (Schilke and Görzen, 2010). The STP capabilities inventory provided through the CLONT-framework can help firms evaluate the different solutions that may help increase the efficiency of their STPs. Hence, it is required that the organisation analyses and implements capabilities, processes and routines that are needed to enhance those business relationships (Mitrega *et al.*, 2012). All in all, the findings of the study at hand may function as a valuable premise for determining choices as to which capabilities management should centre its consideration on to boost the performance of its organisation.

5.2 Limitations and future research

The present literature study is a state-of-the-art systematic review on existing STP knowledge, contributing to a better understanding of its research discipline and illustrating the high relevance of STP capabilities. There are three ways through which the research contributes towards the STP capability literature. Firstly, the review part of the paper at hand represents the first systematic effort to organise the STP capabilities academic literature to help gain a deeper knowledge of STP capabilities and their relevant outcome. Secondly, we provide a classificatory framework that distinguishes and categorises STP capabilities as researched in the relevant literature. Thirdly, based on the contributions to the STP capabilities, we can offer several recommendations for future research on STP. Although built on a literature review, the analysis offers some implications for the further investigation.

We have to note, however, that the present study like every research faces limitations. Firstly, although an SLR is an effective instrument for offering a comprehensive overview by further structuring, refining, and clustering the existing knowledge on a specified topic (Müller-Seitz, 2012; Nijmeijer *et al.*, 2014) the process did not allow to explore deeply each article. Consequently, additional research in this field is needed to further develop our understanding of the STP phenomenon. Several researchers suggest undertaking multimethod studies that combine the strengths of different methods in a series of projects that build on one another (e.g. Creswell and Tashakori, 2007; Feller *et al.*, 2013; Siu and Bao, 2008). A mixed methods research design may positively influence the methodological rigour of a research study since considering both quantitative and qualitative evaluations may deliver a more complete and broader picture (Arora and Stoner, 2009). With respect to STP capabilities, qualitative, exploratory and studies are useful in enrichening the understanding of the complex relationship between STP capabilities and performance (Niesten and Jolink, 2014) while quantitative studies allow for generalisable interferences. Therefore, further qualitative, explorative research on STP, such as case studies and secondary data, in combination with quantitative methods, is needed to better explore specific STP capabilities-performance link issues. This allows exploiting the 'best of both worlds' with an emphasis on international comparative studies, given the inevitable progress of globalisation (Brannen, 2005; Molina-Azorin, 2010). In this context, it would be fruitful for future research to examine inter-industry differences as it constitutes an essential next stage in the STP research sphere (Sivakumar *et al.*, 2011). The next research suggestion is related to the observation that current empirical research frequently studies STP at a particular point in time. Longitudinal research may positively contribute to the study of the evolution of STP by accentuating how companies that implement processes, tools, and structures to develop knowledge and information sharing encourage a common understanding and a clear, long-term focus on combined goals (Kilubi, 2015).

Secondly, we propose several more specific prospects for further research on the identified capabilities based on our review of the literature. To begin with, future research should seek to study the impact of each category of STP capability on performance more systematically based on our proposed CLONT-framework. The causal relationships between the STP capabilities and its resources could be made stronger through future empirical analysis. In addition to that, future studies can advance beyond the effect of STP capabilities on dyadic relationships and analyse the effect of STP between multiple organisations in a company's partnership portfolio (Sarkar *et al.,* 2009). Through future insights, it may also be possible to analyse the impact of STPs upon other attributes, such as complementary resources, partners opportunistic behaviour and trust. We consider the category of complementary capabilities to be a future fundamental requirement for fruitful STP performance in a globalised business world. Since this capability has received less attention in the extant strategic and innovation management literature, a call for more research in this field is in line with other researchers (e.g. Bertrand and Meschi, 2005; Jolink and Niesten, 2012).

An interesting starting point is a research by Davis and Eisenhardt (2011), which demonstrates that alliances generate more new products when associates cooperatively amend STP objectives in a variation of time. Secondly, it is also important to analyse whether an STP can possess multiple capabilities and still excel in all these capabilities. This may help increase our appreciation of the meaning of the diversity of capabilities for the success and survival of STPs (Häussler *et al.*, 2012). More specifically, Noseleit and de Faria (2013) argue that internal R&D efforts become more productive when engaging in STPs in which partners within the same industry or related industries rule – whereupon this effect is stronger when collaborating with companies in related industries. Additionally, they propose future investigations of the positive effects of STP portfolios on company's innovativeness could also advantage from bearing in mind complementarities between STPs and internal R&D efforts. Future research on STP portfolio diversity could profit from taking into account the notion of similar and dissimilar variety (Phene and Tallman, 2012). These findings emphasise the resource-based argument that as companies concurrently collaborate with different types of partners they are more likely to access a wide diversity of capabilities which in turn enhances their internal innovation capabilities (Phelps, 2010; Un *et al.* 2010). In this way, these data may assist the contemporary open innovation paradigm that highlights the impact of external collaboration on internal innovation activities (Faems *et al.*, 2010). Thirdly, several researchers strongly advise authors to perform research on the significance of learning and exploitation in STPs (cf. Harvey and Richey, 2001). This is in line with Beamish and Lupton (2009) who found that the two most cited articles on STP performance examine transfer and learning in STP (Inkpen and Beamish, 1997; Mowery *et al.*, 1996). Likewise, Hagedoorn (1993), as well as Vilkamo and Keil (2003) state that one group of motives for entering a STP is the advancement of research and knowledge diffusion. To gain a better understanding of learning and exploitation capabilities, we encourage future research endeavours to evaluate and compare different practices and techniques with the purpose of exploring and portraying best practices. Thus, future studies are expected to create important measurements of knowledge generation and implementation alongside prevalent constructs of knowledge transfer.

Against this background, we call for the development of quantitative approaches, such as surveys or experiments, to measure, assess, train, and maintain learning and exploitation capabilities of STP partners over time (Andersén, 2011; Schulze *et al.*, 2014). Such measurement constructs may assist to advance further our understanding of how organisations create, accumulate, acquire and exert knowledge in STPs. Schreiner *et al.* (2009) emphasise that the balance between tacit and explicit knowledge needs to be an integral part of a company's decision calculus when it resorts valuable assets for collaborative technology activities. Given that R&D partnerships may add to resource setups in an alternate manner than other forms of strategic partnerships (Eisenhardt and Schoonhoven, 1996), future research should apply our framework to production and marketing alliances, too (Schilke and Görzen, 2010).

In conclusion, the present paper contributes a structured overview of 65 academic peer-reviewed articles from 1992 to the beginning of 2014. The systematic review groups and synthesises the various STP capabilities into five core capabilities and provides a classificatory STP framework, referred to as CLONT-framework and indicates gaps in the literature to target for further scientific development. A considerable stream of research has focused on identifying capabilities beneficial to superior STP performance. Still, substantial fragmentation in empirical study outcomes has restricted theory development and the progression of managerial practice in this significant research field. As a result, the paper's main contribution was to synthesise this multidisciplinary literature by the means of a classificatory framework to provide an enhanced understanding of the interconnected capabilities of STP. The second contribution is the application of a transparent and rigorous review method followed by an analytical synthesis. Newbert (2007) suggests that a systematic framework is necessary to avoid potential subjective bias. Systematic reviews are still relatively rare in literature studies; thus, promoting SLRs to academic reviews assists to develop a higher standard of scientific rigor.

Thirdly, the systematic literature review at hand has the potential to contribute substantially to the current literature both in appraising the existing state of STP and in providing a platform for future developments in the research field. As such, the present SLR delivers valuable insights into the development of the research disciplines and indicates at which points further research is required on the significant topic of STP capabilities. We hope that the present SLR review is stimulating, thought-provoking, and informative for both researchers and practitioners who have an interest in this highly relevant research discipline.

Chapter VI

Bridging the gap between supply chain risk management and strategic technology partnering – insights from two theoretical lenses

Abstract

When companies have to create innovations with new products to remain globally competitive, they also need to consider potential risks in selected supply chain (SC) areas. Hence, the purpose of the paper at hand is to explore the causal nexus of relationships linking supply chain risk management (SCRM) and strategic technology partnering (STP). Through the integration of two complementary theories, namely the resource–based view of the firm (RBV) and the social capital theory (SCT), we examine capabilities that may influence cooperating firms to rely more on STP to mitigate supply chain risks (SCRs). Hence, we use conceptual theory building to create a conceptual framework and to guide future investigation through research propositions. It is proposed that successful SCs operating within STPs are better equipped to handle SCRs. Several SCRM–STP capabilities have been identified in this conceptual paper. However, their mutual links, as well as their links with the three dimensions of social capital, namely structural, cognitive, and relational along with the notion of the RBV, need to be further empirically tested. The present research focuses on the effort to ease bridging the gap between two principal research disciplines and to highlight the potential value of STP and SCRM to manage risks, disruptions and uncertainties. We contribute to the development of the emerging theories of SCRM and STP by integrating notions from the RBV of the firm, the SCT, as well as supply chain management (SCM) and strategic management.

1 Introduction

In the light of the dynamism and intricacy of the current business environment, supply chain risks (SCRs) now represent a notable threat to firms (e.g. Braunscheidel and Suresh, 2009; Christoph and Holweg, 2011; Talluri *et al.*, 2013; Wieland and Wallenburg, 2012). There are numerous and various consequences resulting from SCRs that can be divided into: supply and demand risks, reduction in product quality, reduced service levels, delivery delays, high recovering costs, a negative corporate image, reputation loss, damage to security and health, or financial deficits (Blackhurst *et al.*, 2005; Tang and Tomlin, 2008; Trkman and McCormack, 2009; Tummala and Schönherr, 2001). As our world becomes more and more disordered and turbulent, the management of risks will play a more significant role in both global supply chain (SC) network design and daily operating decision–making. Thus, a better understanding of what accounts for an adequate risk management approach is required (Fawcett *et al.*, 2011). In the same line, it is essential for firms to develop specific organisational capabilities to deliver countermeasures to diverse adversities. For the purpose of this paper, and in accordance with Dosi and Teece (1998, p. 284), we define capabilities as "the reflection of a company's ability to "organize, manage, coordinate, or govern sets of activities". Along these lines, firm capabilities can be associated with several competitive objectives, such as profitable new market entry, lean and agile supply chain management (SCM), effective new product development, excellence in manufacturing technology, etc. Interfirm partnerships may be useful in accomplishing these focused goals through asset exchanges and inter–organisational synergies (Dyer and Hatch, 2006). Nowadays, firms are working increasingly in network environments. By this progress, the network perspective has turned out to be more imperative in supply chain risk management (SCRM) and academic research (Borgatti and Li, 2009; Kim *et al.*, 2011). In addition, social capital that analyses the value actors may derive from their network ties has become increasingly popular in supply chain–related research (Autry and Griffis, 2008; Carter *et al.*, 2007).

Reichhart and Holweg (2007) are of the opinion that uncertainty contributes to processes being inflexible and unresponsive to situational parameters. Supply, demand and technology uncertainty are the three dimensions of environmental uncertainty through which the model set by Chen and Paulraj (2004) is examined and tested. In line with input by Mentzer *et al.* (2001), Terpend *et al.* (2008) elaborated the concepts focusing on how cooperation seemingly impacts risk management and how risks were advised to be shared between the SC actors to decrease uncertainties. In light of this view, it is required to understand how organisations can achieve as well as maintain their competitive advantage. In the present study, we argue that companies engaged in strategic technology partnerships (STP) are better able to mitigate and respond to supply chain risks since uncertainty can be managed through cooperation (Spekman *et al.*, 1998). We focus on creative solutions on how to react to SC disturbances which merit more consideration (Bode *et al.*, 2011). On the basis of conventional and emerging literature, we suppose that both STP and SCRM are critical success factors for company performance and can be seen as massive empowering agents. More precisely, we advocate that the capabilities needed for STP serve as enablers for effective SCRM. This paper focuses on the fusion of the two research streams SCRM and STP as an innovative solution to an ever changing world in the industry environment. Considering the significance of both SCRM and STP as competitive features in turbulent and dynamic market conditions, it is to some degree astounding that the link between these two essential factors has not been sufficiently focused on so far (Bierly *et al.*, 2014). The authors devote to the following main research question: How can the integration of STP and SCRM effectively be used to manage successfully supply chain risks? Stated, the purpose of this analysis is to examine the nexus of linkages between SCRM and STP. Schmenner *et al.* (2009) indicate the necessity for deconstructing theories to build new and superior theories; hence, we use conceptual theory building to create a conceptual framework.

First, we briefly outline the background of our research and provide the theoretical foundations for our propositions. Both the RBV of the firm and the SCT, serving as a theoretical basis, encourage the dialogue between SCRM and STP and inform the generation of the designed conceptual framework. Lastly, conclusions will be drawn where the theoretical implications along with the limitations and future research directions are outlined.

2 Background of the research

Technological innovation, product development networks, distribution or marketing networks and supplier networks belong to STP that exist within inter–organisation networks (Möller and Svahn, 2003). For a long time, a firm's capability to quickly address disruptions has been recognised as being essential for long-term survival and success of the firm (Child, 1972): for easily changing demand cycles and surviving lagging (Fisher, 1997), and greater responsiveness to uncertainty (Stevens and Dimitriadis, 2004). A SC system includes several actors and approaches that include various propensities of risks and vulnerabilities (Hearnshaw and Wilson, 2013) and also tight connections and complex interlinks between these actors and approaches. As a result, SCs become very vulnerable to different risks that could arise from a single or more than one participant and undertakings (Golgeci and Ponomarov, 2013). Hence, it is essential to analyse the role innovativeness plays in common performance results (Hult *et al.*, 2004b), and it is equally important to take into account the increased significance of dealing with major difficulties and disruptions. Disruptions, but also enduring or unexpected adverse events of different intensities and types can occur in almost every SC (Khan *et al.*, 2012). In this context, supply chain resilience has come up as an important capability that is required for companies and their SCs (Golgeci and Ponomarov, 2013).

There can be considerable negative effects of disruptions and risks in SCs for a firm (Hearnshaw and Wilson, 2013). Therefore, Ponomarov and Holcomb (2009) claim that understanding the abilities that lead to a firm's SCR becomes highly important in disruptive and uncertain situations. Consequently, firm innovativeness could be developed, applied, and used to overcome damaging and adverse events that occur in the SC of a firm. Usually, innovative firms have increased opportunities for implementing innovative solutions to be used to neutralise, limit or defeat negative effects of uncertain events that occur in their SCs. Moreover, observing a rare disruptive occurrence raises the perception of its possibility (Tversky and Kahneman, 1973). For that reason, it is important for firms to exhibit innovativeness in the face of uncertain occurrences in the SCs. Subsequently, it is essential for a firm to have the capability to quickly develop ideas to solve problems and to ensure the application of ideas so that long-term solutions against risks could be achieved in times of adversities and disruptions in supply chains (Mitroff and Alpaslan, 2003). Moreover, the delivery of countermeasures to risks requires enthusiasm and vigilance, and it could involve a series of proactive approaches to prevent being in an undesirable situation in the course of disruptions and disasters (Ponomarov and Holcomb, 2009).

The interrelationships exhibited by the principal constructs about the multiple domains at varying levels should be considered regarding their impact on quality, costs, flexibility, and delivery (Narasimhan, 2014). Superior customer value and lower relative cost position may not be mutually exclusive. A strategic, positional advantage can be gained from a high competitive environment, superior product differentiation like superior product quality and fast responsiveness (Lanctot and Swan, 2000). "[…] there is a trend toward changing the locus of innovation in the sector of the economy, moving upstream in the supply chain from assembly (buyer) firms like General Motors Corporation and Toyota to first–tier suppliers like Delphi and Visteon" (Ettlie and Pavlou, 2006, pp. 126–127). The difficulties and disturbances as part of the SC are managed through the creative ability of an organisation since they must continue with their value offerings in an efficient manner (Ketchen and Hult, 2007). It is highly risky to carry out technological innovation and there are only a few products that prove to be promising ideas and finally reach the market as services or products for the customers (Hagedoorn and Duysters, 2002). Hence, the adverse and disruptive incidents faced by firms can be handled through organisational innovativeness using STP. As a result, we provide the first major postulation:

Px: There exists a positive relationship between SCRM and STP.

When the conditions are unfavourable and uncertain, it becomes essential to understand the capabilities that may enhance the performance of the organisation (Ponomarov and Holcomb, 2009). Any disastrous or disruptive issues subjected to the SC of the organisation can benefit from the building, deployment and leverage of organisational innovativeness (Hearnshaw and Wilson, 2013). Figure VI-1 displays the tentative conceptual framework for the SCRM–STP integration. On the left-hand side we have the SCRM domain whereas on the right-hand side we have the STP domain. Both domains have specific capabilities inherent that lead to enhanced organisational performance. Considering the significance of both SCRM and STP as competitive features in turbulent and dynamic market conditions, it is to some degree surprising that the linkage between these two concepts has not been sufficiently researched on so far. To bridge this gap we use theory building to create a conceptual framework that integrates SCRM and STP.

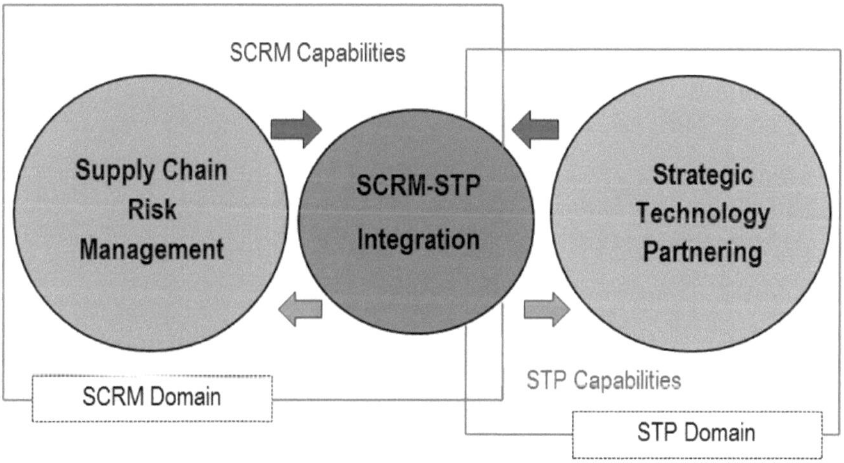

Figure VI-1: A tentative conceptual framework for the SCRM-STP integration.
Source: Own illustration.

3 Theoretical foundations

The concept of STP is usually analysed by researchers by combining two or more theoretical lenses. The resource–based view (RBV) of the firm and the social capital theory (SCT) are the two primary theories integrated into many managerial studies (Ahuja, 2000a; Zaheer and Bell, 2005). They have the ability to explain a vast spectrum of concepts present in research trends and reduce the gap between research paradigms (Di Guardo and Harrigan, 2012). Hence, the RBV and the SCT are the two complementary theoretical bases used to explore the nexus of SCRM and STP in the present study. Within strategic management, the RBV is considered most dominant (Barney and Mackey, 2005; Newbert, 2007). The strategic management initiative of RBV revolves around performing better than the competitors and achieving a competitive advantage. Thus, the internal resources such as human, organisational, intangible, technological, physical and financial resources are the competitive advantages of an organisation as part of the classical RBV (Fey and Birkinshaw, 2005; Rothaermel and Hess, 2007). Following Rindova and Fombrun (1999, p. 694), the RBV "attributes advantage in an industry to a firm's control over bundles of unique material, human, organisational and locational resources and skills that enable unique value–creating strategies". Therefore, the resources of a firm are considered to be a wellspring to the extent that they are valuable, rare, distinct, uncommon, and hard to copy or substitute (Amit and Schoemaker, 1993; Barney, 1991). The social capital, on the other hand, is considered as the largest growing area of the organisation network research. This concept has been symbiotically able to return the favour and increased interest in social networks (Kim *et al.*, 2011). Social capital describes the benefits that actors can gain from their partnership ties and the network in which they are rooted (Baker, 1990; Burt, 1992; Bourdieu, 1986; Coleman, 1988). For this paper, we embrace a definition of social capital as offered by Nahapiet and Ghoshal (1998), viewed as "the sum of the actual and potential resources embedded within, available through, and derived from the network of relationships possessed by an individual or social unit" (p. 243). The central logic of this perspective can be considered in the example of a company that forms network ties of relationships with other organisations that are valuable resources for the respective company, such as a purchasing contract (Zaheer *et al.*, 2010). Relational ties are formed with stakeholders such as suppliers, government agencies, unions and competitors as part of the relational resource. The existing variations as part of the relational resources are considered a natural outcome of the SC competition (Borgatti and Li, 2009). We demonstrate the significance of merging the two theories of RBV and SCT, while taking into account the inner capabilities of the partners within a network combined with capabilities they exploit from the network structure at the same time. These two underpinning theoretical lenses informing the present study will be elaborated in the following. Table VI-1 provides an overview of the RBV and the SCT in the SCRM and STP context.

Theoretical perspective	SCRM	STP	Author(s) in this issue
Resource–based view	Adopting the RBV perspective, supply chain linkages that ensure quality materials from suppliers to the organisation or the customers show valuable resources and provide the organisation with enhanced performance.	The complementary assets, organisation routines or the skills which are differentiated allow an organisation to manage certain activities that form a competitive advantage basis in several or particular markets. The related capabilities, competencies, and resources are configured together as part of the resource–based view.	Holcomb and Hitt, 2007; Wynstra *et al.*, 2014; Zhang and Dhaliwal, 2009; Eisenhardt and Schoonhoven, 1996; Amit and Schoemaker, 1993; Barratt and Oke, 2007; Lanctot and Swan, 2000; Rungtusanatham *et al.*, 2003; Dyer and Singh, 1998; Steinle and Schiele, 2008; Rothaermel and Hess, 2007; Miotti and Sachwald, 2003; Ketchen and Hult, 2007; Kim and Song, 2007; Noseleit and de Faria, 2013; Phene and Tallman, 2012; Chen *et al.*, 2013; Lorenzoni and Lipparini, 1999; Ettlie and Pavlou, 2006; Huang and Yu, 2011; Lee *et al.*, 2001; Ahuja, 2000a; Dogsen, 1993; Morrow *et al.*, 2005; Kale and Singh, 2007; Tidd, 2014; Trott *et al.*, 1995; Vilkamo *et al.*, 2003; Mowery *et al.*, 1996, Zaheer and Bell, 2005; Barney and Mackey, 2005; Newbert, 2007; Fey and Birkinshaw, 2005; Rindova and

Theoretical perspective	SCRM	STP	Author(s) in this issue
			Fombrun, 1999; Barney, 1991; Wernerfelt, 1984; Peteraf, 1993; Ketchen and Hult, 2007b; Grant, 1991; Lavie, 2006; Zaheer and Bell, 2005
Social Capital Theory	Risks and costs can be reduced through the long–term supply chain effectiveness that has been established through mutually beneficial relationships, shared values, and trust. The social capital is used to strengthen supplier relationships, knowledge transfer promotion and the regional production networks.	According to the social capital theory, the external network of an organisation is an active contributor towards its performance. Quality and price competitive products are created for the customers and for this purpose the organisation transacts with suppliers as well as other partners to attain valuable external resources.	Brass and Burkhardt, 1993; Autry and Griffis, 2008; Krause *et al.*, 2007; Hunt and Davis, 2012; Leenders and Gabbay, 1999; Pennings and Lee, 1999; Pennings *et al.*, 1998; Uzzi, 1996; Vasileiou and Morris, 2006; Granovetter, 1985; Inkpen and Tsang, 2005; Romo and Schwartz, 1995; Johnson *et al.*, 2013; Larson, 1992; Hagedoorn *et al.*, 2006; Carey, *et al.*, 2011; Lee *et al.*, 2001; Borgatti and Foster, 2002; Koka and Prescott, 2002; Lawson *et al.*, 2008; Villena *et al.*, 2011; Mukherjee *et al.*, 2013; Siu and Bao, 2008; Lechner *et al.*, 2010; Parra–Requena *et al.*, 2010; Woolcock, 1998; Zaheer and Bell, 2005; Bourdieu, 1986; Coleman, 1988; Baker, 1990; Burt, 1992; Granovetter, 1985; Nahapiet and Ghoshal, 1998; Bolino *et al.* 2002; Zaheer *et al.*, 2010; Prusak and Cohen, 2001; Lin, 2005; Hogg and Terry, 2000; Tsai and Goshal, 1998; Min *et al.*, 2008; Burt *et al.*, 2000; Powell *et al.*, 1996; Athanassiou and Nigh, 1999; Markovsky *et al.*, 1993; Yli–Renko, 2001; Coleman, 1990; Adler and Kwon, 2002; Oh *et al.*, 2006; Petersen *et al.*, 2008

Table VI-1: Linkage between SCRM and STP through the RBV and the SCT.
Source: Own illustration.

3.1 Integrating SCRM and STP: The Resource–based View

There is a two–fold logic attached to the RBV, which is the reason we have applied it as one of the two theoretical frameworks for the present study. First, the inter–firm relationships are represented by the SC interactions (cf. Carter *et al.*, 2007). The second logic is that other forms of inter–firm relationships like STPs have been also explored with the help of RBV (e.g. Caloghirou *et al.*, 2004; Chen *et al.*, 2013; Huang and Yu, 2011; Kim and Song, 2007; Miotti and Sachwald, 2003; Noseleit and de Faria, 2013; Phene and Tallman, 2012). In this light, R&D co–operation is primarily initiated by firms that are carrying out risky, complex and expensive research projects which are mostly present in the high–technologies industries (Miotti and Sachwald, 2003). However, the classical RBV of the firm has several extensions due to the current dissatisfaction with the purely firm–internal resource perspective (Chisholm and Nielsen, 2009). These theoretical extensions make it possible to view suppliers as a part of firms' valuable resource base (Steinle and Schiele, 2008). Both SC linkages and the connection between the SC entities are regarded as critical. Hence, the operational performance impact of the SC interactions can also be clearly understood through the RBV in a pragmatic and conceptual manner (Barratt and Oke, 2007). The results are not surprising since the resource–based view may be the dominant theoretical standpoint within strategic management (Ketchen *et al.*, 2007), and it represents a central perspective in the research field of entrepreneurship as well (Alvarez and Busenitz, 2001).

Interestingly, Hult *et al.* (2004b) report a significantly high positive relationship between shared meaning and shorter cycle time, proposing that executives should overthink concepts such as quality and speed (e.g. through greater emphasis on information sharing and personal communications) to enhance SC performance. According to Feller *et al.* (2013), new products should be offered to the markets with high levels of flexibility, reliability and speed. Thus, firms should possess the ability to respond in a quick and speedy manner towards updated conditions of the market (Merschmann and Thonemann, 2011). Following Ingham and Mothe (1998), companies that build capabilities to manage their external STP are perceived to leave behind their contenders when it comes to lowering transaction costs, improving the flexibility of their collaborative relationships, and reducing their dependence on the market environment. Enablers towards higher flexibility and greater efficiency through complementary capabilities, mentioned by Vilkamo and Keil (2003), are sharing of risks, shared objectives of partners, and explicit contributions from each partner involved. Tang and Tomlin (2008) have examined the benefits of different flexibility strategies in the SCRM context. They showed that through mitigation of supply, process, and demand risks, most of the benefits are achieved at low levels of flexibility. Braunscheidel and Suresh (2009) show that augmenting SC agility serves as a critical driver for mitigating SCRs. According to them, agility is of value for both response and mitigation strategies, highlighting fast, proactive measures when confronted with SCRs. Wieland and Wallenburg (2013), who collected survey data from 270 manufacturing companies in their empirical study, found that SCRM is necessary for the agility and robustness of a firm to improve performance. Hence, superior performance is maintained upon the specialised capabilities that are attained using external relationships (Morrow *et al.*, 2005; Holcomb and Hitt, 2007).

Alliances contribute to the sharing of risks amongst stakeholders which is related to performance rather than relational aspects (Das, 2001). Aspects of SC flexibility have been evaluated by multiple authors (e.g. Vickery *et al.*, 1999; Sánchez and Pérez, 2005; Swafford *et al.*, 2006) who have concluded that a flexible SC model is quickly able to adapt to changing scenarios. Swafford *et al.* (2006) propose that SC flexibility impacts organisational capability in multiple ways and is demonstrated by the rate in which organisations respond to sudden changes in the market composition. The interrelationships between aspects of the environment, SC, and their impact on firms' processes have been evaluated by Vickery *et al.* (1999) and Sánchez and Pérez (2005), respectively. Direct associations in this regard indicate that high levels of environmental uncertainty contribute to higher degrees of SC flexibility that leads to greater performance efficiency (Merschmann and Thonemann, 2011). Quality and price competitive products are created for the customers, and for this purpose the organisation transacts with suppliers as well as other partners to attain external resources (Burt, 1992; Pennings *et al.*, 1998; Pennings and

Lee, 1999). Following Wheelwright and Clark (1992), new product and process technologies consist of three competitive imperatives for their development; these are speed, quality and efficiency. Likewise, Ketchen and Hult (2007) consider the total value of speed, quality, costs, and flexibility as competitive priorities of best value supply chains. Consequently, we postulate the following:

P1: SCRM in STP leads to reduced supply chain risks of firms through the higher value of competitive priorities (quality, speed, costs, and flexibility).

Powell *et al.* (1996) claim that multifunctional teams and active collaborations in technology with external partners lead to novel innovations and a generation of improved products, and thus in turn to higher sales. Likewise, Lee *et al.* (2001), who examined the influence of internal innovative capabilities in combination with external networks on firm performance, have found a statistically significant effect on performance leading to firm growth and high returns. Furthermore, Faems *et al.* (2010) argue that firms with superior innovation ability yield higher financial rents. This is in line with Feller *et al.* (2013) who conclude that for companies operating in chaotic and risky business environments, viable competitive advantage derive mainly from their technological capability. Notwithstanding, the graveness of disturbances may represent a beneficial effect on the activating of an organisation's responsive innovation capabilities since innovative companies are portrayed as ready to react rapidly and adequately (Craighead *et al.*, 2007a). For that reason, firm innovativeness may be constructed, conveyed, and utilised against troublesome and adverse happenings occurring in the SC network of the organisation. Instinctive, innovative and inventive firms are inclined to embrace creative answers to impede, to hold off, or surmount adverse impacts of unreckoned misfortunes that endanger the efficiency of their SCs (Golgeci and Ponomarov, 2014). Thus, a firm's capacity to develop rapid problem-solving solutions could be obligatory when confronted with SC disruptions. Likewise, firm innovativeness is clearly connected with compelling reaction to exceptional economic changes (Mainela and Puhakka, 2008). Accordingly, Christensen *et al.* (1998) state that firm innovativeness is one of the essential drivers of lasting viability.

Hence, we formulate the second propositions as follows:

P2: SCRM in STP leads to reduced supply chain risks of firms through enhanced technological and innovative capability.

3.2 Integrating SCRM and STP: The Social Capital Theory

Nahapiet and Ghoshal (1998) have developed an approach to cluster attributes of social capital in three distinct categories which has been widely adopted in the fields of operations, SCM and strategic management (e.g. Hagedoorn *et al.*, 2006; Inkpen and Tsang, 2005; Borgatti and Foster, 2003; Koka and Prescott, 2002; Lawson *et al.*, 2008; Mukherjee *et al.*, 2013; Siu and Bao, 2008). They describe attributes of social capital, clustering them into three categories: a) structural, b) cognitive, and c) relational. In the following we will derive our next propositions from these dimensions as they form the core of our conceptual framework presented later on. The structural element refers to the arrangements of linkages between network members. The cognitive element stands for shared understanding and meaning between the members of networks; and lastly, the relational element involves partnership, trust, reciprocity, and mutual respect derived from long–term interactions (Yli–Renko, 2001).

3.2.1 Structural dimension of Social Capital

In total, structural social capital considers the focal points resulting from the arrangement of the system of contacts inside of a given social structure. Partners that upgrade the relations and communication with different contacts at diverse levels (e.g. technical and managerial) and several functions (e.g. quality, engineering and sales) permit the formation of a social structure that favours both sides of the partnership (Cousins *et al.*, 2006). The structural dimension is a variant of social capital studies in a structuralist and topological manner. At the actor's level, the central position of the actor in the network and the associated benefits (e.g., Burt *et al.*, 2000; Powell *et al.*, 1996; Brass and Burkhardt, 1993) constitute the main focus of these studies. Structural capital is often discussed in terms of the wider network of different actors with which a firm holds ties (Autry and Griffis, 2008;

Granovetter, 1973). To maximise gain, the actor, in this case, is an active agent who exploits his position and is known to be rational (Prusak and Cohen, 2001). The local network topology is the principal function of the actor that provides benefits and ties that are subliminally perceived of as forming leverageable structures (Athanassiou and Nigh, 1999; Markovsky *et al.*, 1993). The business-related information exchange is stronger with the increase in the social interaction between the firm and the exchange partner (Larson, 1992). In the similar vein, the sharing of information for optimised capacity management can be informed by SCT, based on which information is passed back and forth between the supplier and buyer to develop a well–informed capacity plan (Yli–Renko, 2001). Nooraie and Parast (2015) demonstrate that increased visibility in SCs offers tremendous costs savings when SC disturbances occur. Their results show that a high level of visibility is alluring because it creates efficiency in a SC and reduces both risks and costs. Without visibility of upstream and downstream flows, managers are uncertain about the demand forecasts and order cycle time, etc. However, according to Bowersox *et al.* (2003) and Chen *et al.* (2013), information sharing is the starting point of SC collaboration. Through structural capital, an essential benefit gained by actors is the access to information (Coleman, 1990). "Fundamental to the ability to plan is the exchange of large amounts of information within and between SC entities" (Kilubi and Haasis, 2015, p. 46).

Informal interpersonal relationships help establish connectivity between the network numbers in an industrial district (Inkpen and Tsang, 2005). The speed of information transfer is influenced by the configuration and the network ties that also concern the resource alternatives and opportunities existent amongst the SC members (Johnson and Elliott, 2011). At MIT (Massachusetts Institute of Technology), Bavelas (1950) conducted a research, focusing on the examination of the relationship between group performance and centralisation. Better performance was observed when frequent and intensive communication was present due to strong ties amongst firms established through high structural capital levels (Lawson *et al.*, 2008). We consider risk information sharing and risk sharing devices as two vital SCRM procedures since the open exchange of information provides the cornerstone that holds the SC together (Lee *et al.*, 2004). Hence, it can be concluded that risk informationsharing, as well as risk sharing mechanisms, contribute to financial efficiency. Correspondingly, the former is further reinforced by consideration of the duration of the relationship and the extent of the suppliers' trust, while the latter element is reinforced by consideration of correctly perceiving SCRM aspects (Li *et al.*, 2015). That leads us to the next proposition:

P3: SCRM in STP leads to reduced supply chain risks of firms through enhanced information–sharing, communication, and visibility.

3.2.2 Cognitive dimension of Social Capital

The resources that have the ability to provide shared systems of interpretations, representations, and meanings amongst the parties are referred to as social capital cognitive dimension (Villena *et al.*, 2011). The joint understanding of fundamental assumptions and concepts, as well as shared language, are the basis for cognitive capital (Bolino *et al.*, 2002). Hence, it provides free communication, resource exchange through common interests and objectives (Parra–Requena *et al.*, 2010). Between two actors, there are high levels of cognitive capital according to research, while the definition and clarity may vary according to the task, network type and outcomes (Lechner *et al.*, 2010). The partners form a STP based on cultural compromise as there are usually distinct cultures that converge. In addition to that, when uncertainty is present, communication is enhanced through shared codes based on mutual rules, goals, values, narratives, and common language (Spender, 1989; Inkpen and Tsang, 2005). A collaborative effort between buyers and their strategic suppliers is maintained through the development of mutual understanding. Thus, higher levels of collaboration can be gained through SCs with rich relational and cognitive resources, increasing the value creation process across the SC (Hunt and Davis, 2012; Uzzi, 1996). Hult *et al.* (2004a) claim that in SCs, shared denotation is related to both subjective and objective measures of lead time decline. The aforementioned contentions assume that when purchasers and their key suppliers have comparable objectives and tenets concerning their relationship, cognitive capital will decisively influence performance (Weick *et al.*,

1995). Collaboration within the SC is influenced by the cognitive capital that represents the shared values and goals (Krause *et al.*, 2007). In addition to that, collaboration generates new knowledge through joint product design, collaborative research, or collective process innovation, which enhances the capability of the SC to respond promptly to environmental changes (Christopher and Holweg, 2012). According to Rajesh *et al.* (2015), when the operations of two firms are well–coordinated, the capability of suppliers and their performance are improved, the continuity of supply is ensured, and supply–side risks are reduced. Finally, Chen *et al.* (2013) examine SC collaboration as a risk mitigation strategy. Their evaluation reveals that each type of collaboration reduces its respective SCR. At this point, the members of the SC share their understandings and explain how improvements may take place and how tasks may be efficiently completed (Handfield and Bechtel, 2002). Hence, we formulate the fourth proposition as follows:

P4: SCRM in STP leads to reduced supply chain risks of firms through higher levels of collaboration.

Three case studies conducted by Ingham and Mothe (1998) have shown that, among other things, learning by doing, trust between partners, member's involvement and motivation are necessary prerequisites to foster a culture of learning within STPs. Thus, firm success is based on the organisational learning and knowledge (Senge *et al.*, 2001). Huang and Yu's (2011) findings suggest that learning in R&D partnerships can profoundly contribute to innovativeness. Similar to differences in STPs, SCs vary in critical competencies such as the learning ability (e.g. McFarland *et al.*, 2008). Companies with better capabilities of securing, embracing, converting and taking advantage of knowledge from external sources may better integrate that gained cognition into new solutions (Kilubi, 2016). Potential advantages of such learning mentioned in the SCM context encompass reciprocal support, risk decline through joint experimentation, exposure to various perceptions and thought-provoking reflections on progress (Bessant *et al.*, 2003). Next, Ettlie and Pavlou (2006) show that interfirm partnership capabilities such as intensive interactions are significantly related to critical NPD success outcomes. Given that cognitive capital diminishes uncertainty, it enhances the effect of relational ties between buyer and supplier (Heide *et al.*, 2007; Poppo and Zenger, 2002). The received acumen on inter–firm capabilities subliminally suggests that the acquirement of technology–based capabilities is a necessary and desired outcome of cross–company collaboration. Thus, the fifth proposition articulates:

P5: SCRM in STP leads to reduced supply chain risks of firms through higher levels learning and exploitation capabilities.

3.2.3 Relational dimension of Social Capital

Recurrent bonds with known companies generate a pattern of interactions in which central companies can access data about the quality and performance of existing and potential partners (Zaheer *et al.*, 1998; Gulati *et al.*, 2000). SCT, in general, applies to the analysis of inter–organisational relationships as firms endeavour to share data, synchronize their plans, and create products conjointly (Galaskiewicz, 2011). In light of the SCT, we conclude that SCRM is – just like STP – an ongoing process that implicates long–term commitment and dedication of all SC members involved (Mahapatra *et al.,* 2010; Giunipero and Eltantawy, 2004; Manuj and Mentzer, 2008b) and requires mutual trust (Bode *et al.*, 2011; Lavastre *et al.*, 2012; Faisal *et al.*, 2006; Tang (2006a). The social quality of the relationships such as mutual identifications, obligations, relational norms, friendship and trust arc part of the relational attributes of the social capital structure (e.g. Cousins *et al.*, 2006; Petersen *et al.*, 2008). Mutual interdependence (Adler and Kwon, 2002), actors' similarity (Rivera, 2010) and geographic proximity (Chetty and Michailova, 2011; Felzensztein *et al.*, 2010) are the factors behind the development of relational capital between at least two actors. A higher degree of relational capital leads to a deeper and more content–rich information flow while reducing monitoring costs (Liu *et al.*, 2010; Spekman and Carraway, 2005). Such an enriched information exchange is valuable to collaboration and excellent performance in inter–organisational partnerships (Hansen, 1999; Cousins *et al.*, 2006). Increased mutual trust and commitment levels contribute to enhancing performance within STPs, regarding both financial and non-financial aspects (Cullen *et al.,* 2000). To that effect, trust exists at multiple levels, including the individual, organisational, inter-organisational and the international level. From the perspective of individual companies, various researchers have concluded that trust significantly contributes to enhancing the quality of relationships (Ring and van den Ven, 1992; Sydow, 1998). Furthermore, it contributes to reducing the negative effects related to opportunistic behaviour, besides enabling partners to integrate their resources more effectively while reducing the requirements of formal contracting (Das, 2001).

The good concern and the openness of the partners along with the confidence in their competence and their mutual reliability are referred to as trust (Mishira, 1996). This aspect lies at the heart of the social capital's relational dimension. Collaboration is facilitated by trust as most parties only collaborate after they have gained confidence in the other party (Zacharia *et al.*, 2009). Hence, when managing flexibility within the SC network, trust building is extremely essential. If it lacks, the information sharing amongst suppliers may be a reluctant process and the resources that support flexibility may not be activated (Faisal *et al.*, 2006; Lavastre *et al.*, 2012). An appropriable company may likewise influence the capabilities of flexibility and responsiveness, giving feasible options in the face of challenging circumstances (Johnson *et al.*, 2013). Capabilities towards higher flexibility and greater efficiency through complementary capabilities mentioned by Vilkamo and Keil (2003) are sharing of risks, common objectives of partners, clear contributions from partners. The operating assets status is also affected by trust in terms of building confidence and exchanging valuable information (Pettit *et al.*, 2010). It helps reduce the issues of unnecessary interventions, overreactions, and inappropriate decisions during risky conditions (Christopher and Lee, 2004). During a crisis, the fast response is influenced through trust by providing rapid information access; without the necessity for formal or contractual requisitions. Instead, there exists an understanding that financial issues might be 'sorted out' subsequently (Johnson and Elliott, 2011).

The effectiveness of SCRM implementation could be affected as the relational aspects may harm the velocity or visibility. Thus, firms have to ensure that collaborative efforts and events are managed promptly through communication (Bartlett *et al.*, 2007). Commitment must also be reinforced by SC members to share valuable information with other SC members as part of visibility (Krause *et al.*, 2007). When a risky situation occurs, trust shows that SC partners allow their fate being taken into the hands of the other party to take action and make appropriate decisions (Inkpen and Tsang, 2005). The network actors are willing to share knowledge, and it is trust that plays a crucial role in that process (Powell *et al.*, 1996). The committed exchange partners must provide free information exchange to show their level of trust as the decision makers must not feel that they need to protect themselves from any opportunistic behaviour that may be shown by the other party (Blau, 1964; Jarillo, 1988). Moreover, trust is process–based, in the sense that firms regularly test each other's integrity, moving from small, discrete exchanges of limited risk to more open–ended deals (Lazerson and Lorenzoni, 1999). The dependence on external knowledge and skills is strongly connected to two elements: the nature of the relationship and the extent of commitment (Siu and Bao, 2008). As a result, trust as a vital constituent of relational capital between network members and a paramount enabler of open information exchange (Gulati and Nickerson, 2008; Ireland and Webb, 2007; Krishnan *et al.*, 2006). Accordingly, we offer the last proposition:

P6: SCRM in STP leads to reduced supply chain risks of firms through mutual trust and commitment.

A summary of the conjoint SCRM–STP capabilities and all the research propositions is provided in Appendix VI and Appendix VII, respectively. The following figure shows a tentative framework (Figure VI-2) illustrating some linkages between SCRM and STP through capabilities that have evolved from our study combining both research streams through RBV and SCT. The most important thing here is that social capital as a theoretical foundation structured into three dimensions relates to several capabilities that lead to improved performance under uncertain and risky conditions by combining SCRM and STP into one research stream.

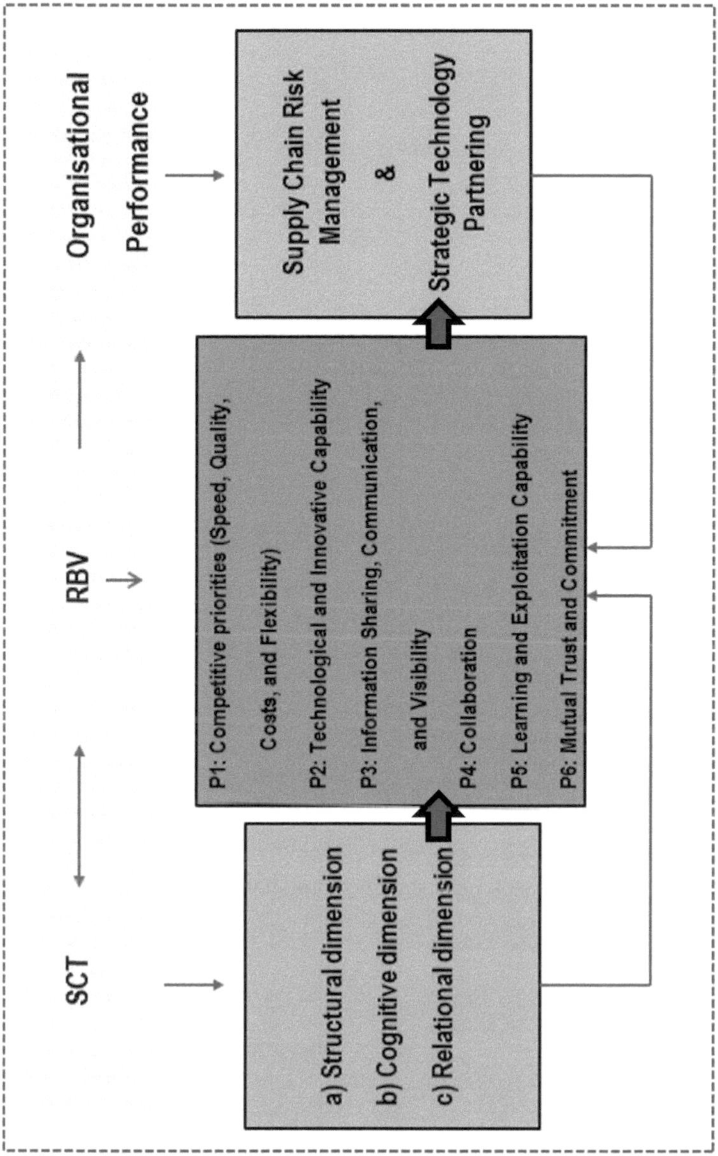

Figure VI-2: SCRM-STP conceptual framework.
Source: Own illustration.

4 Discussion and conclusion

4.1 Theoretical implications

In spite of the incredible advance in SCRM concepts, parallel progression in theory improvement and endeavors to comprehend the social interactions in SCRM has stayed behind. With an end goal to establish a hypothetical ground for the social interactions of SCRM and STP, we drew from the RBV and SCT and developed a conceptual framework that portrays the social procedures that foster enhanced execution and performance in an managed SC (Min *et al.*, 2008). Regarding our formulated research question: How can the integration of STP and SCRM effectively be used to manage successfully supply chain risks? We considered why a company's organisational performance benefits from a SCRM–STP linkage. This is in line with Feller *et al.* (2013) who employ a mixed–method approach and conclude that for companies, operating in chaotic and risky business environments, viable competitive advantage derives largely from their technological capability. On this note, Kleindorfer and Saad (2005) deemed SCRM capabilities such as collaboration, as well as flexibility as crucial for mitigating SCRs. Moreover, Lavastre *et al.* (2012) identified among others, collaboration, and information sharing as one central way of delivering countermeasures to risk exposure. With its derivation and development, the complementarity of the SCRM and the STP has been demonstrated. From a social capital perspective, taking a look at SCRM on the one hand, risks and cost can be reduced through the long-term supply chain effectiveness that has been established through mutually beneficial relationships, shared values, and trust. Taking a look at STP on the other hand, quality and innovative products are created for the customers, and for this purpose the respective organisation transacts with suppliers as well as other partners to attain external resources. As a result, the social capital is used to strengthen supplier relationships and to foster knowledge transfer promotion. The suggested framework may well be applied to develop useful SCRM mitigation strategies while engaged in STPs. Thus, the integration of the two diverse, but yet complementary research streams leads to the achievement of new systems of sustainable competitive advantage that base upon the grounds of the dynamics of the environment.

4.2 Managerial implications

SCRM–STP linkages have quantifiable relational benefits, and it is also essential for managers to realise that they can provide competitive advantages, as well as yield financial rent as herein reported. Specific guidance for the implementation of linking SCRM and STP has not been provided as part of this paper. However, it is highly recommended as part of the organisation's internal operations; thus, SCRM in STP must be continuously engaged in the processes of acquiring knowledge and facilitating managerial actions. The long–term potential performance benefits must be questioned by managers as a principle that goes beyond the immediate advantages and investment costs (Rungtusanatham *et al.*, 2003). A couple of research studies have shown that the innovative capability of an organisation can be used to reduce disruptions in the SC, but the 'how' question remains unanswered. It is this 'how' which needs to be analysed further through investigation and analysis (Wong *et al.*, 2011). SC disruptions may be existent within organisations that have profoundly embedded and interdependent supply chains (Hallikas *et al.*, 2004; Kleindorfer and Saad, 2005; Wagner and Bode, 2006). The same characteristics may be able to provide organisations with innovative capabilities and practical innovation adoptions as well (Capaldo, 2007; Moran, 2005). The processes and practices that link the SCRM and STP must be considered important. Hence, further research must be conducted on the basis of those intricate relationships to help analyse and understand the potential disruptions, as well as the useful capabilities of the SC (Golgeci and Ponomarov, 2013).

5 Limitations and future research

The propositions and conclusions presented must consider the limitations inherent in the study at hand as well. A profound literature analysis has been submitted as a major part of this research study as it is a conceptual article; however, some of the details have been entirely based on anecdotal and scant empirical evidence. At first, future research must take into account the question of how an organisation's innovative capability can be used to reduce disruptions in the SC. The SCT creates an awareness that the benefits of cooperation between firms could be to a great extent due to network resources and their positions within the networks (e.g. cliques, centrality) (Chang, 2003), while the RBV provides the firm with essential capabilities to exploit their valuable resources in an efficient manner (Kale and Singh, 2007; Ettlie and Pavlou, 2006; Santangelo, 2000). Regarding the SCT, all three underlying dimensions and their ability to affect the performance outcomes have been included for improved understanding of how those mechanisms work. On the one hand, from the perspective of the suppliers, the social capital must be analysed in a much more thorough manner (Schiele *et al.*, 2015). On the other hand, the contingency factors that affect relationship performance and social capital like environmental uncertainty may be analysed through future research to gain additional insights (Carey *et al.*, 2011).

As opposed to conducting studies in light of single viewpoints, maybe researchers ought to see each dimension as an important, yet not adequate part for the understanding of knowledge generation (Hult *et al.*, 2004b). All through our discourse, it has become apparent that social capital and resources are multi–level occurrences (Adler and Kwon, 2002; Oh *et al.*, 2006). It would accordingly be beneficial to examine more in–depth how relationships within individual boundary spanners in a SC network form at the firm–level. The proposed conceptual framework is the first concept to connect SCRM and STP to one research stream. The complementarity of the two research streams directs towards a new strategic approach, which should be validated and empirically tested in a large–scale quantitative study. Contrasted with the transaction cost economics perspective that predominates in the SC literature, the SCT provides an open door for the extended comprehension of the complexities of SC connections (Krause *et al.*, 2007). The subject matter to focus on is the process through which the capabilities can be created as well as sustained (Zollo *et al.*, 2002). Hence, a longitudinal comparative case analysis is needed for a thorough understanding of those underlying processes. Longitudinal research can potentially offer a valuable contribution to the research study of the evolution of STP and SCRM capabilities since capability development (such as by investing in R&D) does not necessarily produce immediate performance effects (McGrath and O'Toole, 2013). Given the path– and time–dependent nature of capabilities, it is necessary to investigate the impact of capabilities on long–term performance which could be measured by the organisation's key (both financial and market) performance indicators in comparison to its main competitors or the industry average over a period of five to ten years (Duysters *et al.*, 2012). Moreover, complex challenges ask for exceptional approaches that can be accomplished by strategic thinking and activities in the context of SCRM and STP (Johnson *et al.*, 2013). In addition to aspects of the duration of the relationship, the reliability of the supplier and how the shared understanding of SCRM dimensions contributes to collaborative relationships in STP and influences relationship-specific investment initiatives and how it relates to its interdependence could be further investigated. That would contribute to understanding corresponding SCRM practices and the factors impacting them. In consideration of an absence of systematic effort towards evaluating conjoint SCRM-STP strategies in the available literature, this paper may contribute to filling in certain aspects of these gaps. Thus, we are confident of that by drawing together the RBV and SCT, we gain a fuller and richer explanation of organisational–level effects within strategic networks in SCs. In the end, this investigation has released a novel line of inquiry into this essential zone of SCM and strategic management research. Building on existing organisational theory of social capital and RBV, we allied the two concepts and applied them to SCRM within STP relationships. Finally, it should be noted that the integration of

SCRM and STP has a significant potential to advance theory and practice in managing SCRs and, therefore, constitutes an innovative and novel concept in times of an uncertain business environment.

References

Acedo, F.J. and Casillas, J.C. (2005). "Current paradigms in the international management field: An author co–citation analysis. *International Business Review,* **14**(5), pp. 619–639.

Acedo, F.J., Barroso, C., Casanueva, C. and Galan, J.L. (2006). "Co–authorship in management and organizational studies: An empirical and network analysis". *Journal of Management Studies*, **43**(5), pp. 957–983.

Adler, N.J. and Harzing, A.-W. (2009). "When knowledge wins: Transcending the sense of and nonsense of academic rankings". *Academy of Management Learning and Education*, **8**(1), pp. 72–95.

Adler, P.S. and Kwon, S.–W. (2002). "Social capital: Prospects for a new concept". *Academy of Management Review*, **27**(1), pp. 17–40.

Adobor, H. (2005). "Trust as sensemaking: The microdynamics of trust in interfirm alliances". *Journal of Business Research,* **58**(3), pp. 330–337.

Aggeri, F. and Segrestin, B. (2007). "Innovation and project development: An impossible equation? Lessons from an innovative automobile project development". *R&D Management,* **37**(1), pp. 37–47.

Agrawal, V. and Sheshadri, S. (2000). "Risk intermediation in supply chains". *IIE Transactions,* **32**(9), pp. 819–831.

Agrell, P.J., Lindroth, R. and Norrman, A. (2004). "Risk, information and incentives in telecom supply chains". *International Journal of Production Economics,* **90**(1), pp. 1–16.

Ahuja, G. (2000a). "Collaboration networks, structural holes, and innovation: A longitudinal study. *Administrative Science Quarterly,* **45**(3), pp. 425–455.

Ahuja, G. (2000b). "The duality of collaboration: Inducements and opportunities in the formation of inter–firm linkages". *Strategic Management Journal,* **21**(3), pp. 317–343.

Ahuja, G. and Katila, R. (2001). "Technological acquisitions and the innovation performance of acquiring firms: A longitudinal study". *Strategic Management Journal,* **22**(3), pp. 197–220.

Aksnes, D. and Rip, A. (2009). "Researcher's perceptions of citations". *Research Policy,* **38**(1), pp. 895–905.

Alvarez, S. and Busenitz, L. (2001). "The entrepreneurship of resource–based theory". *Journal of Management,* **27**(6), pp. 755–775.

Ambulkar, S., Blackhurst, J. and Grawe, S. (2015). "Firm's resilience to supply chain disruptions: Scale development and empirical examination". *Journal of Operations Management,* Vol. 33–34, pp. 111–122.

American Heritage Dictionary of the English Language, 5th ed. (2011). Houghton Mifflin: Boston, MA.

Amit, R. and Schoemaker, P.J.H. (1993). "Strategic assets and organizational rent". *Strategic Management Journal,* **14**(1), pp. 33–46.

Anand, B.N. and Khanna, T. (2000). "Do firms learn to create value? The case of alliances". *Strategic Management Journal,* **21**(3), pp. 295–315.

Andersen, J. (2011). "Strategic resources and firm performance". *Management Decision,* **49**(1), pp. 87–98.

Andrews, T. (2012). "What is social constructionism?" *Grounded Theory Review,* **11**(1). pp. 39–46.

Argyris, C. and Schön, D.A. (1978). "Organizational Learning: A theory of action perspective". Addison–Wesley Publishing Company: Reading, MA.

Arora, R. and Stoner, C. (2009). "A mixed method approach to understanding brand personality". *Journal of Product & Brand Management,* **18**(4), pp. 272–283.

Athanassiou, N.A. and Nigh, D. (2000). "Internationalization, tacit knowledge and the top management team of MNCs". *Journal of International Business Studies,* **31**(3), pp. 471–488.

Autry, C.W. and Griffis, S.E. (2008). "Supply chain capital: The impact of structural and relational linkages on firm execution and innovation". *Journal of Business Logistics*, **29**(1), pp. 157–173.

Backhaus, K., Luegger, K. and Koch, M. (2011). "The structure and evolution of business–to–business marketing: A citation and co–citation analysis". *Industrial Marketing Management*, **40**(6, SI), pp. 940–951.

Baker, W.E. (1990). "Market networks and corporate behavior". *American Journal of Sociology*, **96**(3), pp. 589–625.

Bakker, R.M. (2010). "Taking stock of temporary organizational forms: A systematic review and research agenda". *International Journal of Management Reviews,* **12**(4), pp. 466–486.

Bamford, J.D. and Ernst, D. (2002). "Managing an alliance portfolio". *The McKinsey Quarterly,* Vol. 3, pp. 29–39.

Bandaly, D., Satir, A. and Shanker, L. (2014). "Integrated supply chain risk management via operational methods and financial instruments". *International Journal of Production Research,* **52**(7), pp. 2007–2025.

Barney, J. (1991). "Firm resources and sustained competitive advantage". *Journal of Management*, **17**(1), pp. 99–120.

Barney, J.B. and Mackey, T.B. (2005). "Testing Resource–Based Theory". In Ketchen, D.J. and Bergh, D.D. (Eds.). *Research Methodology in Strategy and Management (Research Methodology in Strategy and Management,* 2nd ed. Emerald Group Publishing: Bingley, UK, pp. 1–13.

Barr, P.S. (2004). "Current and potential importance of qualitative methods in strategy research". In Ketchen, D. and Bergh, D. (Eds.). *Research methodology in strategy and management,* 1st ed. Emerald Group Publishing: Bingley, UK, pp. 165–188.

Barratt, M. and Barratt, R. (2011). "Exploring internal and external supply chain linkages: Evidence from the field". *Journal of Operations Management,* **29**(5), pp. 514–528.

Barratt, M. and Oke, A. (2007). "Antecedents of supply chain visibility in retail supply chains: A resource–based theory perspective". *Journal of Operations Management,* **25**(6), pp. 1217–1233.

Barry, J. (2004). "Supply chain risk in an uncertain global supply chain environment". *International Journal of Physical Distribution & Logistics Management,* **34**(9), pp. 695–697.

Bartlett, P.A., Julien, D.M. and Baines, T.S. (2007). "Improving supply chain performance through improved visibility". *International Journal of Logistics Management,* **18**(2), pp. 294–313.

Bartunek, J.M., Rousseau, D.M., Rudolph, J.W. and DePalma, J.A. (2006). "On the receiving end. Sensemaking, emotion, and assessments of an organizational change initiated by others". *Journal of Applied Behavioural Science,* **42**(2), pp. 182–206.

Baum, J.A.C., Calabrese, T. and Silverman, B.S. (2000). "Don't go it alone: Alliance network composition and startups' performance in Canadian biotechnology". *Strategic Management Journal,* **21**(3), pp. 22–29.

Bavelas, A. (1950). "Communication patterns in task–oriented groups". *Journal of the Acoustical Society of America*, **22**(6), pp. 271–282.

Bayer, A.E., Smart, J.C. and McLaughlin, G.W. (1990). "Mapping intellectual structure of a scientific subfield through author co–citations". *Journal of the American Society for Information Science,* **41**(6), pp. 444–452.

Bayona, C., Garcia–Marco, T. and Huerta E. (2001). "Firms' motivations for cooperative R&D: An empirical analysis of Spanish firms". *Research Policy,* **30**(8), pp. 1289–1307.

Bazeley, P. (2008). "Mixed methods in management research". In Holt, R. and Thorpe, R. (Eds.). *Dictionary of qualitative management research.* Sage Publications: London, UK, pp. 133–136.

Beamish, P.W. and Lupton, N.C. (2009). "Managing joint ventures". *Academy of Management Perspectives,* **23**(2), pp. 75–94.

Benavides–Velasco, C.A., Quintana–García, C. and Guzmán–Parra, V.F. (2011). "Trends in family business research". *Small Business Economics*, **40**(1), pp. 41–57.

Berg, E., Knudsen, D. and Norrman, A. (2008). "Assessing performance of supply chain risk management programmes: A tentative approach". *International Journal of Risk Assessment & Management,* **9**(3), pp. 288–310.

Bernardi, L., Kleim, S. and von der Lippe, H. (2007). "Social influences on fertility: A comparative mixed methods study in Eastern and Western Germany". *Journal of Mixed Methods Research*, **1**(1), pp. 23–47.

Bertrand, P. and Meschi, P. (2005). "A transactional analysis of Chinese partners' performance in international joint ventures". *The Chinese Economy,* **38**(2), pp. 16–35.

Bessant, J., Kaplinski, R. and Lamming, R. (2003). "Putting supply chain learning into practice". *International Journal of Operations & Production Management,* **23**(2), pp. 167–184.

Bidault, F. and Cummings, T. (1994). "Innovating through alliances: expectations and limitations". *R&D Management,* **24**(1), pp. 33–45.

Biehl, M., Kim, H. and Wade, M. (2006). "Relationships among the academic business disciplines: A multi–Method citation analysis". *Omega*, **34**(4), pp. 359–371.

Bierly, P., Gallagher, S. and Spender, J.–C. (2014). "Innovation decision making in high–risk organizations: A comparison of the US and Soviet attack submarine programs". *Industrial and Corporate Change,* **23**(3), pp. 759–795.

Blackhurst, J., Craighead, C.W., Elkins, D. and Handfield, R.B. (2005). "An empirically derived agenda of critical research issues for managing supply–chain disruptions". *International Journal of Production Research,* **43**(19), pp. 4067–4081.

Blackhurst, J., Kaitlin, S.D. and Craighead C.W. (2011). "An empirically derived framework of global supply resiliency". *Journal of Business Logistics*, **32**(4), pp. 374-391.

Blau, P.M. (1964). "Exchange and power in social life". John Wiley & Sons: New York, NY.

Bode, C., Wagner, S.M., Petersen, K.J. and Ellram, L.M. (2011). "Understanding responses to supply chain disruptions: Insights from information processing and resource dependency perspectives". *Academy of Management Journal,* **54**(4), pp. 833–856.

Bogataj, D. and Bogataj, M. (2007). "Measuring the supply chain risk and vulnerability in frequency space". *International Journal of Production Economics*, **108**(1–2), pp. 291–301.

Bolino, M.C., Turnley, W.H. and Bloodgood, J.M. (2002). "Citizenship behavior and the creation of social capital in organizations". *Academy of Management Review,* **27**(4), pp. 505–522.

Bonaccorsi, A. and Lipparini, A. (1994). "Strategic partnerships in new product development: an Italian case study". *Journal of Product Innovation Management,* **11**(2), pp. 134–145.

Boote, D. and Bailey, P. (2005). "Scholars before researchers – on the centrality of the literature review in research preparation". *Educational Researcher,* **34**(6), pp. 3–15.

Borgatti, S.P. and Foster, P.C. (2003). "The network paradigm in organizational research: A review and typology". *Journal of Management*, 29(6), pp. 991–1013.

Borgatti, S.P. and Halgin, D.S. (2011). "On network theory". *Organization Science,* **22**(5), pp. 1168–1181.

Borgatti, S.P. and Li, X. (2009). "On social network analysis in a supply chain context". *Journal of Supply Chain Management,* **45**(2), pp. 5–22.

Börner, K., Chen, C. and Boyack, K. (2003). "Visualizing knowledge domains". *Annual Review of Information Science and Technology*, **37**(1), pp. 179–255.

Bourdieu, P. (1986). "The forms of capital". In Richardson, J. (Ed.). *Handbook of Theory and Research for the Sociology of Education.* Greenwood: New York, NY, pp. 83–95.

Bowersox, D.J., Closs, D.J. and Stank, T.P. (2003). "How to master cross–enterprise collaboration". *Supply Chain Management Review,* **7**(4), pp. 18–27.

Bowman, E.H. and Hurry, D. (1993). "Strategy through the options lens: An integrated view of resource investments and the incremental–choice process". *Academy of Management Review,* **18**(4), pp. 760–782.

Boyack, K. and Klavans, R. (2010). "Co–citation analysis, bibliographic coupling, and direct citation: Which citation approach represents the research front most accurately?" *Journal of the American Society for Information Science and Technology*, **61**(12), pp. 2389–2404.

Brandenburg, M., Govindan, K., Sarkis, J. and Seuring, S. (2014). "Quantitative models for sustainable supply chain management: Developments and directions". *European Journal of Operational Research,* Vol. 233 No. 2, pp. 299–312.

Brandman, B. (2002). "Security matters: An interview with Barry Brandman". *Supply Chain Management*, **7**(4), pp. 38–45.

Brannen, J. (2005). "Mixing methods: The entry of qualitative and quantitative approaches into the research process". *International Journal of Social Research Methodology,* **8**(3), pp. 173–184.

Brass, D.J. and Burkhardt, M.E. (1993). "Potential power and power use: An investigation of structure and behavior". *Academy of Management Journal,* **36**(3), pp. 441–470.

Braunscheidel, M.J. and Suresh, N.C. (2009). "The organizational antecedents of a firm's supply chain agility for risk mitigation and response". *Journal of Operations Management,* **27**(2), pp. 119–140.

Brewer, P.C. and Speh, T.W. (2001). "Adapting the balanced scorecard to supply chain management". *Supply Chain Management Review,* **5**(2), pp. 48-56.

Brindley, C. (2004). "Risk focus towards customers". In Brindley, C. (Ed.). *Supply chain risk.* Ashgate Aldershot: Farnham, UK, pp. 66–78.

Briner, R.B. and Denyer, D. (2012). "Systematic review and evidence synthesis as a practice and scholarship tool". In Rousseau, D. (Ed.). *Handbook of Evidence–based Management: Companies, Classrooms and Research.* Oxford University Press: New York, NY, pp. 112–129.

Briner, R.B., Denyer, D. and Rousseau, D.M. (2009). "Evidence–based management: A concept cleanup?" *Academy of Management Perspectives,* **23**(4), pp. 19–32.

Brown, T. (2011). "Journal quality metrics: Options to consider other than impact factors". *The American Journal of Occupational Therapy,* **65**(3), pp. 346–350.

Bruderer, E. and Singh, J.V. (1996). "Organizational evolution, learning, and selection: A genetic-algorithm-based model". *Academy of management Journal*, **39**(5), pp. 1322-1349.

Bryman, A. (2007). "The research question in social research: What is its role?" *International Journal of Social Research Methodology,* **10**(1), pp. 5–20.

Bstieler, L. and Hemmert, M. (2008). "Developing trust in vertical product development partnerships: A comparison of South Korea and Austria". *Journal of World Business*, **43**(1), pp. 35–46.

Burgess, K., Singh, P.J. and Koroglu, R. (2006). "Supply chain management: A structured literature review and implications for future research". *International Journal of Operations & Production Management,* **26**(7), pp. 703–29.

Burt, R.S. (1992). "Structural holes: The social structure of competition". Harvard University Press: Cambridge, MA.

Burt, R.S. (2000). "The network structure of social capital". *Research in Organizational behavior*". **22**(6), pp. 345–423.

Byrne, P.M. (2005). "RFID: Unlocking high performance in supply chain planning". *Logistics Management,* **44**(9), pp. 29–30.

Cachon, G.P. (2004). "The allocation of inventory risk in a supply chain: Push, pull, and advance–purchase discount contracts". *Management Science,* **50**(2), pp. 222–238.

Cadogan, J. (2010). "Comparative, cross-cultural, and cross-national research: A comment on good and bad practice". *International Marketing Review,* **27**(6), pp. 601–605.

Calero–Medina, C. and van Leeuwen, T. (2012). "Seed Journal Citation Network Maps: A method based on network theory". *Journal of the American Society for Information Science and Technology*, **63**(6), pp. 1226–1234.

Callon, M., Courtial, J.–P., Turner, W.A. and Bauin, S. (1983). "From translations to problematic networks: An introduction to co–word analysis". *Social Science Information*, **22**(2), pp. 191–235.

Caloghirou, Y., Kastelli, I. and Tsakanikas, A. (2004). "Internal capabilities and external knowledge sources: Complements or substitutes for innovative performance?" *Technovation,* **24**(1), pp. 29–39.

Campbell, R. Pound, P., Pope, C., Britten, N., Pill, R., Morgan, M. and Donovan, J. (2003). "Evaluating meta–ethnography: A synthesis of qualitative research on lay experiences of diabetes and diabetes care". *Social Science & Medicine,* **56**(4), pp. 671–684.

Campos, H.M., Parellada, F.S. and Palma, Y. (2012). "Mapping the Intellectual Structure of Entrepreneurship Research: revisiting the invisible college". *Revista Brasileira de Gestão de Negócios*, **14**(42), pp. 41–58.

Canon, M., Courtial, J.P. and Penan, H. (1995). "Cienciometria. El estudio cuantitativo de la actividad cientifica: de la bibliometria a la vigilancia tecnologica". [Scientometrics. The quantitative study of the scientific activity: From bibliometry to technological surveillance]. Ediciones Trea: Gijon, Espana.

Capaldo, A. (2007). "Network structure and innovation: The leveraging of a dual network as a distinctive relational capability". *Strategic Management Journal,* **28**(6), pp. 585–608.

Carayannis, E.G., Kassicic, S.K. and Radosevich, R. (2000). "Strategic alliances as a source of early–stage seed capital in new technology–based firms". *Technovation*, **20**(11), pp. 603–615.

Carey, S., Lawson, B. and Krause, D.R. (2011). "Social capital configuration, legal bonds and performance in buyer–supplier relationships". *Journal of Operations Management*, **29**(4), pp. 277–288.

Carr, C. (1999). "Globalisation, strategic alliances, acquisitions and technology transfer. Lessons from ICL=Fujitsu and Rover=Honda and BMW". *R&D Management,* **29**(4), pp. 405–421.

Carter, C.R. and Ellram, L.M. (2003). "Thirty–five years of the Journal of Supply Chain Management: Where have we been and where are we going?" *The Journal of Supply Chain Management,* **39**(2), pp. 27–39.

Carter, C.R., Ellram, L.M. and Tate, W.L. (2007). "The use of social network analysis in logistics research". *Journal of Business Logistics*, **28**(1), pp. 137–168.

Carvalho, M.M., Fleury, A. and Lopes, A.P. (2013). "An overview of the literature on technology roadmapping (TRM): Contributions and trends". *Technological Forecasting and Social Change*, **80**(7), pp. 1418–1437.

Cassiman, B., Di Guardo, M.C. and Valentini, G. (2009). "Organising R&D projects to profit from innovation: Insights from co–opetition". *Long Range Planning,* **42**(2), pp. 216–233.

Cavinato, J.L. (2004). "Supply chain logistics risks: From the back room to the board room". *International Journal of Physical Distribution and Logistics Management,* **34**(5), pp. 383–387.

Chabowski, B.R., Samiee, S. and Hult, G.T.M. (2013). "A bibliometric analysis of the global branding literature and a research agenda". *Journal of International Business Studies*, **44**(6), pp. 622–634.

Chang, Y.–C. (2003). "Benefits of co–operation on innovative performance: Evidence from integrated circuits and biotechnology firms in the UK and Taiwan". *R&D Management,* **33**(4), pp. 425–437.

Chapman, K. and Ellinger, A.E. (2009). "Constructing impact factors to measure the influence of logistics journals". *Journal of Business Logistics,* **30**(2), pp. 197–212.

Chapman, R.L. and Corso, M. (2005). "From continuous improvement to collaborative innovation: The next challenge in supply chain management". *Production Planning & Control,* **16**(4), pp. 339–334.

Charvet, F.F., Cooper, M.C. and Gardner, J.T. (2008). "The intellectual structure of supply chain management: A bibliometric approach". *Journal of Business Logistics,* **29**(1), pp. 47–73.

Chen, G., Bliese, P.D. and Mathieu, J.E. (2005). "Conceptual framework and statistical procedures for delineating and testing multilevel theories of homology". *Organizational Research Methods,* **8**(4), pp. 375–409.

Chen, I.J. and Paulraj, A. (2004). "Towards a theory of supply chain management: the constructs and measurements". *Journal of Operations Management,* **22**(2), pp. 119–150.

Chen, J. Chen, Y. and Vanhaverbeke, W. (2011). "The influence of scope, depth, and orientation of external technology sources on the innovative performance of Chinese firms". *Technovation,* **31**(8), pp. 362–373.

Chen, J., Sohal, A.S. and Prajogo, D.I. (2013). "Supply chain operational risk mitigation: A collaborative approach". *International Journal of Production Research,* **51**(7), pp. 2186–2199.

Cheng, S.K. and Kam, B.H. (2008). "A conceptual framework for analysing risk in supply networks". *Journal of Enterprise Information Management,* **22**(4), pp. 345–359.

Chesbrough, H.W. (2003). "*Open innovation: The new imperative for creating and profiting from technology*". Harvard Business School Press: Cambridge, MA.

Chetty, S. and Michailova, S. (2011). "Geographical proximity and inter–firm collaboration: The role of knowledge access and knowledge acquisition". *Journal of General Management,* **36**(4), pp. 71–87.

Child, J. (1972). "Organizational structure, environment and performance: The role of strategic choice". *Sociology,* **6**(1), pp. 1–22.

Chisholm, A.M. and Nielsen, K. (2009). "Social capital and the resource–based view the firm". *International Studies of Management & Organization,* **39**(2), pp. 7–32.

Cho, H.J. and Pucik, V. (2005). "Relationship between innovativeness, quality, growth, profitability, and market value". *Strategic Management Journal,* **26**(6), pp. 555–575.

Choi, T.Y. and Krause, D.R. (2006). "The supply base and its complexity: Implications for transaction costs, risks, responsiveness, and innovation". *Journal of Operations Management,* **24**(5), pp. 637–652.

Chopra S. and Sodhi, M. (2014). "Reducing the risk of supply chain disruptions". *MIT Sloan Management Review,* **55**(3), pp. 73–80.

Chopra, S. and Sodhi, M.S. (2004). "Managing risk to avoid supply–chain breakdown". *MIT Sloan Management Review,* **46**(1), pp. 53–61.

Christensen, C., Suarez, F. and Utterback, J. (1998). "Strategies for survival in fast-changing industries". *Management Science,* **4**(12), pp. 207-220.

Christopher, M. and Holweg, M. (2011). "Supply Chain 2.0: Managing supply chains in the era of turbulence". *International Journal of Physical Distribution and Logistics Management,* **41**(1), pp. 63–82.

Christopher, M. and Lee, H. (2004). "Mitigating supply chain risk through improved confidence". *International Journal of Physical Distribution & Logistics Management,* **34**(5), pp. 388–396.

Christopher, M. and Peck, H. (2004). "Building the resilient supply chain". *International Journal of Logistics Management,* **15**(2), pp. 1–13.

Christopher, M. and Towill, D.R. (2000). "Supply chain migration from lean and functional to agile and customised". *Supply Chain Management: An International Journal,* **5**(4), pp. 206–213.

Coleman, J. (1990). "Foundations of social theory". Harvard University Press: Cambridge, Massachusetts.

Coleman, J.S. (1988). "Social capital in the creation of human capital". *The American Journal of Sociology*, Vol. 94, pp. 95–120.

Colicchia, C. and Strozzi, F. (2012). "Supply chain risk management: A new methodology for a systematic literature review". *Supply Chain Management: An International Journal,* **17**(4), pp. 403–418.

Connelly, B.L., Ketchen, D.J. and Hult, G.T.M. (2013). "Global Supply Chain Management: Toward a theoretically driven research agenda". *Global Strategy Journal*, **3**(3), pp. 227–243.

Contractor, F.J. and Ra, W. (2002). "How knowledge attributes influence alliance governance choices: A theory development note". *Journal of International Management,* **8**(1), pp. 11–27.

Coombes, P.H. and Nicholson, J.D. (2013). "Business models and their relationship with marketing: A systematic literature review". *Industrial Marketing Management*, **42**(5), pp. 656–664.

Cooper, R., Kuh, D., Hardy, R. and the Mortality Group on behalf of the FALCon and HALCyon study teams (2010). "Objectively measured physical capability levels and mortality: Systematic review and meta–analysis". *British Medical Journal,* Vol. 341, pp. 1–12.

Corley, K.G. and Gioia, D.A. (2011). "Building: What constitutes a theoretical contribution?" *Academy of Management Review,* **36**(1), pp. 12–32.

Cousins, P.D., Handfield, R.B., Lawson, B. and Petersen, K.J. (2006). "Creating supply chain relational capital: The impact of formal and informal socialization processes". *Journal of Operations Management,* **24**(6), pp. 851–863.

Craighead, C.W., Blackhurst, J., Rungtusanatham, M.J. and Handfield, R.B. (2007a). "The severity of supply chain disruptions: Design characteristics and mitigation capabilities". *Decision Sciences,* **38**(1), pp. 131–156.

Craighead, C.W., Hanna, J.B., Gibson, B.J. and Meredith, J.R. (2007b). "Research approaches in logistics: Trends and alternative future directions". *International Journal of Logistics Management*, **18**(1), pp. 22–40.

Creswell, J. and Tashakkori, A. (2007). "Differing perspectives on mixed methods research". *Journal of Mixed Methods Research,* 1(4), pp. 303–308.

Creswell, J.W. and Clark, V.L.P. (2007). "Designing and conducting mixed methods research". Sage Publications: Thousand Oaks, CA.

Crossan, M.M. and Apaydin, M. (2010). "A multidimensional framework of organizational innovation. A systematic review of the literature". *Journal of Management Studies,* **47**(6), pp. 1154–1191.

Cucchiella, F. and Gastaldi, M. (2006). "Risk management in supply chain: A real option approach". *Journal of Manufacturing Technology Management,* **17**(6), pp. 700–720.

Cui, C.C., Ball, D.F. and Coyne, J. (2002). "Working effectively in strategic alliances through managerial fit between partners: Some evidence from Sino–British joint ventures and the implications for R&D professionals". *R&D Management,* **32**(4), pp. 343–357.

Cullen, J.B., Johnson, J.L. and Sakano, T. (2000). "Success through commitment and trust: The soft side of strategic alliance management". *Journal of World Business,* **35**(3), pp. 223–240.

Culnan, M.J. (1986). "The intellectual development of management information systems 1972–1982: A co–citation analysis". *Management Science,* **32**(2), pp. 156–172.

Cuypers, I. and Martin, X. (2010). "What makes and what does not make a real option? A study of equity shares in international joint ventures". *Journal of International Business Studies,* **41**(1), pp. 47–70.

Da Mota Pedrosa, A., Näslund, D. and Jasmand, C. (2012). "Logistics case study based research: towards higher quality". *International Journal of Physical Distribution & Logistics Management,* **42**(3), pp. 275–295.

Daft, R. and Lewin, A. (1990). "Can organizational studies begin to break out of the normal science straitjacket? An editorial essay". *Organization Science,* **1**(1), pp. 1–9.

Das, S., Sen, P.K. and Sengupta, S. (1998). "Impact of strategic alliances on firm valuation". *Academy of Management Journal,* **41**(1), pp. 27–41.

Das, T.K. (2001). "Trust, control, and risk in strategic alliances". *Organization Studies,* **22**(2), pp. 251–283.

Das, T.K. and Teng, B.–S. (1998). "Resource and risk management in the strategic alliance making process". *Journal of Management,* **24**(1), pp. 21–42.

Datta, P., Christopher, M. and Allen, P. (2007). "Agent-based Modelling of Complex Production/Distribution Systems to Improve Resilience". *International Journal of Logistics Research and Applications*, **10**(3), pp. 187–203.

David, R.J. and Han, S.–K. (2004). "A systematic assessment of the empirical support for transaction economics". *Strategic Management Journal,* **25**(1), pp. 39–58.

Davis, J.P. and Eisenhardt, K.M. (2011). "Rotating leadership and collaborative innovation: Recombination processes in symbiotic relationships". *Administrative Science Quarterly,* **56**(2), pp. 159–201.

Day, G.S. (1994). "The capabilities of market–driven organizations". *Journal of Marketing,* **58**(4), pp. 37–52.

De Man, A.–P. and Duysters, G. (2005). "Collaboration and innovation: A review of the effects of mergers, acquisitions and alliances on innovation". *Technovation*, **25**(12), pp. 1377–1387.

Deeds, D.L., De Carolis, D. and Coombs, J. (1999). "Dynamic capabilities and new product development in high technology ventures: An empirical analysis of new biotechnology firms". *Journal of Business Venturing* **15**(3), pp. 211–229.

Delbufalo, E. (2012). "Outcomes of inter-organizational trust in supply chain relationships: A systematic literature review and a meta-analysis of the empirical evidence". *Supply chain Management: An International Journal,* **17**(4), pp. 277–402.

Denyer, D. and Neely, A. (2004). "Introduction to the special issue: Innovation and the productivity performance in the UK". *International Journal of Management Reviews,* **5**(3–4), pp. 131–135.

Denyer, D. and Tranfield, D. (2009). "Producing a systematic review". In Buchanan, D. and Bryman, A. (Eds.). *The Sage Handbook of Organizational Research Methods.* Sage Publications: London, UK, pp. 671–687.

Denyer, D., Tranfield, D. and van Aken, J.E. (2008). "Developing design propositions through research design". *Organization Studies,* **29**(3), pp. 393–413.

Di Guardo, M.C. and Harrigan, K.R. (2012). "Mapping research on strategic alliances and innovation: a co–citation analysis". *The Journal of Technology Transfer*, **37**(6), pp. 789–811.

Di Stefano, G., Verona, G. and Peteraf, M. (2010). "Dynamic capabilities deconstructed: A bibliographic investigation into the origins, development, and future directions of the research domain". *Industrial and Corporate Change*, **18**(3) pp. 1–18.

Dickersin, K., Scherer, R. and Lefebvre, C. (1994). "Identifying relevant studies for systematic reviews". *BMJ: British Medical Journal,* **309**(6964), pp. 1286–1291.

Dickson, P.H. and Weaver, K.M. (1997). "Environmental determinants and individual–level moderators of alliance use". *Academy of Management Journal,* **40**(2), pp. 404–425.

Dogsen, M. (1993). "Learning, trust, and technological collaboration". *Human Relations,* **46**(1), pp. 77–98.

Dosi, G. and Teece, D.J. (1998). "Organizational competences and the Boundaries of the firms". In Arena, R. and C. Longhi, C. (Eds.). *Markets and Organizations.* Springer–Verlag: Berlin/Heidelberg (Germany), New York (NY).

Draulans, J., De Man, A.–P. and Volberda, H.W. (2003). "Building alliance capability: Management techniques for superior alliance performance". *Long Range Planning*, **36**(2), pp. 151−166.

Dubois, A. (2009). "To leap or not to leap: Triads as arbitrary subsets of networks of connected dyads". *Journal of Purchasing & Supply Management,* **15**(4), pp. 267–268.

Duran, B. S. and Odell, P. L. (2013). *Cluster analysis: A survey.* (Vol. 100). Springer Science & Business Media: Luxembourg/Berlin (Germany).

Durisin, B., Calabretta, G. and Parmeggiani, V. (2010). "The intellectual structure of product innovation research: A bibliometric study of the Journal of Product Innovation Management, 1984–2004". *Journal of Product Innovation Management*, **27**(3), pp. 437–451.

Durlak, J.A. and Lipsey, M.W. (1991). "A practitioner's guide to meta–analysis". *American Journal of Community Psychology,* **19**(3), pp. 291–332.

Duysters, G. and Vanhaverbeke, W. (1996). "Strategic interactions in DRAM and RISC technology: A network approach". *Scandinavian Journal of Management*, **12**(4), pp. 437–461.

Duysters, G., Heimeriks, K., Lokshin, B., Meijer, E. and Sabidussi, A. (2012). "Do firms learn to manage alliance portfolio diversity? The diversity–performance relationship and the moderating effects of experience and capability". *European Management Review*, **9**(3), pp. 139–152.

Duysters, G., Kok, G. and Vaandrager, M. (1999). "Crafting successful strategic technology partnerships". *R&D Management,* **29**(4), pp. 343–351.

Dyer, J., Kale, P. and Singh, H. (2004). "When to ally and when to acquire". *Harvard Business Review,* **82**(7–8), pp. 108–115.

Dyer, J.H. and Chu, W. (2000). "The determinants of trust in supplier–automaker relationships in the U.S., Japan, and Korea". *Journal of International Business Studies,* **31**(2), pp. 259–285.

Dyer, J.H. and Hatch, N.W. (2006). "Relation–specific capabilities and barriers to knowledge transfers: Creating advantage through network relationships". *Strategic Management Journal,* **27**(8), pp. 701–719.

Dyer, J.H. and Nobeoka, K. (2002). "Creating and managing a high–performance knowledge–sharing network: The Toyota case". *Strategic Management Journal,* **21**(3), pp. 345–367.

Dyer, J.H., Kale, P. and Singh, H. (2001). "How to make strategic alliances work". *Sloan Management Review,* 42(4), pp. 37–43.

Earley, P.C. and Brittain, J. (1993). "Cross–level analysis of organizations: Social resource management model". In Staw, B.M. and Cummings, L.L. (Eds.). *Research in organizational behavior.* JAI Press: Greenwich, CT, Vol. 15, pp. 357–408.

Eden, L., Hitt, M.A. and Ireland, R.D. (2008). "Friends, acquaintances, or strangers? Partner selection in R&D alliances". *Academy of Management Journal,* **51**(2), pp. 315–334.

Eisenhardt, K.M. and Martin, J.A. (2000). "Dynamic capabilities: What are they?" *Strategic Management Journal,* **21**(10–11), pp. 1105–1121.

Eisenhardt, K.M. and Schoonhoven, C.B. (1996). "Resource–based view of strategic alliance formation: strategic and social effects in entrepreneurial firms". *Organization Science,* **7**(2), pp. 136–150.

Elder, L. and Paul, R. (2009). "A glossary of critical thinking terms of concepts: The critical analytic vocabulary of the English language". Foundation for Critical Thinking: Dillon Beach, CA.

Ellis, S.C., Shockley, J. and Henry, R.M. (2011). "Making sense of supply disruption risk research: A conceptual framework grounded in enactment theory". *Journal of Supply Chain Management,* **47**(2), pp. 65–96.

Ellis, S.C., Henry, R.M. and Shockley, J. (2010). "Buyer perceptions of supply disruption risk: A behavioral view and empirical assessment". *Journal of Operations Management,* **28**(1), pp. 34–46.

Ellram, L.M., Tate, W.L. and Billington, C. (2007). "Services supply management: The next frontier for improved organizational performance". *California Management Review,* **49**(4), pp. 44–65.

Elmquist, M. and Le Masson, P. (2009). "The value of a 'failed' R&D project: An emerging evaluation framework for building innovative capabilities". *R&D Management*, **39**(2), pp. 136–151.

Eom, S.B. (2008). "Author cocitation analysis: Quantitative methods for mapping the intellectual structure of an academic discipline". IGI Global: Hershey, PA.

Ernst & Young (2009). *"Redrawing the map: Globalization and the changing world of business"*. [http://www.ey.com/GL/en/Issues/Business–environment/Redrawing–the–map—globalization–and–the–changing–world–of–business——Five–business–responses–to–globalization] (Accessed online: March 14th, 2014).

Ettlie, J.E. and Pavlou, P.A. (2006). "Technology–based new product development partnerships". *Decision Sciences*, **37**(2), pp. 117–147.

Faems, D., De Visser, M., Andries, P. and van Looy, B. (2010). "Technology alliance portfolios and financial performance: Value–enhancing and cost–increasing effects of open innovation". *Journal of Product Innovation Management,* **27**(6), pp. 785–796.

Fagerberg, J., Fosaas, M. and Sapprasert, K. (2012). "Innovation: Exploring the knowledge base". *Research Policy*, **41**(7), pp. 1132–1153.

Faisal, M.N., Banwet, D.K. and Shankar, R. (2006). "Supply chain risk mitigation: Modeling the enablers". *Business Process Management Journal*, **12**(4), pp. 535–552.

Farr, C.M. and Fischer, W.A. (1992). "Managing international high technology cooperative projects". *R&D Management,* **22**(1), pp. 55–67.

Fawcett, S.E., Calantone, R. and Smith, S.R. (1996). "An investigation of the impact of flexibility on global reach and firm performance". *Journal of Business Logistics,* **17**(2), pp. 167–196.

Fawcett, S.E., Waller, M.A., Miller, J.W., Schwieterman, M.A., Hazen, B.T. and Overstreet, R.E. (2014). "A trail guide to publishing success: Tips on writing influential conceptual, qualitative, and survey research". *Journal of Business Logistics,* **35**(1), pp. 1–16.

Fawcett, S.E., Wallin, C., Allred, C., Fawcett, A.M. and Magnan, G.M. (2011). "Information technology as an enabler of supply chain collaboration: A dynamic capabilities perspective". *Journal of Supply Chain Management*, **47**(1), pp. 38–56.

Felekoglu, B. and Moultrie, J. (2013). "Top management involvement in new product development: A review and synthesis". *Journal of Product Innovation Management,* **31**(1), pp. 159–175.

Feller, J., Parhankangas, A., Smeds, R. and Jaatinen, M. (2013). "How companies learn to collaborate: The emergence of improved inter–organizational processes in R&D alliances". *Organization Studies*, **34**(3), pp. 313–343.

Felzensztein, C., Gimmon, E. and Carter, S. (2010). "Geographical co–location, social networks and inter–firm marketing co–operation: The case of the salmon industry". *Long Range Planning*. **43**(5–6), pp. 675–690.

Fey, C.F. and Birkinshaw, J. (2005). "External sources of knowledge, governance mode, and R&D performance". *Journal of Management,* **31**(4), pp. 597–621.

Finch, P. (2004). "Supply chain risk management". *Supply Chain Management: An International Journal,* **9**(2), pp. 183–96.

Fink, A. (2005). "Conducting research literature reviews: From paper to the internet". Sage Publications: Thousand Oaks, CA.

Fischbach, K., Putzke, J. and Schoder, D. (2011). "Co–authorship networks in electronic markets research". *Electronic Markets*, **21**(1), pp. 19–40.

Fisher, M.L. (1997). "What is the right supply chain for your product?" *Harvard Business Review*, March–April, pp. 105–116.

Flynn, B.B., Sakakibara, S. and Schroeder, R.G. (1995). "Relationship between JIT and TQM: Practices and performance". *The Academy of Management Journal,* **38**(5). pp. 1325–1360.

Flynn, B.B., Sakakibara, S., Schroeder, R.G., Bates, K.A. and Flynn, E.J. (1990). "Empirical research in operations management". *Journal of Operations Management*, **9**(2), pp. 250–284.

Folke, C., Carpenter, S., Elmqvist, T., Gunderson, L., Holling, C.S. and Walker, B. (2002). "Resilience and sustainable development: Building adaptive capacity in a world of transformations". *AMBIO: A Journal of the Human Environment,* **31**(5), pp. 437–440.

Forrest, J.E. and Martin, M. J. C (1992). "Strategic alliances between large and small research intensive organizations: Experiences in the biotechnology industry". *R&D Management* **22**(1), pp. 41–53.

Franceschet, M. (2010). "A comparison of bibliometric indicators for computer science scholars and journals on Web of Science and Google Scholar". *Scientometrics,* **83**(1), pp. 243–258.

Franklin, J.J. and Johnston, R. (1988). "Co–citation bibliometric modeling as a tool for S&T policy and R&D management: Isues, applications, and developments". In Raan, A.F.J. (Ed.). *Handbook of quantitative studies of science and technology.* Elsevier: Amsterdam, The Netherlands, pp. 325–389.

Friedmann, H. (2005). "From colonialism to green capitalism: Social movements and emergence of food regimes". In Buttel, F.H. and McMichael, P. (Eds.). *New Directions in the Sociology of Global Development (Research in Rural Sociology and Development),* 11th ed. Emerald Group Publishing: Bingley, UK, pp. 227–264.

Furrer, O., Thomas, H. and Goussevskaia, A. (2008). "The structure and evolution of the strategic management field: A content analysis of 26 years of strategic management research". *International Journal of Management Reviews,* **10**(1), pp. 1–23.

Galaskiewicz, J. (2011). "Studying supply chains from a social network perspective". *Journal of Supply Chain Management,* **47**(1), pp. 4–8.

Galvagno, M. (2011). "The intellectual structure of the anti–consumption and consumer resistance field: An author co–citation analysis". *European Journal of Marketing*, **45**(11–12), pp. 1688–1701.

Gammelgaard, B. and Flint D. (2012). "Qualitative research in logistics and supply chain management: beyond the justification for using qualitative methods". *International Journal of Physical Distribution & Logistics Management*, **42**(8/9).

Gassmann O. (2006). "Innovation und Risiko - zwei Seiten einer Medaille". In: Gassmann O., Kobe C. (Eds.). *Management von Innovation und Risiko.* Springer Verlag: Berlin, Germany, pp. 3-24.

Gerdsri, N., Kongthon, A. and Vatananan, R.S. (2013). "Mapping the knowledge evolution and professional network in the field of technology roadmapping: A bibliometric analysis". *Technology Analysis & Strategic Management*, **25**(4), pp. 403–422.

Ghadge, A., Dani, S. and Kalawasky, R. (2012). "Supply chain risk management: present and future scope". *The International Journal of Logistics Management,* **23**(3), pp. 313–339.

Gimenez, C., Elcio, M. and Tachizawa, E.M. (2012). "Extending sustainability to suppliers: A systematic literature review". *Supply Chain Management: An International Journal,* **17**(5), pp. 531–543.

Giunipero, L.C. and Eltantawy, R.A. (2004). "Securing the upstream supply chain: A risk management approach". *International Journal of Physical Distribution & Logistics Management*, **34**(9), pp. 698–713.

Giunipero, L.C., Hooker, R.E., Joseph–Matthews, S., Yoon, T.E. and Brudvig, S. (2008). "A decade of SCM literature: Past, present and future implications". *Journal of Supply Chain Management*, **44**(4), pp. 66–86.

Gligor, D.M. and Holcomb, M.C. (2012). "Understanding the role of logistics capabilities in achieving supply chain agility: A systematic literature review". *Supply Chain Management: An International Journal,* **17**(4), pp. 438–453.

Gmür, M. (2003). "Co–citation analysis and the search for invisible colleges: A methodological evaluation". *Scientometrics*, **57**(1), pp. 27–57.

Goh, M., Lim, J. and Meng, F. (2007). "A stochastic model for risk management in global supply chain networks". *European Journal of Operational Research,* **182**(1), pp. 64–173.

Golgeci, I. and Ponomarov, S.Y. (2013). "Does firm innovativeness enable effective responses to supply chain disruptions? An empirical analysis". *Supply Chain Management: An international Journal,* **18**(6), pp. 604–617.

Golgeci, I. and Ponomarov, S.Y. (2014). "How does firm innovativeness enable supply chain resilience? The moderating role of supply uncertainty and interdependence". *Technology Analysis & Strategic Management,* **27**(3), pp. 267-282.

Golicic, S.L. and Davis, D.F. (2012) "Implementing mixed methods research in supply chain management". *International Journal of Physical Distribution & Logistics Management,* **42**(8/9), pp. 726–741.

Gosling, J. and Naim, M.M. (2009). "Engineer–to–order supply chain management: A literature review and research agenda". *International Journal of Production Economics,* **122**(2), pp. 741–754.

Granovetter, M. (1973). "The strength of weak ties". *American Journal of Sociology*, **78**(6), pp. 1360–1380.

Grant, R.M. (1991). "The resource–based theory of competitive advantage: Implications for strategy formulation". *California Management Review,* **33**(3), pp. 114–135.

Grant, R.M. (1996). "Toward a knowledge–based theory of the firm". *Strategic Management Journal,* **17**(S2), pp. 109–122.

Grant, R.M. and Baden–Fuller, C. (2004). "A knowledge theory of strategic alliances". *Journal of Management studies,* **41**(1), pp. 61–84.

Greening, P. and Rutherford, C. (2011). "Disruptions and supply networks: A multi-level, multi-theoretical relational perspective". *The International Journal of Logistics Management,* **22**(1), pp. 104–126.

Grégoire, D.A., Corbett, A.C. and McMullen, J.S. (2011). "The cognitive perspective in entrepreneurship: An agenda for future research". *Journal of Management Studies*, **48**(6), pp. 1443–1477.

Grötsch, V.M., Blome, C. and Schleper, M.C. (2013). "Antecedents of proactive supply chain risk management – A contingency perspective". *International Journal of Production Research,* **51**(10), pp. 2842–2867.

Gulati, R. (1995). "Does familiarity breed trust? The implications of repeated ties for contractual choice in alliances". *Academy of Management Journal,* **38**(1), pp. 85–112.

Gulati, R. (1998). "Alliances and networks". *Strategic Management Journal,* **19**(4), pp. 293–317.

Gulati, R. and Gargiulo, M. (1999). "Where do interorganizational networks come from?" *American Journal of Sociology,* **104**(5), pp. 1439-1493.

Gulati, R. and Nickerson, J.A. (2008). "Interorganizational trust, governance choice and exchange performance". *Organization Science,* **19**(5), pp. 688–708.

Gulati, R. and Singh, H. (1998). "The architecture of cooperation: Managing coordination costs and appropriation concerns in strategic alliances". *Administrative Science Quarterly.* **43**(4), pp. 781–814.

Gulati, R., Nohria, N. and Zaheer, A. (2000). "Strategic Networks". *Strategic Management Journal,* **21**(3), pp. 203–215.

Gundolf, K. and Filser, M. (2012). "Management research and religion: A citation analysis". *Journal of Business Ethics,* **112**(1), pp. 177–185.

Hackman, J.R. (2003). "Learning more by crossing levels: Evidence from airplanes, hospitals, and orchestras". *Journal of Organizational Behaviour,* **24**(8), pp. 905–922.

Hafeez, K., Zhang, Y.B. and Malak, N. (2002). "Determining key capabilities of a firm using analytic hierarchy process". *International Journal of Production Economics,* **76**(1), pp. 39–51.

Hagedoorn, J. (1993). "Understanding the rationale of strategic technology partnering: Nterorganizational modes of cooperation and sectoral differences". *Strategic management journal*, **14**(5), pp. 371-385.

Hagedoorn, J. (2002). "Inter–firm R&D partnerships: an overview of major trends and patterns since 1960". *Research Policy,* **31**(4), pp. 477–492.

Hagedoorn, J. and Duysters, G. (2002). "External sources of innovative capabilities: The preference for strategic alliances or mergers and acquisitions". *Journal of Management Studies,* **39**(2), pp. 167–188.

Hagedoorn, J. and Schakenraad, J. (1994). "The effect of strategic technology alliances on company performance". *Strategic Management Journal,* **15**(4), pp. 291–309.

Hagedoorn, J., Roijakkers, N. and Van Kranenburg, H. (2006). "Inter–Firm R&D networks: The importance of strategic network capabilities for high–tech partnership formation". *British Journal of Management,* **17**(1), pp. 39–53.

Hallikas, J., Karvonen, I., Pulkkinen, U., Virolainen, V.–M. and Tuominen, M. (2004). "Risk management process in supplier networks". *International Journal of Production Economics,* **90**(1), pp. 47–58.

Hallikas, J., Virolainen, V.–M. and Tuominen, M. (2002). "Risk analysis and assessment in network environments: A dyadic case study". *International Journal of Production Economics*, **78**(1), pp. 45–55.

Hambrick, D.C. (1994). "What if the academy actually mattered?" *Academy of Management Review,* **19**(1), pp. 11–16.

Hamel, G. and Valikangas, L. (2003). "The quest for resilience". *Harvard Business Review,* **81**(9), pp. 52–63.

Handfield, R.B. and Bechtel, C. (2002). "The role of trust and relationship structure in improving supply chain responsiveness". *Industrial Marketing Management,* **31**(4), pp. 367–382.

Handfield, R.B. and Nichols, E.L. (2002). "Supply chain redesign: Transforming supply chains into integrated value systems". Prentice–Hall: Upper Saddle River, NJ.

Hanisch, B. and Wald, A. (2012). "A bibliometric view on the use of contingency theory in project management research". *Project Management Journal*, **43**(3), pp. 4–23.

Hansen, B.E. (1999). "Threshold effects in non–dynamic panels: Estimation, testing, and inference". *Journal of Econometrics,* **93**(2), pp. 345–368.

Harland, C., Brenchley, R. and Walker, H. (2003). "Risk in supply networks". *Journal of Purchasing & Supply Management*, **9**(2), pp. 51–62.

Harzing, A.-W. (2015). *"Journal Quality List". 53rd edition"*. [http://www.harzing.com/download/jql_journal.pdf] (Accessed online: 10th March, 2015).

Hassini, E., Surti, C. and Searcy, C. (2012). "A literature review and a case study of sustainable supply chains with a focus on metrics". *International Journal of Production Economics,* **140**(1), pp. 69–82.

Häusler, J., Hohn, H.–W. and Lütz, S. (1994). "Contingencies of innovative networks: A case study of successful interfirm R&D collaboration". *Research Policy,* **23**(1), pp. 47–66.

Häussler, C. and Higgins, M.J. (2014). "Strategic alliances: Trading ownership for capabilities". *Journal of Economics and Management Strategy,* **23**(1), pp. 178–203.

Häussler, C., Patzelt, H. and Zahra, S. (2012). "Strategic alliances and product development in high technology new firms: The moderating effect of technological capabilities". *Journal of Business Venturing,* **27**(2), pp. 217–233.

Hearnshaw, E.J.S. and Wilson, M.M.J. (2013). "A complex network approach to supply chain network theory". *International Journal of Operations & Production Management,* **33**(4), pp. 442 –469.

Heckmann, I., Comes, T. and Nickel, S. (2015). "A critical review on supply chain risk – Definition, measure and modeling". *Omega,* Vol. 52, pp. 119–132.

Heimeriks, K. and Duysters, G. (2007). "Alliance capability as a mediator between experience and alliance performance: An empirical investigation into the alliance capability development process". *Journal of Management Studies*, **44**(1), pp. 25–49.

Heimeriks, K., Klijn, E. and Reuer, J. (2009). "Building capabilities for alliance portfolios". *Long Range Planning*, **42**(1), pp. 96–114.

Hendricks, K.B. and Singhal, V.R. (2005). "An empirical analysis of the effect of supply chain disruptions on long–run stock price performance and equity risk of the firm". *Production and Operations Management,* **14**(1), pp. 35–52.

Hendricks, K.B. and Singhal, V.R. (2012). "Supply chain disruptions and corporate performance". In: Gurnani, H., Mehrotra, A. and Ray, S. (Eds.). *Supply chain disruptions: Theory and practice of managing risks.* Springer: London, UK, pp. 1–19.

Hennart, J.–F. (1988). "A Transaction cost theory of equity joint–ventures". *Strategic Management Journal,* **9**(4), pp. 361–374.

Hennart, J.–F. (1991). "The transaction cost theory of joint–ventures. An empirical study of Japanese subsidiaries in the United States". *Management Science,* **37**(4), pp. 483–97.

Herbst, U., Voeth, M. and Meister, C. (2011). "What do we know about buyer–seller negotiations in marketing research? A status quo analysis". *Industrial Marketing Management*, **40**(6), pp. 967–978.

Higgins, M.J. and Rodriguez, D. (2006). "The outsourcing of R&D through acquisitions in the pharmaceutical industry". *Journal of Financial Economics,* **80**(2), pp. 351–383.

Hill, C.W.L. and Rothaermel, F.T. (2003). "The performance of incumbent firms in the face of radical technological innovation". *Academy of Management Review,* **28**(2), pp. 257–274.

Hitt, M.A., Tihanyi, L., Miller, T. and Connelly, B. (2006). "International diversification: Antecedents, outcomes, and moderators". *Journal of Management*, **32**(6), pp. 831–867.

Hoang, H. and Rothaermel, F.T. (2005). "The effect of general and partner-specific alliance experience on joint R&D project performance". *Academy of Management Journal*, **48**(2), pp. 332-345.

Hoffman, D.L. and Holbrook, M.B. (1993). "The intellectual structure of consumer research – A bibliometric study of author cocitations in the first 15 years of the Journal of Consumer Research". *Journal of Consumer Research*, **19**(4), pp. 505–517.

Hoffmann, P., Schiele, H. and Krabbendam, K. (2013). "Uncertainty, supply risk management and their impact on performance". *Journal of Purchasing & Supply Management,* **19**(3), pp. 199–211.

Holcomb, T.R. and Hitt, M.A. (2007). "Toward a model of strategic outsourcing". *Journal of Operations Management,* **25**(2), pp. 464–481.

Holtbrügge, D. and Dögl, C. (2012). "How international is corporate environmental responsibility? A literature review". *Journal of International Management,* **18**(2), pp. 80–195.

Huang, K.F. and Yu, C.M.J. (2011). "The effect of competitive and non–competitive R&D collaboration on firm innovation". *Journal of Technology Transfer*, **36**(4), pp. 383–403.

Hult, G.T.M., Hurley, R.F. and Knight, G.A. (2004a). "Innovativeness: Its antecedents and impact on business performance". *Industrial Marketing Management,* **33**(5), pp. 429–438.

Hult, G.T.M., Ketchen Jr., D.J. and Slater, S.F. (2004b). "Information processing, knowledge development, and strategic supply chain performance". *Academy of Management Journal,* **47**(2), pp. 241–253.

Hunt, S.D. and Davis, D.F. (2012). "Grounding supply chain management in resource–advantage theory: In defense of a resource–based view of the firm". *Journal of Supply Chain Management,* **48**(2), pp. 14–20.

Ingham, M. and Mothe, C. (1998). "How to learn in R&D partnerships?" *R&D Management,* **28**(4), pp. 249–261.

Inkpen, A.C. and Beamish, P.W. (1997). "Knowledge, bargaining power, and the instability of international joint ventures". *Academy of Management Review,* **22**(1), pp. 177–202.

Inkpen, A.C. and Tsang, E.W.K. (2005). "Social capital, networks and knowledge transfer". *Academy of Management Review*, **30**(1), pp. 146–165.

Ireland, R.D. and Webb, J.W. (2007). "A multi–theoretic perspective on trust and power in strategic supply chains". *Journal of Operations Management*, **25**(2), pp. 482–497.

Ishfaq, R. (2012). "Resilience through flexibility in transportation operations". *International Journal of Logistics Research and Applications,* **15**(4), pp. 215–229.

Jarillo, J.C. (1988). "On strategic networks". *Strategic Management Journal,* **9**(1), pp. 31-41.

Jarneving, B. (2005). "A comparison of two bibliometric methods for mapping of the research front". *Scientometrics*, **65**(2), pp. 245–263.

Jiang, B., Baker, R.C. and Frazier, G.V. (2009). "An analysis of job dissatisfaction and turnover to reduce global supply chain risk: Evidence from China". *Journal of Operations Management*, **27**(2), pp. 169–184.

Johnson, B. and Onwuegbuzie, A. (2004). "Mixed methods research: A research paradigm whose time has come". *Educational Researcher,* **33**(7), pp. 14–26.

Johnson, B., Onwuegbuzie, A. and Turner, L. (2007). "Toward a definition of mixed methods research". *Journal of Mixed Methods Research,* **1**(2), pp. 112–133.

Johnson, M.E. (2001)". Learning from toys: Lessons in managing supply chain risk from the toy industry". *California Management Review,* **43**(3), pp. 106–124.

Johnson, N. (2013). "Exploring the role of social capital in facilitating supply chain resilience". *Supply Chain Management: An International Journal,* **18**(3), pp. 324–336.

Johnstone, M. (2007). "Journal impact factors: Implications for the nursing profession". *International Nursing Review,* **54**(1), pp. 35–40.

Jolink, A. and Niesten, E. (2012). "Recent qualitative advances on hybrid organizations: Taking stock, looking ahead". *Scandinavian Journal of Management,* **28**(2), pp. 1149–1161.

Jones, S., Fawcett, S.E., Fawcett, A.M. and Wallin, C. (2010). "Benchmarking trust signals in supply chain alliances: Moving toward a robust measure of trust". *Benchmarking: An International Journal,* **17**(5), pp. 705–27.

Jüttner, U. (2005). "Supply chain risk management: Understanding the business requirements from a practitioner perspective". *The International Journal of Logistics Management,* **16**(1), pp.120–141.

Jüttner, U., Peck, H. and Christopher, M. (2003). "Supply chain risk management: Outlining an agenda for future research". *International Journal of Logistics Research and Applications*, **6**(4), pp. 197–210.

Kalaignanam, K., Shankar, V. and Varadarajan, R. (2007). "Asymmetric new product development alliances: Win–win or win–lose partnerships?" *Management Science,* **53**(3), pp. 357–374.

Kale, P. and Singh, H. (2007). "Building firm capabilities through learning: The role of the alliance learning process in alliance capability and firm–level alliance success". *Strategic Management Journal,* **28**(10), pp. 981–1000.

Kale, P., Dyer, J. and Singh, H. (2002). "Alliance capability, stock market response, and long–term alliance success: The role of the alliance function". *Strategic Management Journal*, **23**(8), pp. 747–768.

Kamal, M.M. and Irani, Z. (2014). "Analysing supply chain integration through a systematic literature review: A normative perspective". *Supply Chain Management: An International Journal,* **19**(5/6), pp. 523–557.

Katila, R. and Ahuja, G. (2002). "Something old, something new: A longitudinal study of search behavior and new product introduction". *Academy of Management Journal,* **45**(6), pp. 1183–1194.

Keil, T., Maula, M., Schildt, H. and Zahra, S.A. (2008). "The effect of governance modes and relatedness of external business development activities on innovation performance". *Strategic Management Journal*, **29**(8), pp. 895–907.

Kern, D., Moser, R., Hartmann, E. and Moder, M. (2012). "Supply risk management: Model development and empirical analysis". *International Journal of Physical Distribution & Logistics Management,* **42**(1), pp. 60–82.

Ketchen Jr., D.J. and Hult, G.T.M. (2007). "Bridging organization theory and supply chain management: The case of best value supply chains". *Journal of Operations Management,* **25**(2), pp. 573–580.

Ketchen Jr., D.J., Ireland, R.D. and Snow, C.C. (2007). "Strategic entrepreneurship, collaborative innovation, and wealth creation". *Strategic Entrepreneurship Journal,* **1**(3–4), pp. 371–385.

Keupp, M.M., Palmié, M. and Gassmann, O. (2012). "The strategic management of innovation: A systematic review and paths for future research". *International Journal of Management Reviews*, **14**(4), pp. 367–390.

Khan, O. and Burnes, B. (2007). "Risk and supply chain management: Creating a research agenda". *International Journal of Logistics Management,* **18**(2), pp. 197–216.

Khan, O., Christopher, M. and Burbes, B. (2008). "The impact of product design on supply chain risk: A case study". *International Journal of Physical Distribution &Logistics Management,* **38**(5), pp. 412–432.

Khan, O., Christopher, M. and Creazza, A. (2012). "Aligning product design with the supply chain: A case study". *Supply Chain Management,* **17**(3), pp. 323–336.

Khan, O., Christopher, M. and Burbes, B. (2008). "The impact of product design on supply chain risk: A case study". *International Journal of Physical Distribution & Logistics Management,* **38**(5), pp. 412–32.

Kilduff, M. (2006). "Editor's comments: Publishing theory". *Academy of Management Review*, **31**(2), pp. 252–55.

Kilubi, I. (2015). "Strategic technology partnering: A framework extension". *The Journal of High Technology Management Research,* **26**(1), pp. 27–37.

Kilubi, I. (2015). "Strategic technology partnering: A framework extension".

Kilubi, I. (2016). "Strategic technology partnering capabilities: A systematic review of the empirical evidence over two decades". *Journal of Strategy and Management,* **9**(2), pp. 216-255.

Kilubi, I. and Haasis, H.-D. (2015). "Supply chain risk management enablers – A framework development through systematic review of the literature from 2000 to 2015". *International Journal of Business Science and Applied Management,* **10**(1), pp. 35-54.

Kilubi, I. and Haasis, H.-D. (2016). "26 years of strategic technology partnering: Trends, patterns and future prospects in research through frequency analysis". *International Journal of Innovation and Technology Management,* **13**(2), pp. 1-44.

Kim, C. and Song, J. (2007). "Creating new technology through alliances: An empirical investigation of joint patents". *Technovation*, **27**(8), pp. 461–470.

Kim, C.–S. and Inkpen, A.C. (2005). "Cross–border R&D alliances, absorptive capacity and technology learning". *Journal of International Management,* **11**(3), pp. 313–329.

Kim, Y. and Lee, K. (2003). "Technological collaboration in the Korean electronics parts industry: patterns and key success factors". *R&D Management,* **33**(1), pp. 59–77.

Kim, Y., Choi, T.Y., Yan, T. and Dooley, K. (2011). "Structural investigation of supply networks: A social network analysis approach". *Journal of Operations Management*, **29**(3), pp. 194–211.

Kleindorfer, P.R. and Saad, G.H. (2005). "Managing disruption risks in supply chains". *Production and Operations Management,* **14**(1), pp. 53–68.

Knemeyer, A.M., Zinn, W., and Eroglu, C. (2009). "Proactive planning for catastrophic events in supply chains". *Journal of Operations Management,* **27**(2), pp. 141–153.

Kogut, B. and Zander, U. (1996). "What firms do? Coordination, identity, and learning". *Organization Science,* **7**(5), pp. 502–518.

Koka, B.R. and Prescott, J.E. (2002). "Strategic alliances as social capital: A multidimensional view". *Strategic Management Journal,* **23**(9), pp. 795–816.

Kotabe, M. and Swan, K.S. (1995). "The role of strategic alliances in high–technology new product development". *Strategic Management Journal,* **16**(8), pp. 621–636.

Kousha, K. and Thelwall, M. (2007). "Google Scholar citations and Google Web/URL citations: A multi–discipline exploratory analysis". *Journal of the American Society for Information Science and Technology,* **58**(7), pp. 1055–1065.

Koza, M.P. and Lewin, A.Y. (1998). "The co–evolution of strategic alliances". *Organization Science,* **9**(3), pp. 255–264.

Kozlowski, S.W.J. and Klein, K.J. (2000). "A multilevel approach to theory and research in organizations: Contextual, temporal, and emergent processes". In Klein, K.J. and Kozlowski, S.W.J. (Eds.). *Multilevel theory, research and methods in organizations: Foundations, extensions, and new directions.* Jossey–Bass: San Francisco, CA, pp. 3–90.

KPMG (2012). "*Global Manufacturing Outlook 2012: Fostering growth through innovation*". [http://www.kpmg.com/Global/en/IssuesAndInsights/ArticlesPublications/global–manufacturing–outlook/Documents/fostering–growth–through–innovation.pdf] (Accessed online: June 14th, 2014).

Krause, D.R., Handfield, R.B. and Tyler, B.B. (2007). "The relationships between supplier development, commitment, social capital accumulation and performance improvement". *Journal of Operations Management,* **25**(2), pp. 528–545.

Krishnan, R., Martin, X. and Noorderhaven, N.G. (2006). "When does trust matter to alliance performance?" *Academy of Management Journal,* **49**(5), pp. 894–917.

Krugman, P. (1991). "Geography and Trade". MIT Press: Cambridge, MA.

Kuhn, T.S. (1996). "The structure of scientific revolutions". 3rd ed. Chicago: University of Chicago Press.

Lai, G., Debo, L.G., and Sycara, K. (2009). "Sharing inventory risk in supply chain: The implication of financial constraint". *Omega,* **37**(4), pp. 811–825.

Lanctot, A. and Swan, K.S. (2000). "Technology acquisition strategy in an internationally competitive environment". *Journal of International Management,* **6**(3), pp. 187–215.

Landis, J.R. and Koch, G.G. (1977). "The measurement of observer agreement for categorical data". *Biometrics,* Vol. 33, pp. 159–174.

Landström, H., Harirchi, G. and Aström, F. (2012). "Entrepreneurship: Exploring the knowledge base". *Research Policy*, **41**(7), pp. 1154–1181.

Lapide, L. (2000). "True measures of supply chain performance". *Supply Chain Management Review,* **4**(3), pp. 25–28.

Larson, A. (1992). "Network dyads in entrepreneurial settings: A study of the governance of exchange relationships". *Administrative Science Quarterly*, **37**(1), pp. 76–104.

Lattin, J.M., Carroll, J.D. and Green, P.E. (2003). "Analyzing multivariate data". Thomson Brooks/Cole, Pacific Grove, CA.

Lavastre, O., Gunasekaran, A. and Spalanzani, A. (2012). "Supply chain risk management in French companies". *Decision Support Systems,* **52**(4), pp. 828–838.

Lavie, D. (2006). "The competitive advantage of interconnected firms: An extension of the resource–based view". *Academy of Management Review,* **31**(3), pp. 638–658.

Lawson, B., Tyler, B.B. and Cousins, P.D. (2008). "Antecedents and consequences of social capital on buyer performance improvement". *Journal of Operations Management*, **26**(3), pp. 446–460.

Lazerson, M.H. and Lorenzoni, G. (1999). "The firms that feed industrial districts: A return to the Italian source". *Industrial and Corporate Change,* **8**(2), pp. 235–266.

Lechner, C., K. Frankenberger and S.W. Floyd (2010). "Task contingencies in the curvilinear relationship between inter–group networks & performance". *The Academy of Management Journal*, **53**(4), pp. 865–889.

Lee, C., Lee, K. and Pennings, J.M. (2001). "Internal capabilities, external networks, and performance: A study on technology–based ventures". *Strategic Management Journal,* **22**(6–7), pp. 615–640.

Lee, G.K. and Cole, R.E. (2003). "From a firm–based to a community–based model of knowledge creation: The case of the Linux Kernel development". *Organization Science,* **14**(6), pp. 633–649.

Lee, H.L. (2002). "Aligning supply chain strategies with product uncertainties". *California Management Review,* **44**(3), pp. 105–119.

Leenders, R.T.A.J. and Gabbay, S.M. (1999). "Corporate social capital and liability". Kluwer Academic Publishers: Boston, MA.

Leiblein, M.J. (2003). "The choice of organizational governance form and performance: Predictions from transaction cost, resource–based, and real options theories". *Journal of Management,* **29**(6), pp. 937–961.

Lenartowicz, T. and Roth, K. (2001). "Does subculture within a country matter? A cross–cultural study of motivational domains and business performance in Brazil". *Journal of International Business Studies,* **32**(2), pp. 305–325.

Leone, R.P., Robinson, L.M., Bragge, J. and Somervuori, O. (2012). "A citation and profiling analysis of pricing research from 1980 to 2010". *Journal of Business Research*, **65**(7), pp. 1010–1024.

Leseure, M.J., Bauer, J., Birdi, K., Neely, A.D. and Denyer, D. (2004). "Adoption of promising practices: A systematic review of the evidence". *International Journal of Management Reviews*, **5**(3–4), pp. 169–190.

Leyesdorff, L. and Vaughan, L. (2006). "Co–occurrence matrices and their implications in information science: Extending ACA to the Web environment". *Journal of the American Society for Information Science and Technology,* **57**(12), pp. 1616–1628.

Li, D., Eden, L., Hitt, M.A. and Ireland, R.D. (2008). "Friends, acquaintances, or strangers? Partner selection in R&D alliances". *Academy of Management Journal,* **51**(2), pp. 315–334.

Li, G., Fan, H., Lee, P.K.C. and Cheng, T.C.E. (2015). "Joint supply chain risk management: An agency and collaboration perspective". *International Journal of Production Economics,* Vol. 164, pp. 83–94.

Li, X. and Barnes, I. (2008). "Proactive supply risk management methods for building a robust supply selection process when sourcing from emerging markets". *Strategic Outsourcing: An International Journal*, **1**(3), pp. 252-267.

Light, R.J. and Pillemer, D.B. (1984). "Summing up: The science of reviewing research". Harvard University Press: Cambridge, MA.

Lightfoot, H., Baines, T. and Smart, P. (2013). "The servitization of manufacturing: A systematic literature review of interdependent trends". *International Journal of Operations and Production Management*, **33**(11), pp. 1408–1434.

Liker, J.K. and Choi, T.Y. (2004). "Building deep supplier relationships". *Harvard Business Review,* **82**(12), pp. 104–113.

Link, A.N. and Siegel, D.S. (*2007*). "*Innovation, entrepreneurship,* and *technological change".* Oxford University Press: Oxford, UK.

Link, A.N. and Siegel, D.S. (2007*).* "Innovation, entrepreneurship, and technological Change*".* Oxford, UK: Oxford University Press.

Linton, J.D. and Thongpapanl, N.T. (2004). "Ranking the technology innovation management journals". *Journal of Product Innovation Management,* **21**(2), pp. 123–139.

Liu, C.–L., Ghauri, P.N. and Sinkovics, R.R. (2010). "Understanding the impact of relational capital and organizational learning on alliance outcomes". *Journal of World Business,* **45**(3), pp. 237–249.

Lo Nigro, G. and Abbate, L. (2011). "Risk assessment and profit sharing in supply networks". *International Journal of Production Economics*, **131**(1), pp. 234–241.

Lockamy III, A. and McCormack, K. (2010). "Analysing risks in supply networks to facilitate outsourcing decisions". *International Journal of Production Research,* **48**(2), pp. 593–611.

Lorenzoni, G. and Lipparini, A. (1999). "The leveraging of interfirm relationships as a distinctive organizational capability: A longitudinal study". *Strategic Management Journal,* **20**(4), pp. 317–338.

Lummus, R.R., Vokurka, R.J. and Duclos, L.K. (2006). "The produce–process matrix revisited: Integrating supply chain trade–offs". *SAM Advanced Management Journal*, **71**(2), pp. 4–10.

Lynn, G., Reilly, R.R. and Akgün, A.E. (2000). "Knowledge Management in new products team: practices and outcomes". *IEEE Transactions on Engineering Management,* **47**(2), pp. 221–231.

MacInnis, D.J. (2004). "Where have all the papers gone? Reflections on the decline of conceptual articles". *Association for Consumer Research Newsletter*, (Spring), pp. 1–3.

MacInnis, D.J. (2011). "A framework for conceptual contributions in marketing". *Journal of Marketing,* **75**(4), pp. 136–154.

Macpherson, A. and Jones, O. (2010). "Strategies for the development of international journal of management reviews". *International Journal of Management Reviews,* **12**(2), pp. 107–113.

Mahapatra, S., Narasimhan, R. and Barbieri, P. (2010). "Strategic interdependence, governance effectiveness and supplier performance: A case study investigation and theory development". *Journal of Operations Management,* **28**(6), pp. 537–552.

Maitlis, S. and Lawrence, T.B. (2007). "Triggers and enablers of sensegiving in organizations". *Academy of Management Journal,* **50**(1), pp. 57–84.

Makino, S., Takehiko, I. and Chan, C.M. (2004). "Does country matter?" *Strategic Management Journal,* **25**(10), pp. 1027–1043.

Malik, K. (2002). "Aiding the technology manager: A conceptual model for intra–firm technology transfer". *Technovation,* **22**(7), pp. 427–436.

Mangan, J., Lalwani, C. and Gardner, B. (2004). "Combining quantitative and qualitative methodologies in logistics research". *International Journal of Physical Distribution & Logistics Management*, **34**(7), pp. 565–78.

Manuj, I. (2013). "Risk management in global sourcing: Comparing the business world and the academic world". *Transportation Journal*, **52**(1), pp. 80–107.

Manuj, I. and Mentzer, J.T. (2008a). "Global supply chain risk management". *Journal of Business Logistics*, **29**(1), pp. 133–155.

Manuj, I. and Mentzer, J.T. (2008b). "Global supply chain risk management strategies". *International Journal of Physical Distribution & Logistics Management,* **38**(3), pp. 192–223.

Manuj, I., Esper, T.L. and Stank, T.S. (2014). "Supply chain risk management approaches under different conditions of risk". *Journal of Business Logistics,* **35**(3), pp. 241–258.

Markovsky, B., Skovoretz, J., Willer, D., Lovaglia, M.J. and Erger, J. (1993). "The seeds of weak power: An extension of network exchange theory". *American Sociological Review,* **58**(2), pp. 197–209.

Markusen, J.R. (1995). "The boundaries of multinational enterprises and the theory of international trade". *Journal of Economic Perspectives*, **9**(2), pp. 169–189.

Marley, K.A., Ward, P.T. and Hill, J.A. (2014). "Mitigating supply chain disruptions – A normal accident perspective". *Supply Chain Management: An International Journal,* **19**(2), pp. 142–152.

Martha, J. and Subbakrishna, S. (2002). "Targeting a just–in–case supply chain for the inevitable next disaster". *Supply Chain Management Review,* **6**(5), pp. 18–23.

Martin, B. R., Nightingale, P. and Yegros–Yegros, A. (2012). "Science and technology studies: Exploring the knowledge base". *Research Policy*, **41**(7), pp. 1182–1204.

Mason–Jones, R., Naylor, B. and Towill, D.R. (2000). "Lean, agile, or leagile? Matching your supply chain to the marketplace". *International Journal of Production Research,* **38**(17), pp. 4061–4070.

Mays, N., Pope, C. and Popay, J. (2005). "Systematically reviewing qualitative and quantitative evidence to inform management and policy–making in the health field". *Journal of Health Services Research Policy,* **10**(1), pp. 6–20.

McCain, K.W. (1990). "Mapping authors in intellectual space: A technical overview". *Journal of the American Society for Information Science*, **41**(6), pp. 433–443.

McFarland, R.G., Bloodgood, J.M. and Payan, J.M. (2008). "Supply chain contagion". *Journal of Marketing*, **72**(2), pp. 63–79.

McGrath, H. and O'Toole (2013). "Enablers and inhibitors of the development of network capability in entrepreneurial firms: A study of the Irish micro–brewing network". *Industrial Marketing Management,* **42**(7), pp. 1141–1153.

McKinnon, A.C. (2013). "Starry–eyed: Journal rankings and the future of logistics research". *International Journal of Physical Distribution & Logistics Management,* **43**(1), pp. 6–17.

Meier, M. (2011). "Knowledge management in strategic alliances: A review of empirical evidence". *International Journal of Management Reviews,* **13**(1), pp. 1–23.

Mentzer, J.T., Dewitt, W., Keebler, J.S., Min, S., Nix, N.W., Smith, C.D. and Zacharia, Z.G. (2001). "Defining supply chain management". *Journal of Business Logistics*, **22**(2), pp. 1–26.

Merschmann, U. and Thonemann, U.W. (2011). "Supply chain flexibility, uncertainty and firm performance: An empirical analysis of German manufacturing firms". *International Journal of Production Economics,* **130**(1), pp. 43.53.

Miles, I.D. (2005). "Innovation in Services". In Fagerberg, J. Mowery, D. and R Nelson, R (Eds.). *The Oxford Handbook of Innovation*. Oxford University Press: Oxford, UK.

Min, K., Stephen, K. and Chen, H. (2008). "Developing social identity and social capital for supply chain management". *Journal of Business Logistics*, **29**(1), pp. 283–304.

Miotti, L. and Sachwald, F. (2003). "Co–operative R&D: Why and with whom? An integrated framework of analysis". *Research Policy,* **32**(8), pp. 1481–1499.

Mishra, A.K. (1996). "Organizational responses to crisis: The centrality of trust". In Kramer, R.M. and Thomas Tyler (Eds.). *Trust in organizations.* Sage Publications: Newbury Park, CA, pp. 261–287.

Mitrega, M., Forkmann, S., Ramos, C. and Henneberg, S.C. (2012). "Networking capability in business relationships – Concept and scale development". *Industrial Marketing Management,* **41**(5), pp. 739–751.

Mitroff, I.I. and Alpaslan, M.C. (2003). "Preparing for evil". *Harvard Business Review,* **81**(4), pp. 109–115.

Molina–Azorin, J.F. (2010). "Mixed methods research in strategic management: Impact and applications". *Organizational research methods,* **15**(1), pp. 33–56.

Möller, K. and Svahn, S. (2003). "Managing strategic nets: A capability perspective". *Marketing Theory*, **3**(2), pp. 209–234.

Monroe, R.W., J.M. Teets and P.R. Martin (2014). "Supply Chain Risk Management: An analysis of sources of risk and mitigation strategies". *International Journal of Applied Management Science,* **6**(1), pp. 4–21.

Moran, P. (2005). "Structural vs. relational embeddedness: Social capital and managerial performance". *Strategic Management Journal*, **26**(12), pp. 1129–1151.

Morgeson, F.P. and Hofmann, D.A. (1999). "The structure of collective constructs: Implications for multilevel research and theory development". *The Academy of Management Review,* **24**(2), pp. 249–265.

Morrow, J.L., Simon, D.G, Hitt, M.A and Holcomb, T.R. (2005). "Creating value in the face of declining performance: Designing actions to effect organizational recovery". Paper presented at the Strategic Management Society in Orlando, Florida.

Mowery, D.C., Oxley, J.E. and Silverman, B.S. (1996). "Strategic alliances and interfirm knowledge transfer". *Strategic Management Journal,* **17**(S2), pp. 77–91.

Moya, F., Jiménez, E. and Moneda, M. (1998). "Research fronts in library and information science in Spain 1985–1994". *Scientometrics,* **42**(2), pp. 229–246.

Mukherjee, D., Gaur, A.S., Gaur, S.S. and Schmid, F. (2013). "External and internal influences on R&D alliance formation: Evidence from German SMEs". *Journal of Business Research,* **66**(11), pp. 2178–2185.

Müller–Seitz, G. (2012). "Leadership in interorganizational networks: A literature review and suggestions for future research". *International Journal of Management Reviews,* **14**(4), pp. 428–443.

Mulrow, C.D. (2001). "Rationale for systematic reviews". *BMJ: British Medical Journal,* **309**(6954), pp. 597–599.

Nag, R., Hambrick, D.C. and Chen, M. (2007). "What is strategic management, really? Inductive derivation of a consensus definition of the field". *Strategic Management Journal,* **28**(9), pp. 935–955.

Nagurney, A. and Matsypura, D. (2005). "Global supply chain network dynamics with multicriteria decision–making under risk and uncertainty". *Transportation Research Part E: Logistics and Transportation Review,* **41**(6), pp. 585–612.

Nahapiet, J. and Ghoshal, S. (1998). "Social capital, intellectual capital and the organizational advantage". *Academy of Management Review*, **23**(2), pp. 242–266.

Narasimhan, R. (2014). "Theory development in operations management: Extending the frontiers of a mature discipline via qualitative research". *Decision Sciences,* **45**(2), pp. 209–227.

Narasimhan, R. and Narayanan, S. (2013). "Perspectives on supply chain enabled innovation". *Journal of Supply Chain Management*, **49**(4), pp. 27–42.

Narasimhan, R. and Talluri, S. (2009). "Perspectives on risk management in supply chains". *Journal of Operations Management,* **27**(2), pp. 114–118.

Narula, R. and Duysters, G. (2004). "Globalisation and trends in international R&D alliances". *Journal of International Management,* **10**(2), pp. 199–218.

Narasimhan, R. (2014). "Theory development in operations management: Extending the frontiers of a mature discipline via qualitative research". *Decision Sciences,* **45**(2), pp. 209–227.

Narasimhan, R. and Talluri, S. (2009). "Perspectives on risk management in supply chains". *Journal of Operations Management,* **27**(2), pp. 114–118.

Natarajarathinam, M., Capar, I. and Narayanan, A. (2009). "Managing supply chains in times of crisis: Review of literature and insights". *International Journal of Physical Distribution and Logistics Management,* **39**(7), pp. 535–73.

Neiger, D., Rotaru, K. and Churilov, L. (2009). "Supply chain risk identification with value–focused process engineering". *Journal of Operations Management,* **27**(2), pp. 154–168.

Nerur, S.P., Rasheed, A.A. and Natarajan, V. (2008). "The intellectual structure of the strategic management field: An author co–citation analysis". *Strategic Management Journal*, **29**(3), pp. 319–336.

Newbert, S.L. (2007). "Empirical research on resource–based view of the firm: An assessment and suggestions for future research". *Strategic Management Journal,* **28**(2), pp. 121–46.

Niesten, E. and Jolink, A. (2014). "The impact of alliance management capabilities on alliance attributes and performance: A literature review". *International Journal of Management Reviews,* 17(1), pp. 69–100.

Nijmeijer, K.J., Fabbricotti, I.N. and Huijsman, R. (2014). "Making franchise work: A framework based on a systematic review". *International Journal of Management Reviews,* **16**(1), pp. 62–83.

Nooraie, S.V. and Parast, M.M. (2015). "A multi–objective approach to supply chain risk management: Integrating visibility with supply and demand risk". *International Journal of Production Economics,* Vol. 161, pp. 192–200.

Nordin, A. and Agndal, H. (2008). "Business service sourcing: A literature review and agenda for future research". *International Journal of Integrated Supply Management,* **4**(3–4), pp. 378–405.

Norrman, A. and Jansson, U. (2004). "Ericsson's proactive supply chain risk management approach after a serious sub–supplier accident". *International Journal of Physical Distribution & Logistics Management,* **34**(5), pp. 434–56.

Noseleit, F. and de Faria, P. (2013). "Complementarities of internal R&D and alliances with different partner types". *Journal of Business Research,* **66**(10), pp. 2000–2006.

Nosella, A., Cantarello, S. and Filippini, R. (2012). "The intellectual structure of organizational ambidexterity: A bibliographic investigation into the state of the art". *Strategic Organization*, **10**(4), pp. 450–465.

Nueno, P. and Oosterveld, J. (1988). "Managing technology alliances". *Long Range Planning*, **21**(3), pp. 11–17.

Oh, H., Labianca, G. and Chung, M.–H. (2006). "A multilevel model of group social capital". *Academy of Management Review*, **31**(3), pp. 569–582.

Ohmae, K. (1989). "The global logic of strategic alliances". *Harvard Business Review,* **67**(2), pp. 143–154.

Ordanini, A., Rubera, G. and DeFillippi, R. (2008). "The many modes of interorganizational imitation. A critical review". *International Journal of Management Reviews,* **10**(4), pp. 375–398.

Ostlund, U., Wengstrom, Y. and Rowa–Dewar, N. (2011). "Combining qualitative and quantitative research within mixed method research designs: A methodological view". *International Journal of Nursing Studies,* **48**(3), pp. 369–383.

Oxley, J.E. and Sampson, R.C. (2004). "The scope and governance of international R&D alliances". *Strategic Management Journal,* **25**(8–9), pp. 723–749.

Ozman, M. (2009). "Inter–firm Networks and Innovation: A survey of literature". *Economics of Innovation and New Technology,* **18**(1), pp. 39–67.

Palmatier, R.W. (2008). "Interfirm relational drivers of customer value". *Journal of Marketing,* **72**(4), pp. 76–89.

Papadakis, I.S. (2006). "Financial performance of supply chains after disruptions: An event study". *Supply Chain Management: An International Journal,* **11**(1), pp. 25–33.

Park, N.K., Mezias, J.M. and Song, J. (2004). "A resource–based view of strategic alliances and firm value in the electronic marketplace". *Journal of Management,* **30**(1), pp. 7–27.

Parkhe, A. (1993). "Strategic alliance structuring: A game theoretic and transaction cost examination of interfirm cooperation". *The Academy of Management Journal,* **36**(4), pp. 794–829.

Parra–Requena, G., Molina–Morales, F.X. and Garcia–Villaverde, P.M. (2010). "The mediating effect of cognitive social capital on knowledge acquisition in clustered firms". *Growth and Change,* **41**(1), pp. 59–84.

Patton, M.Q. (1990). "Qualitative evaluation and research methods". Sage Publications: Newbury Park, CA.

Peck, H. (2005). “Drivers of supply chain vulnerability: an integrated framework”. *International Journal of Physical Distribution & Logistics Management,* **35**(4), pp. 210 – 232.

Pennings, J.M. and Harianto, F. (1992). “Technological networking and innovation implementation”. *Organization Science,* **3**(3), pp. 356–382.

Pennings, J.M. and Lee K. (1999). “Social capital of organization: Conceptualization, level of analysis, and performance implications”. In Leenders, R.T.A.J. and Gabbay, S.M. (Eds.). *Corporate social capital and liability.* Kluwer: New York, NY, pp. 43–67.

Pennings, J.M., Lee, K. and van Witteloostuijn, A. (1998). “Human capital, social capital, and firm dissolution”. *Academy of Management Journal,* **41**(4), pp. 425–440.

Peteraf, M.A. (1993). “The cornerstone of competitive advantage: A resource–based view”. *Strategic Management Journal,* **14**(3), pp. 179–191.

Petersen, K.J., Handfield, R.B., Lawson, B. and Cousins, P.D. (2008). “Buyer dependency and relational capital formation: The mediating effects of socialization processes and supplier integration”. *Journal of Supply Chain Management*, **44**(4), pp. 53–65.

Peterson, M.F., Arregle, J.–L. and Martin, X. (2012). “Multilevel models in international business research”. *Journal of International Business Studies*, **43**(5), pp. 451–457.

Petticrew, M. (2001). “Systematic reviews from astronomy to zoology: Myths and misconceptions”. *BMJ: British Medical Journal,* **322**(7278), pp. 98–101.

Petticrew, M. and Roberts, H. (2006). “Systematic reviews in the social sciences: A practical guide”. Blackwell Publishing: Oxford, UK.

Pettit, T.J., Fiksel, J. and Croxton, K.L. (2010). “Ensuring supply chain resilience: Development of a conceptual framework”. *Journal of Business Logistics,* **31**(1), pp. 1–22.

Pfohl, H., Koehler, H. and Thomas, D. (2010). “State of the art in supply chain risk management research: Empirical and conceptual findings and a roadmapfor the implementation in practice”. *Logistics Research,* **2**(1), pp. 33–44.

Phelps, C.C. (2010). "A longitudinal study of the influence of alliance network structure and composition on firm exploratory innovation". *Academy of Management Journal,* **53**(4), pp. 890–913.

Phene, A. and Tallman, S. (2010). "Complexity, context and governance in biotechnology alliances". *Journal of International Business Studies*, **43**(1), pp. 61–83.

Pierce, S.J. (1990). "Disciplinary work and interdisciplinary areas: Sociology and bibliometrics". In Borgman, C.L. (Ed.). *Scholarly communication and bibliometrics*. Sage: Newbury Park, CA, pp. 84–106.

Pilbeam, C., Alvarez, G. and Wilson, H. (2012). "The governance of supply networks: A systematic literature review". *Supply Chain Management: An International Journal,* **17**(4), pp. 358–376.

Pilkington, A. and Liston–Heyes, C. (1999). "Is production and operations management a discipline? A citation/co–citation study". *International Journal of Operations & Production Management,* **19**(1), pp. 7–20.

Pilkington, A. and Meredith, J. (2009). "The evolution of the intellectual structure of operations management–1980–2006: A citation/co–citation analysis". *Journal of Operations Management*, **27**(3), pp. 185–202.

Pittaway, L., Robertson, M., Munir, K., Denyer, D. and Neely, A. (2004). "Networking and innovation: A systematic review of the evidence". *International Journal of Management Reviews,* **5–6**(3–4), pp. 137–168.

Podsakoff, P.M., MacKenzie, S.B., Bachrach, D.G. and Podskaff, N.P. (2005). "The influence of management journals in the 1980s and 1990s". *Strategic Management Journal*, **26**(5), pp. 473–488.

Ponomarov, S.Y. (2012). "Antecedents and consequences of supply chain resilience: A dynamic capabilities perspective". Ph.D. dissertation (Business Administration). *The University of Tennessee*, Knoxville, TN.

Ponomarov, S.Y. and Holcomb, M.C. (2009). "Understanding the concept of supply chain resilience". *The International Journal of Logistics Management,* **20**(1), pp. 124–143.

Ponzi, L.J. (2002). "The intellectual structure and interdisciplinary breadth of knowledge management: A bibliometric study of its early stage of development". *Scientometrics,* **55**(2), pp. 259–272.

Popay, J., Roberts, H., Petticrew, M., Arai, L., Rodgers, M. and Brittens, N. (2006). "Guidance on the conduct of narrative synthesis in systematic reviews: Final report". ESRC Methods Programme: Swindon, UK.

Popay, J., Rogers, A. and Williams, G. (1998). "Rationale and standards for the systematic review of qualitative literature in health services research". *Qualitative Health Research,* **8**(3), pp. 341–351.

Poppo, L. and Zenger, T. (2002). "Do formal contracts and relational governance function as substitutes or complements?" *Strategic Management Journal*, **23**(8), pp. 707–725.

Porter, M. E. (1998). "Competitive strategy: Techniques for analyzing industries and competitors". Free Press: New York, NY.

Powell, W.W. (1998). "Learning from collaboration: knowledge and networks in the biotechnology and pharmaceutical industries". *California Management Review,* **40**(3), pp. 228–240.

Powell, W.W., Koput, K.W. and Smith–Doerr, L. (1996). "Interorganizational collaboration and the locus of innovation: Networks of learning in biotechnology". *Administrative Science Quarterly,* **41**(1), pp. 116–145.

Prusak, L. and Cohen, D. (2001). "How to invest in social capital". *Harvard Business Review,* **79**(6), pp. 86–93.

Pujawan, N. and Geraldin, L.H. (2009). "House of risk: A model for proactive supply chain risk management". *Business Process Management Journal,* **15**(6), pp. 953–967.

Punniyamoorthy, M., Thamaraiselvan, N. and Manikandan, L. (2013). "Assessment of supply chain risk: Scale development and validation". *Benchmarking: An International Journal,* **20**(1), pp. 79–105.

PwC (2010). "*The ever–changing global service–provider industry: Key findings for 2010.*" [http://www.pwc.com/us/en/increasing–it–effectiveness/assets/the–ever–changing–global–service–provider–industry.pdf] (Accessed online: June 14th, 2014).

Quinn, R.E. and Cameron, K.S. (1988). "Paradox and transformation". Bollinger: Cambridge, MA.

Raasch, C., Lee, V., Spaeth, S. and Herstatt, C. (2013). "The rise and fall of interdisciplinary research: The case of open source innovation". *Research Policy,* **42**(5), pp. 1138–1151.

Rajesh, R. and Ravi, V. (2015). "Modeling enablers of supply chain risk mitigation in electronic supply chains: A Grey–DEMATEL approach". *Computers & Industrial Engineering,* Vol. 87, pp. 126–139.

Rajesh, R., Ravi, V. and Rao, R.V. (2015). "Selection of risk mitigation strategy in electronic supply chains using grey theory and digraph–matrix approaches". *International Journal of Production Research,* **53**(1), pp. 238–257.

Ralston, D.A., Holt, D.H., Terpstra, R.H. and Kai–Cheng, Y. (1997). "The impact of national culture and economic ideology on managerial work values: A study of the United States, Russia, Japan, and China". *Journal of International Business Studies,* **28**(1), pp. 177–207.

Ramamoorthy, N., Kulkarni, S.P., Gupta, A. and Flood, P.C. (2007). "Individualism–collectivism orientation and employee attitudes: A comparison of employees from the high–technology sector in India and Ireland". *Journal of International Management,* **13**(2), pp. 187–203.

Ramos-Rodríguez, A.R. and Ruíz-Navarro, J. (2004). "Changes in the intellectual structure of strategic management research: A bibliometric study of the Strategic Management Journal". 1980–2000. Strategic Management Journal, **25**(10), pp. 981-1004.

Rao, S. and Goldsby, T.J. (2009). "Supply chain risks: A review and typology". *The International Journal of Logistics Management,* **20**(1), pp. 97–123.

Rashman, L., Withers, E. and Hartley, J. (2009). "Organizational learning and knowledge in public service organizations: A systematic review of the literature". *International Journal of Management Reviews,* **11**(4), pp. 463–494.

Raynaud, E., Sauvée, L. and Valeschini, E. (2009). "Aligning branding strategies and governance of vertical transactions in agri–food chains". *Industrial and Corporate Change,* **24**(3), pp. 251–273.

Reichart, A. and Holweg, M. (2007). "Creating the customer responsive supply chain: A reconciliation of concepts". *The International Journal of Operations and Production Management,* **27**(12), pp. 1144–1172.

Reus, T.H. and Rottig, D. (2009). "Meta–analyses of international joint venture performance determinants". *Management International Review,* **49**(5), pp. 607–640.

Rice, J.B. and Caniato, F. (2003). "Building a secure and resilient supply network". *Supply Chain Management Review,* **7**(5), pp. 22–30.

Richards, M. and De Carolis, D.M. (2003). "Joint venture research and development activity: An analysis of the international biotechnology industry“. *Journal of International Management*, **9**(1), pp. 33–49.

Rindova, V.P. and Violina, C.J. (1999). "Constructing competitive advantage: The role of firm–constituent interactions". *Strategic Management Journal,* **20**(8), pp. 691–710.

Ring, P.S. and van de Ven, A.H. (1994). "Developmental process of cooperative interorganizational relationships". *Academy of Management,* **19**(1), pp. 90–118.

Ritala, P., Armila, L. and Blomqvist, K. (2009). "Innovation orchestration capability defining the organizational and individual level determinants". *International Journal of Innovation Management,* **13**(4), pp. 569–591.

Ritchie, B. and Brindley, C. (2007). "Supply chain risk management and performance: A guiding framework for future development". *International Journal of Operations& Production Management,* **27**(3), pp. 303–322.

Ritchie, B. and Brindley, C. (2007b). "An emergent framework for supply chain risk management and performance measurement". *Journal of the Operational Research Society*, **58**(11), pp. 1398–1411.

Ritter, T., Wilkinson, I.F. and Johnston, W.J. (2002). "Measuring network competence: Some international evidence". *Journal of Business & Industrial Marketing,* **17**(2/3), pp. 119–138.

Rivera, M.T., Soderstrom, S.B. and Uzzi, B. (2010). "Dynamics of dyads in social networks: Assortative, relational, and proximity mechanisms". *Annual Review of Sociology,* **36**(1), pp. 91–115.

Robertson, C.J. and Crittenden, W.F. (2003). "Mapping moral philosophies: Strategic implications for multinational firms". *Strategic Management Journal,* **24**(4), pp. 385–392.

Robertson, T.S. and Gatignon, H. (1998) "Technology development mode: A transaction cost conceptualization". *Strategic Management Journal,* **19**(6), pp. 515–531.

Rogers, H., Ghauri, P.N. and Pawar, K.S. (2005). "Measuring international new product development projects: An evaluation process". *Journal of Business and Industrial Marketing,* **20**(2), pp. 79–87.

Romo, F.P. and Schwartz, M. (1995). "The structural embeddedness of business decisions: The migration of manufacturing plants in New York State, 1960–1985". *American Sociological Review,* **60**(6), pp. 874–907.

Rothaermel, F.T. (2001). "Incumbent's advantage through exploiting complementary assets via interfirm cooperation". *Strategic Management Journal,* **22**(6–7), pp. 687–699.

Rothaermel, F.T. and Deeds, D.L. (2006). "Alliance type, alliance experience and alliance management capability in high–technology ventures". *Journal of Business Venturing*, **21**(4), pp. 429–460.

Rothaermel, F.T. and Hess, A.M. (2007). "Building Dynamic Capabilities: Innovation driven by individual–, firm–, and network–level effects". *Organization Science,* **18**(6), pp. 898–921.

Rousseau, D. M. and Fried, Y. (2001). "Location, location, location: Contextualizing organizational research". *Journal of Organizational Behavior,* **22**(1), pp. 1–13.

Rousseau, D.M. (1985). "Issues of level in organizational research: Multi–level and cross–level perspectives". *Research in Organizational Behaviour,* Vol. 7, pp. 1–37.

Rousseau, D.M., Manning, J. and Denyer, D. (2008). "Evidence in management and organizational science: Assembling the field's full weight of scientific knowledge through syntheses". *The Academy of Management Annals,* **2**(1), pp. 475–515.

Rowlands, I. (1999). "Patterns of author co–citation in information policy: Evidence of social, collaborative and cognitive structure". *Scientometrics,* **44**(3), pp. 533–546.

Rozas, L.W. and Klein, W.C. (2010). "The value and purpose of the traditional qualitative literature review". *Journal of Evidence–Based Social Work,* **7**(5), pp. 387–99.

Rungtusanatham, M., Salvador, F., Forza, C. and Choi, T.Y. (2003). "Supply–chain linkages and operational performance: A resource–based–view perspective". *International Journal of Operations & Production Management,* **23**(9), pp. 1084–1099.

Rynes, S.L., Bartunek, J.M. and Daft, R.L. (2001). "Across the great divide: Knowledge creation and transfer between practitioners and academics". *Academy of Management Journal*, **44**(2), pp. 340–355.

Sampson, R.C. (2007). "R&D alliances and firm performance: The impact of technological diversity and alliance organization on innovation". *Academy of Management Journal,* **50**(2), pp. 364–386.

Sánchez, A.M. and Pérez, M.P. (2005). "Supply chain flexibility and firm performance: A conceptual model and empirical study in the automotive industry". *International Journal of Operations & Production Management,* **25**(7), pp. 681–700.

Sanders, N.R. and Primus, R. (2005). "Modeling the relationship between firm IT capability, collaboration, and performance". *Journal of Business Logistics,* **26**(1), pp. 1–23.

Santangelo, G.D. (2000). "Corporate strategic technological partnerships in the European information and communications technology industry". *Research Policy,* **29**(9), pp. 1015–1031.

Sarkar, M.B., Aulakh, P.S. and Madhok A. (2009). "Process capabilities and value generation in alliance portfolios". *Organization Science*, **20**(3), pp. 583–600.

Sarkis, J. Zhu, Q. and Lai, K.–H. (2011). "An organizational theoretic review of green supply chain management literature". *International Journal of Production Economics,* **130**(1), pp. 1–15.

Saxton, T. (1997). “The effects of partner and relationship characteristics on alliance outcomes”. *The Academy of Management Journal,* **40**(2), pp. 443–461.

Scandura, T.A. and Williams, E.A. (2000). “Research methodology in management: Current practices, trends, and implications for future research”. *Academy of Management Journal,* **43**(6), pp. 1248–1264.

Schiele, H., Ellis, S.C., Eßig, M., Henke, J.W. and Thomas, J.K. (2015). “Managing supplier satisfaction: Social capital and resource dependence frameworks”. *Australasian Marketing Journal,* **23**(2), pp. 132–138.

Schilke, O. and Görzen, A. (2010). “Alliance management capability: An investigation of the construct and its measurement”. *Journal of Management,* **36**(5), pp. 1192–1219.

Schilling, M.A. and Phelps, C.C. (2007). “Interfirm collaboration networks: The impact of large–scale network structure on firm innovation”. *Management Science,* **53**(7), pp. 1113–1126.

Schmenner, R.W., van Wassenhove, L., Ketokivi, M., Heyl, J. and Lusch, R. (2009). “Too much theory, not enough understanding”. *Journal of Operations Management,* **27**(5), pp. 339–343.

Schmitt, A.J. and Singh, M. (2012). “A quantitative analysis of disruption risk in a multi–echelon supply chain”. *International Journal of Production Economics,* **139**(1), pp. 22–32.

Schmitt, A.J., Sun, S.A., Snyder, L.V. and Shen, Z.J.M. (2015). “Centralization versus decentralization: Risk pooling, risk diversification, and supply chain disruptions”. *Omega,* Vol. 52, pp. 201–212.

Schneider, B., Hanges, P.J., Smith, D.B. and Salvaggio, A.N. (2003). “Which comes first: Employee attitudes or organizational financial and market performance?” *Journal of Applied Psychology,* **88**(5), pp. 836–851.

Schoenherr, T., Tummala, V.M.R. and Harrison, T.P. (2008). “Assessing supply chain risks with the analytic hierarchy process: Providing decision support for the offshoring decision by a US manufacturing company”. *Journal of Purchasing & Supply Management,* **14**(2), pp. 100–111.

Schoenmakers, W. and Duysters, G. (2006). "Learning in strategic alliances". *Technology Analysis & Strategic Management,* **18**(2), pp. 245–264.

Schrader, U. and Hennig–Thurau, T. (2009). "VHB–JOURQUAL2: Method, results, and implications of the German Academic Association for Business Research's Journal Ranking". *BuR – Business Research*, **2**(2), pp. 180–204.

Schreiner, M., Kale, P. and Corsten, D. (2009). "What really is alliance management capability and how does it impact alliance outcomes and success?" *Strategic Management Journal,* **30**(13), pp. 1395–1419.

Schulze, A., Brojerdi, G. and von Krogh, G. (2014). "Those Who Know, Do. Those who understand, teach. Disseminative capability and knowledge transfer in the automotive industry". *Journal of Product Innovation Management,* **31**(1), pp. 79–97.

Seppanen, R., Blomqvist, K. and Sundqvist, S. (2007). "Measuring Inter–Organizational Trust – A critical review of the empirical research in 1990–2003". *Industrial Marketing Management,* **36**(2), pp. 249–65.

Seuring, S. (2011). "Supply chain management for sustainable products – Insights from research applying mixed methodologies". *Business strategy and the environment,* **20**(7), pp. 471–484.

Seuring, S. and Gold, S. (2012). "Conducting content–analysis based literature reviews in supply chain management". *Supply Chain Management: An International Journal,* **17**(5), pp. 544–555.

Shafique, M. (2013). "Thinking inside the box? Intellectual structure of the knowledge base of innovation research (1988–2008)". *Strategic Management Journal*, **34**(1), pp. 62–93.

Shao, X.-F. (2013). "Supply chain characteristics and disruption mitigation capability: An empirical investigation in China". *International Journal of Logistics Research and Applications*, **16**(4), pp. 277-295.

Sheffi, Y. and Rice Jr., J.B. (2005). "A supply chain view of the resilient enterprise". *MIT Sloan Management Review,* **47**(1), pp. 41–48.

Silberschatz, A., Korth, H.F. and Sudarshan, S. (1997). "Database research faces the information explosion". *Communications from the ACM (CACM),* **40**(2), pp. 139–142.

Silva, J. and Reddy, S. (2011). "A framework for reducing disaster risks in supply chains". *International Journal of Business Research,* **11**(4), pp. 112–117.

Sinha, P.R., Whitman, L.E. and Malzahn, D. (2004). "Methodology to mitigate supplier risk in an aerospace supply chain". *Supply Chain Management: An International Journal,* **9**(2), pp. 154–168.

Sinkovics, R.R. and Roath, A.S. (2004). "Strategic orientation, capabilities, and performance in manufacturer – 3PL relationships". *Journal of Business Logistics,* **25**(2), pp. 43–64.

Siu, W.–S. and Bao, Q. (2008). "Network strategies of small Chinese high–technology firms: A qualitative study". *Journal of Product Innovation Management,* **25**(1), pp. 79–102.

Sivadas, E. and Dwyer, F.R. (2000). "An examination of organizational factors influencing new product success in internal and alliance–based processes". *Journal of Marketing,* **64**(1), pp. 31–49.

Sivakumar, K., Roy, S., Zhu, J. and Hanvanich, S. (2011). "Global innovation generation and financial performance in business–to–business relationships: The case of cross–border alliances in the pharmaceutical industry". *Journal of the Academy of Marketing Science,* **39**(5), pp. 757–776.

Skipper, J.B. and Hanna, J.B. (2009). "Minimizing supply chain disruption risk through enhanced flexibility". *International Journal of Physical Distribution and Logistics Management*, **39**(5), pp. 404–27.

Sluyts, K., Matthyssens, P., Martens, R. and Streukens, S. (2011). "Building capabilities to manage strategic alliances". *Industrial Marketing Management,* **40**(6), pp. 875–886.

Small, H. (1973). "Co–citation in the scientific literature: A new measure of the relationship between two documents". *Journal of the American Society for Information Science*, **24**(4), pp. 265–269.

Small, H. (1999). "Visualizing science by citation mapping". *Journal of the American Society for Information Science and Technology*, **50**(9), pp. 799–813.

Smith, R. and Sharif, N. (2007). "Understanding and acquiring technology assets for global competition". *Technovation,* **27**(11), pp. 643–649.

Søderberg, A.M., Krishna, S. and Bjørn, P. (2013). "Global software development: Commitment, trust and cultural sensitivity in strategic partnerships". *Journal of International Management,* **19**(4), pp. 347–361.

Sodhi, M.S. (2005)". Managing demand risk in a tactical supply chain planning for global Consumer Electronics company". *Production and Operations Management,* **14**(1), pp. 69–79.

Sodhi, M.S. and Lee, S. (2007). "An analysis of sources of risk in the consumer electronics industry". *Journal of the Operational Research Society,* **58**(11), pp. 1430–1439.

Sodhi, M.S., Son, B.G. and Tang, C.S. (2012). "Researchers' perspectives on supply chain risk management". *Production and Operations Management,* **21**(1), pp. 1–13.

Speier, C., Whipple, J.M., Closs, D.J. and Voss, M.D. (2011). "Global supply chain design considerations: Mitigating product safety and security risks". *Journal of Operations Management,* **29**(7–8), pp. 721–736.

Spekman, R. and Davis, E. (2004). "Risky business: Expanding the discussion on risk and the extended enterprise". *International Journal of Physical Distribution and Logistics Management,* **34**(5), pp. 414–433.

Spekman, R.E. and Carraway, R. (2005). "Making the transition to collaborative buyer–seller relationships: An emerging framework". *Industrial Marketing Management,* **35**(1), pp. 10–19.

Spekman, R.E., Kamauff Jr., J.W. and Myhr, N. (1998). "An empirical investigation into supply chain management: A perspective on partnerships". *International Journal of Physical Distribution & Logistics Management,* **28**(8), pp. 630–650.

Spender, J.-C. (1989). "Industry recipes: The nature and sources of managerial judgement". Basil Blackwell: Oxford, UK and Cambridge, MA.

Spicer, A. and Bailey, W.J. (2007). "When does national identity matter? Convergence and divergence in international business ethics". *The Academy of Management Journal,* **50**(6), pp. 1462–1480.

Stank, T., Keller, S.B. and Closs, D.J. (2001). "Performance benefits of supply chain logistical integration". *Transportation Journal,* **41**(2/3), pp. 32–46.

Stanley, T.D., Doucouliagos, C. and Jarrell, S.B. (2008). "Meta–regression analysis as the socio–economics of economics research". *The Journal of Socio–Economics,* **37**(1), pp. 276–92.

Starbuck, W.H. (2005). "How much better are the most–prestigious journals? The statistics of academic publication". *Organization Science,* **16**(2), pp. 180–200.

Steensma, H.K. and Corley, K.G. (2000). "On the performance of technology–sourcing partnerships: The interaction between partner interdependence and technology attributes". *Academy of Management Journal,* **43**(6), pp. 1045–1067.

Steinle, C. and Schiele, H. (2008). "Limits to global sourcing? Strategic consequences of dependency on international suppliers: Cluster theory, resource–based view and case studies". *Journal of Purchasing & Supply Management,* **14**(1), pp. 3–14.

Stevens, E. and Dimitriadis, S. (2004). "New service development through the lens of organisational learning: Evidence from longitudinal case studies". *Journal of Business Research,* **57**(10), pp. 1074–1084.

Stewart, D.W. and Zinkhan, G.M. (2006). "Enhancing marketing theory in academic research". *Journal of the Academy of Marketing Science*, **34**(4), pp. 477–80.

Stuart, T.E. (2005). "Interorganizational technology". In Baum, J.A. (Ed.). *The Blackwell companion to organizations.* Blackwell Publishing: Oxford, UK.

Sutton, R.I. and Staw, B.M. (1995). "What theory is not". *Administrative Science Quarterly*, **40**(3), pp. 371–384.

Svensson, G. (2004). "Key areas, causes and contingency planning of corporate vulnerability in supply chains". *International Journal of Physical Distribution & Logistics Management,* **34**(9), pp. 728–748.

Swafford, P.M., Ghosh, S. and Murthy, N. (2006). "The antecedents of supply chain agility of a firm: Scale development and model testing". *Journal of Operations Management,* **24**(2), pp. 170–188.

Swink, M. and Zsidisin, G. (2006). "On the benefits and risks of focused commitment to suppliers". *International Journal of Production Research,* **44**(20), pp. 4223–4240.

Sydow, J. (1998). "Understanding the constitution of interorganizational trust". In Lane, C. and Bachmann, R. (Eds.). *Trust within and between organizations: Conceptual issues and empirical applications.* Oxford University Press: Oxford, UK, pp. 31–63.

Talluri, S., Kull, T.J., Yildiz, H. and Yoon, J. (2013). "Assessing the efficiency of risk mitigation strategies in supply chains". *Journal of Business Logistics,* **34**(4), pp. 253–269.

Tang, C.S. (2006a). "Perspectives in supply chain risk management". *International Journal of Production Economics,* **103**(2), pp. 451–488.

Tang, C.S. (2006b). "Robust strategies for mitigating supply chain disruptions". *International Journal of Logistics: Research and Applications,* **9**(1), pp. 33–45.

Tang, C.S. and Tomlin, B. (2008). "The power of flexibility for mitigating supply chain risks". *International Journal of Production Economics,* **116**(1), pp. 12–27.

Tang, O. and Musa, S.N. (2011). "Identifying risk issues and research advancements in supply chain risk management". *International Journal of Production Economics,* **133**(1), pp. 25–34.

Teece, D.J., Pisano, G. and Shuen, A. (1997). "Dynamic capabilities and strategic management". *Strategic Management Journal,* **18**(7), pp. 509–533.

Teichert, T. (2010). "Investigating research streams of conjoint analysis: A bibliometric study". *Business Research,* **3**(1), pp. 49–68.

Terpend, R., Tyler, B.B., Krause, D.R. and Handfield, R.B. (2008). "Buyer–supplier relationships: Derived value over two decades". *The Journal of Supply Chain Management,* **44**(2), pp. 28–55.

Thorpe, R., Gold, J., Holt, R. and Clarke, J. (2006). "Immaturity: The constraining of entrepreneurship". *International Small Business Journal,* **24**(3), pp. 232–252.

Thorpe, R., Holt, R., Macpherson, A. and Pittaway, L. (2005). "Using knowledge within small and medium–sized firms: A systematic review of the evidence"**.** *International Journal of Management Reviews.* **7**(4), pp. 257–281.

Thun, J.–H. and Hoenig, D. (2011). "An empirical analysis of supply chain risk management in the German automotive industry". *International Journal of Production Economics,* **131**(1), pp. 242–249.

Tidd, J. (2014). "Conjoint innovation: Building a bridge between innovation and entrepreneurship". *International Journal of Innovation Management,* **18**(1), pp. 1–20.

Tippins, M.J. and Sodhi, R.S. (2003). "IT competency and firm performance: Is organizational learning a missing link?" *Strategic Management Journal,* **24**(8), pp. 745–761.

Tomlin, B. (2006). "On the value of mitigation and contingency strategies for managing supply chain disruption risks". *Management Science,* **52**(5), pp. 639–657.

Tranfield, D. and Starkey, K. (1998). "The nature, social organization and promotion of management research: Towards policy". *British Journal of Management,* **9**(4), pp. 341–353.

Tranfield, D., Denyer, D. and Smart, P. (2003). "Towards a methodology for developing evidence informed management knowledge by means of systematic review". *British Journal of Management,* **14**(3), pp. 207–222.

Trkman, P. and McCormack, K. (2009). "Supply chain risk in turbulent environments – A conceptual model for managing supply chain network risk". *International Journal Production Economics,* **119**(2), pp. 247–258.

Trott, P., Cordey–Hayes, M. and Seaton, R.A.F. (1995). "Inward technology transfer as an interactive process". *Technovation,* **15**(1), pp. 25–43.

Tsai, W. and Ghoshal, S. (1998). "Social capital and value creation: The role of intrafirm networks". *Academy of Management Journal*, **41**(4), pp. 464–476.

Tse, Y.K. and Tan, K.H. (2011). "Managing product quality risk in a multi–tier global supply chain". *International Journal of Production Research*, **49**(1), pp. 139–158.

Tukamuhabwa, B. R., Stevenson, M., Busby, J. and Zorzini, M. (2015). "Supply chain resilience: definition, review and theoretical foundations for further study". *International Journal of Production Research*, **53**(18), pp. 5592-5623.

Tummala, R. and Schoenherr, T. (2011). "Assessing and managing risks using the Supply Chain Risk Management Process (SCRMP)". *Supply Chain Management: An International Journal,* **16**(6), pp. 474–483.

Un, C.A. and Cuervo–Cazurra, A. (2004). "Strategies for knowledge creation in firms". *British Journal of Management*, **15**(S1), pp. 27–41.

Un, C.A., Cuervo–Cazurra, A. and Asakawa, K. (2010). "R&D collaborations and product innovation". *Journal of Product Innovation Management,* **27**(5), pp. 673–689.

Uzzi, B. (1997). "Social structure and competition in interfirm networks: The paradox of embeddedness". *Administrative Science Quarterly,* **42**(1), pp. 35–67.

van Aken, J.E. (2004). "Management research based on the paradigm of the design sciences: The quest for field–tested and grounded technological rules". *Journal of Management Studies*, **41**(2), pp. 219–246.

van de Ven, A. and Poole, M.S. (1995). "Explaining development and change in organizations". *Academy of Management Review,* **20**(3), pp. 510–540.

van de Vrande, V., Vanhaverbeke, W. and Duysters, G. (2011). "Technology in–sourcing and the creation of pioneering technologies". *Journal of Product Innovation Management,* **28**(6), pp. 974–987.

Vanany, I., Zailani, S. and Pujawan, N. (2009). "Supply chain risk management: Literature review and future research". *International Journal of Information Systems and Supply Chain Management,* **2**(1), pp. 16–33.

Vasileiou, K. and Morris, J. (2006). "The sustainability of the supply chain for fresh potatoes in Britain". *Supply Chain Management: An International Journal,* **11**(4), pp. 317–327.

Verbeek, A., Debackere, K., Luwel, M. and Zimmermann, E. (2002). "Measuring progress and evolution in science and technology–I: The multiple uses of bibliometric indicators". *International Journal of Management Reviews,* **4**(2), pp. 179–211.

Vesalainen, J. and Hakala, H. (2014). "Strategic capability architecture: The role of network capability". *Industrial Marketing Management,* **43**(6), pp. 938–950.

Vickery, S.K., Calantone, R. and Dröge, C. (1999). "Supply chain flexibility: An empirical study". *The Journal of Supply Chain Management: A Global Review of Purchasing and Supply,* **7**(3). pp. 16–24.

Vilkamo, T. and Keil, T. (2003). "Strategic technology partnering in high–velocity environments – Lessons from a case study". *Technovation,* **23**(3), pp. 193–204.

Vilko, J., Ritala, P. and Edelmann, J. (2014). "On uncertainty in supply chain risk management". *International Journal of Logistics Management,* **25**(1), pp. 3–19.

Vilko, J.P.P. and Hallikas, J.M. (2012). "Risk assessment in multimodal supply chains". *International Journal of Production Economics*, **140**(2), pp. 586–595.

Villena, V.H., Revilla, E. and Choi, T.Y. (2011). "The dark side of buyer–supplier relationships: A social capital perspective". *Journal of Operations Management,* **29**(6), pp. 561–576.

Vitell, S.J., Nwachukwu, S.L. and Barnes, J.H. (1993). "The effects of culture on ethical decision–making: An application of Hofstede's typology". *Journal of Business Ethics*, **12**(10), pp. 753–759.

Vogel, R. (2012). "The visible colleges of management and organization studies: A bibliometric analysis of academic journals". *Organization Studies*, **33**(8), pp. 1015–1043.

Vogel, R. and Güttel, W.H. (2013). „The dynamic capability view in strategic management: A bibliometric review". *International Journal of Management Reviews*, **15**(4), pp. 426–446.

Vokurka, R.J. and O'Leary–Kelly, S.W. (2000). "A review of empirical research on manufacturing flexibility". *Journal of Operations Management,* **18**(4), pp. 485–501.

Volberda, H.W., Foss, N.J. and Lyles, M.A. (2010). "Absorbing the concept of absorptive capacity: How to realize its potential in the organization field". *Organization Science,* **21**(4), pp. 931–951.

von Krogh, G. (1998). "Care in knowledge creation". *California Management Review,* **40**(3), pp. 133.

Vonortas, N.S. (1997). "Research joint ventures in the US". *Research Policy,* **26**(4–5), pp. 577 595.

Wagner, S.M. and Bode, C. (2008). "An empirical investigation of supply chain performance along several dimensions of risk". *Journal of Business Logistics,* **29**(1), pp. 307–325.

Wagner, S.M. and Neshat, N. (2012). "A comparison of supply chain vulnerability indices for different categories of firms". *International Journal of Production Research,* **50**(11), pp. 2877–2891.

Wakolbinger, T. and Cruz, J.M. (2011). "Supply chain disruption risk management through strategic information acquisition and sharing and risk–sharing contracts". *International Journal of Production Research,* **49**(13), pp. 4063–4084.

Walker, K. (2010). "A systematic review of the corporate reputation literature: Definition, measurement, and theory". *Corporate Corporation Review,* **12**(4), pp. 357–387.

Waller, M.A., Fawcett, S.E., and Van Hoek, R. (2012). "Thought leaders and thoughtful leaders: Advancing logistics and supply chain management". *Journal of Business Logistics,* **33**(2), pp. 75–77.

Wallin, J.A. (2005). "Bibliometric methods: Pitfalls and possibilities". *Basic & Clinical Pharmacology & Toxicology,* **97**(5), pp. 261–275.

Walter, A., Auer, M. and Ritter, T. (2006). "The impact of network capabilities and entrepreneurial orientation on university spin–off performance". *Journal of Business Venturing,* **21**(4), pp. 541–567.

Walter, C. and Ribière, V. (2013). "A citation and co–citation analysis of 10 years of KM theory and practices". *Knowledge Management Research & Practice*, **11**(3), pp. 221–229.

Walter, J., Kellermanns, F.W. and Lechner, C. (2012). "Decision making within and between organizations: Rationality, politics, and alliance performance". *Journal of Management*, **38**(5), pp. 1582–1610.

Walters, W.H. (2007). "Google scholar coverage of a disciplinary field". *Information Processing & Management,* **43**(4), pp. 1121–1132.

Wang, C.L. and Ahmed, P.K. (2007). "Dynamic capabilities: A review and research agenda". *International Journal of Management Reviews,* **9**(1), pp. 31–51.

Wang, C.L. and Chugh, H. (2014). "Entrepreneurial learning: Past research and future challenges". *International Journal of Management Reviews,* **16**(1), pp. 24–61.

Wassmer, U. (2010). "Alliance portfolio: A review and research agenda". *Journal of Management*, **38**(1), pp. 141–171.

Waters, D. (2007). "Supply chain risk management: Vulnerability and resilience in logistics". Kogan Page: London, UK and Philadelphia, PA.

Webster Jr., F.E. (2005). "A perspective on the evolution of marketing management". *Journal of Public Policy & Marketing*, **24**(1), pp. 121–26.

Weick, K.E. (1979). "The social psychology of organizing". 2nd ed. Addison–Wesley: Reading, MA.

Weick, K.E. (1989). "Theory construction as disciplined imagination". *Academy of Management Review,* **14**(4), pp. 516–531.

Weick, K.E. (1995). "Sensemaking in Organizations". Sage Publications: Thousand Oaks, CA.

Wenger, E. (2000). "Communities of practice and social learning systems". *Organization,* **7**(2), pp. 225–246.

Wernerfelt, B. (1984). "A resource–based view of the firm". *Strategic Management Journal,* **5**(2), pp. 171–180.

Wever, M., Wognum, P.M., Trienekens, J.H. and Omta, S.W.F. (2012). "Supply chain–wide consequences of transaction risks and their contractual solutions: Towards an extended transaction cost economics framework". *Journal of Supply Chain Management,* **48**(1), pp. 73–91.

Wheelwright, S.C. and Clark, K.B. (1992). "Revolutionizing product development – Quantum leaps in speed, efficiency, and quality". The Free Press Inc.: New York, NY.

Whetten, D.A. (1989). "What constitutes a theoretical contribution". *Academy of Management Review,* **14**(4), pp. 490–495.

Whetten, D.A., Felin, T. and King, B.G. (2009). "The practice of theory borrowing in organizational studies: Current issues and future directions". *Journal of Management,* **35**(3), pp. 537–563.

Whipple, J.M., Griffis, S.E. and Daugherty, P.J. (2013). "Conceptualizations of trust: Can we trust them?" *Journal of Business Logistics,* **34**(2), pp. 117–130.

White, H.D. and Griffith, B.C. (1981). "Author co–citation: A literature measure of intellectual structure". *Journal of the American Society for Information Science,* **32**(3), 163–171.

White, H.D. and McCain, K.W. (1998). "Visualizing a discipline: An author co–citation analysis of information science, 1972–1995". *Journal of the American Society for Information Science*, **49**(4), pp. 327–355.

White, S. and Lui, S.S. (2005). "Distinguishing costs of cooperation and control in alliances". *Strategic Management Journal*, **26**(10), pp. 913–932.

Whitley, R. (1984). "The scientific status of management research as a practi cally–oriented social science". *Journal of Management Studies,* **21**(4), pp. 369–390.

Wieland, A. (2013). "Selecting the right supply chain based on risks". *Journal of Manufacturing Technology Management,* **24**(5), pp. 652–668.

Wieland, A. and Wallenburg, C.M. (2012). "Dealing with supply chain risks: Linking risk management practices and strategies to performance". *International Journal of Physical Distribution and Logistics Management*, **42**(10), pp. 887–905.

Wildgoose, N., Brennan, P. and Thompson, S. (2012). "Understanding your supply chain to reduce the risk of supply chain disruption". *Journal of Business Continuity & Emergency Planning*, **6**(1), pp. 55–67.

Wilkinson L. (2002). "Multidimensional scaling". *In Systat 10.2 Statistics II.* Systat Software: Richmond, CA, pp. 119–145.

Williamson, O. (1991). "Comparative economic organization: The analysis of discreet structural alternatives". *Administrative Science Quarterly,* **36**(2), pp. 269–296.

Wilson, M.C. (2007). "The impact of transportation disruptions on supply chain performance". *Transportation Research Part E: Logistics and Transportation Review,* **43**(4), pp. 295–320.

Wong, C., Skipworth, H., Godsell, J. and Achimugu, N. (2012). "Towards a theory of supply chain alignment enablers: A systematic literature review". *Supply Chain Management: An International Journal,* **17**(4), pp. 419–437.

Wong, C.Y., Boon–Itt, S. and Wong, W.Y. (2011). "The contingency effects of environmental uncertainty on the relationship between supply chain integration and operational performance". *Journal of Operations Management,* **29**(6), pp. 604–615.

Woolcock, M. (1998). "Social capital and economic development: Toward a theoretical synthesis and policy framework". *Theory and Society,* **27**(2), pp. 151–208.

Woolf, S.H., Battista, R.N., Anderson, G.M., Logan, A.G. and Wang, E. (1990). "Assessing the clinical effectiveness of preventative maneuvers: Analytic principles and systematic methods in reviewing evidence and developing clinical practice recommendations". *Journal of Clinical Epidemiology,* **43**(9), pp. 891–905.

Wu, B. and Knott, A.M. (2006). "Entrepreunerial risk market and entry". *Management Science,* **52**(9), pp. 1315–1330.

Wu, D. and Olson, D.L. (2008). "Supply chain risk, simulation, and vendor selection". *International Journal of Production Economics,* 114(2), pp. 646–655.

Wu, T., Wu, Y. C. J., Chen, Y. J. and Goh, M. (2014). Aligning supply chain strategy with corporate environmental strategy: A contingency approach. *International Journal of Production Economics*, **147** (Part B), pp. 220-229.

Yadav, M. (2010). "The decline of conceptual articles and implications for knowledge development". *Journal of Marketing,* **74**(1), pp. 1–19.

Yamin, M. and Otto, J. (2004). "Patterns of knowledge flows and MNE innovative performance". *Journal of International Management,* **10**(2), pp. 239–258.

Yang, B. and Yang, Y. (2010). "Postponement in supply chain risk management: A complexity perspective". *International Journal of Production Research,* **48**(7), pp. 1901–12.

Yang, B., Burns, N.D. and Backhouse, C.J. (2004). "Postponement: A review and an integrated framework". *International Journal of Operations & Production Management,* **24**(5), pp. 468–487.

Yli–Renko, H., Autio, E. and Sapienza, H.J. (2001). "Social capital, knowledge acquisition, and knowledge exploitation in young technology–based firms". *Strategic Management Journal*, **22**(6–7), pp. 587–613.

You, F., Wassick, J.M. and Grossmann, I.E. (2009). "Risk management for a global supply chain planning under uncertainty". *AIChE Journal,* **55**(4), pp. 931–946.

Yu, H., Zeng, A.Z. and Zhao, L. (2009). "Single or dual sourcing: Decision–making in the presence of supply chain disruption risks". *Omega,* **37**(4), pp. 788–800.

Yu, M.–C. and Goh, M. (2014). "A multi–objective approach to supply chain visibility". *European Journal of Operational Research,* **233**(1), pp. 125–130.

Zacharia, Z.G., Nix, N.W. and Lusch, R.F. (2009). "An analysis of supply chain collaborations and their effect on performance outcomes". *Journal of Business Logistics,* **30**(2), pp. 101–123.

Zaheer, A. and Bell, G.G. (2005). “Benefiting from network position: Firm capabilities, structural holes and performance”. *Strategic Management Journal*, **26**(9), pp. 809–825.

Zaheer, A., Gozubuyuk, R. and Milanov, H. (2010). “It’s the connections: The network perspective in inter–organizational research”. *Academy of Management Journal*, **24**(1), pp. 62–77.

Zaheer, A., McEvily, B. and Perrone, V. (1998). ”Does trust matter? Exploring effects of interorganizational and interpersonal trust on performance”. *Organization Science,* **9**(2), pp. 141–159.

Zahra, S.A. and Sharma, P. (2004). “Family business research: A strategic reflection”. *Family Business Review,* **17**(4), pp. 331–346.

Zald, M. (1993). “Organization studies as a scientific and humanistic enterprise”. *Organization Science*, **4**(4), pp. 513–530.

Zhang, C. and Dhaliwal, J. (2009). “An investigation of resource–based and institutional factors in technology adoption for operations and supply chain management”. *International Journal of Production Economics,* **120**(1), pp. 252–269.

Zhang, J. and Baden–Fuller, C. (2010). “The influence of technological knowledge base and organizational structure on technology collaboration”. *Journal of Management Studies,* **47**(4), pp. 679–704.

Zhang, Q., Vonderembse, M.A. and Lim, J.–S. (2002). “Value chain flexibility: A dichotomy of competence and capability”. *International Journal of Production Research,* **40**(3), pp. 561–583.

Zhang, Q., Vonderembse, M.A. and Lim, J.–S. (2003). “Manufacturing flexibility: Defining and analyzing relationships among competence, capability, and customer satisfaction”. *Journal of Operations Management,* **21**(2), pp. 173–191.

Zhao, L., Huo, B., Sun, L. and Zhao, X. (2013). “The impact of supply chain risk on supply chain integration and company performance: A global investigation”. *Supply Chain Management: An International Journal,* **18**(2), pp. 115–131.

Zhou, C. and Li, J. (2008). "Product innovation in emerging market–based international joint ventures: An organizational ecology perspective". *Journal of International Business Studies,* **39**(7), pp. 1114–1132.

Zitt, M. and Bassecoulard, E. (1994). "Development of a method for detection and trend analysis of research fronts built by lexical or cocitation analysis". *Scientometrics,* **30**(1), pp. 333–351.

Zollo, M., Jeffrey J. Reuer, J.J. and Singh, H. (2002). "Interorganizational routines and performance in strategic alliances". *Organization Science,* **13**(6), pp. 701–713.

Zsidisin, G.A. and Ellram, L.M. (2003). "An agency theory investigation of supply risk management". *Journal of Supply Chain Management*, **39**(3), pp. 15–27.

Zsidisin, G.A. and Ritchie, B. (2008). "Supply chain risk. A handbook of assessment, management, and performance". Springer Science and Business Media: New York, NY.

Zsidisin, G.A. and Smith, M.E. (2005). "Managing supply risk with early supplier involvement: A case study and research propositions". *Journal of Supply Chain Management,* **41**(4), pp. 44–57.

Zsidisin, G.A. and Wagner, S.M. (2010). "Do perceptions become reality? The moderating role of supply risk resiliency on disruption occurrence". *Journal of Business Logistics,* **31**(2), pp. 1–20.

Zsidisin, G.A., Melnyk, S. A. and Ragatz, G.L. (2005). "An institutional theory perspective of business continuity planning for purchasing and supply management". *International Journal of Production Research*, **43**(16), pp. 3401-3420.

Zsidisin, G.A., Panelli, A. and Upton, R. (2000). "Purchasing organization involvement in risk assessments, contingency plans, and risk management: An exploratory study". *Supply Chain Management: An International Journal,* **5**(4), pp. 187–202.

Zsidisin, G.A., Wagner, S.M., Melnyk, S.A., Ragatz, G.L. and Burns, L.A. (2008). "Supply risk perceptions and practices: An exploratory comparison of German and US supply management professionals". *International Journal of Technology, Policy and Management,* **8**(4), pp. 401–419.

Zsisdin, G.A., Ellram, L.M., Carter, J.R. and Cavinato, J.L. (2004). "An analysis of supply risk assessment techniques". *International Journal of Physical Distribution & Logistics Management,* **34**(5), pp. 397–413.

Zupic, I. and Cater, T. (2014). "Bibliometric methods in management and organization". *Organizational Research Methods,* **18**(3), pp. 429–472.

Appendix I: Set of the 32 most frequently co–cited journal articles listed by number of citations

Author	Year	Journal	Title	Citations
Tang (2006a)	2006	*International Journal of Production Economics*	"Perspectives in supply chain risk management"	312
Kleindorfer and Saad	2005	*Production and Operations Management*	"Managing disruption risks in supply chains"	267
Tomlin	2006	*Management Science*	"On the value of mitigation and contingency strategies for managing supply chain disruption risks"	237
Chopra and Sodhi	2004	*MIT Sloan Management Review*	"Managing risk to avoid supply–chain breakdown"	221
Cachon	2004	*Management Science*	"The allocation of inventory risk in a supply chain: Push, pull, and advance–purchase discount contracts"	175
Hendricks and Singhal	2005	*Production and Operations Management*	"An empirical analysis of the effect of supply chain disruptions on long–run stock price performance and equity risk of the firm"	164
Hallikas *et al.*	2004	*International Journal of Production Economics*	"Risk management processes in supplier networks"	130
Faisal *et al.*	2006	*Business Process Management Journal*	"Supply chain risk mitigation: Modeling the enablers"	111
Agrawal and Seshadri	2000	*IIE Transactions*	"Risk intermediation in supply chains"	90
Wu and Olson	2008	*International Journal of Production Economics*	Supply chain risk, simulation, and vendor selection"	82

Author	Year	Journal	Title	Citations
Braunscheidel and Suresh	2009	*Journal of Operations Management*	"The organizational antecedents of a firm's supply chain agility for risk mitigation and response"	78
Manuj and Mentzer	2008a	*International Journal of Physical Distribution & Logistics Management*	"Global Supply Chain Risk Management"	78
Johnson	2001	*California Management Review*	"Learning from toys: Lessons in managing supply chain risk from the toy industry"	76
Manuj and Mentzer	2008b	*Journal of Business Logistics*	"Global Supply Chain Risk Management"	67
Tang and Tomlin	2008	*International Journal of Production Economics*	"The power of flexibility for mitigating supply chain risks"	67
Cucchiella and Gastaldi	2006	*Journal of Manufacturing Technology Management*	"Risk management in supply chain: A real option approach"	57
Ritchie and Brindley	2007a	*International Journal of Operations & Production Management*	"Supply chain risk management and performance – A guiding framework for future development"	53
You *et al.*	2009	*AIChE Journal*	"Risk management for a global supply chain planning under uncertainty: Models and algorithms"	50
Finch	2004	*Supply Chain Management: An International Journal*	"Supply chain risk management"	49
Hallikas *et al.*	2002	*International Journal of Production Economics*	"Risk analysis and assessment in network environments: A dyadic case"	43
Nagurney and Matsypura	2005	*Transportation Research Part E: Logistics and Transportation Review*	"Global supply chain network dynamics with multicriteria decision–making under risk and uncertainty"	43

Author	Year	Journal	Title	Citations
Rao and Goldsby	2009	*International Journal of Logistics Management*	"Supply chain risks: A review and typology"	42
Sodhi	2005	*Production and Operations Management*	"Managing demand risk in tactical supply chain planning for a global consumer electronics company"	42
Sinha *et al.*	2004	*Supply Chain Management: An International Journal*	"Methodology to mitigate supplier risk in an aerospace supply chain"	41
Trkman and McCormack	2009	*International Journal of Production Economics*	"Supply chain risk in turbulent environments – A conceptual model for managing supply chain network risk"	41
Bogataj and Bogataj	2007	*International Journal of Production Economics*	"Measuring the supply chain risk and vulnerability in frequency space"	38
Neiger *et al.*	2009	*Journal of Operations Management*	"Supply chain risk identification with value–focused process engineering"	35
Narasimhan and Talluri	2009	*Journal of Operations Management*	"Perspectives on risk management in supply chains"	34
Thun and Hoenig	2011	*International Journal of Production Economics*	"An empirical analysis of supply chain risk management in the German automotive industry"	32
Jiang *et al.*	2009	*Journal of Operations Management*	"An analysis of job dissatisfaction and turnover to reduce global supply chain risk: Evidence from China"	31
Khan *et al.*	2008	*International Journal of Physical Distribution & Logistics Management*	"The impact of product design on supply chain risk: A case study"	24
Lockamy III and McCormack	2010	*International Journal of Production Research*	"Analysing risks in supply networks to facilitate outsourcing decisions"	23

Appendix II: The applied co–citation matrix

	D1	D2	D3	D4	D5	D6	D7	D8	D9	D10	D11	D12	D13	D14	D15	D16	D17	D18	D19	D20	D21	D22	D23	D24	D25	D26	D27	D28	D29	D30	D31	D32
D1	0	5	4	6	1	8	7	2	0	2	1	2	5	3	1	0	0	0	3	1	5	0	2	3	1	1	2	1	0	1	1	1
D2	5	0	4	11	0	5	4	4	1	1	0	1	3	2	0	0	0	0	2	0	0	0	4	1	0	1	1	0	0	1	2	1
D3	4	4	0	5	1	2	3	1	0	1	0	1	1	1	0	0	0	0	1	1	2	0	3	1	0	0	1	0	0	1	1	1
D4	6	11	5	0	2	9	7	1	2	1	0	1	3	3	0	0	0	0	4	1	2	0	3	5	0	1	1	0	0	1	2	1
D5	1	0	1	2	0	1	1	0	1	1	1	0	1	1	0	0	0	0	1	1	1	0	0	1	0	0	0	0	0	0	0	0
D6	8	5	2	9	1	0	5	2	1	2	2	1	4	2	1	0	0	0	2	1	3	0	1	2	1	1	1	1	0	1	1	0
D7	8	4	3	7	1	5	4	3	0	2	2	2	4	2	1	0	0	0	6	2	2	0	2	5	1	0	2	1	0	1	2	1
D8	2	4	1	1	0	2	3	0	0	2	1	0	2	1	1	0	0	0	1	0	0	0	0	1	1	0	0	1	0	0	1	0
D9	0	1	0	2	1	1	0	0	0	0	0	0	2	1	0	0	0	0	0	1	0	0	0	0	0	0	0	0	0	0	0	0
D10	2	1	1	1	0	2	2	2	0	0	2	0	1	1	1	0	0	0	1	0	0	0	0	1	1	0	1	1	0	0	0	0
D11	1	0	0	0	0	2	2	1	0	2	0	0	1	1	1	0	0	0	0	0	0	0	0	0	0	0	0	0	0	0	0	0
D12	2	1	1	1	0	1	3	0	0	0	0	0	1	1	0	0	0	0	1	0	0	0	1	1	0	0	0	0	0	1	0	0
D13	5	2	1	3	1	4	4	2	2	1	1	1	0	3	1	0	0	0	3	1	2	0	2	1	1	1	1	1	0	1	2	0
D14	3	2	1	3	1	2	2	1	1	1	0	1	3	0	1	0	0	0	2	0	0	0	0	2	1	0	1	1	0	0	1	0
D15	1	0	0	0	0	1	1	1	0	0	1	0	1	1	0	0	0	0	1	0	0	0	0	1	1	0	1	1	0	0	1	0
D16	0	0	0	0	0	0	0	0	0	0	0	0	0	0	0	0	0	0	0	0	0	0	0	0	0	0	0	0	0	0	0	0
D17	0	0	0	0	0	0	0	0	0	0	0	0	0	0	0	0	0	0	0	0	0	0	0	0	0	0	0	0	0	0	0	0
D18	0	0	0	0	0	0	0	0	0	0	0	0	0	0	0	0	0	0	0	0	0	0	0	0	0	0	0	0	0	0	0	0
D19	3	2	1	4	0	2	6	1	0	1	1	1	3	2	1	0	0	0	1	0	0	0	1	3	1	0	1	1	0	1	0	0
D20	1	0	1	1	1	1	2	0	1	0	0	0	1	0	0	0	0	0	0	1	0	0	1	0	0	0	0	0	0	0	2	0
D21	5	1	2	2	1	3	2	0	0	0	0	0	2	0	0	0	0	0	0	1	0	0	1	1	0	0	0	0	0	0	0	0
D22	0	0	0	0	0	0	0	0	0	0	0	0	0	0	0	0	0	0	0	0	0	0	0	0	0	0	0	0	0	0	0	0
D23	2	4	3	3	0	1	2	0	0	0	0	1	2	11	1	0	0	0	0	0	0	0	1	0	0	0	0	0	0	1	0	0
D24	3	1	1	5	1	2	5	1	0	1	1	0	1	2	1	0	0	0	3	1	1	0	0	2	1	0	1	1	0	0	0	0
D25	1	0	0	0	0	1	1	1	0	1	1	0	1	1	0	0	0	0	1	0	0	0	0	1	1	0	1	1	0	0	1	0
D26	1	1	0	1	0	1	0	0	0	0	0	0	1	0	0	0	0	0	0	0	0	0	0	0	0	0	0	0	0	0	0	0

	D1	D2	D3	D4	D5	D6	D7	D8	D9	D10	D11	D12	D13	D14	D15	D16	D17	D18	D19	D20	D21	D22	D23	D24	D25	D26	D27	D28	D29	D30	D31	D32
D27	2	1	1	1	0	1	2	1	0	1	1	0	1	1	1	0	0	0	1	0	0	0	0	1	0	0	0	1	0	0	0	1
D28	1	0	0	0	0	1	1	1	0	1	1	0	1	1	1	0	0	0	1	0	0	0	0	1	0	0	1	0	0	0	0	0
D29	0	0	0	0	0	0	0	0	0	0	0	0	0	0	0	0	0	0	0	0	0	0	0	0	0	0	0	0	0	0	0	0
D30	1	1	1	1	0	1	1	0	0	0	0	1	1	1	0	0	0	0	1	0	0	0	1	0	0	0	0	0	0	1	1	0
D31	2	1	1	2	0	1	2	1	0	0	0	0	2	1	0	1	0	0	0	2	0	0	0	0	1	0	0	0	0	1	0	0
D32	1	1	1	1	0	0	1	0	0	1	0	0	0	0	0	0	0	0	0	0	0	0	0	0	0	0	1	0	0	0	0	0

Appendix III: Results of the cluster analysis: Ward's method dendrogram

Case/Label **Rescaled distance cluster combined**

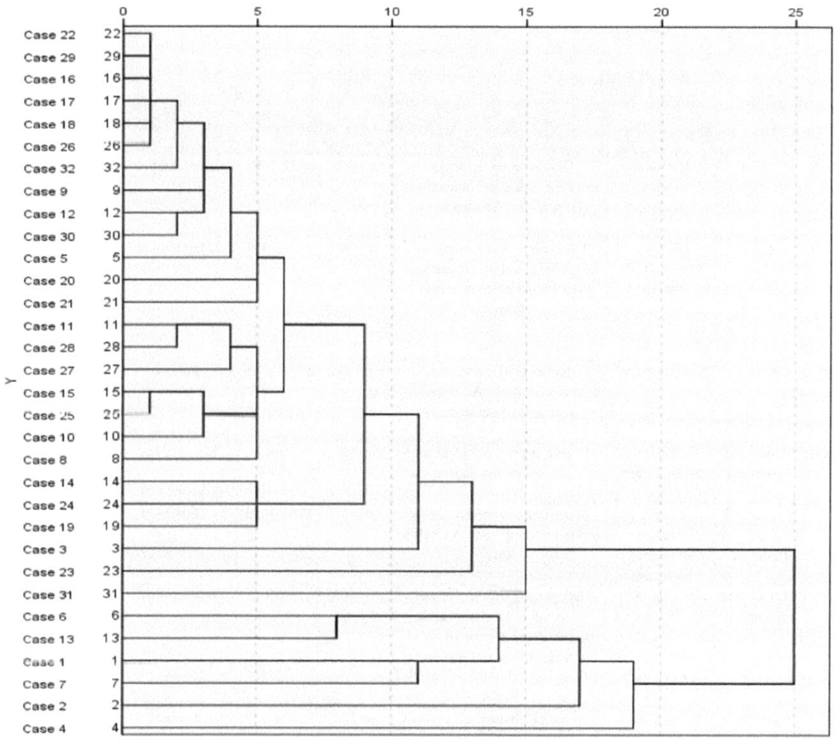

Appendix IV: Summary of the journal articles included in the review

Year	Author	Journal	Study	Sample size	Period	Regional focus of research	Industry/Sector
2000a	Ahuja	*Administrative Science Quarterly*	Collaboration networks, structural holes, and Innovation: A longitudinal study	n = 97	1971-1991	International	Chemicals
2000b	Ahuja	*Strategic Management Journal*	The duality of collaboration: Inducements and opportunities in the formation of interfirm linkages	n = 97	1979-1991	International	Chemicals
2001	Bayona	*Research Policy*	Firms' motivations for cooperative R&D: An empirical analysis of Spanish firms	n = 1652	1994-1996	Europe	N/S
1994	Bidault and Cummings	R&D Management	Innovating through alliances: Expectations and limitations	n = 5	N/S	Not specified	Information Technology
1994	Bonaccorsi and Lipparani	Journal of Product Innovation Management	Strategic partnerships in new product development: An italian case	n = 1	1991-1992	Europe	Machinery
2008	Bstieler and Hemmert	Journal of World Business	Developing trust in vertical product development partnerships: A comparison of South Korea and Austria	n = 100	N/S	International	N/S
2004	Caloghirou et al.	*Technovation*	Internal capabilities and external knowledge sources: Complements	n = 556	2000	Europe	Diverse
1999	Carr	R&D Management	Globalisation, strategic alliances, acquisitions and technology transfer. Lessons from ICL=Fujitsu and Rover=Honda and BMW	n = 2	1982-1995	International	Automotive, ICT, Semiconductor
2009	Cassiman et al.	*Long Range Planning*	Organising R&D projects to profit from innovation: Insights from co-opetition	n=1	1998-2003	Europe	Semiconductor

Level of analysis Multilevel (ML) Economy/Society (ES) Industry/Market (IM) Network Level (NW) Organisation (ON)	**Type of partnership** Cooperation/Contractual (CL) Collaboration (CN) Alliance (AL) Acquisition (AQ) Merger (MR) Mergers & Acquisition (MA) Joint Ventures (JV) Consortia (CA) Licensing (LC)	**Theory** Economics and Evolution (EE) Game Theory (GT) (Social) Network Theory (SKT) Knowledge-based View (KBV) Organisational Learning (OL) Transaction Cost Economy (TCE) Resource-based View (RBV) Social/Relational Capital Theory (SCT) Real Options Theory (ROT)	**Paper type** Literature review (LR) Case study (CS) Conceptual (CO) Secondary database research (SR) Survey/Questionnaire (SQ) Empirical (Theory-testing) (TT) Empirical (Theory-building) (TB)
ML (NW, ON)	CN	SKT	SR, TT, LS
ON	CN	RBV, SKT	SR, TT, LS
IM	CL	KBV	SQ, TT
ON	AL, CL	N/S	CS, TB
ON	AQ	N/S	CS, TB
ML (ES, ON)	CL	N/S	SQ, TT
ON	CL	RBV	SQ, TT
NW	AL, AQ, MR	N/S	CS, TB
ON	CL	GT	CS, TB

Appendix IV: Summary of the journal articles included in the review

Year	Author	Journal	Study	Sample size	Period	Regional focus of research	Industry/Sector
2003	Chang	*R&D Management*	Benefits of co-operation on innovative performance: Evidence from integrated circuits and biotechnology firms in the UK and Taiwan	n = 400	1996-1998	International	Diverse
2011	Chen et al.	Technovation	The influence of scope, depth, and orientation of external technology sources on the innovation performance of Chinese firms	n = 209	2006-2007	Asia	Diverse
2002	Ciu et al.	*R&D Management*	Working effectively in strategic alliances through managerial fit between partners: some evidence from Sino-British joint ventures and the implications for R&D professionals	n = 72	1993-1998	International	N/S
1993	Dogsen	*Human Relations*	Learning, trust, and technological collaboration	n = 2	1988-1993	Europe	Biotechnology
1999	Duysters et al.	*R&D Management*	Crafting successful strategic technology partnerships	N/A	N/A	N/A	N/A
2006	Ettlie and Pavlou	*Decision Sciences*	Technology-based new product development partnerships	n = 72	2002	International	Diverse
1992	Farr and Fischer	*R&D Management*	Managing international high technology cooperative projects	n = 14	N/S	N/S	N/S
2005	Fey and Birkinshaw	*Journal of Management*	External sources of knowledge, governance mode, and R&D performance	n = 107	N/S	Europe	Diverse

Level of analysis Multilevel (ML) Economy/Society (ES) Industry/Market (IM) Network Level (NW) Organisation (ON)	**Type of partnership** Cooperation/Contractual (CL) Collaboration (CN) Alliance (AL) Acquisition (AQ) Merger (MR) Mergers & Acquisition (MA) Joint Ventures (JV) Consortia (CA) Licensing (LC)	**Theory** Economics and Evolution (EE) Game Theory (GT) (Social) Network Theory (SKT) Knowledge-based View (KBV) Organisational Learning (OL) Transaction Cost Economy (TCE) Resource-based View (RBV) Social/Relational Capital Theory (SCT) Real Options Theory (ROT)	**Paper type** Literature review (LR) Case study (CS) Conceptual (CO) Secondary database research (SR) Survey/Questionnaire (SQ) Empirical (Theory-testing) (TT) Empirical (Theory-building) (TB)
ON	CL	RBV	SQ, TT
NW	CN & CL	RBV	SQ, TT
ES	JV, AL	SKT	SQ, TT
ON	CN	OL, RBV, Contingency Theory	SQ, TT
ON	AL	N/S	SQ, TT
NW	CN	RBV	SR, TT
ON	CL	N/S	SQ, TT
ON	AL, CL	KBV	SR, TT

Appendix IV: Summary of the journal articles included in the review

Year	Author	Journal	Study	Sample size	Period	Regional focus of research	Industry/Sector
1992	Forrest and Martin	R&D Management	Strategic alliances between large and small research intensive organizations: Experiences in the biotechnology industry	n = 70	N/S	USA	Biotechnology
1994	Hagedoorn and Schakenraad	Strategic Management Journal	The effect of strategic technology alliances on company performance	n = 346	1980-1987	International	Diverse
2006	Hagedoorn et al.	*British Journal of Management*	Inter-Firm R&D networks: the importance of strategic network capabilities for high-tech partnership formation	n = 230	1991-1998	N/S	Biotechnology
2012	Häussler et al.	*Journal of Business Venturing*	Strategic alliances and product development in high technology new firms: The moderating effect of technological capabilities	n=199	N/S	Europe	Biotechnology
2011	Huang and Yu	*Journal of Technology Transfer*	The effect of competitive and non-competitive R&D collaboration on firm innovation	n = 165	2002-2003	Asia	ICT
1998	Ingham and Mothe	*R&D Management*	How to learn in R& partnerships?	n = 3	N/S	International	N/S
2007	Kalaignanam et al.	*Management Science*	Asymmetric new product development Alliances: Win-win or win-lose partnerships?	n = 167	1993 & 2004	USA	ICT
2007	Kale and Singh	*Strategic Management Journal*	Building firm capabilities through learning: The role of the alliance learning process on alliance capability and firm-level alliance	n = 175	1994-1998	USA	ICT

Level of analysis Multilevel (ML) Economy/Society (ES) Industry/Market (IM) Network Level (NW) Organisation (ON)	**Type of partnership** Cooperation/Contractual (CL) Collaboration (CN) Alliance (AL) Acquisition (AQ) Merger (MR) Mergers & Acquisition (MA) Joint Ventures (JV) Consortia (CA) Licensing (LC)	**Theory** Economics and Evolution (EE) Game Theory (GT) (Social) Network Theory (SKT) Knowledge-based View (KBV) Organisational Learning (OL) Transaction Cost Economy (TCE) Resource-based View (RBV) Social/Relational Capital Theory (SCT) Real Options Theory (ROT)	**Paper type** Literature review (LR) Case study (CS) Conceptual (CO) Secondary database research (SR) Survey/Questionnaire (SQ) Empirical (Theory-testing) (TT) Empirical (Theory-building) (TB)
IM	AL, CN	N/S	SQ, TT
ON	AL	N/S	SR, TT
ML (ON, NW, IM)	CN	SKT	SR, TT
ON	AL	RBV	SR, TT, LS
NW	CN	RBV	SR, TT, LS
ML (ON, NW)	CA	OL	SR, TT
ML (IM, NW)	AL	N/S	SR, TT
ON	AL	KBV, RBV	SQ, TT

Appendix IV: Summary of the journal articles included in the review

Year	Author	Journal	Study	Sample size	Period	Regional focus of research	Industry/Sector
2002	Kale et al.	*Strategic Management Journal*	Alliance capability, stock market response, and long-term alliance success: the role of the alliance function	n = 78	1997	N/S	Computers, Telecommunications, Pharmaceuticals, Chemicals, Electronics, and Services
2007	Ketchen et al.	Strategic Entrepreneurship Journal	Strategic entrepreneurship, collaborative innovation, and wealth creation	N/A	N/A	N/A	N/A
2003	Kim and Lee	*R&D Management*	Technological collaboration in the Korean electronic parts industry: Patterns and key success factors	n = 82	N/S	Asia	Elecctronic Parts
2007	Kim and Song	*Technovation*	Creating new technology through alliances: An empirical investigation of joint patents	n = 516	1988-1995	International	Pharmaceutical
2001	Lee et al.	*Strategic Management Journal*	Internal capabilities, external networks, and performance: a study on technologybased ventures	n = 188	1998	International	Diverse
2008	Li et al.	*Academy of Management Journal*	Friends, acquaintances, or strangers? Partner selection in R&D alliances	n = 1.159	1994-2003	N/S	Diverse
2003	Miotti and Sachwald	*Research Policy*	Co-operative R&D: why and with whom? An integrated framework of analysis	n = 4215	1994-1996	Europe	N/S
1996	Mowery et al.	*Strategic Management Journal*	Strategic alliances and interfirm knowledge transfer	n = 792	1985-1986	International	N/S

Level of analysis Multilevel (ML) Ecomomy/Society (ES) Industry/Market (IM) Network Level (NW) Organisation (ON)	Type of partnership Cooperation/Contractual (CL) Collaboration (CN) Alliance (AL) Acquisition (AQ) Merger (MR) Mergers & Acquisition (MA) Joint Ventures (JV) Consortia (CA) Licensing (LC)	Theory Economics and Evolution (EE) Game Theory (GT) (Social) Network Theory (SKT) Knowledge-based View (KBV) Organisational Learning (OL) Transaction Cost Economy (TCE) Resource-based View (RBV) Social/Relational Capital Theory (SCT) Real Options Theory (ROT)	Paper type Literature review (LR) Case study (CS) Conceptual (CO) Secondary database research (SR) Survey/Questionnaire (SQ) Empirical (Theory-testing) (TT) Empirical (Theory-building) (TB)
ON	AL	OL, RBV, EE	SQ, TT
ML (ON, NW)	CN	SKT, KBV, RBV, RO	LR
NW	CN	GT, OL	SR, TT
IM	AL	RBV, EE	SQ, TT
NW	AL, CL	RBV, SCT	SQ, TT
ON	AL, JV	OL, TCE	SQ, TT
ES	CL	RBV	CO
ON	AL	RBV, KBV	CS, TB

Appendix IV: Summary of the journal articles included in the review

Year	Author	Journal	Study	Sample size	Period	Regional focus of research	Industry/Sector
2013	Mukherjee et. al.	*Journal of Business Research*	External and internal influences on R&D alliance formation: Evidence from German SMEs	n = 763	1999-2006	Europe	N/S
2013	Noseleit and de Faria	*Journal of Business Research*	Complementarities of internal R&D and alliances with different partner types	n = 60	1990-2004	USA	Electrical & Electronical
1988	Nueno and Oosterveld	Long Range Planning	Managing technology alliances	n = 15	N/S	Europe	Diverse
1992	Pennings and Harianto	*Organization Science*	Technological networking and innovation implementation	n = 152	1977-1987	USA	Financial Services
2010	Phelps	*Academy of Management Journal*	A longitudinal study of the influence of alliance network structure and composition on firm exploratory innovation	n = 77	1987-1997	USA	Telecommunications Equipment
2012	Phene and Tallman	*Journal of International Business Studies*	Complexity, context and governance in biotechnology alliances	n = 413	1990-2009	International	Biotechnology
1996	Powell et al.	*Administrative Science Quarterly*	Interorganizational collaboration and the locus of innovation: Networks of learning in biotechnology	n = 225	1990-1994	International	Biotechnology
2001	Rothaermel	*Strategic Management Journal*	Incumbent's advantage through exploiting complementary assets via interfirm cooperation	n = 889	1970-1997	N/S	Biopharmaceutical
2007	Rothaermel and Hess	*Organization Science*	Building dynamic capabilities: Innovation driven by individual-, firm-, and network-level effects	n = 81	1980-2001	International	Pharmaceutical

Level of analysis Multilevel (ML) Economy/Society (ES) Industry/Market (IM) Network Level (NW) Organisation (ON)	Type of partnership Cooperation/Contractual (CL) Collaboration (CN) Alliance (AL) Acquisition (AQ) Merger (MR) Mergers & Acquisition (MA) Joint Ventures (JV) Consortia (CA) Licensing (LC)	Theory Economics and Evolution (EE) Game Theory (GT) (Social) Network Theory (SKT) Knowledge-based View (KBV) Organisational Learning (OL) Transaction Cost Economy (TCE) Resource-based View (RBV) Social/Relational Capital Theory (SCT) Real Options Theory (ROT)	Paper type Literature review (LR) Case study (CS) Conceptual (CO) Secondary database research (SR) Survey/Questionnaire (SQ) Empirical (Theory-testing) (TT) Empirical (Theory-building) (TB)
IM	AL	SCT, TCE	SQ, TT
IM	AL, CN	RBV	SQ, TT
ES	AL	N/S	CS, TB
ON	JV, CL, LC	Dynamic Theory of Innovation	CS, TB, LS
NW	AL	KBV	SQ, TT, LS
ON	AL	TCE, RBV, KBV	SQ, TT
ML (IM, NW, ON)	CN	OL	SQ, TT
ML (IM, NW)	AL, CL	N/S	SQ, TT
ML (e.g. ON, NW)	Not specified	RBV	SR, TT

Appendix IV: Summary of the journal articles included in the review

Year	Author	Journal	Study	Sample size	Period	Regional focus of research	Industry/Sector
2007	Sampson	*Academy of Management Journal*	R&D alliances and firm performance: the impact of technological diversity and alliance organization on innovation	n = 463	1991-1993	International	Telecommunications
1999	Santangelo	*Research Policy*	Corporate strategic technological partnerships in the European information and communications technology industry	n = 14	1978-1995	USA	ICT
1997	Saxton	*Academy of Management Journal*	The effects of partner and relationship characteristics on alliance outcomes	n = 98	N/S	International	N/S
2007	Schilling and Phelps	Management Science	Interfirm collaboration networks: The impact of large-scale network structure on firm innovation	n = 1.106	1990-2000	USA	Diverse
2014	Schulze et al.	*Journal of Product Innovation Management*	Those who know, do. Those who understand, teach. disseminative capability and knowledge transfer in the automotive industry	n = 60	N/S	International	Automotive
2008	Siu and Bao	*Journal of Product Innovation Management*	Network strategies of small chinese high-technology firms: A qualitative study	n = 12	N/S	Asia	N/S
2000	Sividas and Dwyer	*Journal of Marketing*	An examination of organizational factors influencing new product success in internal and alliance-based processes	n = 147	N/S	N/S	Semiconductor, Health Care

Level of analysis Multilevel (ML) Economy/Society (ES) Industry/Market (IM) Network Level (NW) Organisation (ON)	Type of partnership Cooperation/Contractual (CL) Collaboration (CN) Alliance (AL) Acquisition (AQ) Merger (MR) Mergers & Acquisition (MA) Joint Ventures (JV) Consortia (CA) Licensing (LC)	Theory Economics and Evolution (EE) Game Theory (GT) (Social) Network Theory (SKT) Knowledge-based View (KBV) Organisational Learning (OL) Transaction Cost Economy (TCE) Resource-based View (RBV) Social/Relational Capital Theory (SCT) Real Options Theory (ROT)	Paper type Literature review (LR) Case study (CS) Conceptual (CO) Secondary database research (SR) Survey/Questionnaire (SQ) Empirical (Theory-testing) (TT) Empirical (Theory-building) (TB)
ON	AL	KBV, TCE	SR, TT, LS
ML (IM, NW)	CN	RBV	SR, TT
ON	AL	KBV	SR, TT
NW	AL, CN	SKT	SR, TT
ON	AL	KBV	SQ, TT
ON	CN	SCT	SQ, TT
ON	AL	KBV, Organisational Theory	CS, TB

Appendix IV: Summary of the journal articles included in the review

Year	Author	Journal	Study	Sample size	Period	Regional focus of research	Industry/Sector
2000	Steensma and Corley	*Academy of Management Journal*	On the performance of technology-sourcing partnerships: The interaction between partner interdependence and technology attributes	n = 193	1993-1994	N/S	Diverse
2014	Tidd	*International Journal of Innovation Management*	Conjoint innovation: building a bridge between innovation and entrepreneurship	n = 15	N/A	International	Diverse
1995	Trott et al.	*Technovation*	Inward technology transfer as an interactive process	n = 1	N/S	Europe	Chemicals & Polymers
2010	Un et al.	*Journal of Product Innovation Management*	R&D collaborations and product innovation	n = 781	1998-2002	Europe	Manufacturing (N/S)
2011	van de Vrande et al.	Journal of Product Innovation Management	Technology in-sourcing and the creation of pioneering technologies	n = 153	1985-2000	N/S	Pharmaceutical
2003	Vilkamo and Keil	*Technovation*	Strategic technology partnering in high-velocity environments — Lessons from a case study	n = 1	N/S	Europe	Mobile Phone
2010	Zhang and Baden-Fuller	*Journal of Management Studies*	The influence of technological knowledge base and organizational structure on technology collaboration	n = 78	1993–2002	International	Biotechnology

Level of analysis Multilevel (ML) Ecomomy/Society (ES) Industry/Market (IM) Network Level (NW) Organisation (ON)	Type of partnership Cooperation/Contractual (CL) Collaboration (CN) Alliance (AL) Acquisition (AQ) Merger (MR) Mergers & Acquisition (MA) Joint Ventures (JV) Consortia (CA) Licensing (LC)	Theory Economics and Evolution (EE) Game Theory (GT) (Social) Network Theory (SKT) Knowledge-based View (KBV) Organisational Learning (OL) Transaction Cost Economy (TCE) Resource-based View (RBV) Social/Relational Capital Theory (SCT) Real Options Theory (ROT)	Paper type Literature review (LR) Case study (CS) Conceptual (CO) Secondary database research (SR) Survey/Questionnaire (SQ) Empirical (Theory-testing) (TT) Empirical (Theory-building) (TB)
ON	AQ, CL	KBV	SQ, TT
ON	Not specified	RBV	SQ, TT
ON	AL, AQ	RBV	CS, TB
ML	CN	KBV	CS, TB
IM	AL	OL, ROT	SR, TT
ON	AL, CN	RBV, Complexity Theory	SQ, TT
ON	CN	OL	CS, TB

Appendix IV: Summary of the journal articles included in the review

Year	Author	Journal	Study	Sample size	Period	Regional focus of research	Industry/Sector
2008	Zhou and Li	Journal of International Business Studies	Product innovation in emerging market-based international joint ventures: An organizational ecology perspective	n = 3555	1999-2003	Asia	N/S
2002	Zollo et al.	*Organization Science*	Interorganizational Routines and Performance in Strategic Alliances	n = 145	1982-1994	N/S	Biotech and pharmaceutical

Level of analysis Multilevel (ML) Ecomomy/Society (ES) Industry/Market (IM) Network Level (NW) Organisation (ON)	Type of partnership Cooperation/Contractual (CL) Collaboration (CN) Alliance (AL) Acquisition (AQ) Merger (MR) Mergers & Acquisition (MA) Joint Ventures (JV) Consortia (CA) Licensing (LC)	Theory Economics and Evolution (EE) Game Theory (GT) (Social) Network Theory (SKT) Knowledge-based View (KBV) Organisational Learning (OL) Transaction Cost Economy (TCE) Resource-based View (RBV) Social/Relational Capital Theory (SCT) Real Options Theory (ROT)	Paper type Literature review (LR) Case study (CS) Conceptual (CO) Secondary database research (SR) Survey/Questionnaire (SQ) Empirical (Theory-testing) (TT) Empirical (Theory-building) (TB)
ML (IM and ON)	JV	Organizational Ecology Theory	SR, TT
ON	AL, CL	EE, TCE	SR, TT

Appendix V: All capabilities as mentioned originally in the 65 selected articles

STP Capabilities	Capabilities	Fre-quency	Description	Author(s)
Comple-mentary Capabilities	*Complementary capa-bilities* (see all author(s))	**12**	Complementary ca-pabilities imply the pooling of distinct skills and know-how, or technologi-cal diversity be-tween partners which inspire crea-tivity and novel ap-proaches to preva-lent challenges. Thus, they consti-tute the extent to which companies get along and ap-preciate anticipated synergies that are critical to an opera-tion's success.	Deeds *et al.*, 1999; Kale and Singh, 2007; Malik, 2002; Noseleit and de Faria, 2013; Phelps, 2010; Sampson, 2007; Santangelo (2006), 2000; Saxton, 1997; Tidd, 2014; Un *et al.*, 2010; Vilkamo and Keil, 2003; Zollo *et al.*, 2000
Learning and exploitation Capabilities	*Learning capability* Ingham and Mothe (1998); Ketchen *et al.* (2007); Lorenzoni and Lipparini (1999); Phene and Tallman (2012); Powell *et al.* (1999) *Exploitation capability* Ingham and Mothe (1998) *Knowledge-(based) ca-pabilities* Mowery *et al.* (1996); Sampson (2007); Trott *et al.* (1995)	**13**	Firms with superior capabilities of ob-taining, integrating, converting and lev-eraging knowledge from external sources are better in transforming the as-similated knowledge into su-perior innovations. Learning and ex-ploitation capabili-ties are thus, seen as	Fey and Birkin-shaw, 2005; Hagedoorn *et al.*, 2006; Huang and Yu, 2011; Ingham and Mothe, 1998; Ketchen *et al.*, 2007; Lo-renzoni and Lipparini, 1999; Miotti and Sachwald, 2003; Mowery *et al.*, 1996;

STP Capabilities	Capabilities	Fre-quency	Description	Author(s)
	Knowledge transfer/dis-seminative capability Schulze *et al.* (2014) *Endogenous capabili-ties* Hagedoorn *et al.* (2006) *Cognitive capabilities* Fey and Birkinshaw (2005)		endogenous capa-bilities. The central point is that over time organisations build up a body of knowledge and skills through expe-rience and learning-by-doing.	Phene and Tall-man, 2012; Powell *et al.*, 1999; Sampson, 2007; Schulze *et al.*, 2014; Trott *et al.*, 1995
Organisa-tional Capabilities	*Organisational capabil-ities* Deeds *et al.* (1999); Kim and Song (2007); Pennings and Harianto (1992); Ketchen *et al.* (2007); Malik (2002); Phene and Tallman (2012); Sivadas and Dwyer (2000); Trott *et al.* (1995); Zollo *et al.* (2002) *Coordination capabili-ties* Ettlie and Pavlou (2006); Phene and Tall-man (2012) *Management capability* Cassiman *et al.* (2009) *Managerial capabilities* Forrest and Martin (1992)	**12**	The organisational capabilities base upon practiced rou-tines and represent a set of functional capabilities coordi-nated through busi-ness processes and activities. As a re-sult, the organisa-tional capabilities required for the generation and ap-plication of new technology typi-cally becomes em-bodied in a set of experienced pro-cesses, structures, and formalised pro-cedures within a firm.	Cassiman *et al.*, 2009; Deeds *et al.*, 1999; Ettlie and Pavlou, 2006; Forrest and Martin, 1992; Ketchen *et al.*, 2007; Kim and Song, 2007; Malik, 2002; Pennings and Harianto, 1992; Sivadas and Dwyer, 2000; Trott *et al.*, 1995; Phene and Tallman, 2012; Zollo *et al.*, 2002
Network, alliance, and part-nership Capabilities	*Relational capabilities* Kale *et al.* (2002); Kale and Singh (2007); Lo-renzoni and Lipparini (1999); Schreiner *et al.* (2009); Siu and Bao (2008);	**23**	Are defined as the abilities of a com-pany to effectively manage a multitude of interfirm partner-ships. They can be	Capaldo, 2007; De Man and Duysters, 2005; Duysters *et al.*, 1999; Duysters,

STP Capabilities	Capabilities	Fre-quency	Description	Author(s)
	Sivadas and Dwyer (2000)		understood as company-specific capabilities that enable an organisation to position itself in a broad portfolio and network of partnerships with various firms and the capacity to handle, build, and manage relationships. Hence, network and partnership capabilities are predominantly related to the particular brainpower of firms concerning their network arrangements and the selection of the right external partners.	2012; Ettlie and Pavlou, 2006; Faems, 2010; Feller *et al.*, 2013; Hagedoorn *et al.*, 2006; Häussler and Higgins, 2014; Heimeriks and Duysters, 2007; Kalaignanam *et al.*, 2007; Kale *et al.*, 2002; Kale and Singh, 2007; Lorenzoni and Lipparini, 1999; Mitrega *et al.*, 2012; Rothaermel and Deeds, 2006; Sarkar, 2009; Schilke and Görzen, 2010; Schreiner *et al.*, 2009; Sivadas and Dwyer, 2000; Siu and Bao, 2008; Sluyts *et al.*, 2011; Heimeriks *et al.*, 2009
	Interfirm capabilities Ettlie and Pavlou (2006)			
	Integration capabilities Mowery *et al.* (1996)			
	Alliance (management) capabilities Häussler and Higgins (2014); Kalaignanam *et al.* (2007); Kale *et al.* (2002); Kale and Singh (2007); Duysters *et al.* (1999); Feller *et al.* (2013); Rothaermel and Deeds (2006); Heimeriks and Duysters (2007)			
	Partnership capabilities Ettlie and Pavlou (2006); Hagedoorn *et al.* (2006)			
	(Strategic) network capabilities Hagedoorn *et al.* (2006)			
Technological, innovative and internal Capabilities	*Technological capabilities* Ahuja (2000b); Cassiman *et al.* (2009); Carr (1999); Deeds *et al.* (1999); Fey and Birkinshaw (2005); Häussler *et al.* (2012); Malik (2002); Mowery	**31**	Refer to the level of expertise within a technological territory that encompass the different scientific techniques available to the organisation; i.e. the	Ahuja, 2000a; Bayona *et al.*, 2001; Caloghirou *et al.*, 2004; Cassiman *et al.*, 2009; Carr, 1999; Ciu *et al.*, 2002; Deeds *et al.*, 1999;

STP Capabilities	Capabilities	Frequency	Description	Author(s)
	et al. (1996); Lee *et al.* (2001); Sampson (2007); Steensma and Corley (2000); Zhang and Baden-Fuller (2010) *Innovative capabilities* Hagedoorn and Duysters (2002); Hagedoorn and Schakenraad (1994); Miotti and Sachwald (2003); Zhou and Li (2008) *Internal capabilities* Bayona *et al.* (2001); Caloghirou *et al.* (2004); Cassiman *et al.* (2009); Lanctot and Swan (2000); Lee *et al.* (2001); Miotti and Sachwald (2003); Powell *et al.* (1996); Rothaermel and Hess (2007); Santangelo (2000); Zhang and Baden-Fuller (2010) *(Scientific) research capabilities* Deeds *et al.* (1999) *In-house capabilities* Forrest and Martin (1992) *(Product) development capabilities* Deeds *et al.* (1999); Carr (1999) *Engineering capabilities* Carr (1999)		ability to continually create new products, technologies, and processes depends on a company's technological and scientific capabilities. Furthermore, they point to skills for the successful transformation of inputs into outputs.	Duysters *et al.*, 2012; Faems *et al.*, 2010; Feller *et al.*, 2013; Fey and Birkinshaw, 2005; Häussler *et al.*, 2012; Häussler and Higgins, 2014; Hagedoorn and Duysters, 2002; Hagedoorn and Schakenraad, 1994; Huang and Yu, 2011; Ketchen *et al.*, 2007; Malik, 2002; Lanctot and Swan, 2000; Lee *et al.*, 2001; Li *et al.*, 2008; Miotti and Sachwald, 2003; Mowery *et al.*, 1996; Powell *et al.*, 1996; Rothaermel, 2001; Ritala *et al.*, 2009; Rothaermel and Hess, 2007; Steensma and Corley, 2000; Zhang and Baden-Fuller, 2010; Zhou and Li, 2008; Capaldo, 2007

STP Capabilities	Capabilities	Frequency	Description	Author(s)
	Design and manufacturing capabilities Ketchen *et al.* (2007)			
	Technical capabilities Carr (1999); Li *et al.* (2008); Forrest and Martin (1992); Ketchen *et al.* (2007)			
	Commercialization, manufacturing, distribution and marketing capabilities Häussler and Higgins (2014)			
	Market capabilities Rothaermel (2001)			
	Manufacturing capabilities Malik (2002); Saxton (1997)			
	Manufacturing and marketing capabilities Forrest and Martin (1992)			
	Design capabilities Carr (1999)			
	Research and design, manufacturing, marketing, and after-sales service capabilities Chang (2003)			
	R&D capability Feller *et al.* (2013); Huang and Yu (2011)			

Appendix VI: The conjoint SCRM–STP capabilities

Conjoint SCRM–STP Capabilities	Author(s) in this issue
Quality, Speed (including Agility and Responsiveness), Costs, and Flexibility	Feller *et al.* (2013); Vilkamo and Keil (2003); Tang and Tomlin (2008); Kleindorfer and Saad (2005); Ketchen and Hult (2007); Wheelwright and Clark (1992); Merschmann and Thonemann (2011); Braunscheidel and Suresh (2009); Wieland and Wallenburg (2013); Johnson *et al.* (2013); Ketchen *et al.* (2007); Rungtusanatham *et al.* (2003); Lanctot and Swan (2000); Burt, (1992); Pennings and Lee (1999); Pennings *et al.* (1998); Uzzi (1996)
Technological and Innovative Capability	Lee *et al.* (2001); Feller *et al.* (2013); Huang and Yu's (2011); Capaldo (2007); Moran (2005); Fey and Birkinshaw (2005); Rothaermel and Hess (2007); Ahuja (2000a)
Information Sharing, Communication, and Visibility	Johnson *et al.* (2013); Johnson and Elliott (2011); Inkpen and Tsang (2005); Larson (1992); Yli–Renko (2001); Koka and Prescott (2002); Capaldo (2007); Tsai and Ghoshal (1998); Krause *et al.* (2007); Lawson *et al.* (2008); Parra–Requena *et al.* (2010); Spender (1989); Nooraie and Parast (2015); Faisal *et al.* (2006); Lavastre *et al.* (2012); Bowersox *et al.* (2003); Chen *et al.* (2013); Liu *et al.* (2010); Spekman and Carraway (2005); Hansen (1999); Cousins *et al.*, (2006); Carey *et al.* (2011)
Collaboration	Christopher and Lee (2004); Johnson *et al.* (2013); Krause *et al.* (2007); Weick (2005); Inkpen and Tsang (2005); Rothaermel and Hess (2007); Powell *et al.* (1996); Bowersox *et al.* (2003); Chen *et al.* (2013); Hunt and Davis (2012); Uzzi (1996); Hansen (1999); Cousins *et al.* (2006); Lawson *et al.* (2008); Carey *et al.* (2011)
Learning and Exploitation Capability	McFarland *et al.* (2008); Ingham and Mothe (1998); Senge *et al.* (2001), Ettlie and Pavlou (2006); Huang and Yu (2011)
Trust and Commitment	Jarillo (1988); Coleman (1990); Johnson and Elliott (2011); Christopher and Lee (2004); Zacharia *et al.* (2009); Cousins *et al.* (2006); Nahapiet and Ghoshal (1998); Ingham and Mothe (1998); Allee (2003); Vasileiou and Morris (2006); Woolcock (1998); Bode *et al.* (2011); Lavastre *et al.* (2012); Faisal *et al.* (2006); Tang (2006a); Petersen *et al.* (2008); Pettit *et al.* (2010); Inkpen and Tsang (2005); Powell *et al.* (1996); Mishira (1996); Saxton (1997); Lazerson and Lorenzoni (1999); Gulati and Nickerson (2008); Ireland and Webb (2007); Krishnan *et al.* (2006); Vilkamo and Keil (2003); Mahapatra *et al.* (2010); Giunipero and Eltantawy (2004); Manuj and Mentzer (2008b); Siu and Bao (2008)

Appendix VII: Summary of the research propositions

SUMMARY OF THE RESEARCH PROPOSITIONS	
P1	SCRM in STP leads to reduced supply chain risks of firms through higher value of competitive priorities (quality, speed, costs, and flexibility).
P2	SCRM in STP leads to reduced supply chain risks of firms through enhanced technological and innovative capability.
P3	SCRM in STP leads to reduced supply chain risks of firms through enhanced information sharing, communication, and visibility.
P4	SCRM in STP leads to reduced supply chain risks of firms through higher levels of collaboration.
P5	SCRM in STP leads to reduced supply chain risks of firms through higher levels learning and exploitation capabilities.
P6	SCRM in STP leads to reduced supply chain risks of firms through mutual trust and commitment.

Veröffentlichungen

Internationale peer-reviewed Fachbeiträge

** Fachbeiträge in der Dissertation inkludiert (wesentliche Teile der Dissertation wurden in den nachfolgenden Publikationen veröffentlicht bzw. zur Publikation angenommen oder befinden sich im Review-Prozess)*

***Kilubi, I.** (2016). "Bridging the gap between supply chain risk management and strategic technology partnering – Insights from two theoretical lenses". *Supply Chain Management: An international Journal* (under review).

***Kilubi, I.** (2016). "Strategic technology partnering capabilities: A systematic review of the empirical evidence over two decades". *Journal of Strategy and Management,* **9**(2), pp. 216-255.

***Kilubi, I. and Haasis, H.-D.** (2016). "26 years of strategic technology partnering: Trends, patterns and future prospects in research through frequency analysis". *International Journal of Innovation and Technology Management,* **13**(2), pp. 1-44.

***Kilubi, I.** (2016). "Investigating current paradigms in supply chain risk management: A bibliometric study". *Business Process Management Journal,* **22**(4), pp.662-692.

***Kilubi, I.** (2016). "The strategies of supply chain risk management – A synthesis and classification". *International Journal of Logistics Research and Applications,* **19**(6), pp. 1-26.

Kilubi, I. and Haasis, H.-D. (2015). "Supply chain risk management enablers – A framework development through systematic review of the literature from 2000 to 2015". *International Journal of Business Science & Applied Management*, **10**(1), pp. 35-54.

Kilubi, I. and Haasis, H-D. (2016). "Supply chain risk management research: Avenues for further studies. *International Journal of Supply Chain and Operations Resilience*, **2**(1), pp. 51-71.

Kilubi, I. (2015). "Strategic technology partnering: A framework extension". *Journal of High Technology Management Research*, **26**(1), pp. 27-37.

Monographien und Buchbeiträge

Kilubi, I. (2015). "Services supply chain management & organisational performance: An exploratory mixed-method investigation of service and manufacturing organisations". *Wissenschaftlicher Verlag Berlin (wvb)*; Auflage 1, July 2015.

Konferenzbeiträge & Vorträge

Kilubi, I. (2015). "The role of supply chain risk management and strategic technology partnering: Critical success factors through joint forces". BVL *(Bundesverband Logistik e.V). 20th Doctoral Workshop within the 32nd German Logistics Convention.* Berlin (Germany), 28th – 30th October 2015.

Kilubi, I. and Haasis, H.-D. (2015). "The capabilities of strategic technology partnering: Past, present and future scope". *Proceedings of the British Academy of Management Conference* (BAM associated with AOM, *Academy of Management*): *"The value of pluralism in advancing management research, education and practice".* Portsmouth (UK), 8th – 10th September 2015.

Kilubi, I. (2015). "Supply chain risk management enablers: What do we know now, and where do we go from here?" *Proceedings of the British Academy of Management Conference* (BAM associated with AOM, *Academy of Management*): *"The value of pluralism in advancing management research, education and practice".* Portsmouth (UK), 8th – 10th September 2015.

Kilubi, I. (2015). "Merging strategic technology partnering and supply chain risk management through the social capital theory". Paper presented at the Doctoral Workshop of the *British Academy of Management Conference* (BAM associated with AOM, *Academy of Management): "The value of pluralism in advancing management research, education and practice".* Portsmouth (UK), 7th September 2015.

Kilubi, I. and Haasis, H-D. (2015). "Linking supply chain risk management and strategic technology partnering – Towards a conceptual framework for improved organisational performance". *Proceedings of the 20th International Symposium on Logistics* (ISL): *"Reflections on Supply Chain Research and Practice".* Bologna (Italy), 5th – 8th July 2015.

Kilubi, I. (2015). “Mapping the research fronts of supply chain risk management – A co-citation analysis”. Research paper presented at the *Council of Supply Chain Management Professionals* (CSCMP) *European Research Seminar* (ERS) *on Logistics and SCM.* Copenhagen (Denmark), 23rd – 24th April 2015.

Gutachtertätigkeiten

International Journal of Physical Distribution & Logistics Management (IJPDLM)

International Journal of Innovation and Technology Management (IJITM)

Technology Analysis & Strategic Management (TAS)

Journal of Strategy and Management (JSM)

British Academy of Management, BAM (associated with AOM, *Academy of Management*)

MIX
Papier aus verantwortungsvollen Quellen
Paper from responsible sources
FSC® C105338

If you have any concerns about our products,
you can contact us on
ProductSafety@springernature.com

In case Publisher is established outside the EU,
the EU authorized representative is:
Springer Nature Customer Service Center GmbH
Europaplatz 3, 69115 Heidelberg, Germany

Printed by Libri Plureos GmbH
in Hamburg, Germany